MW01147823

BIBLEFORCE®

THE FIRST HEROES BIBLE

BibleForce® The First Heroes Bible

Visit Tyndale's website for kids at tyndale.com/kids.

Tyndale is a registered trademark of Tyndale House Ministries. The Tyndale Kids logo is a trademark of Tyndale House Ministries.

Copyright © 2021 North Parade Publishing Ltd. and International Publishing Services Pty Ltd.

North Parade Publishing
4 North Parade, Bath BA1 1LF, United Kingdom
www.nppbooks.co.uk
International Publishing Services Pty Ltd.
Sydney, Australia
www.ipsoz.com

Previously published under ISBN 978-1-8392-3497-2. First printing by Tyndale House Publishers in 2024.

BibleForce® was created by Wayne McKay and Peter Hicks.
BibleForce® is a wholly owned registered trademark of International Publishing Services, Sydney, Australia.

All rights reserved. No portion of this book may be reproduced, stored in a retrieval system, or transmitted in any form or by any means—electronic, mechanical, photocopy, recording, scanning, or other—except for brief quotations in critical reviews or articles, without the prior written permission of the publisher.

BibleForce is a graphic adaptation of the Holy Bible. It closely follows the biblical text but is not a word-for-word adaptation. In a few places, scenes and conversations are included which can be inferred or imagined from the biblical text and from history.

Scripture quotations are taken from the *Holy Bible*, New Living Translation, copyright © 1996, 2004, 2015 by Tyndale House Foundation. Used by permission of Tyndale House Publishers, Carol Stream, Illinois 60188. All rights reserved.

Publishers: Wayne McKay and Peter Hicks
Consulting Author and General Editor: Janice Emmerson
Editorial Team: Mark Friedman, John Perritano, and Fraser Emmerson-Hicks
Design Team: Directed by Janice Emmerson

ISBN 978-1-4964-8887-9

Printed in China

30 29 28 27 26 25 24
7 6 5 4 3 2 1

BIBLEFORCE®

THE FIRST HEROES BIBLE

www.bibleforce.net

Contents

List of Maps

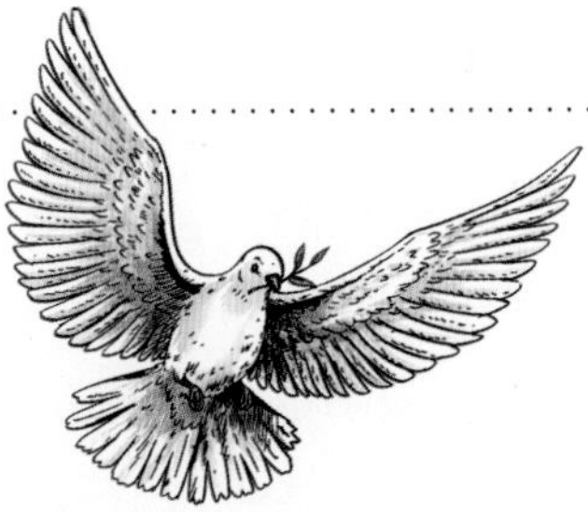

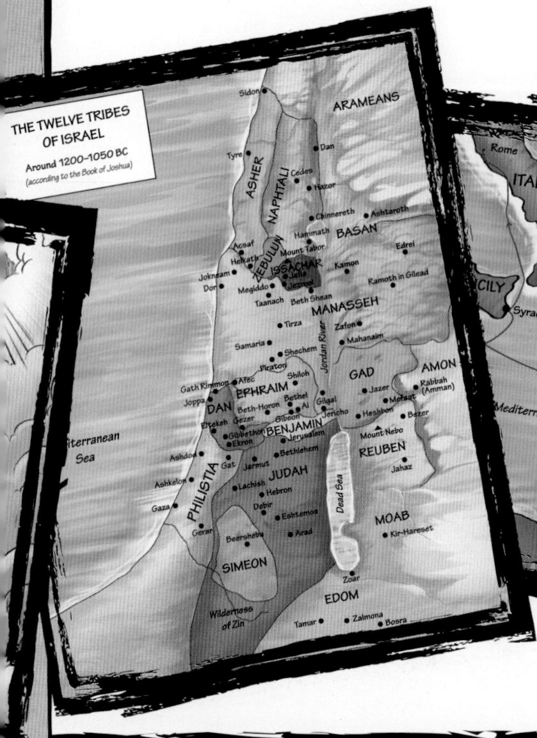

THE TWELVE TRIBES OF ISRAEL
Around 1200–1050 BC
(according to the Book of Joshua)
Sidon
ARAMEANS
Dan
Tyre
ASHER
NAPHTALI
Hazor
Chinnereth
Ashtaroth
BASAN
Edrei
ZEBULUN
ISSACHAR
Megiddo
Beth Shean
MANASSEH
Ramoth in Gilead
Tirza
Samaria
Shechem
Mahanaim
Shiloh
EPHRAIM
GAD
AMON
Rabbah (Amman)
Joppa
DAN
Bethel
Gilgal
Jericho
Gezer
Gibeon
BENJAMIN
Jerusalem
Heshbon
Mount Nebo
Bezer
REUBEN
Ashdod
Ashkelon
Gaza
PHILISTIA
Bethlehem
JUDAH
Lachish
Hebron
Dead Sea
MOAB
Kir-Hareset
Beersheba
Arad
SIMEON
Zoar
EDOM
Wilderness of Zin
Tamar
Zalmona
Bosra
Mediterranean Sea
Jordan River

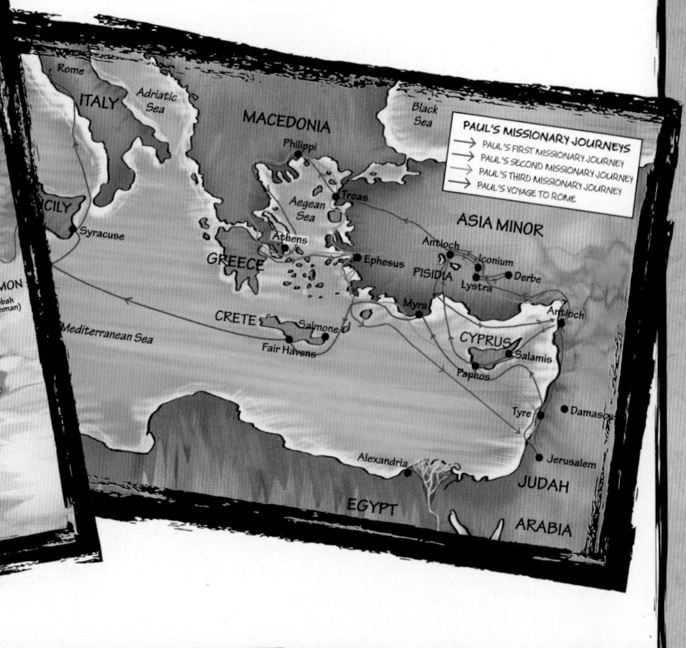

Rome
ITALY
Adriatic Sea
MACEDONIA
Black Sea
PAUL'S MISSIONARY JOURNEYS
PAUL'S FIRST MISSIONARY JOURNEY
PAUL'S SECOND MISSIONARY JOURNEY
PAUL'S THIRD MISSIONARY JOURNEY
PAUL'S VOYAGE TO ROME
Philippi
Aegean Sea
Troas
ASIA MINOR
Syracuse
Athens
GREECE
Ephesus
Antioch
Iconium
PISIDIA
Lystra
Derbe
Myra
CRETE
Salmone
Fair Havens
Mediterranean Sea
CYPRUS
Salamis
Paphos
Tyre
Damascus
Alexandria
Jerusalem
JUDAH
EGYPT
ARABIA

"Your word is a lamp to my feet and a light to my path."

Psalm 119:105

An Introduction to the Bible

NOT ONE BOOK, BUT A WHOLE LIBRARY!

YOU MIGHT THINK OF THE BIBLE AS ONE LARGE VOLUME, BUT IT IS ACTUALLY 66 INDIVIDUAL BOOKS, WRITTEN BY MANY DIFFERENT AUTHORS OVER MANY CENTURIES!

THERE ARE LOTS OF DIFFERENT STYLES, FROM POETRY TO LISTS AND FROM HISTORY BOOKS TO LETTERS. THERE ARE BOOKS BY KINGS, DOCTORS, PRIESTS, AND SHEPHERDS. SOME WERE WRITTEN IN THE TIME OF THE ROMAN EMPIRE. OTHERS WERE BEGUN NEARLY 3,500 YEARS AGO!

YET WHILE THESE BOOKS WERE WRITTEN BY HUMAN BEINGS, THEY WERE INSPIRED BY GOD. GOD SPOKE THROUGH ALL THESE DIFFERENT PEOPLE TO CREATE A WRITTEN VERSION OF HIS WORD. HE USED PEOPLE WHOSE WORLDS AND CULTURES WERE VASTLY DIFFERENT. BUT THROUGH IT ALL, GOD'S UNIVERSAL MESSAGE OF LOVE AND REDEMPTION IS PRESENT FROM GENESIS TO REVELATION.

SOME OF THE OLDEST SURVIVING WRITTEN PARTS OF THE BIBLE ARE FROM THE DEAD SEA SCROLLS.

IT'S LIKELY THAT MOST OF THE OLD TESTAMENT WAS PASSED DOWN BY WORD OF MOUTH THROUGH THE GENERATIONS UNTIL SCRIBES WROTE THE TEXT THAT BECAME THE BIBLE. SOME OF THE OLD TESTAMENT WAS WRITTEN IN HEBREW, WHILE A FEW PASSAGES WERE WRITTEN IN A SIMILAR LANGUAGE CALLED ARAMAIC.

THE EARLIEST TRANSLATION OF THE OLD TESTAMENT WAS FROM HEBREW MANUSCRIPTS INTO GREEK. IT WAS LATER TRANSLATED INTO LATIN AROUND THE FOURTH CENTURY AD WHILE THE FIRST ENGLISH VERSION WAS TRANSLATED AROUND 1,000 YEARS LATER. THE "KING JAMES BIBLE" (ALSO KNOWN AS THE "AUTHORIZED VERSION") WAS COMPLETED IN AD 1611.

TODAY THE FULL BIBLE HAS BEEN TRANSLATED INTO WELL OVER 600 LANGUAGES. THE NEW TESTAMENT HAS BEEN TRANSLATED INTO OVER 1,400 LANGUAGES, SPREADING THE MESSAGE OF GOD'S LOVE ALL ACROSS OUR WORLD!

THE OLD TESTAMENT

CHRISTIANS TRADITIONALLY DIVIDE THE BOOKS OF THE OLD TESTAMENT INTO FOUR GROUPINGS:

THE BOOKS OF THE OLD TESTAMENT

The Law
- Genesis
- Exodus
- Leviticus
- Numbers
- Deuteronomy

History
- Joshua
- Judges
- Ruth
- 1 Samuel
- 2 Samuel
- 1 Kings
- 2 Kings
- 1 Chronicles
- 2 Chronicles
- Ezra
- Nehemiah
- Esther

Poetry & Wisdom
- Job
- Psalms
- Proverbs
- Ecclesiastes
- Song of Solomon

The Prophets
- Isaiah
- Jeremiah
- Lamentations
- Ezekiel
- Daniel
- Hosea
- Joel
- Amos
- Obadiah
- Jonah
- Micah
- Nahum
- Habakkuk
- Zephaniah
- Haggai
- Zechariah
- Malachi

LAW AND HISTORY

THE FIRST FIVE BOOKS OF THE BIBLE ARE KNOWN AS EITHER THE LAW, THE PENTATEUCH, OR THE TORAH. THEY COVER THE PERIOD FROM THE CREATION, THE STORY OF THE ANCESTORS OF THE ISRAELITES, AND THE EARLY HISTORY OF THE ISRAELITES. THEY OFFER MANY LAWS ABOUT HOW THEY WERE TO BUILD THEIR SOCIETY.

THE NEXT TWELVE BOOKS, OR THE HISTORICAL BOOKS, COVER ABOUT 800 YEARS OF ISRAEL'S HISTORY, FROM THE POSSESSION OF THE PROMISED LAND, THE RISE AND FALL OF THE KINGDOM, AND THE EXILE TO THE RETURN TO JERUSALEM.

TRADITIONALLY, THE FIRST FIVE BOOKS IN THE BIBLE WERE ATTRIBUTED TO MOSES.

POETRY AND WISDOM

THE FIVE POETICAL BOOKS, FROM JOB TO SONG OF SOLOMON, RELATE TO ISRAEL'S SPIRITUAL LIFE AND DEAL WITH QUESTIONS OF SUFFERING, LOVE, WISDOM, AND THE NATURE OF GOD. THEY ARE ALSO KNOWN AS THE WRITINGS OF WISDOM.

MANY OF THE WORDS OF WISDOM IN THE BOOK OF PROVERBS ARE ATTRIBUTED TO KING SOLOMON.

The Lord is my shepherd;
I shall not want.
He makes me to lie down
in green pastures;
He leads me beside the still waters.
He restores my soul;
He leads me in the paths of
righteousness
For His name's sake.
Yea, though I walk through
the valley of the shadow of death,
I will fear no evil;
For You are with me;
Your rod and Your staff,
they comfort me.

Psalm 23:1–4

DAVID, WHO WENT FROM SHEPHERD BOY TO KING OF ISRAEL, IS BELIEVED TO HAVE WRITTEN MANY OF THE PSALMS INCLUDED IN THE OLD TESTAMENT. THE WORDS SPEAK FROM THE HEART AND OFFER COMFORT AND HOPE EVEN IN TIMES OF DESPAIR.

THE PROPHETS

IN THE OLD TESTAMENT, A SERIES OF BOOKS BEAR THE NAMES OF PROPHETS. THEY ARE DIVIDED INTO THE FOUR MAJOR PROPHETS (ISAIAH, JEREMIAH, EZEKIEL, AND DANIEL) AND THE TWELVE MINOR PROPHETS. THEY ARE DESIGNATED "MAJOR" AND "MINOR" MOSTLY BASED ON THE LENGTH OF THEIR WRITINGS.

PROPHETS WERE PEOPLE CHOSEN TO BE SPOKESMEN FOR GOD. THEY WERE ALSO KNOWN AS SEERS, WATCHMEN, OR SERVANTS OF THE LORD.

WHILE MANY OF THE PROPHETS' MESSAGES FOCUSED ON THE FUTURE, THEY WERE ALSO CONCERNED WITH PRESENT-DAY EVENTS, SUCH AS SOCIAL LIFE AND POLITICS.

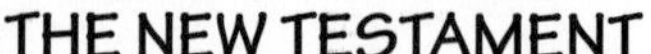

THE NEW TESTAMENT

THE NEW TESTAMENT CAN BE DIVIDED INTO FOUR SECTIONS:

THE BOOKS OF THE NEW TESTAMENT

Gospels: Matthew, Mark, Luke, John

History: Acts

Letters: Romans, 1 Corinthians, 2 Corinthians, Galatians, Ephesians, Philippians, Colossians, 1 Thessalonians, 2 Thessalonians, 1 Timothy, 2 Timothy, Titus, Philemon, Hebrews, James, 1 Peter, 2 Peter, 1 John, 2 John, 3 John, Jude

Prophecy: Revelation

THE GOSPELS

THE NEW TESTAMENT BEGINS WITH THE GOSPELS. THESE HISTORICAL DOCUMENTS GIVE US DETAILS ABOUT THE BIRTH, LIFE, DEATH, AND RESURRECTION OF JESUS. WHILE EACH BOOK IS WRITTEN FROM AN INDIVIDUAL PERSPECTIVE, MATTHEW, MARK, AND LUKE'S WRITINGS BROADLY COVER THE SAME MATERIAL AND ARE KNOWN AS THE SYNOPTIC GOSPELS. "SYNOPTIC" IS A GREEK WORD MEANING "HAVING A COMMON VIEW."

THE FOURTH GOSPEL IS TRADITIONALLY ATTRIBUTED TO JOHN THE APOSTLE, OFTEN IDENTIFIED AS "THE BELOVED DISCIPLE." WRITING SLIGHTLY LATER, JOHN DOES NOT CONCENTRATE ON ALL THE SAME EVENTS MENTIONED IN THE OTHER GOSPELS AND TENDS TO BE MORE REFLECTIVE AND POETIC, FOCUSING ON CHRIST'S DIVINE IDENTITY AS THE SON OF GOD.

TOGETHER THESE FOUR EYEWITNESS ACCOUNTS PRESENT A FULLER PICTURE OF THE LIFE AND TEACHINGS OF JESUS.

HISTORY

THE BOOK OF ACTS IS WRITTEN BY THE SAME AUTHOR AS THE BOOK OF LUKE—THE DOCTOR AND COMPANION OF THE APOSTLE PAUL. LUKE TELLS US WHAT HAPPENED AFTER THE DEATH AND RESURRECTION OF CHRIST AND OF THE BIRTH AND GROWTH OF THE CHURCH.

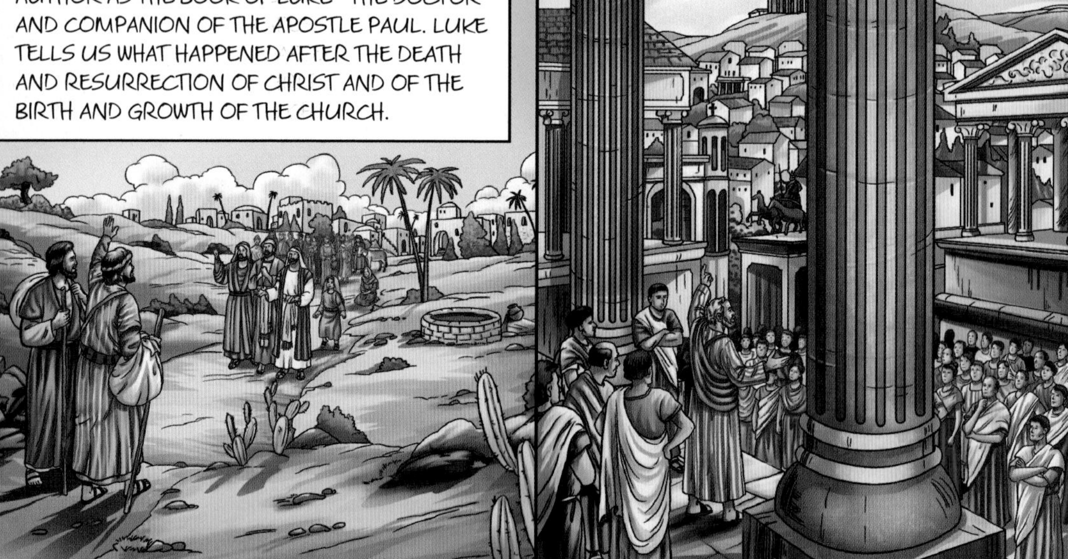

LETTERS

OF THE 27 BOOKS THAT MAKE UP THE NEW TESTAMENT, 21 ARE IN THE GROUP CALLED THE EPISTLES, OR LETTERS. MANY OF THESE WERE WRITTEN BY THE APOSTLE PAUL. SOME LETTERS WERE WRITTEN TO CHURCHES AND WERE DESIGNED TO GUIDE THE NEW BELIEVERS AND ANSWER THEIR QUESTIONS. OTHERS WERE MORE PERSONAL AND WERE DIRECTED TO INDIVIDUALS.

WHETHER PERSONAL OR GENERAL, THE LETTERS OFFERED ADVICE, GUIDANCE, COMFORT, AND HOPE TO THE NEW CHURCH. THEY CONTINUE TO BE RELEVANT AND USEFUL TO PEOPLE TODAY.

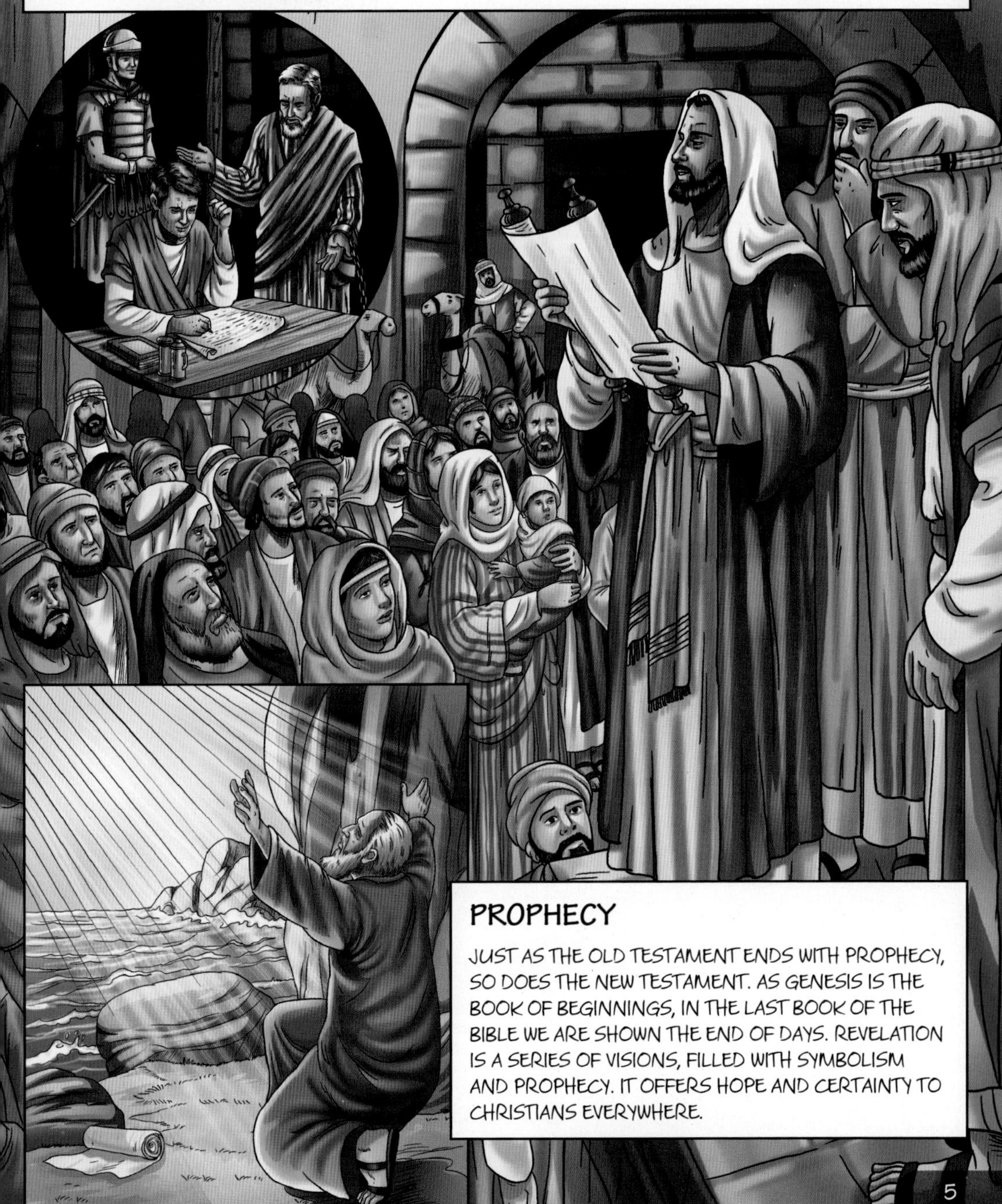

PROPHECY

JUST AS THE OLD TESTAMENT ENDS WITH PROPHECY, SO DOES THE NEW TESTAMENT. AS GENESIS IS THE BOOK OF BEGINNINGS, IN THE LAST BOOK OF THE BIBLE WE ARE SHOWN THE END OF DAYS. REVELATION IS A SERIES OF VISIONS, FILLED WITH SYMBOLISM AND PROPHECY. IT OFFERS HOPE AND CERTAINTY TO CHRISTIANS EVERYWHERE.

What Happened When?

THE STORIES IN THE BIBLE TAKE PLACE OVER MANY CENTURIES. IT IS HARD TO KNOW THE EXACT DATES OR LOCATIONS OF KEY EVENTS. HERE IS A TIMELINE OF FAMOUS BIBLE STORIES, AND ESTIMATES OF WHEN THEY HAPPENED! (ALL DATES ARE APPROXIMATE)

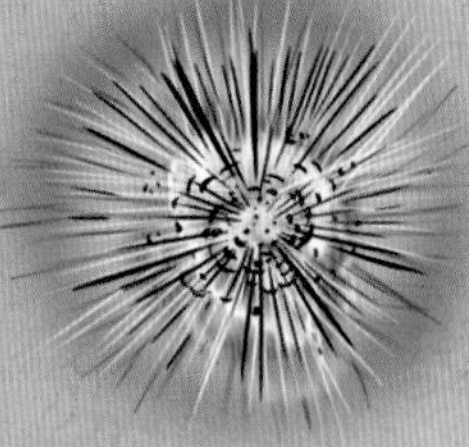

CREATION
DATES UNKNOWN

NOAH SURVIVES THE GREAT FLOOD
BEFORE 2500 BC

ABRAHAM IS BORN
1996 BC

SODOM IS DESTROYED
1897 BC

JACOB AND ESAU ARE BORN
1837 BC

MOSES IS BORN
1530 BC

THE ISRAELITES LEAVE EGYPT
1491 BC

GOD GIVES MOSES THE TEN COMMANDMENTS
1491 BC

DEATH OF SAUL
1010 BC

DAVID IS KING OF ISRAEL
1010 BC

SOLOMON BUILDS THE TEMPLE
960 BC

NEBUCHADNEZZAR TAKES CAPTIVES TO BABYLON
605 BC
OCTAVIUS APPOINTED FIRST EMPEROR OF ROMAN EMPIRE
27 BC
JESUS IS BORN
4–6 BC
JOHN THE BAPTIST BAPTIZES JESUS
AD 26–27
BOOK OF NEHEMIAH WRITTEN
430 BC
EMPIRE OF ALEXANDER THE GREAT
336–323 BC
JESUS CALLS HIS DISCIPLES
AD 27–29
MINISTRY OF JESUS
AD 27–30
JESUS ASCENDS TO HEAVEN
AD 30
JESUS IS CRUCIFIED AND RISES FROM THE DEAD
AD 30
BOOK OF REVELATION IS WRITTEN
AD 95
PAUL IS CONVERTED ON THE ROAD TO DAMASCUS
AD 35
PAUL IS EXECUTED IN ROME
AD 67

The World of the Bible

N
W
E
S
Caspian Sea
CAUCASUS
Black Sea
ARMENIA
ASSYRIA
GALATIA
Anti-Taurus Mountains
PERSIA
Nineveh
Tarsus
MESOPOTAMIA
Tigris
CILICIA
Zagros Mountains
Antioch
Euphrates
CYPRUS
Paphos
SYRIA
Susah
Sidon
Damascus
Babylon
ISRAEL
Sea of Galilee
Jerusalem
Dead Sea
EGYPT
EDOM
ARABIA
Red Sea
Thebes

The Old Testament

"In the beginning God created the heavens and the earth."

Genesis 1:1

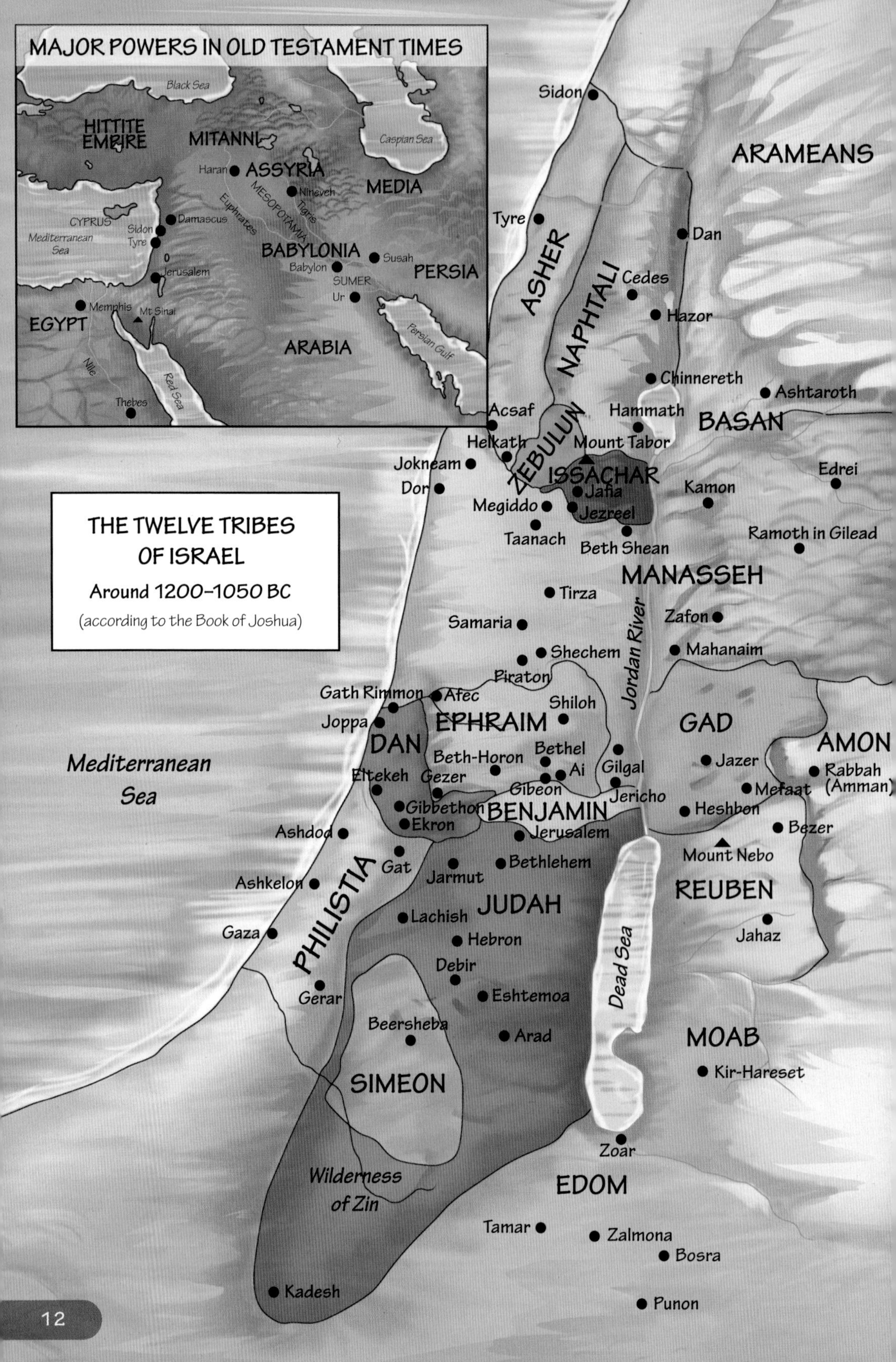

MAJOR POWERS IN OLD TESTAMENT TIMES
Black Sea
HITTITE EMPIRE
MITANNI
Caspian Sea
Haran
ASSYRIA
Nineveh
MEDIA
MESOPOTAMIA
Tigris
Euphrates
CYPRUS
Damascus
Sidon
Tyre
Mediterranean Sea
BABYLONIA
Susah
Babylon
PERSIA
Jerusalem
SUMER
Ur
Memphis
Mt Sinai
EGYPT
ARABIA
Persian Gulf
Nile
Red Sea
Thebes
THE TWELVE TRIBES OF ISRAEL
Around 1200–1050 BC
(according to the Book of Joshua)
Sidon
ARAMEANS
Tyre
ASHER
Dan
NAPHTALI
Cedes
Hazor
Chinnereth
Ashtaroth
Acsaf
ZEBULUN
Hammath
BASAN
Helkath
Mount Tabor
Jokneam
ISSACHAR
Edrei
Dor
Jafia
Kamon
Megiddo
Jezreel
Taanach
Beth Shean
Ramoth in Gilead
MANASSEH
Tirza
Jordan River
Samaria
Zafon
Shechem
Mahanaim
Piraton
Gath Rimmon
Afec
Shiloh
Joppa
EPHRAIM
GAD
DAN
Bethel
AMON
Mediterranean Sea
Beth-Horon
Jazer
Rabbah (Amman)
Eltekeh
Gezer
Ai
Gilgal
Gibeon
Mefaat
Jericho
Gibbethon
BENJAMIN
Heshbon
Ekron
Bezer
Ashdod
Jerusalem
Mount Nebo
Gat
Bethlehem
Jarmut
Ashkelon
PHILISTIA
REUBEN
JUDAH
Lachish
Jahaz
Gaza
Hebron
Dead Sea
Debir
Gerar
Eshtemoa
Beersheba
Arad
MOAB
Kir-Hareset
SIMEON
Zoar
Wilderness of Zin
EDOM
Tamar
Zalmona
Bosra
Kadesh
Punon

In the Beginning

EARLIEST SOURCES FOR GENESIS MOST LIKELY DATE FROM 1000 BC.

THE BOOK TOOK ITS CURRENT FORM IN THE 400s BC.

BEHIND THE NAME

THE ORIGINAL HEBREW TITLE OF THE BOOK MEANS "IN BEGINNING." HOWEVER, THE NAME WE NOW KNOW IT BY, GENESIS, COMES FROM THE GREEK WORD **GENESEOS** MEANING "ORIGIN, GENERATION, OR BEGINNING." THIS TITLE WAS USED BY GREEK SCHOLARS WHEN THEY TRANSLATED THE BOOK IN THE 200s BC.

BEHIND THE PEN

BASED ON TRADITION, MOSES WROTE THE FIRST FIVE BOOKS OF THE BIBLE (ALSO CALLED THE PENTATEUCH OR LAW).

God Creates the World

Genesis 1–2

ON THE SECOND DAY, GOD SEPARATED THE WATER FROM THE SKY.
ON THE THIRD DAY, GOD SAID, "LET DRY GROUND APPEAR." AND IT DID. HE CALLED THE DRY GROUND "LAND." AND THE WATER THE "SEAS."
GOD LIKED WHAT HE SAW.
GOD CREATED TREES, FLOWERS, AND ALL TYPES OF PLANTS.

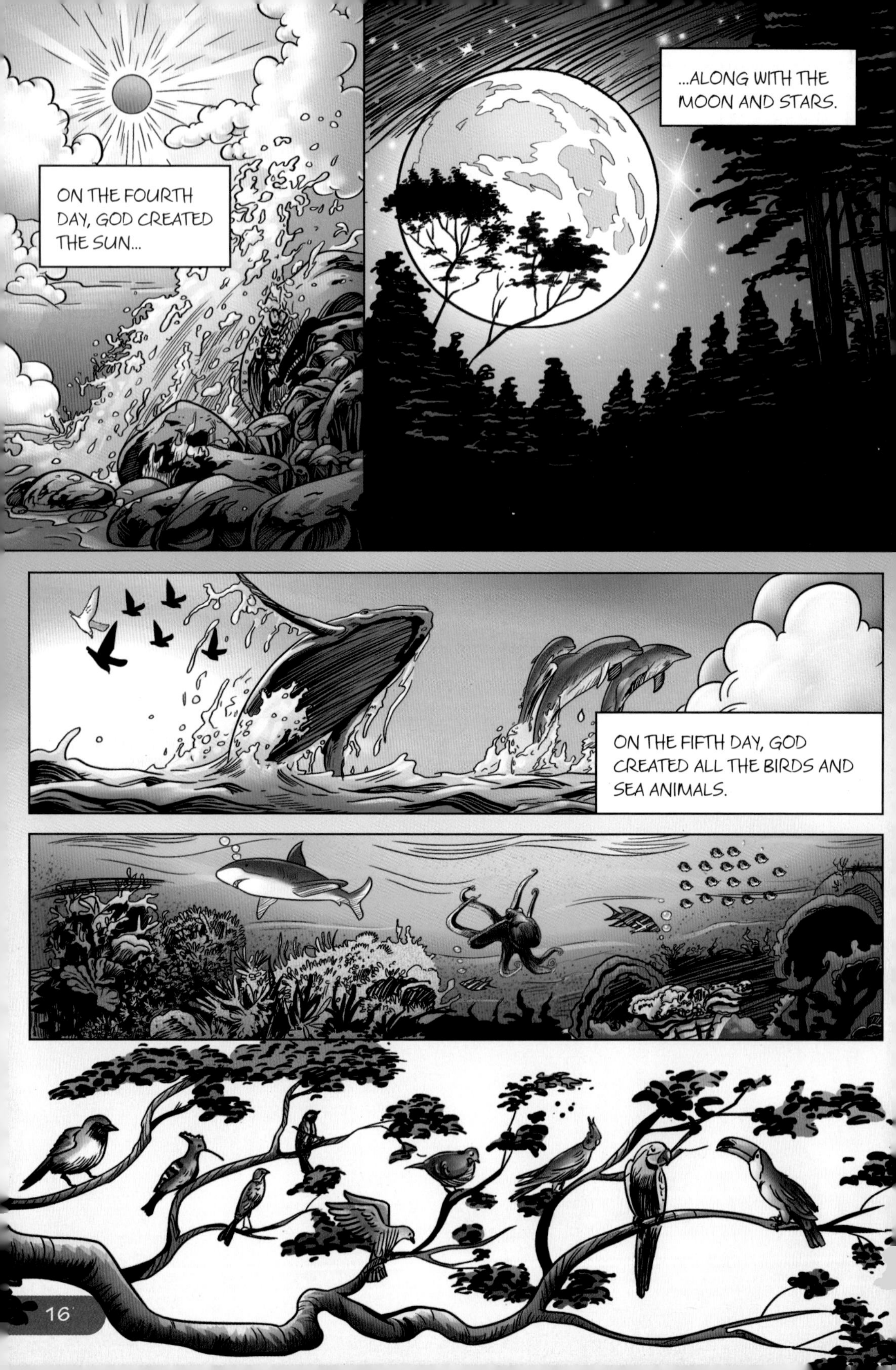

ON THE FOURTH DAY, GOD CREATED THE SUN...

...ALONG WITH THE MOON AND STARS.

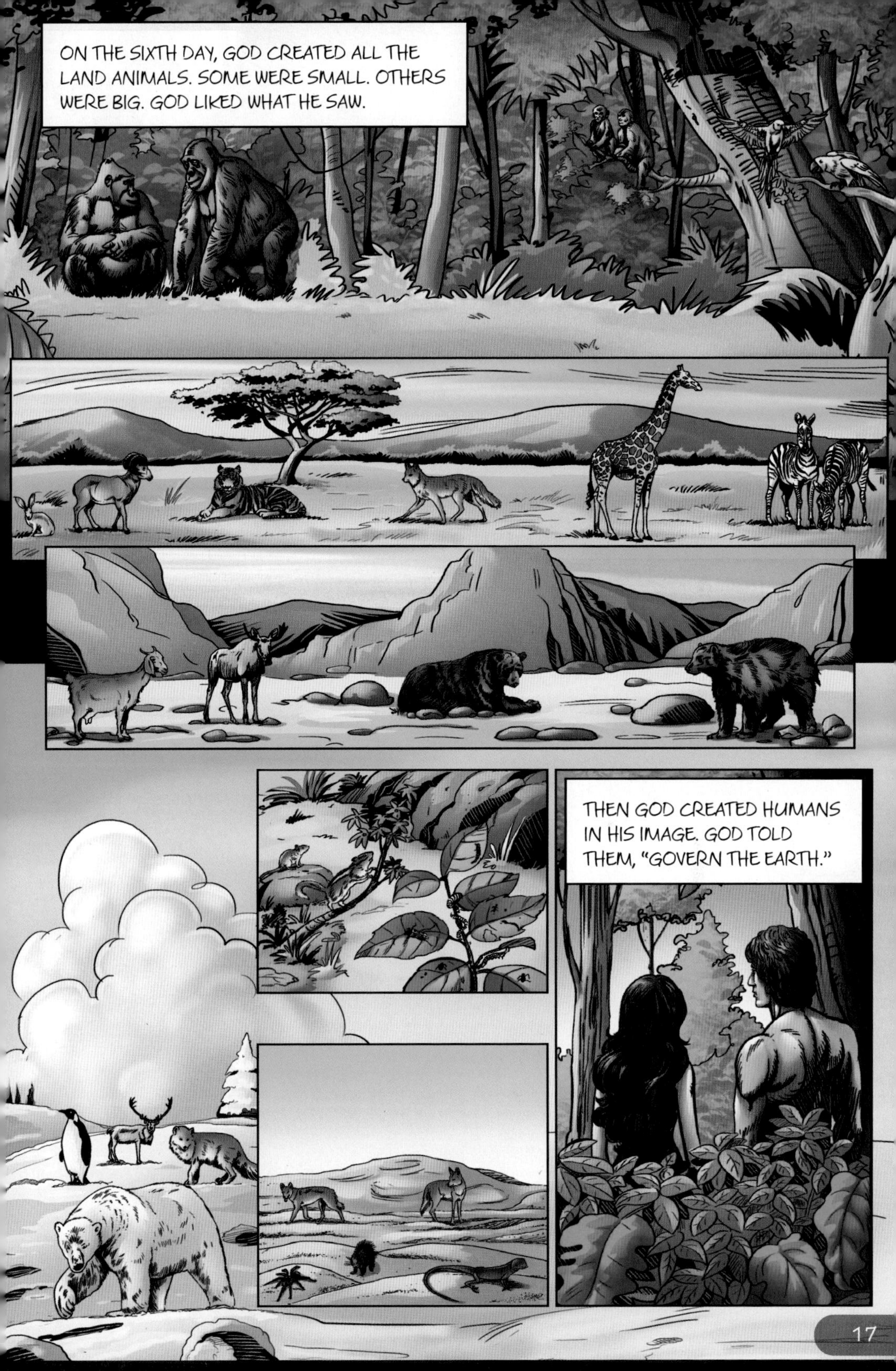
ON THE SIXTH DAY, GOD CREATED ALL THE LAND ANIMALS. SOME WERE SMALL. OTHERS WERE BIG. GOD LIKED WHAT HE SAW.
THEN GOD CREATED HUMANS IN HIS IMAGE. GOD TOLD THEM, "GOVERN THE EARTH."

GOD SAW ALL THAT HE HAD MADE AND WAS VERY HAPPY. HIS WORK WAS DONE. ON THE SEVENTH DAY, GOD RESTED. HE DECLARED THE SEVENTH DAY HOLY.

The Garden of Eden
Genesis 2
HOW DID GOD CREATE HUMANS?
GOD FORMED MAN OUT OF THE DUST.
THE LORD BREATHED LIFE INTO HIM, AND THE MAN LIVED.
THE FIRST MAN WAS CALLED ADAM. GOD CREATED ADAM IN HIS OWN IMAGE.

THEN GOD PLANTED A GARDEN IN EDEN. IT WAS A PEACEFUL PLACE WITH BEAUTIFUL FRUIT TREES.
YOU MAY EAT THE FRUIT FROM ANY OF THE TREES...
...EXCEPT THIS ONE, THE TREE OF THE KNOWLEDGE OF GOOD AND EVIL.
IF YOU EAT ITS FRUIT, YOU WILL DIE!

GOD SAW THAT ADAM WAS ALONE. HE TOLD ADAM TO NAME ALL THE ANIMALS.
I WILL CALL YOU BIRDS...
...YOU ARE HORSES...
...CATTLE...
...DOGS...

GOD SAW THAT ADAM WAS STILL ALONE AND DECIDED TO MAKE A HELPER FOR HIM.
GOD CAUSED ADAM TO SLEEP...
...GOD TOOK ONE OF ADAM'S RIBS...
...AND CREATED A WOMAN.
THE WOMAN'S NAME WAS EVE.

Banished from Eden
Genesis 3
EVE AND ADAM WERE NAKED. BUT THEY WERE NOT ASHAMED.
THEY WERE NOT AFRAID OF THE ANIMALS.
THE SNAKE WAS THE CLEVEREST OF ALL THE ANIMALS.

PSSSSSSSST.
DID GOD SAY YOU MUST NOT EAT FROM ANY TREES?
WE MAY EAT THE FRUIT FROM ANY TREE, EXCEPT THIS ONE: THE TREE OF THE KNOWLEDGE OF GOOD AND EVIL.
WHAT WILL HAPPEN IF YOU DO?
GOD SAID WE WOULD DIE!
PSSSSSSSST.
YOU **WILL NOT** DIE!

GOD KNOWS THAT IF YOU EAT THE FRUIT, **YOUR EYES WILL BE OPENED!**
YOU WILL BE LIKE GOD HIMSELF! **PSSSSSSSST.**

AFTER EVE ATE THE FRUIT FROM THE TREE, SHE TURNED TO ADAM...
...AND GAVE HIM THE FRUIT TO EAT. HE ATE SOME TOO.

RIGHT THEN, THEIR EYES WERE OPENED. THEY FELT SHAME AT BEING NAKED, SO THEY COVERED THEMSELVES.

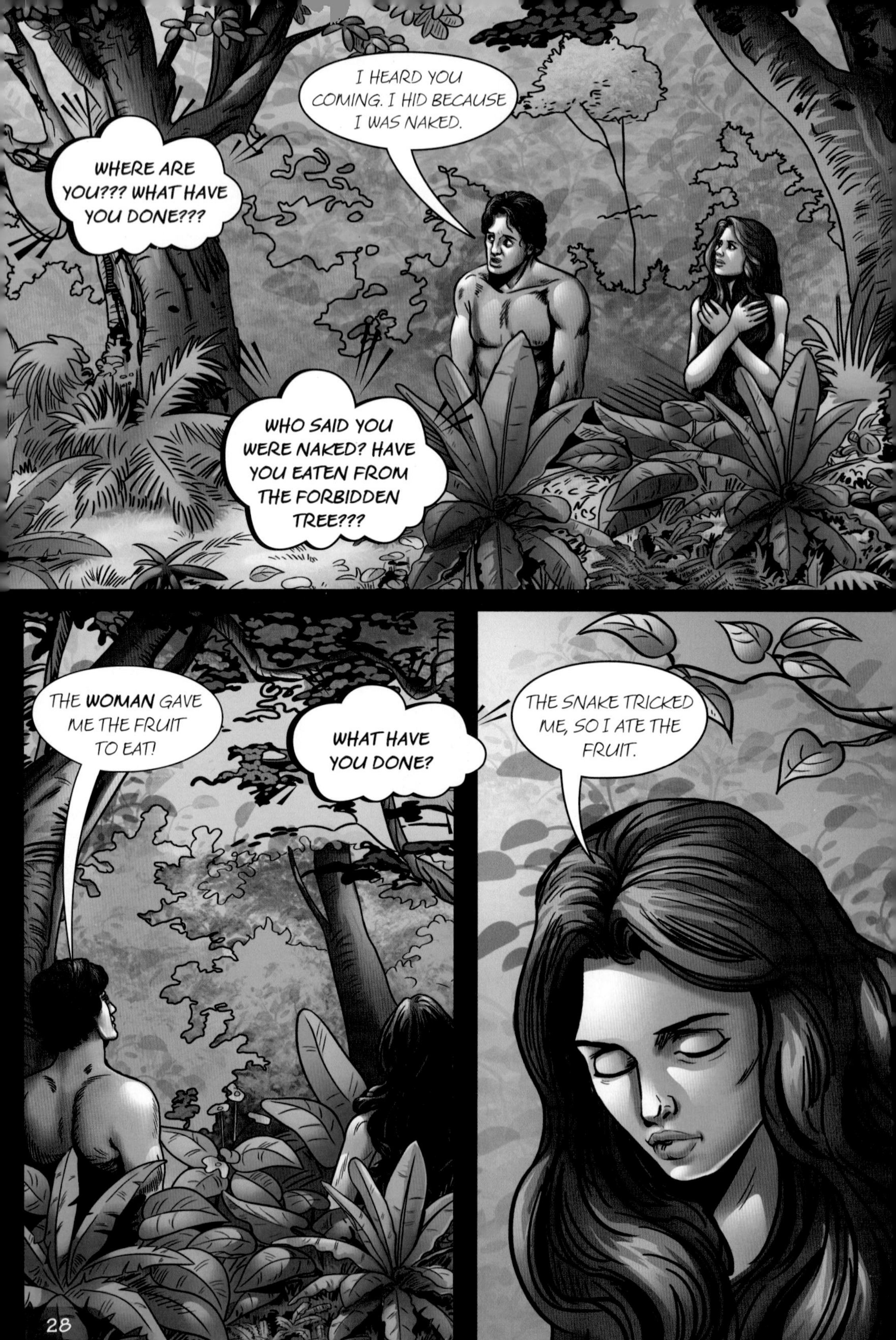

WHERE ARE YOU??? WHAT HAVE YOU DONE???

I HEARD YOU COMING. I HID BECAUSE I WAS NAKED.

WHO SAID YOU WERE NAKED? HAVE YOU EATEN FROM THE FORBIDDEN TREE???

THE LORD TOLD THE SNAKE HE WAS THE LOWEST ANIMAL ON EARTH.
YOU WILL CRAWL ON YOUR BELLY!
THEN GOD PUNISHED EVE...
BECAUSE YOU DISOBEYED ME, YOUR HUSBAND WILL RULE OVER YOU...
...AND CHILDBIRTH WILL BE PAINFUL FOR YOU!
...AND ADAM.
CURSED IS THE GROUND BECAUSE OF YOU! YOU WILL NOW STRUGGLE TO GROW YOUR FOOD FROM THE GROUND. FROM THE DUST I CREATED YOU, AND TO THE DUST YOU WILL RETURN!

GOD MADE CLOTHES FOR ADAM AND EVE. THEN HE SENT THEM OUT OF THE GARDEN.
BECAUSE ADAM AND EVE HAD SINNED, ALL HUMANS WOULD HAVE TO WORK AND SUFFER.

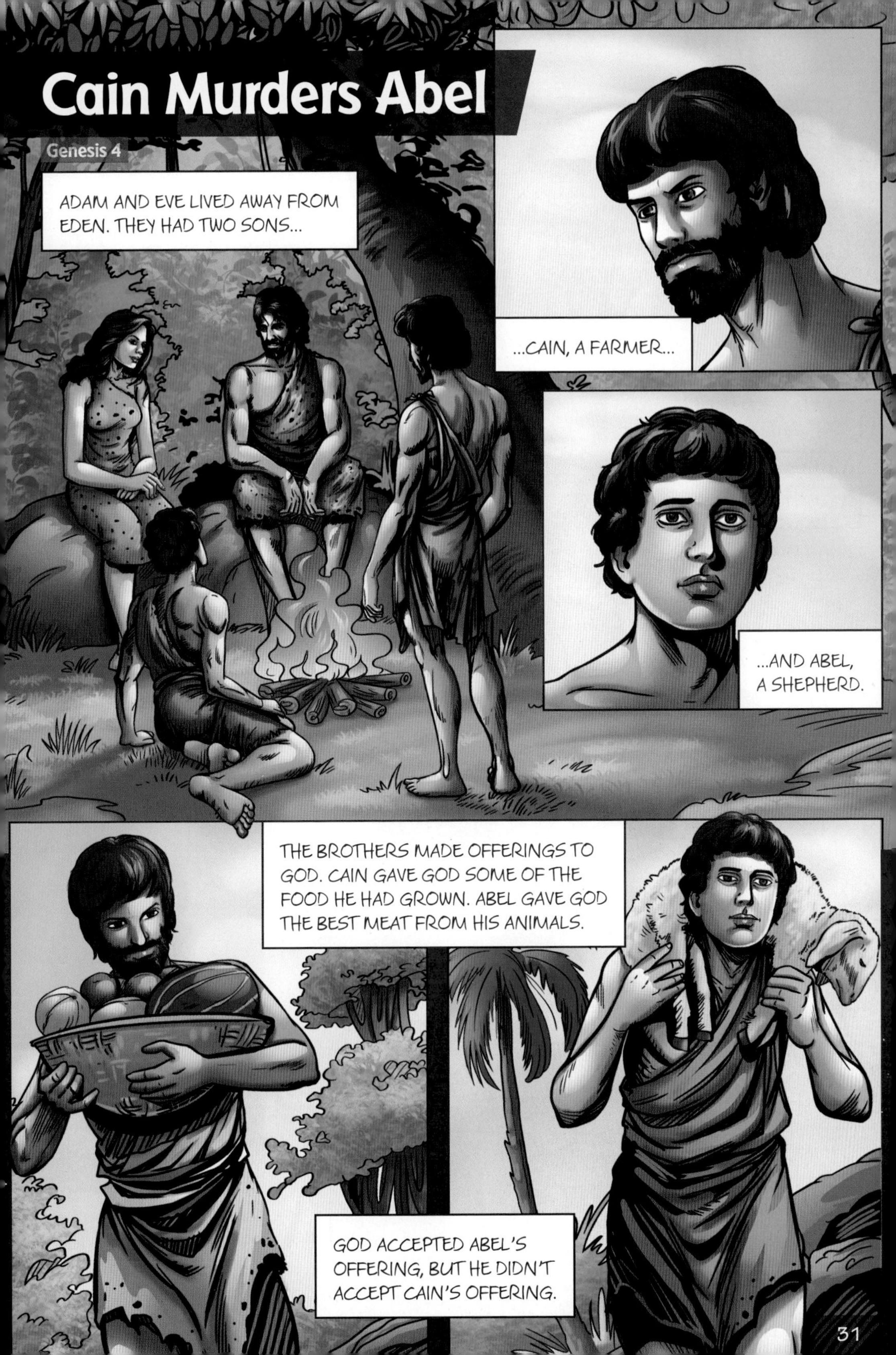
Cain Murders Abel
Genesis 4
ADAM AND EVE LIVED AWAY FROM EDEN. THEY HAD TWO SONS...
...CAIN, A FARMER...
...AND ABEL, A SHEPHERD.
THE BROTHERS MADE OFFERINGS TO GOD. CAIN GAVE GOD SOME OF THE FOOD HE HAD GROWN. ABEL GAVE GOD THE BEST MEAT FROM HIS ANIMALS.
GOD ACCEPTED ABEL'S OFFERING, BUT HE DIDN'T ACCEPT CAIN'S OFFERING.

CAIN WAS ANGRY BECAUSE GOD ACCEPTED ABEL'S GIFT AND NOT HIS.
CAIN LURED HIS BROTHER OUT INTO A FIELD...
...AND MURDERED HIM.
CAIN! WHERE IS YOUR BROTHER?
I DON'T KNOW! AM I IN CHARGE OF MY BROTHER?
THE LORD KNEW CAIN HAD MURDERED ABEL.
CAIN LEFT HIS HOME AND WENT TO LIVE IN THE LAND OF NOD, EAST OF EDEN.

Hero Profile
Noah—The Last Good Man

FATHER: LAMECH, A DESCENDANT OF ADAM

SONS: SHEM, HAM, JAPHETH

LIFE SPAN: DIED AT AGE 950

GENERATION GAP

NOAH WAS THE GRANDSON OF METHUSELAH, THE OLDEST PERSON IN THE BIBLE, WHO DIED AT AGE 969 IN THE YEAR OF THE FLOOD. NOAH WAS 500 YEARS OLD WHEN HE BECAME A FATHER.

WHERE IS MOUNT ARARAT?

THE MOUNTAINS OF ARARAT, THE LANDING PLACE OF NOAH'S ARK, ARE A MOUNTAIN RANGE IN THE EXTREME EASTERN PART OF TURKEY. THEY ARE SEVERAL HUNDRED MILES NORTH OF WHERE MANY SCHOLARS BELIEVE CIVILIZATION BEGAN IN MESOPOTAMIA. FOR CENTURIES EXPLORERS HAVE SEARCHED FOR THE REMAINS OF NOAH'S GREAT BOAT ON THESE MYSTERIOUS MOUNTAIN PEAKS.

Noah and the Great Flood

Genesis 6–8

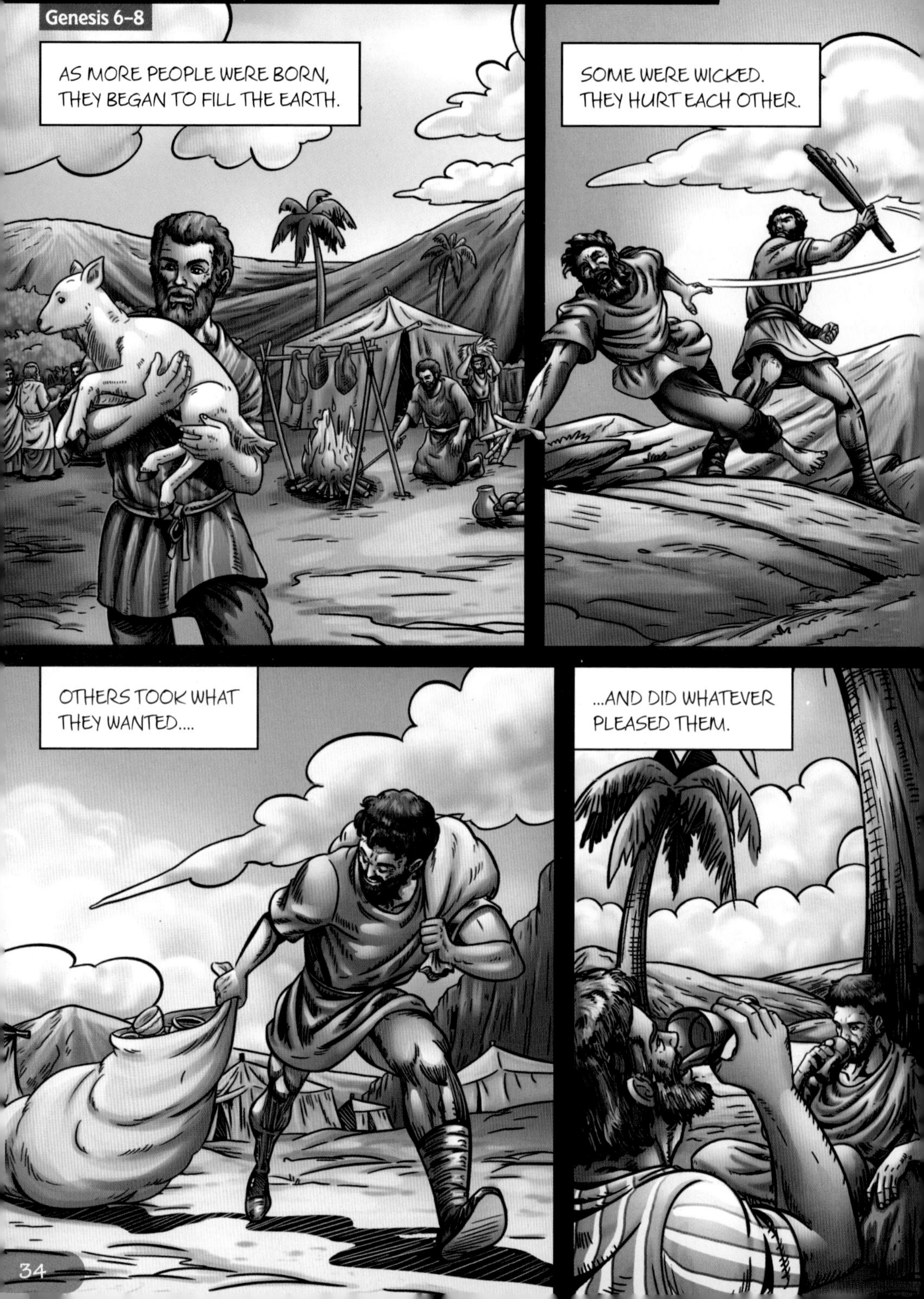

AS MORE PEOPLE WERE BORN, THEY BEGAN TO FILL THE EARTH.

SOME WERE WICKED. THEY HURT EACH OTHER.

GOD SAW THAT PEOPLE WERE EVIL. YET THERE WAS ONE RIGHTEOUS MAN. HIS NAME WAS NOAH. HE HAD A WIFE AND THREE SONS—SHEM, HAM, AND JAPHETH.

GOD TOLD NOAH HE WAS GOING TO DESTROY EVERY LIVING CREATURE ON EARTH.
HE WOULD SEND RAIN AND A GREAT FLOOD. HE WOULD WIPE FROM THE EARTH EVERYTHING THAT BREATHES.
GOD PROMISED TO SPARE NOAH AND HIS FAMILY.
I DON'T UNDERSTAND!
HOW WILL MY FAMILY SURVIVE THE FLOOD?

GOD SPOKE TO NOAH. HE TOLD NOAH HOW TO BUILD AN ARK—A GREAT SHIP IN WHICH NOAH AND HIS FAMILY WOULD SURVIVE THE FLOOD.

THIS IS HOW BIG THE ARK HAS TO BE.

IT CAN'T BE DONE. IT'S NOT POSSIBLE!
FATHER, IT IS TOO LARGE!
IT WILL NEVER FLOAT!

NOAH AND HIS FAMILY WORKED HARD FOR A LONG TIME BUILDING THE ARK.

NOAH DID EVERYTHING ACCORDING TO ALL THAT GOD COMMANDED HIM TO DO.

NOAH! ANIMALS WILL COME TO YOU, MALE AND FEMALE OF EACH KIND. TAKE THEM INTO THE ARK. THEY WILL SURVIVE WITH YOU THERE.
NOAH AND HIS FAMILY, ALONG WITH ALL THE ANIMALS THAT GOD COMMANDED HIM TO TAKE ON THE ARK, BOARDED THE GIANT SHIP.

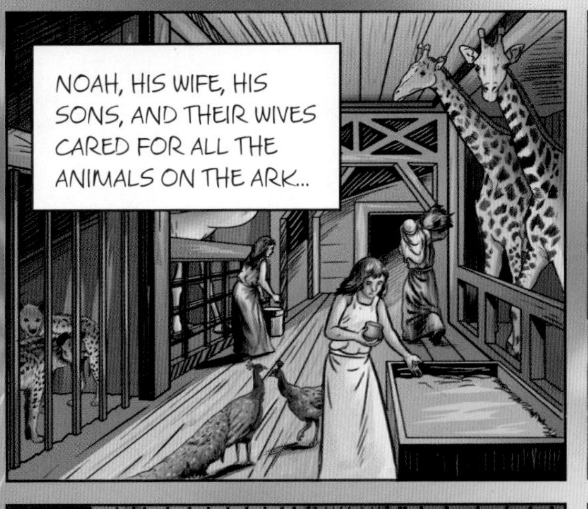

THE RAIN BEGAN TO FALL, AND THE EARTH'S SPRINGS BURST OPEN. IT RAINED FOR FORTY DAYS AND NIGHTS.

FLOODWATERS COVERED THE EARTH—TOWNS AND CITIES, FORESTS AND MOUNTAINS. THE FLOOD KILLED EVERY LIVING BEING ON THE PLANET.

NOAH AND HIS FAMILY WERE SAFE IN THE BOAT. THEY WERE THE ONLY PEOPLE TO SURVIVE.
EVEN AFTER THE RAIN STOPPED, THE FLOOD LASTED 150 DAYS. BUT GOD REMEMBERED NOAH AND THE ANIMALS ON THE BOAT. HE MADE THE FLOODWATERS RECEDE.
I WILL SEND OUT A BIRD TO FIND DRY GROUND.

THE ARK CAME TO REST ON THE MOUNTAINS OF ARARAT. IT TOOK MONTHS FOR THE FLOODWATERS TO SLOWLY RECEDE. THEN NOAH RELEASED A RAVEN AND A DOVE.

AT FIRST THE DOVE COULD FIND NOWHERE TO LAND, FOR THE EARTH WAS STILL COVERED IN WATER. AFTER SEVEN DAYS, NOAH TRIED AGAIN. WHEN THE BIRD RETURNED THIS TIME, IT CARRIED A LEAF IN ITS BEAK.

GOD TOLD NOAH TO LEAVE THE ARK WITH HIS FAMILY AND ALL THE ANIMALS. NOAH OBEYED GOD.

FATHER, WE HAVE BEEN DELIVERED. GOD HAS SPARED US.
WE MUST BUILD AN ALTAR AND **MAKE A SACRIFICE** TO THE LORD.

God's Covenant with Noah

Genesis 8–9

GOD SAID NOAH'S FAMILY COULD HUNT ANY ANIMAL...
...CATCH ANY FISH...
...EAT ANY PLANT.

THEN GOD MADE A PROMISE—A COVENANT.
I MAKE MY COVENANT WITH YOU. NEVER AGAIN WILL A FLOOD DESTROY THE EARTH.
GOD PLACED A RAINBOW IN THE CLOUDS AS THE SIGN OF HIS COVENANT. GOD PROMISED THAT THE RAINBOW WOULD REMIND HIM OF HIS COVENANT WITH EVERY LIVING CREATURE.

The Tower of Babel

Genesis 11

SO THE PEOPLE WENT TO WORK BUILDING A GREAT CITY—BABEL.
THEY LEARNED TO MAKE STRONG BRICKS. THEY USED THESE BRICKS TO BUILD TALLER BUILDINGS THAN ANYONE HAD EVER BUILT.
PUT THOSE BRICKS OVER HERE!
BUILDING A GREAT CITY IS HARD WORK!
IT IS TOUGH WORK, BUT THE CITY WILL BE BEAUTIFUL. OUR BUILDINGS WILL BE **MAGNIFICENT**!

WE NOW HAVE A HOME!
WE WILL NO LONGER MOVE FROM PLACE TO PLACE.
WE HAVE BUILT A GREAT CITY, BUT WE SHOULD NOT STOP! WE SHOULD BUILD A **GREAT TOWER THAT REACHES INTO THE SKY!**
YES! A TALL TOWER WILL MAKE US FAMOUS!
IT WILL KEEP US FROM BEING SCATTERED ALL OVER!

AND SO THEY BEGAN BUILDING A GREAT BRICK TOWER—THE **TOWER OF BABEL**.
THE PEOPLE WERE VERY AMBITIOUS.
WHAT A **GLORIOUS** TOWER THIS WILL BE!
WE ARE ACHIEVING **GREATNESS**!

GOD SAID, "THE PEOPLE ARE UNITED, AND THEY ALL SPEAK THE SAME LANGUAGE. AFTER THIS, NOTHING WILL BE IMPOSSIBLE FOR THEM!"
SO GOD MADE SURE THEY COULD NOT UNDERSTAND EACH OTHER. PEOPLE SPOKE TO EACH OTHER, BUT EACH SPOKE A DIFFERENT LANGUAGE. WORK ON THE TOWER STOPPED.
I DON'T UNDERSTAND WHAT YOU'RE SAYING!
WHAT ARE YOU TALKING ABOUT???
GOD SPREAD THE PEOPLE OVER THE WHOLE EARTH. THEY POPULATED THE WORLD.

Hero Profile
Abraham—The Chosen One

NAME: ABRAHAM (MEANING "FATHER OF MANY PEOPLE")

ALSO KNOWN AS: ABRAM (MEANING "GREAT FATHER") AND THE FATHER OF THE HEBREW PEOPLE, OR JEWISH NATION

AGE: LIVED TO THE AGE OF 175

FATHER: TERAH

WIFE: SARAH (SARAI)

BORN: THE CITY OF UR IN BABYLONIA

SONS: ISHMAEL AND ISAAC

NEPHEW: LOT

A FOUNDING "FATHER"

GOD USED ABRAHAM TO SHOW THAT SALVATION COMES ONLY BY FAITH IN THE ONE TRUE GOD. THE NEW TESTAMENT EXPLAINS THAT ABRAHAM'S TRUST IN GOD'S PROMISE WAS AN EXAMPLE OF GREAT FAITH. WE, TOO, CAN HAVE FAITH IN GOD THROUGH HIS SON, JESUS CHRIST (ROMANS 4).

FAMOUS ABRAHAM

MANY PEOPLE HAVE BEEN NAMED ABRAHAM THROUGHOUT HISTORY. PERHAPS NONE HAS BEEN MORE FAMOUS THAN ABRAHAM LINCOLN, THE 16TH PRESIDENT OF THE UNITED STATES. HE GUIDED THE NATION THROUGH THE CIVIL WAR, CHAMPIONED HUMAN RIGHTS, AND FREED THE AMERICAN SLAVES.

The Call of Abraham
Genesis 12
ONE OF NOAH'S DESCENDANTS WAS A MAN NAMED ABRAHAM. HE GREW UP IN MESOPOTAMIA UNTIL HIS FATHER MOVED THE FAMILY TO THE CITY OF HARAN.
ABRAHAM AND HIS WIFE, SARAH, ENJOYED A GOOD LIFE FILLED WITH MANY BLESSINGS.
ONE DAY, GOD CALLED TO ABRAHAM: "LEAVE YOUR FATHER'S FAMILY, AND GO TO THE LAND I WILL SHOW YOU."
WHY, LORD? WHY MUST WE LEAVE?
GOD SAID, "I WILL MAKE YOU INTO A GREAT NATION. I WILL BLESS YOU. ALL THE FAMILIES ON EARTH WILL BE BLESSED THROUGH YOU."

ABRAHAM HAD GREAT FAITH IN GOD. HE SET OUT FOR CANAAN WITH HIS WIFE AND HIS NEPHEW, LOT. ABRAHAM WAS 75 YEARS OLD.
ALTHOUGH THE JOURNEY WAS DIFFICULT, GOD GUIDED THEM TO THE LAND HE PROMISED.
ABRAHAM, LOOK! I THINK WE HAVE REACHED CANAAN!
GOD IS TRULY MAGNIFICENT. WE HAVE ARRIVED! LET US THANK HIM. LET US WORSHIP HIM.
I WILL GIVE THIS LAND TO YOUR DESCENDANTS.
ABRAHAM BUILT AN ALTAR AND PRAYED.

GOD IS WONDERFUL. HE HAS PROMISED THIS LAND TO US, TO OUR CHILDREN, AND TO THEIR CHILDREN!
SARAH MUST HAVE WONDERED HOW GOD COULD PROMISE THE LAND TO THEIR CHILDREN, SINCE THEY HAD NONE.
I AM **TOO OLD** TO HAVE CHILDREN!
SARAH, HAVE FAITH IN GOD. I DO. I TRUST IN HIM. HE WILL PROVIDE.

Lot Leaves

Genesis 13

LOT LEFT WITH HIS HERDS. HE SET OFF FOR THE FERTILE JORDAN VALLEY.
ABRAHAM STAYED IN CANAAN.

God's Covenant with Abraham

Genesis 15

GOD TOLD ABRAHAM TO BRING HIM A COW...
...A FEMALE GOAT...
...A TURTLEDOVE...
...A RAM...
...AND A PIGEON.

ABRAHAM DID AS GOD ASKED. HE CUT THE COW, GOAT, AND RAM IN TWO.
ABRAHAM FELL ASLEEP, AND A DARKNESS FELL OVER HIM. AS HE SLEPT, GOD TOLD HIM ABOUT THE FUTURE.
YOU CAN BE SURE THAT YOUR DESCENDANTS WILL BE STRANGERS IN A FOREIGN LAND, WHERE THEY WILL BE SLAVES...
...BUT I WILL PUNISH THE NATION THAT ENSLAVES THEM, AND YOUR DESCENDANTS WILL RETURN HERE TO THIS LAND.
AS A SIGN OF HIS COVENANT, GOD PASSED A SMOKING FIREPOT WITH A FLAMING TORCH BETWEEN THE DIVIDED ANIMALS.

A Son Is Born

Genesis 16

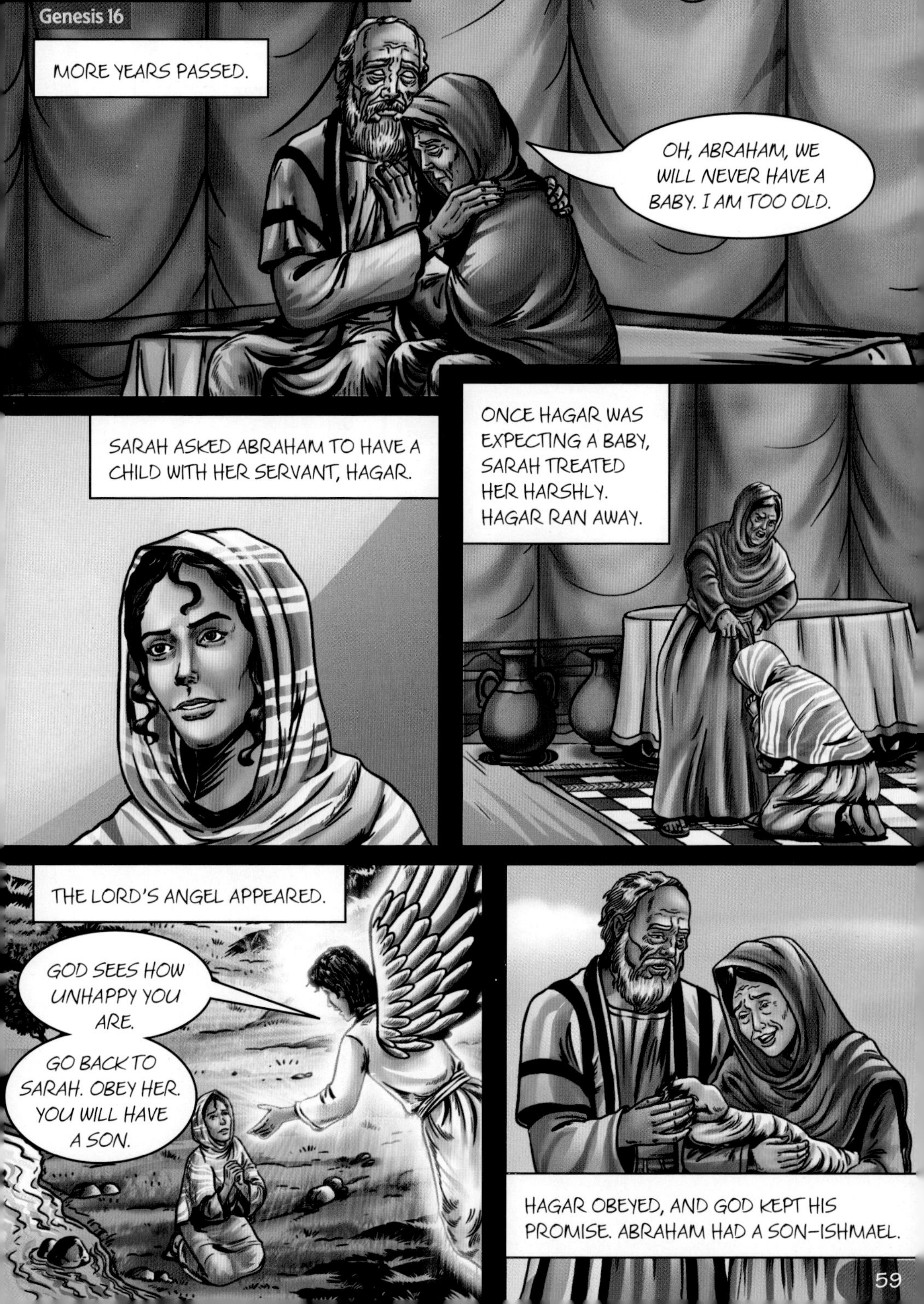

MORE YEARS PASSED.

OH, ABRAHAM, WE WILL NEVER HAVE A BABY. I AM TOO OLD.

SARAH ASKED ABRAHAM TO HAVE A CHILD WITH HER SERVANT, HAGAR.

ONCE HAGAR WAS EXPECTING A BABY, SARAH TREATED HER HARSHLY. HAGAR RAN AWAY.

The Destruction of Sodom and Gomorrah

Genesis 18–19

THE PEOPLE IN EACH CITY WERE WICKED AND IMMORAL.
GIVE ME YOUR **MONEY!**
MANY WERE CRUEL.
YOU DON'T BELONG HERE. **GET OUT!**
OTHERS WERE MEAN AND DID NOT WELCOME PEOPLE FROM THE OUTSIDE.

GOD WAS ANGRY. HE TOLD ABRAHAM HE WOULD DESTROY THE CITIES...
...AND HE WOULD KILL EVERY LIVING BEING IN THE CITIES, YOUNG AND OLD.
BUT MY NEPHEW LIVES IN SODOM!
WILL YOU SWEEP AWAY THE **RIGHTEOUS** WITH THE **WICKED?**
WILL YOU KILL THE **INNOCENT** WITH THE **GUILTY?**

SUPPOSE THERE WERE 50 GOOD PEOPLE IN THE CITY.
WOULD YOU TREAT THE 50 **GOOD** PEOPLE AS YOU WOULD TREAT THE **WICKED?**
GOD SAID, "IF I FIND 50 RIGHTEOUS PEOPLE, I WILL SPARE THE CITY."

WHAT IF THERE WERE **45** RIGHTEOUS PEOPLE?
WILL YOU DESTROY THE **WHOLE** CITY?
I WILL NOT DESTROY IT IF I FIND 45 THERE.
WHAT IF **TEN RIGHTEOUS PEOPLE** WERE FOUND THERE?
GOD SAID, "I WILL NOT DESTROY IT FOR THE SAKE OF THE TEN."

THAT EVENING TWO ANGELS APPEARED BEFORE LOT AT THE GATE OF SODOM.
ABRAHAM'S NEPHEW INVITED THEM TO HIS HOUSE.
A MOB SURROUNDED LOT'S HOUSE.
BRING THOSE MEN OUT!
LEAVE THESE MEN ALONE!
THE TWO ANGELS PULLED LOT BACK INSIDE AND LOCKED THE DOOR. THEN THEY STRUCK THE MOB WITH BLINDNESS.
LOT, YOU AND YOUR FAMILY MUST **LEAVE NOW!** GOD HAS SENT US TO DESTROY THIS CITY.
FLEE FOR YOUR LIFE! **DO NOT LOOK BACK AT THIS WICKED PLACE!**

THE ANGELS RUSHED LOT, HIS WIFE, AND THEIR DAUGHTERS OUT OF THE CITY SAFELY.
GOD RAINED FIRE ON SODOM AND GOMORRAH, DESTROYING BOTH CITIES AND THE PEOPLE IN THEM.
BUT LOT'S WIFE LOOKED BACK. AS SOON AS SHE LOOKED BEHIND HER, SHE TURNED INTO A PILLAR OF SALT.

God Tests Abraham
Genesis 18, 21–22
THE SUMMER SUN WAS HOT AS ABRAHAM SAT AT THE ENTRANCE OF HIS TENT.
AS HE LOOKED UP, ABRAHAM SAW THREE STRANGERS.
LET ME BRING YOU SOME WATER TO WASH YOUR FEET.
LET ME BRING YOU A LITTLE FOOD TO REFRESH YOURSELVES.

WHERE IS SARAH, YOUR WIFE?
SARAH WAS INSIDE THE TENT, LISTENING TO ABRAHAM AND THE STRANGER TALK.
I WILL RETURN TO YOU AT THIS TIME NEXT YEAR.
WHEN I COME BACK, **SARAH WILL HAVE A SON.**
SARAH LAUGHED WHEN SHE HEARD THE STRANGER'S PREDICTION.
THE LORD HAD PROMISED ABRAHAM THAT SARAH WOULD HAVE A SON.
I AM TOO OLD TO HAVE A CHILD.

GOD KEPT HIS PROMISE. HE GAVE SARAH AND ABRAHAM A SON, DESPITE THEIR AGE.
GOD HAS MADE ME LAUGH. EVERYONE WHO HEARS ABOUT THIS WILL LAUGH WITH ME!
THE BABY BOY WAS NAMED ISAAC, WHICH MEANS "HE LAUGHS."
NOW THAT SARAH HAD A CHILD OF HER OWN, SHE TOLD ABRAHAM TO SEND HAGAR AND ISHMAEL AWAY. ABRAHAM WAS SAD BUT DID AS SHE ASKED.
GOD LOOKED AFTER ISHMAEL IN THE DESERT AS HE GREW UP.

ISAAC ALSO GREW. HE WAS A HAPPY BOY. SARAH AND ABRAHAM LOVED HIM VERY MUCH.
ABRAHAM!
HERE I AM!
TAKE YOUR SON ISAAC, WHOM YOU LOVE, AND GO TO THE LAND OF MORIAH. SACRIFICE HIM AS AN OFFERING.
ABRAHAM WAS DEVASTATED TO HEAR GOD'S COMMAND. BUT HE TRUSTED GOD...

...AND THE NEXT DAY, HE TOOK ISAAC TO THE MOUNTAIN CALLED MORIAH.
ABRAHAM TOLD ISAAC TO COME WITH HIM TO WORSHIP GOD.
FATHER, IF WE ARE TO MAKE A SACRIFICE TO GOD, DON'T WE NEED AN ANIMAL?
GOD WILL PROVIDE, MY SON.
THEY ARRIVED AT THE PLACE GOD HAD DESCRIBED TO ABRAHAM. THEY BUILT AN ALTAR.
ABRAHAM THEN TOOK ISAAC...
AND ABRAHAM TIED ISAAC HIS SON AND PLACED HIM ON THE ALTAR.

JUST AS ABRAHAM WAS ABOUT TO CARRY OUT GOD'S COMMAND, AN ANGEL APPEARED!
ABRAHAM! ABRAHAM!
HERE I AM!
RELEASE HIM AND LET HIM LIVE! SACRIFICE THAT RAM INSTEAD.

ABRAHAM RELEASED HIS SON...
...AND WENT TO FETCH THE RAM.
ABRAHAM MADE A BURNT OFFERING OF THE RAM. THIS WAS HIS SACRIFICE TO GOD. THE ANGEL REAPPEARED.
GOD KNOWS THAT YOU TRUST HIM BECAUSE YOU WERE WILLING TO SACRIFICE YOUR CHERISHED SON.
GOD HAS **REAFFIRMED HIS COVENANT** TO YOU BECAUSE YOU OBEYED HIS COMMAND. GOD BLESSES YOU AND ALL YOUR DESCENDANTS!

Isaac and Rebekah

Genesis 24

ABRAHAM'S SERVANT SET OUT ON HIS MISSION.
HE BROUGHT GIFTS OF ALL KINDS TO OFFER TO ISAAC'S BRIDE, WHOEVER SHE MIGHT BE.
HE WORRIED THAT HE WOULD NOT FIND THE WOMAN WHO WAS MEANT FOR ISAAC.
HE PRAYED TO GOD TO SEND HIM A SIGN. HE PRAYED THAT A WOMAN WOULD OFFER WATER TO HIS CAMELS.
THE SERVANT STOPPED TO REST WHEN HE SAW A BEAUTIFUL YOUNG WOMAN.
HER NAME WAS REBEKAH.
DRINK, SIR. THIS WATER WILL REFRESH YOU.
I WILL ALSO DRAW **WATER FOR YOUR CAMELS**. THEY NEED TO DRINK TOO.

WHOSE DAUGHTER ARE YOU? WOULD YOUR FATHER HAVE ANY ROOM FOR MY CAMELS AND ME TO STAY THE NIGHT?
I AM THE DAUGHTER OF BETHUEL.
PLEASE, SIR. COME MEET MY FATHER AND MY FAMILY. WE LIVE NEARBY.
ABRAHAM'S SERVANT SPENT THE NIGHT AT REBEKAH'S FATHER'S HOUSE.
GOD HAS CHOSEN YOUR DAUGHTER TO BE THE WIFE OF MY MASTER'S SON!
THEY LISTENED AS HE TOLD OF HOW HE HAD PRAYED TO GOD FOR A SIGN AND GOD HAD ANSWERED.
CAN REBEKAH COME BACK WITH ME AND MARRY MY MASTER'S SON?
YES, I WILL GO.

REBEKAH TRAVELED BACK WITH ABRAHAM'S SERVANT.
WHO IS THAT MAN OVER THERE?
THAT IS ISAAC, MY MASTER'S SON.
REBEKAH AND ISAAC KNEW THEY WERE MEANT TO BE TOGETHER. ISAAC TOOK REBEKAH AS HIS WIFE, AND HE LOVED HER. NOW THE GENERATIONS OF ABRAHAM WOULD CONTINUE THROUGH ISAAC'S DESCENDANTS.

Hero Profile
Jacob—Father of a Nation

AGE: LIVED TO THE AGE OF 147

FATHER: ISAAC, SON OF ABRAHAM

MOTHER: REBEKAH

BROTHER: ESAU

WIVES: LEAH, RACHEL

CHILDREN: SONS—REUBEN, SIMEON, LEVI, JUDAH, DAN, NAPHTALI, GAD, ASHER, ISSACHAR, ZEBULUN, JOSEPH, BENJAMIN; DAUGHTER—DINAH

TWELVE TRIBES OF ISRAEL

JACOB'S TWELVE SONS WOULD BECOME THE ANCESTORS OF THE TWELVE TRIBES OF ISRAEL—CALLED "ISRAEL" BECAUSE GOD CHANGED JACOB'S NAME TO "ISRAEL."

ISRAEL

THE MODERN STATE OF ISRAEL WAS FORMED IN 1948 AS THE ONLY JEWISH COUNTRY IN THE WORLD.

The Birth of Jacob and Esau
Genesis 25
ISAAC AND REBEKAH LIVED THEIR LIVES. BUT SOMETHING WAS MISSING—A CHILD.
OH, ISAAC, HOW I LONG TO HAVE A BABY!
YES, WE MUST HAVE CHILDREN AND CONTINUE MY FATHER'S LINE.
I WILL PRAY TO GOD. HE BLESSED ME AFTER MY FATHER, ABRAHAM, DIED.
DEAR LORD, HEAR MY PRAYERS.
MY WIFE WANTS A SON TO LOVE.
GOD HEARD ISAAC'S PRAYERS, AND REBEKAH BECAME PREGNANT WITH TWINS.

THE TWINS REBEKAH CARRIED STRUGGLED TOGETHER INSIDE HER. SHE WONDERED WHAT WAS HAPPENING, SO SHE ASKED GOD ABOUT IT.

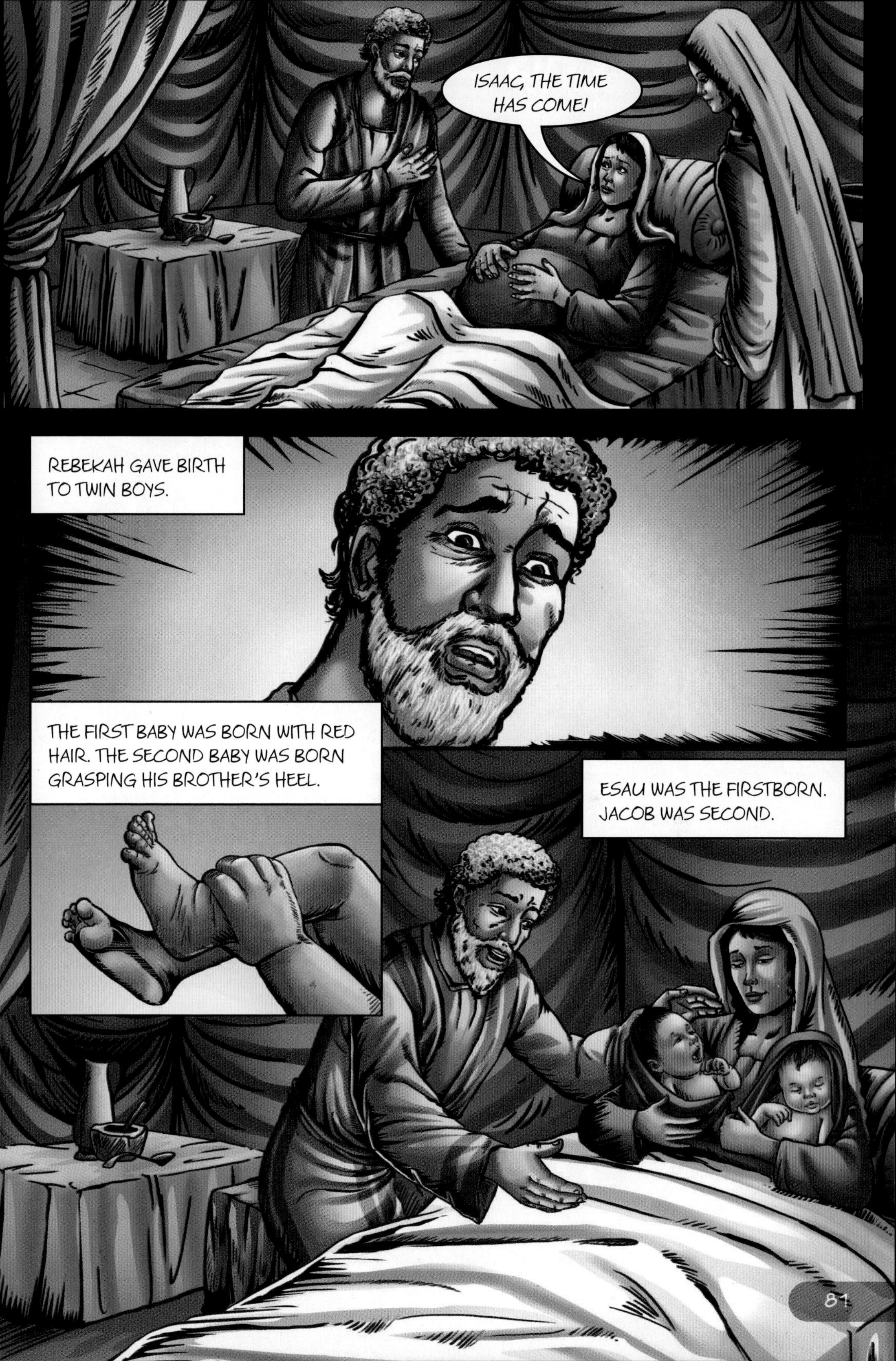
ISAAC, THE TIME HAS COME!
REBEKAH GAVE BIRTH TO TWIN BOYS.
THE FIRST BABY WAS BORN WITH RED HAIR. THE SECOND BABY WAS BORN GRASPING HIS BROTHER'S HEEL.
ESAU WAS THE FIRSTBORN. JACOB WAS SECOND.

Esau Sells His Birthright

Genesis 25, 27

ESAU, YOU ARE MY FAVORITE SON.
I LOVE YOU THE MOST, JACOB.

BROTHER, I AM SO HUNGRY! GIVE ME SOME OF THAT RED STEW YOU ARE COOKING!
YOU CAN HAVE THE STEW, ESAU. BUT YOU MUST GIVE ME YOUR BIRTHRIGHT.
MY BIRTHRIGHT? WHY SHOULD I GIVE YOU ALL MY RIGHTS AS THE FIRSTBORN SON?
TRADE ME YOUR BIRTHRIGHT FOR THE STEW.
WELL, I AM STARVING! WHAT GOOD IS MY BIRTHRIGHT IF I STARVE TO DEATH?
I SWEAR TO YOU, JACOB, YOU WILL HAVE ALL MY RIGHTS AS THE FIRSTBORN.
NOW GIVE ME THE STEW.

THE YEARS PASSED, AND ISAAC GREW OLD AND BLIND.
ISAAC CALLED FOR ESAU AND TOLD HIM TO GO OUT AND HUNT FOR SOME GAME.
AFTER YOU HUNT, PREPARE MY FAVORITE FOOD...
...SO THAT I MAY GIVE YOU MY BLESSING BEFORE I DIE.
SO ESAU WENT OUT TO HUNT AS HIS FATHER REQUESTED.
REBEKAH, HOWEVER, WAS MAKING OTHER PLANS.

LISTEN TO ME, JACOB. BRING ME TWO GOATS, AND I WILL PREPARE YOUR FATHER'S FAVORITE MEAL. THEN YOU WILL SERVE IT TO HIM.
BUT WHY, MOTHER?
HE WILL THINK YOU ARE ESAU...
...AND HE WILL GIVE YOU HIS BLESSING!
ESAU'S SKIN IS HAIRY. MY SKIN IS SMOOTH. FATHER WILL KNOW I'M NOT ESAU!
HE WILL **CURSE** ME, NOT **BLESS** ME!
I HAVE AN IDEA, JACOB. JUST GO GET THE GOATS. AND HURRY!

The Stolen Blessing

Genesis 27

IS THAT YOU, ESAU? COME CLOSER, MY SON, SO THAT I MIGHT FEEL YOU.
YES, I AM ESAU.
THE VOICE IS JACOB'S, BUT THE HANDS ARE ESAU'S.
GIVE ME MY DINNER SO THAT I MIGHT BLESS YOU.
COME CLOSE AND KISS ME, MY SON. YOU SMELL LIKE THE OUTDOORS THAT THE LORD HAS BLESSED.
I DO BLESS YOU, MY FIRSTBORN SON!
ISAAC BLESSED JACOB. THIS ENSURED THAT THE YOUNGER SON WOULD RULE OVER THE OLDER SON, JUST AS GOD HAD PROMISED WHEN HE SPOKE TO REBEKAH.

Stairway to Heaven
Genesis 27–32
ISAAC HAD BLESSED JACOB, AND ESAU WAS FURIOUS. HE VOWED REVENGE.
I'LL **KILL** MY BROTHER!
REBEKAH OVERHEARD ESAU AND WARNED HER BELOVED JACOB.
YOU MUST **LEAVE. NOW!**
GO VISIT YOUR UNCLE IN HARAN. I WILL SEND WORD WHEN IT IS SAFE FOR YOU TO RETURN.
JACOB LEFT, ALTHOUGH HE DID NOT WANT TO.

JACOB STOPPED IN A PLACE CALLED BETHEL AND FELL ASLEEP.
AS HE SLEPT, JACOB DREAMED OF A STAIRWAY TO HEAVEN. ANGELS WALKED UP AND DOWN THE STEPS.
THEN GOD SPOKE TO HIM.
I AM THE GOD OF ABRAHAM AND THE GOD OF ISAAC. THIS LAND WILL BE YOURS. YOUR DESCENDANTS WILL BE AS NUMEROUS AS THE DUST OF THE EARTH.

THE NEXT MORNING JACOB MADE A PROMISE TO FOLLOW GOD.
HE CONTINUED HIS JOURNEY. ONE DAY HE CAME UPON A GROUP OF SHEPHERDS AT A WELL.
BROTHERS, DO YOU KNOW MY UNCLE, LABAN?
YES, WE DO! AND HERE COMES HIS DAUGHTER, RACHEL.
LABAN IS MY FATHER. I WILL TAKE YOU TO MEET HIM.
RACHEL AND JACOB FELL IN LOVE.
JACOB ASKED LABAN IF HE COULD MARRY HIS DAUGHTER.
I WILL WORK FOR YOU **BECAUSE I LOVE RACHEL** WITH ALL MY HEART.
YOU CAN MARRY RACHEL, BUT ONLY IF YOU WORK FOR ME FOR **SEVEN YEARS**.

HOWEVER, LABAN TRICKED JACOB. INSTEAD OF MARRYING RACHEL, JACOB MARRIED LABAN'S OLDER DAUGHTER, LEAH.
LABAN SAID JACOB COULD MARRY RACHEL TOO...

...BUT ONLY IF JACOB AGREED TO WORK FOR FREE FOR ANOTHER SEVEN YEARS.
JACOB NOW HAD TWO WIVES, BUT HE LOVED RACHEL MORE.

JACOB WORKED FOR LABAN ANOTHER SEVEN YEARS.
JACOB HAD MANY CHILDREN WITH LEAH AND TWO SERVANT WOMEN. RACHEL COULD NOT BEAR CHILDREN, SO SHE PRAYED TO GOD.

FINALLY, GOD GAVE HER A SON, JOSEPH

I HAVE WORKED HARD FOR YOU FOR MANY YEARS, LABAN. PLEASE LET ME TAKE MY WIVES AND CHILDREN AND RETURN TO MY HOME COUNTRY.
WHAT CAN I PAY YOU?
LABAN AND JACOB HAD DISAGREEMENTS. JACOB GATHERED HIS FAMILY AND PREPARED TO SECRETLY LEAVE FOR HOME.
MESSENGERS, TRAVEL AHEAD OF US AND GIVE WORD TO MY BROTHER, ESAU. TELL HIM I AM COMING HOME!
THE MESSENGERS WENT TO ESAU AND RETURNED TO JACOB. THEY TOLD HIM THAT ESAU WAS COMING TO MEET JACOB, ACCOMPANIED BY 400 OF HIS MEN!
JACOB FEARED HIS BROTHER WAS COMING FOR REVENGE, NOT REUNION.

GOD OF MY GRANDFATHER, ABRAHAM...
...RESCUE ME FROM ESAU.
DELIVER MY FAMILY AND ME FROM AN **ALMOST CERTAIN DEATH!**
JACOB CAME UP WITH A PLAN. HE TOLD HIS SERVANTS TO MEET HIS BROTHER AND GIVE ESAU SOME OF JACOB'S ANIMALS.
HE HOPED THE GIFT WOULD SOFTEN ESAU'S HEART.

Wrestling with God
Genesis 32–33
JACOB THEN SENT HIS FAMILY ACROSS THE RIVER SO THEY WOULD BE SAFE FROM ESAU'S VENGEANCE. JACOB WAITED ALONE ON THE OPPOSITE BANK. HE PREPARED HIMSELF FOR DEATH.
A STRANGER SUDDENLY APPEARED AND FOUGHT WITH JACOB.
WHO ARE YOU? WHAT DO YOU WANT?
THE TWO FOUGHT UNTIL DAWN. THE STRANGER TOUCHED JACOB'S HIP, INJURING HIM, BUT JACOB FOUGHT ON. HE REFUSED TO LET THE STRANGER GO UNTIL HE HAD BLESSED JACOB.

THEY CONTINUED TO FIGHT. JACOB ASKED THE STRANGER TO BLESS HIM.
WHAT IS YOUR NAME?
MY NAME IS JACOB.
NOW YOU WILL BE CALLED ISRAEL, BECAUSE YOU HAVE FOUGHT WITH GOD AND MEN AND HAVE WON.
I HAVE SEEN THE **FACE OF GOD,** AND I AM STILL ALIVE!
JACOB FINALLY MET HIS BROTHER.
I AM SO HAPPY TO SEE YOU!
ACCEPT THE GIFTS I HAVE SENT TO YOU.
I SHALL, MY BROTHER.
JACOB AND ESAU WEPT AS THEY WERE REUNITED AS BROTHERS AGAIN.

Hero Profile
Joseph—The Dreamer with a Coat

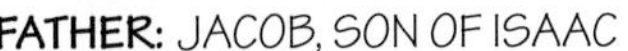

FATHER: JACOB, SON OF ISAAC

MOTHER: RACHEL

BROTHERS: REUBEN, SIMEON, LEVI, JUDAH, DAN, NAPHTALI, GAD, ASHER, ISSACHAR, ZEBULUN, BENJAMIN

INTERPRETER OF DREAMS

JOSEPH IS ONE OF MANY OLD TESTAMENT HEROES WHO ARE GIVEN THE GIFT OF INTERPRETING THE MEANINGS OF DREAMS OR VISIONS. PROPHETS SUCH AS DANIEL, ISAIAH, AND EZEKIEL ARE SHOWN FUTURE EVENTS OR MESSAGES FROM GOD THROUGH VISIONS OR DREAMS.

MOVIE SCRIPT

THE STORY OF JOSEPH AND HIS FAMILY READS LIKE A SCRIPT OF A CLIFF-HANGER MOVIE. HIS LIFE IS A SNAPSHOT OF HOW MESSY, COMPLICATED, AND PAINFUL FAMILY LIFE CAN BE. BUT GOD HAD A PLAN. HE BROUGHT FORGIVENESS, BLESSING, AND HEALING TO JOSEPH AND HIS FAMILY.

Favorite Son

Genesis 35, 37

TO SHOW HIS LOVE AND DEVOTION, JACOB GAVE JOSEPH A BEAUTIFUL COAT.
BECAUSE YOU ARE THE SON OF MY OLD AGE, THIS COAT IS YOURS.
YOU ARE MY FAVORITE SON.
ONE NIGHT, JOSEPH HAD A DREAM. HIS BUNDLE OF GRAIN STOOD STRAIGHT UP, WHILE HIS BROTHERS' BUNDLES BOWED BEFORE IT.

JOSEPH TOLD HIS BROTHERS HIS DREAM.
WE WERE ALL WORKING IN THE FIELD.
MY BUNDLE OF GRAIN STOOD UP.
YOUR BUNDLES BOWED DOWN TO IT.
SO YOU THINK YOU WILL **RULE** OVER US?
YOU THINK YOU WILL BE OUR **KING?**
JOSEPH HAD ANOTHER DREAM, IN WHICH THE MOON, THE SUN, AND 11 STARS BOWED DOWN TO HIM.
DO YOU REALLY EXPECT YOUR MOTHER AND ME TO BOW DOWN TO YOU?
AND YOUR BROTHERS TOO?
JOSEPH'S BROTHERS GREW TO HATE HIM. THEY WERE JEALOUS OF THEIR FATHER'S LOVE FOR HIM. THEY BEGAN TO PLOT AGAINST HIM.

ONE AFTERNOON JACOB SENT JOSEPH TO THE FIELDS TO CHECK ON HIS BROTHERS.
HERE COMES THE DREAMER. **LET'S KILL HIM.**
WE'LL THROW HIS BODY DOWN THE WELL!
WAIT! IT'S NOT RIGHT TO KILL HIM. WHY SHOULD WE CARRY THE GUILT OF HIS MURDER ALL OUR DAYS?
JUST AS JOSEPH APPROACHED, HIS BROTHERS GRABBED HIM AND RIPPED HIS COAT FROM HIS SHOULDERS.
THEN THEY THREW JOSEPH INTO THE PIT.

Bound for Slavery

Genesis 37

AND SO THE BROTHERS PULLED JOSEPH FROM THE PIT...
...AND SOLD HIM FOR 20 PIECES OF SILVER.
HE WILL MAKE A GOOD SLAVE.

JOSEPH WAS TAKEN AWAY, FAR FROM HIS HOME AND FAMILY.

MEANWHILE, HIS BROTHERS PLOTTED HOW THEY WOULD EXPLAIN JOSEPH'S DISAPPEARANCE TO THEIR FATHER, JACOB.

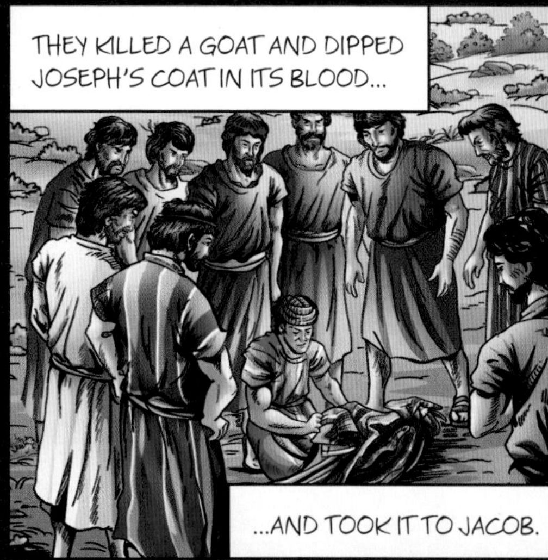
THEY KILLED A GOAT AND DIPPED JOSEPH'S COAT IN ITS BLOOD...
...AND TOOK IT TO JACOB.

FATHER, WE FOUND THIS COAT IN THE FIELD. IS IT JOSEPH'S?
YES! IT IS MY SON'S COAT! A WILD ANIMAL MUST HAVE EATEN HIM!

JACOB WAS OVERWHELMED WITH GRIEF. HE TORE OFF HIS CLOTHES AND WRAPPED HIMSELF IN BURLAP. HE WEPT.
FATHER, PLEASE DON'T BE SO SAD.
OH, FATHER, JOSEPH WAS A GOOD BOY. I KNOW HOW MUCH YOU LOVED HIM.
JACOB COULD NOT BE COMFORTED. HE DID NOT KNOW THAT JOSEPH WAS ALIVE AND WOULD SOON BECOME A VERY IMPORTANT MAN.

Joseph in Prison

Genesis 39

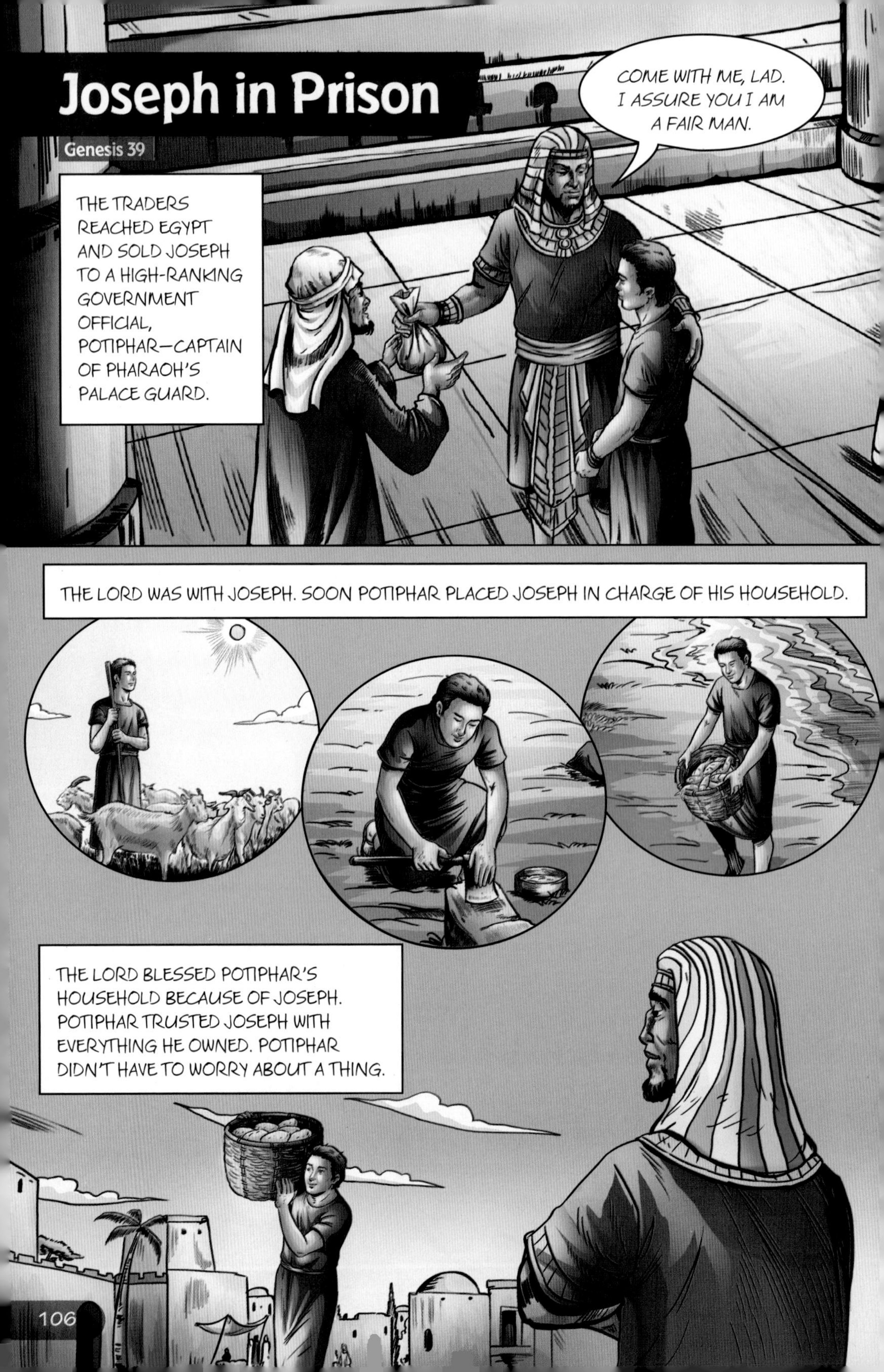

THE TRADERS REACHED EGYPT AND SOLD JOSEPH TO A HIGH-RANKING GOVERNMENT OFFICIAL, POTIPHAR—CAPTAIN OF PHARAOH'S PALACE GUARD.

THE LORD WAS WITH JOSEPH. SOON POTIPHAR PLACED JOSEPH IN CHARGE OF HIS HOUSEHOLD.

THE LORD BLESSED POTIPHAR'S HOUSEHOLD BECAUSE OF JOSEPH. POTIPHAR TRUSTED JOSEPH WITH EVERYTHING HE OWNED. POTIPHAR DIDN'T HAVE TO WORRY ABOUT A THING.

POTIPHAR'S WIFE NOTICED THAT JOSEPH WAS VERY HANDSOME AND STRONG.
JOSEPH, I WANT YOU TO SLEEP WITH ME.
NO! YOU ARE MY MASTER'S WIFE.
IT WOULD BE WRONG! IT WOULD BE A SIN AGAINST GOD!
POTIPHAR'S WIFE PRESSURED JOSEPH DAY AFTER DAY TO SLEEP WITH HER. JOSEPH REFUSED AND ONCE HAD TO RUN FROM THE ROOM.
HOW DARE YOU REFUSE ME!
SHE WANTED REVENGE AGAINST JOSEPH.
GUARDS! JOSEPH TRIED TO ATTACK ME! BUT I SCREAMED, AND HE RAN AWAY.
LOOK! HERE IS HIS CLOAK!

POTIPHAR'S WIFE TOLD HER HUSBAND HER LIE ABOUT JOSEPH.
DESPITE HIS LOVE FOR HIS FAVORITE SERVANT, POTIPHAR BELIEVED HIS WIFE.
JOSEPH, HOW **DARE** YOU DISRESPECT MY WIFE!
YOU CAN ROT IN THIS CELL FOR WHAT YOU HAVE DONE!
BUT EVEN AS JOSEPH WAS LOCKED IN PRISON, THE LORD WAS WITH HIM.

THE HEAD JAILER LIKED JOSEPH...

...AND PUT HIM IN CHARGE OF ALL THE PRISONERS.

The Interpreter of Dreams

Genesis 40–41

I DREAMED I WAS SQUEEZING JUICE FOR PHARAOH'S WINE CUP FROM GRAPES ON THREE BRANCHES.
WHAT DOES IT MEAN?
GOD IS SAYING THAT IN THREE DAYS YOU WILL BE IN PHARAOH'S FAVOR ONCE MORE.
SPEAK WELL OF ME TO PHARAOH WHEN YOU SEE HIM.
IN MY DREAM, I WAS CARRYING THREE BASKETS OF BAKED GOODS FOR PHARAOH, BUT THE BIRDS WERE EATING THEM.
GOD IS SAYING THAT IN THREE DAYS PHARAOH WILL CUT OFF YOUR HEAD AND PUT YOUR BODY ON A POLE, WHERE THE BIRDS WILL PECK AT IT.
SO IT CAME TO PASS. IN THREE DAYS' TIME, THE CUPBEARER BEGAN WORKING FOR PHARAOH, AND THE BAKER WAS KILLED.

JOSEPH STAYED IN PRISON FOR TWO YEARS. THEN PHARAOH HAD A DREAM ABOUT SEVEN HEALTHY COWS GRAZING BY THE NILE RIVER. THEY WERE DEVOURED BY SEVEN HUNGRY COWS.
THEN PHARAOH DREAMED ABOUT SEVEN PLUMP HEADS OF GRAIN ON A SINGLE STALK, WHICH WERE SWALLOWED BY SEVEN THIN HEADS OF GRAIN WITHERED BY THE EAST WIND.
WHAT DO THESE DREAMS MEAN?
WE DO NOT HAVE AN ANSWER FOR YOU, PHARAOH.

THE CUP-BEARER STEPPED FORWARD.
PHARAOH, I KNOW A MAN WHO CAN INTERPRET YOUR DREAMS!
WHO IS THIS MAN??? BRING HIM TO ME!
PHARAOH TOLD JOSEPH HIS DREAMS. WITH GOD'S HELP, JOSEPH THEN TOLD PHARAOH WHAT THEY MEANT.
EGYPT WILL HAVE SEVEN YEARS OF BOUNTIFUL HARVESTS...
...FOLLOWED BY SEVEN YEARS OF TERRIBLE FAMINE.
PLAN WISELY, PHARAOH, AND YOU SHALL SAVE YOUR PEOPLE!

Joseph Feeds His Family

Genesis 41–45

PHARAOH GAVE JOSEPH THE JOB OF PREPARING ALL OF EGYPT FOR THE FAMINE HE HAD PREDICTED. HE BECAME MORE POWERFUL THAN ANY MAN IN EGYPT OTHER THAN PHARAOH.
JOSEPH TRAVELED ACROSS EGYPT, COLLECTING FOOD FROM THE FIELDS AND STORING IT IN THE CITIES.
FOR SEVEN YEARS, JOSEPH COLLECTED THE FOOD. THERE WAS SO MUCH THAT HE HAD TO STOP MEASURING IT.
FINALLY, THE SEVEN YEARS OF ABUNDANCE CAME TO AN END.

THE YEARS OF PLENTY WERE FOLLOWED BY SEVEN YEARS OF FAMINE.
BECAUSE OF JOSEPH, HOWEVER, THE PEOPLE HAD ENOUGH TO EAT.
PEOPLE SUFFERING IN OTHER COUNTRIES CAME TO EGYPT FOR FOOD.

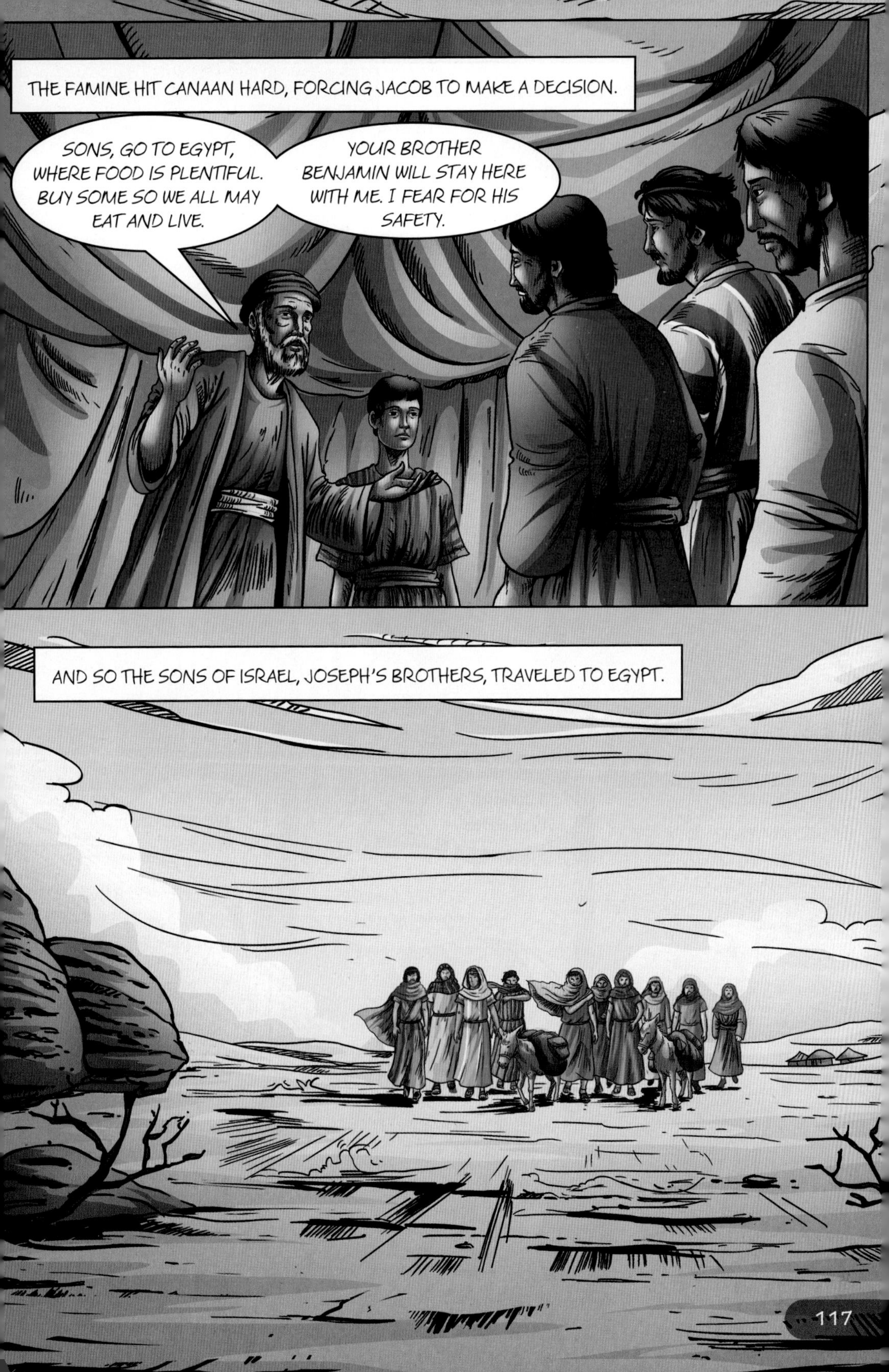
THE FAMINE HIT CANAAN HARD, FORCING JACOB TO MAKE A DECISION.
SONS, GO TO EGYPT, WHERE FOOD IS PLENTIFUL. BUY SOME SO WE ALL MAY EAT AND LIVE.
YOUR BROTHER BENJAMIN WILL STAY HERE WITH ME. I FEAR FOR HIS SAFETY.
AND SO THE SONS OF ISRAEL, JOSEPH'S BROTHERS, TRAVELED TO EGYPT.

WHEN THEY ARRIVED, THEY BOWED AT JOSEPH'S FEET.
MY BROTHERS COME BEGGING, BUT THEY DO NOT RECOGNIZE ME!
SIR, WE'VE COME FROM THE LAND OF CANAAN TO BUY GRAIN.
OUR PEOPLE ARE STARVING. PLEASE— CAN YOU HELP US?
YOU ARE LIARS! SPIES!
YOU'VE COME TO SEE WHERE EGYPT IS WEAK!
NO! NO! WE ARE HONEST.
WE ARE BROTHERS, NOT SPIES! WE ARE THE SONS OF ONE MAN. OUR YOUNGEST BROTHER IS STILL AT HOME WITH OUR FATHER.

IF YOU WISH TO LIVE, PROVE YOUR STORY. BRING ME YOUR YOUNGEST BROTHER.
ONE OF YOU WILL STAY HERE IN PRISON UNTIL THE OTHERS RETURN. THAT WAY I WILL KNOW YOU ARE NOT SPIES.
WE ARE BEING PUNISHED BECAUSE OF WHAT WE DID TO JOSEPH.
JOSEPH OVERHEARD HIS BROTHERS' CONVERSATION. HE WEPT.
JOSEPH ORDERED THAT THE BROTHERS—EXCEPT SIMEON—RETURN HOME WITH GRAIN TO FEED THEIR FAMILY. JOSEPH ALSO PLACED IN THEIR SACKS THE MONEY THEY HAD BROUGHT TO PAY FOR THE GRAIN. THE BROTHERS WENT BACK TO CANAAN WITH THE GRAIN, BUT WHEN THEY GOT HOME, THEY WERE HORRIFIED TO FIND THAT THE MONEY THEY HAD TAKEN TO PAY FOR THE GRAIN WAS IN THEIR SACKS. NOW THEY WERE SCARED TO GO BACK.

EVENTUALLY, THE FAMILY RAN OUT OF GRAIN AND HAD NOTHING TO EAT. IN DESPERATION, THEY RETURNED TO EGYPT, BRINGING BENJAMIN AS JOSEPH HAD DEMANDED.
JOSEPH WAS SO HAPPY THAT HE HELD A MAGNIFICENT FEAST.
JOSEPH TESTED HIS BROTHERS AGAIN. HE TOLD HIS PALACE MANAGER TO PUT THEIR MONEY BACK IN THEIR SACKS AND FILL THEIR SACKS WITH GRAIN.
JOSEPH ALSO TOLD HIS MANAGER TO PLACE JOSEPH'S OWN SILVER CUP IN BENJAMIN'S SACK.

AFTER SAYING FAREWELL, THE BROTHERS LEFT TO RETURN HOME. BUT JOSEPH SENT HIS PALACE MANAGER TO SEARCH THEIR SACKS. HE FOUND THE CUP IN BENJAMIN'S SACK.
BENJAMIN STOLE FROM ME! HE WILL BE MY **SLAVE!**
PLEASE, TAKE ME INSTEAD!, I **BEG OF YOU!** MY FATHER HAS ALREADY LOST ONE SON. IF HE LOSES BENJAMIN, HE WILL DIE!
AT LAST JOSEPH KNEW HIS BROTHERS COULD BE FORGIVEN.
FEAR NOT, **FOR I AM YOUR BROTHER JOSEPH!** GOD SENT ME HERE AHEAD OF YOU TO SAVE LIVES.
BRING MY FATHER HERE TO EGYPT, WHERE FOOD IS PLENTIFUL!

SO JACOB AND HIS FAMILY MOVED TO EGYPT,
WHERE HE WAS REUNITED WITH HIS FAVORITE SON.
JACOB AND HIS FAMILY WERE GIVEN GOOD GRAZING LAND FOR THEIR ANIMALS. JACOB LIVED TO BE 147. HE BLESSED HIS SONS BEFORE HE DIED. HIS DESCENDANTS INCREASED GREATLY IN NUMBER IN EGYPT.

Hero Profile
Moses—The Deliverer

FATHER: AMRAM

MOTHER: JOCHEBED

BROTHERS/SISTERS: AARON AND MIRIAM

FIRST WIFE: ZIPPORAH

SONS: GERSHOM, ELIEZER

WHO WAS PHARAOH?

LIKE JOSEPH, MOSES AND HIS BROTHER, AARON, DEALT WITH AN EGYPTIAN KING CALLED "PHARAOH" IN THE BIBLE. JUST WHO THIS PHARAOH WAS REMAINS A MYSTERY, ALTHOUGH HE MAY HAVE BEEN RAMESES II, WHO RULED EGYPT AROUND 1300 BC.

THE PASSOVER RITUAL

FOR CENTURIES, THE JEWISH PEOPLE HAVE CELEBRATED THE ISRAELITES' SURVIVAL OF THE FINAL PLAGUE DESCRIBED IN EXODUS. FOR MANY JEWS, PASSOVER IS A SEVEN-DAY CELEBRATION HIGHLIGHTED BY A MEAL CALLED A "SEDER" IN WHICH THE EVENTS OF THE EXODUS ARE RETOLD.

A Baby in a Basket

Exodus 1–2

A NEW PHARAOH RULED OVER EGYPT. HE KNEW NOTHING ABOUT JOSEPH OR HOW HE HAD HELPED EGYPT IN THE PAST. JOSEPH'S PEOPLE, THE ISRAELITES (ALSO CALLED HEBREWS), LIVED IN THE LAND OF GOSHEN. THERE WERE SO MANY ISRAELITES THAT PHARAOH BECAME CONCERNED.

THE HEBREWS ARE MORE NUMEROUS THAN WE ARE!

THEY MIGHT JOIN OUR ENEMIES TO FIGHT AGAINST US.

PHARAOH ENSLAVED THE ISRAELITES AND FORCED THEM TO BUILD CITIES. IT WAS BACK-BREAKING WORK.

STILL, THE ISRAELITE POPULATION CONTINUED TO GROW, FORCING PHARAOH TO TAKE MORE DRASTIC ACTION.

YOU ARE MIDWIVES TO THE HEBREW WOMEN.

IF THE WOMEN GIVE BIRTH TO BOYS, **KILL THEM!**

AS YOU COMMAND.

BUT THE MIDWIVES FEARED GOD AND REFUSED TO OBEY PHARAOH'S EVIL ORDER.

PHARAOH ORDERED THE EGYPTIANS TO THROW EVERY NEWBORN HEBREW BOY INTO THE NILE RIVER.

NO! DO NOT KILL MY BABY! PLEASE, I'LL DO ANYTHING!

ONE HEBREW MOTHER, JOCHEBED, HID HER BABY BOY FROM THE EGYPTIANS. FOR THREE MONTHS SHE KEPT HIM SAFE. BUT HE GREW FAST AND SOON BECAME TOO BIG TO HIDE.

TO SAVE HER BABY'S LIFE, THE MOTHER PLACED HIM IN A BASKET MADE OF PAPYRUS REEDS AND PUT IT IN THE RIVER.

MAY THE LORD PROTECT YOU, MY SON.

THE BOY'S SISTER, MIRIAM, WATCHED THE BASKET FROM A DISTANCE. AT THAT TIME, PHARAOH'S DAUGHTER WAS BATHING. SHE SAW THE BASKET.

IT IS ONE OF THE HEBREW BABIES!

MIRIAM APPROACHED THE PRINCESS.

SHALL I FIND A HEBREW WOMAN TO NURSE HIM?

YES, GO!

TAKE THIS CHILD AND NURSE HIM UNTIL HE IS OLDER, AND I WILL PAY YOU.

AS YOU WISH!

THE BABY'S OWN MOTHER TOOK HIM HOME AND CARED FOR HIM.

WHEN THE BOY GREW OLDER, PHARAOH'S DAUGHTER ADOPTED HIM AS HER SON. SHE NAMED HIM MOSES.
OH, MOSES, YOU WILL BE A GREAT MAN IN A GREAT LAND—A PRINCE WHO WILL LEAD HIS PEOPLE.

Moses the Prince

Exodus 2

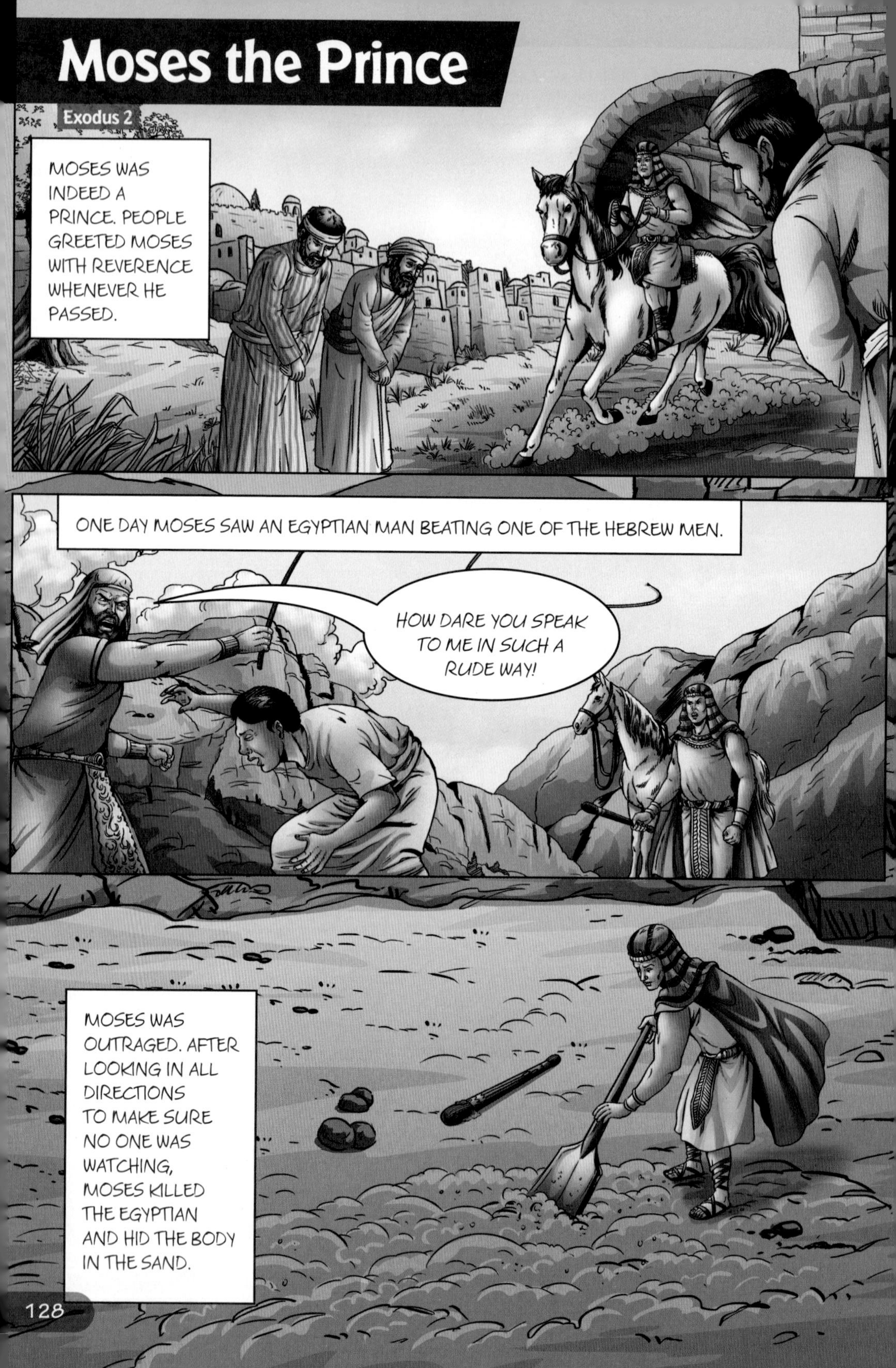

THE NEXT DAY MOSES SAW TWO HEBREW MEN FIGHTING.
WHY ARE YOU BEATING UP YOUR FRIEND?
WHO ARE **YOU** TO JUDGE US?
ARE YOU GOING TO **KILL US** LIKE YOU KILLED THE EGYPTIAN?
IF THEY KNOW I KILLED THE EGYPTIAN, THEN PHARAOH MUST ALSO KNOW.
MOSES KILLED ONE OF MY SUBJECTS? **MOSES?** HOW COULD HE? HOW DARE HE???
MOSES WILL PAY DEARLY WITH HIS LIFE.

The Burning Bush
Exodus 2–4
WITH HIS LIFE IN DANGER, MOSES FLED FROM EGYPT. HE TRAVELED EAST TO MIDIAN, WHERE HE EVENTUALLY BECAME A SHEPHERD. HERE'S HOW THAT HAPPENED.
ONE DAY MOSES WAS SITTING NEAR A WELL. HE SAW SEVEN WOMEN APPROACHING WITH THEIR SHEEP.
YOU WOMEN! GET OUT OF HERE!
YOU CANNOT WATER YOUR ANIMALS HERE.
WE'VE JUST COME TO WATER OUR FATHER'S FLOCK.
MOSES CAME TO THE DEFENSE OF THE WOMEN.
WHO ARE YOU TO DENY THESE WOMEN WATER FOR THEIR FLOCK?
THEY HAVE EVERY RIGHT TO BE HERE!

WHY ARE YOU BACK SO SOON TODAY?
AN EGYPTIAN RESCUED US FROM THE SHEPHERDS.
HE DREW WATER FOR US AND OUR ANIMALS.
WHY DID YOU LEAVE THE MAN THERE? GO TO HIM AND BRING HIM BACK.
INVITE HIM TO EAT WITH US.
MOSES ACCEPTED THEIR INVITATION AND STAYED WITH THEM.
THE FATHER LIKED MOSES SO MUCH THAT HE GAVE HIS DAUGHTER, ZIPPORAH, TO HIM AS A BRIDE.

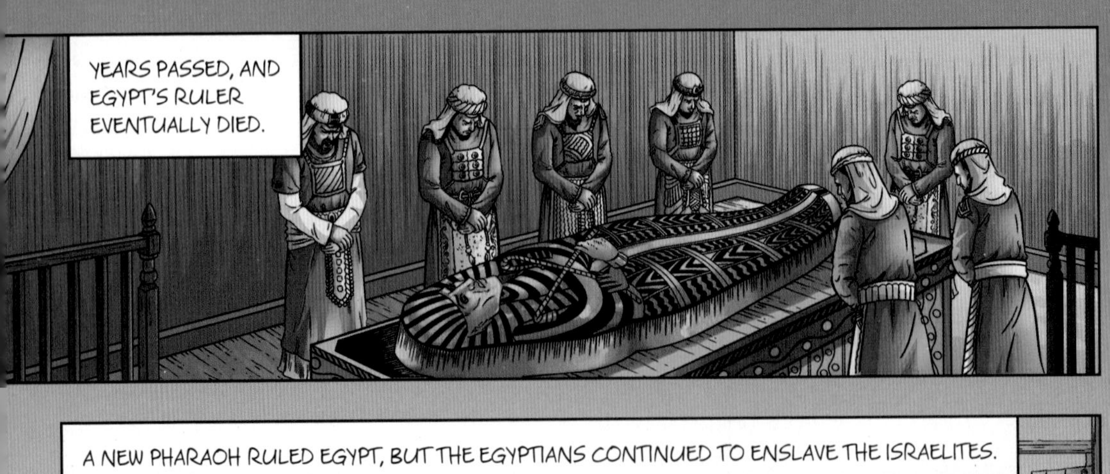

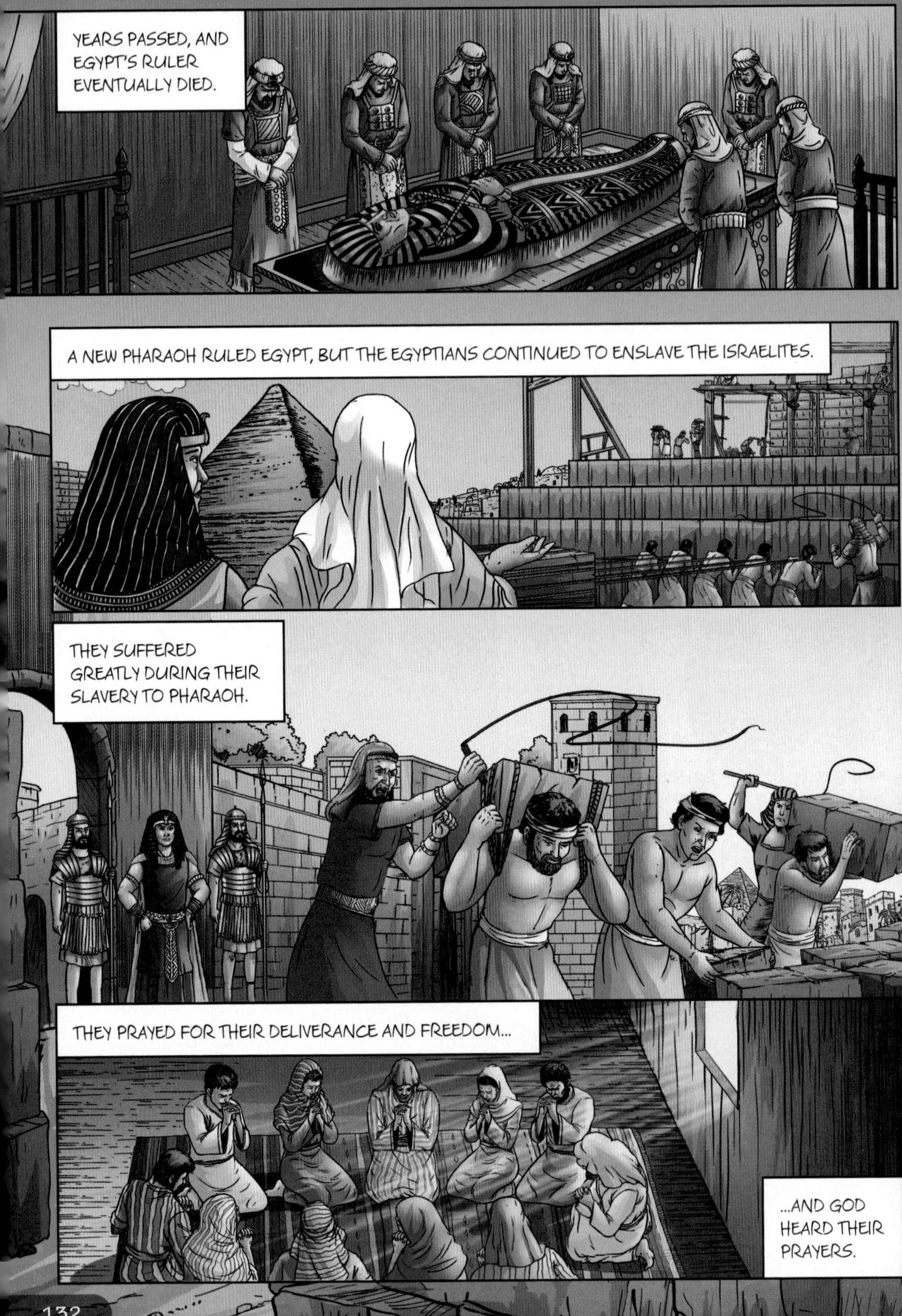

A NEW PHARAOH RULED EGYPT, BUT THE EGYPTIANS CONTINUED TO ENSLAVE THE ISRAELITES.

THEY SUFFERED GREATLY DURING THEIR SLAVERY TO PHARAOH.

THEY PRAYED FOR THEIR DELIVERANCE AND FREEDOM...

...AND GOD HEARD THEIR PRAYERS.

AS THE HEBREWS SUFFERED IN EGYPT, MOSES LIVED WITH HIS FAMILY IN MIDIAN.
ONE DAY MOSES WAS LEADING HIS FATHER-IN-LAW'S FLOCK TO MOUNT SINAI, THE MOUNTAIN OF GOD.
HE ENCOUNTERED A BUSH THAT WAS ON FIRE, YET IT DIDN'T BURN UP.
WHY DOESN'T THE FIRE BURN UP THIS BUSH?
THEN GOD CALLED OUT TO MOSES. THE LORD'S VOICE CAME FROM THE BURNING BUSH.
MOSES!
HERE I AM!
DO NOT COME CLOSER. TAKE OFF YOUR SANDALS, FOR YOU ARE STANDING ON HOLY GROUND.
I AM THE GOD OF YOUR FATHER...
...THE GOD OF ABRAHAM....
...THE GOD OF ISAAC, AND THE GOD OF JACOB.

MOSES COVERED HIS FACE BECAUSE HE WAS AFRAID TO LOOK AT GOD.
I HAVE HEARD THE CRIES OF MY PEOPLE IN EGYPT.
I HAVE SEEN THEIR SUFFERING BECAUSE OF THE SLAVE DRIVERS.
I HAVE COME TO RESCUE THEM AND LEAD THEM TO A LAND FLOWING WITH MILK AND HONEY.
GOD TOLD MOSES TO GO TO PHARAOH AND DEMAND HE SET THE ISRAELITES FREE.

WHO AM I TO GO TO PHARAOH? WHO AM I TO LEAD THE ISRAELITES OUT OF EGYPT?
I WILL BE WITH YOU!
WHEN PEOPLE ASK WHO SENT ME, WHAT IS THE NAME OF THE GOD I SHOULD GIVE?
I AM WHO I AM!
MOSES WAS STILL UNSURE. THE LORD TOLD HIM TO THROW HIS STAFF ON THE GROUND. WHEN THE STAFF HIT THE GROUND, IT TURNED INTO A SNAKE.
PERFORM THIS SIGN. THEN THEY WILL BELIEVE THAT THE LORD APPEARED TO YOU.
I CANNOT SPEAK AS SKILLFULLY AS I SHOULD. I BEG YOU, LORD, SEND SOMEONE ELSE!
YOUR BROTHER, AARON, WILL BE YOUR SPOKESMAN. I WILL BE WITH BOTH OF YOU.
TAKE YOUR STAFF, AND PERFORM THE SIGNS I HAVE SHOWN YOU.

Moses Speaks for God

Exodus 4–7

GOD TOLD MOSES IT WOULD NOT BE EASY TO CONVINCE PHARAOH TO LET THE ISRAELITES GO.

MOSES AND AARON MET AT THE MOUNTAIN OF GOD.

GOD HAS TOLD US TO DELIVER OUR PEOPLE FROM BONDAGE.

HE HAS TOLD US TO RETURN TO EGYPT, BROTHER.

MOSES AND AARON ARRIVED IN EGYPT AND MET WITH A GROUP OF HEBREW ELDERS. MOSES PERFORMED FOR THEM THE SIGNS THAT GOD HAD GIVEN HIM.

MOSES, I HAVE SEEN **THE POWER OF GOD** IN YOU!

YOU MUST **GO TO PHARAOH** AND CONVINCE HIM TO SET US FREE!

MOSES AND AARON APPEARED BEFORE PHARAOH.
THE LORD GOD OF ISRAEL WANTS YOU TO LET HIS PEOPLE GO!
THEY WILL THEN GO INTO THE WILDERNESS AND HOLD A FESTIVAL IN HIS HONOR.
WHO IS THIS LORD, THAT I SHOULD OBEY HIM AND LET ISRAEL GO?
I DO NOT KNOW YOUR GOD...
...AND I WILL NOT LET ISRAEL GO!

PHARAOH DECIDED TO MAKE LIFE EVEN MORE DIFFICULT FOR THE ISRAELITES.
THE HEBREWS ARE LAZY AND WANT TO AVOID THEIR WORK.
YOU SHALL NO LONGER SUPPLY THE HEBREWS WITH STRAW.
AS YOU WISH, MIGHTY PHARAOH!
THE ISRAELITES HAD TO GATHER THEIR OWN STRAW TO MAKE PHARAOH'S BRICKS.
FINISH YOUR WORK! YOU MUST MAKE THE SAME AMOUNT OF BRICKS AS BEFORE!
WHY HAVE YOUR PEOPLE NOT MADE AS MANY BRICKS AS YESTERDAY?
IT IS IMPOSSIBLE. WE...WE...DO NOT HAVE ENOUGH STRAW!

PHARAOH CALLS US LAZY. HIS MEN BEAT US! HE WANTS US TO MAKE JUST AS MANY BRICKS. BUT WE HAVE NO STRAW!
IT IS **YOUR FAULT!** YOU HAVE MADE PHARAOH ANGRY WITH US.
MOSES ASKED GOD FOR HELP.
I SPOKE TO PHARAOH IN YOUR NAME. WILL DELIVERANCE EVER COME?
GOD TOLD MOSES TO GO SEE PHARAOH AGAIN AND TELL HIM TO FREE THE ISRAELITES.

The Plagues

Exodus 7–10

THE NEXT MORNING MOSES AND AARON WENT TO SEE PHARAOH AGAIN.
I WILL STRIKE THE NILE WITH MY STAFF, AND IT WILL TURN INTO BLOOD. **LET GOD'S PEOPLE GO!**
PHARAOH REFUSED, AND THE **NILE RIVER TURNED TO BLOOD**. PEOPLE RAN FROM ITS BANKS BECAUSE OF ITS SICK SMELL. THOUSANDS OF FISH WASHED UP ON THE SHORE—**DEAD!**

PHARAOH'S HEART WAS STILL HARD. SO MOSES TOLD AARON TO STRETCH OUT HIS HAND WITH HIS STAFF OVER THE WATERS OF EGYPT. SOON THE LAND WAS OVERRUN WITH MILLIONS OF **FROGS**.
STILL, PHARAOH REFUSED TO LET GOD'S PEOPLE GO!

THE LORD, THROUGH MOSES, SENT PLAGUE AFTER PLAGUE ON EGYPT.
MILLIONS OF **GNATS** TORMENTED BOTH HUMAN AND BEAST.
THICK SWARMS OF **FLIES** ENTERED PHARAOH'S PALACE AND THE HOMES OF ALL THE EGYPTIANS.
STILL, PHARAOH WOULD NOT FREE THE ISRAELITES.

A DEADLY DISEASE THEN SWEPT OVER EGYPT, KILLING HERDS OF ANIMALS OWNED BY THE EGYPTIANS.
BUT THE LIVESTOCK OF THE ISRAELITES SURVIVED.
AARON AND MOSES TOOK HANDFULS OF ASHES FROM A KILN AND SCATTERED IT IN THE WIND...
...AND THEN FESTERING, PAINFUL **BOILS** APPEARED ON PEOPLE AND ANIMALS.

NEXT CAME A PLAGUE OF **HAIL** THAT DESTROYED FIELDS OF CROPS...
...AND SWARMS OF **LOCUSTS** THAT ATE WHAT THE HAIL DID NOT DAMAGE.
WHEN THOSE PLAGUES FAILED TO MOVE PHARAOH, A PLAGUE OF **DARKNESS** COVERED THE LAND FOR THREE DAYS. ONLY THE ISRAELITES HAD LIGHT WHERE THEY LIVED.

The Final Plague

Exodus 10–12

GOD HAD SAID THAT EVERY FIRSTBORN SON IN EGYPT—INCLUDING PHARAOH'S SON AND EVEN THE FIRSTBORN ANIMALS—WOULD DIE. EVERY EGYPTIAN FAMILY WOULD BE STRUCK BY THE PLAGUE. ONLY THE HEBREWS WOULD BE SPARED.
A LOUD WAIL WILL RISE THROUGHOUT EGYPT, A WAIL LIKE NO ONE HAS HEARD BEFORE OR WILL EVER HEAR AGAIN.

GOD HAD INSTRUCTED MOSES TO TELL EACH HEBREW FAMILY TO FIND A ONE-YEAR-OLD MALE LAMB.
THEY WERE TO SLAUGHTER THE LAMB...
...AND PUT THE ANIMAL'S BLOOD ON THE DOORFRAME OF THEIR HOUSE.
THAT NIGHT EACH FAMILY WAS TO EAT THE LAMB AND WAIT FOR DEATH TO PASS OVER.

MOSES NOW TOLD PHARAOH OF GOD'S PLAN. MOSES HOPED THE EGYPTIAN RULER WOULD CHANGE HIS MIND AND LET THE ISRAELITES GO.
GOD WILL SEND **ONE LAST PLAGUE** UPON YOUR KINGDOM!
AT MIDNIGHT, THE LORD WILL PASS OVER EGYPT AND **KILL EVERY FIRSTBORN SON IN EGYPT**.
THE WAILS FROM SCREAMING PARENTS WILL ECHO IN YOUR EARS FOREVER!
HOW DARE YOU THREATEN ME!
MOSES STORMED OUT OF THE PALACE FOR THE LAST TIME. HE TOLD THE ELDERS OF ISRAEL TO PREPARE SO THAT GOD'S PLAGUE WOULD PASS OVER THEM.

AT MIDNIGHT, GOD'S PLAGUE SPREAD THROUGH EGYPT, STRIKING DOWN THE FIRSTBORN SONS. AS DEATH CAME, MOTHERS AND FATHERS, SISTERS AND BROTHERS CRIED AND SCREAMED.
BUT GOD PASSED OVER THE HEBREW HOMES THAT WERE MARKED WITH LAMB'S BLOOD. THEIR LIVES WERE SPARED.

PHARAOH WAS AWAKENED BY THE CRIES OF HIS PEOPLE.

HE RUSHED TO HIS SON'S BEDCHAMBER...

...ONLY TO FIND THE BOY'S LIFELESS BODY.

PHARAOH KNEW HE HAD BEEN BEATEN. HIS POWER WAS NOT GREATER THAN THE GOD OF MOSES.

YOU AND YOUR PEOPLE ARE TO LEAVE EGYPT AT ONCE.
GO AND SERVE YOUR GOD, AS YOU SAID.
TAKE YOUR ANIMALS.
GO NOW!

Out of Egypt

Exodus 12–13

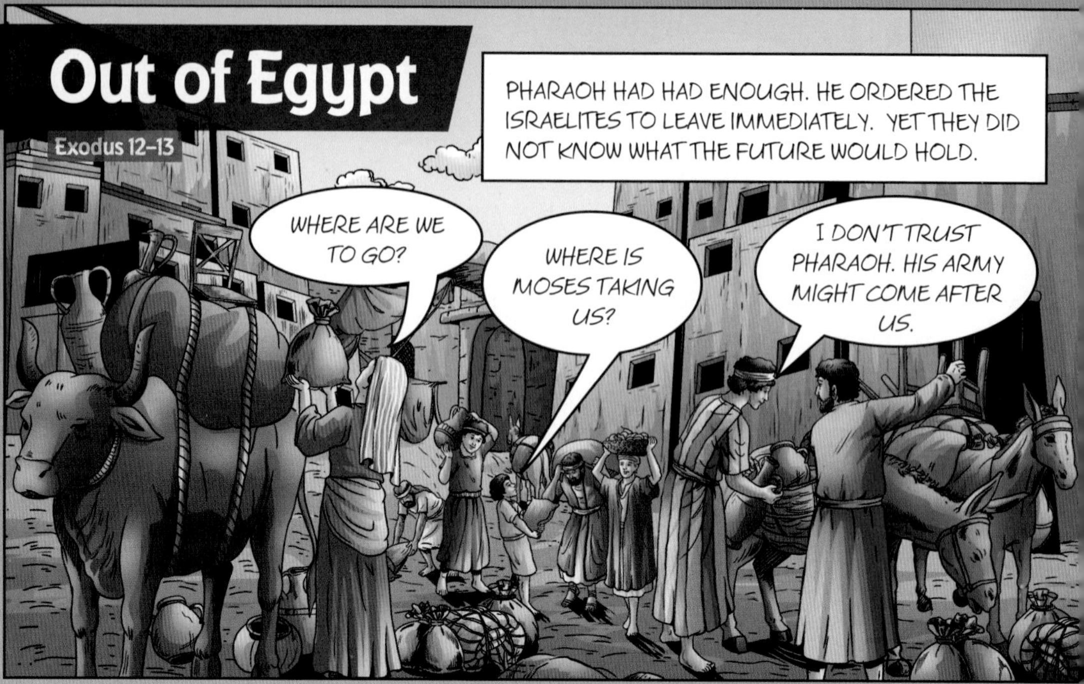

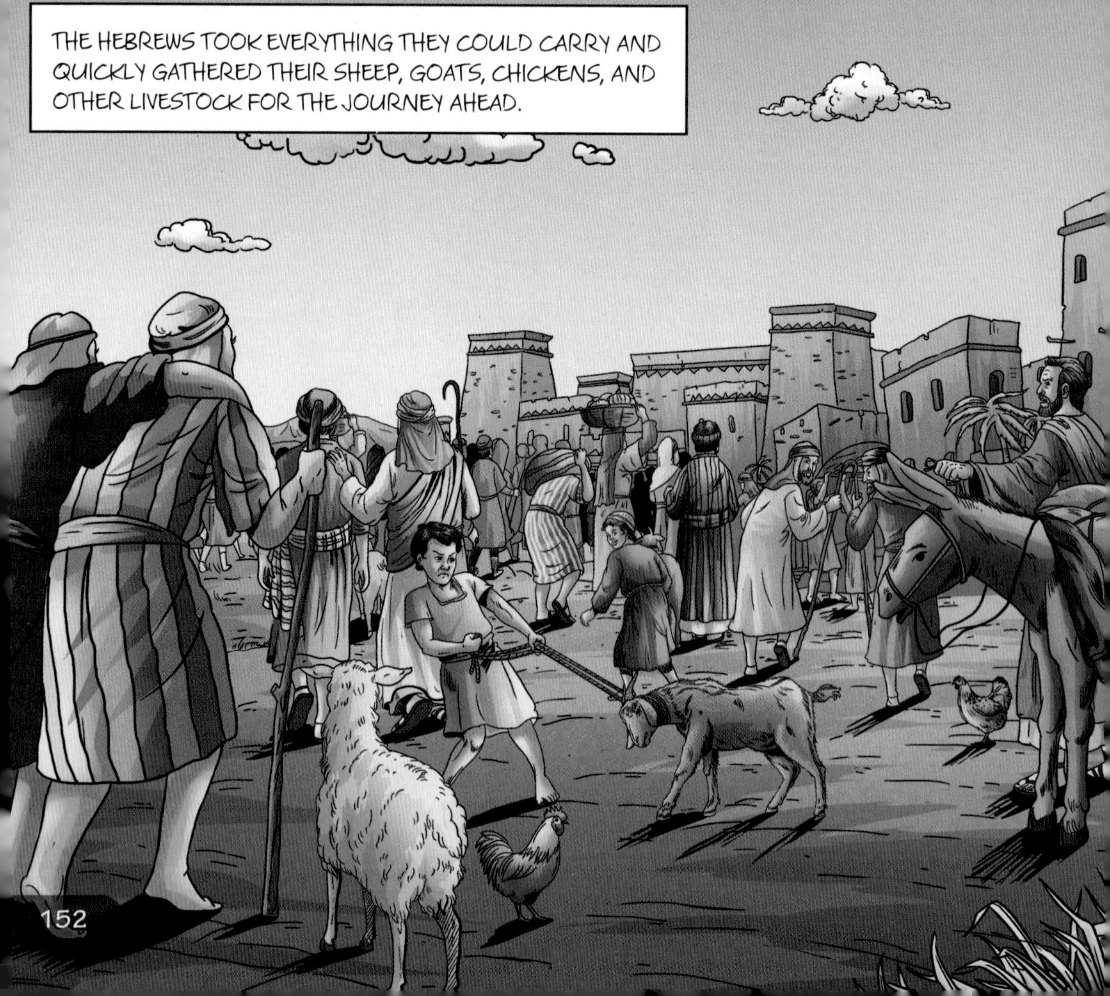

PHARAOH HAD HAD ENOUGH. HE ORDERED THE ISRAELITES TO LEAVE IMMEDIATELY. YET THEY DID NOT KNOW WHAT THE FUTURE WOULD HOLD.

THE HEBREWS TOOK EVERYTHING THEY COULD CARRY AND QUICKLY GATHERED THEIR SHEEP, GOATS, CHICKENS, AND OTHER LIVESTOCK FOR THE JOURNEY AHEAD.

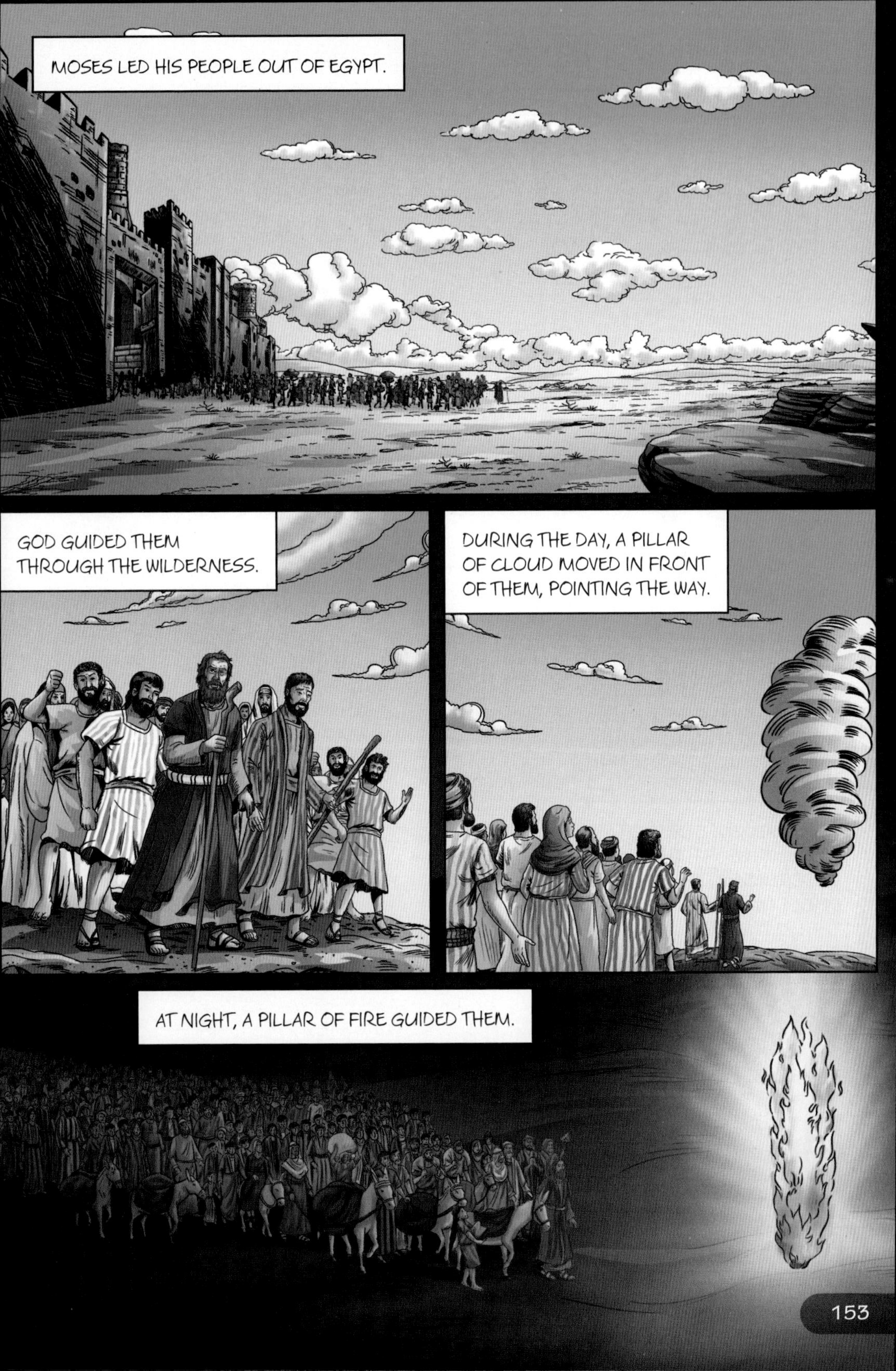

MOSES LED HIS PEOPLE OUT OF EGYPT.

AT NIGHT, A PILLAR OF FIRE GUIDED THEM.

THE HEBREWS' JOURNEY

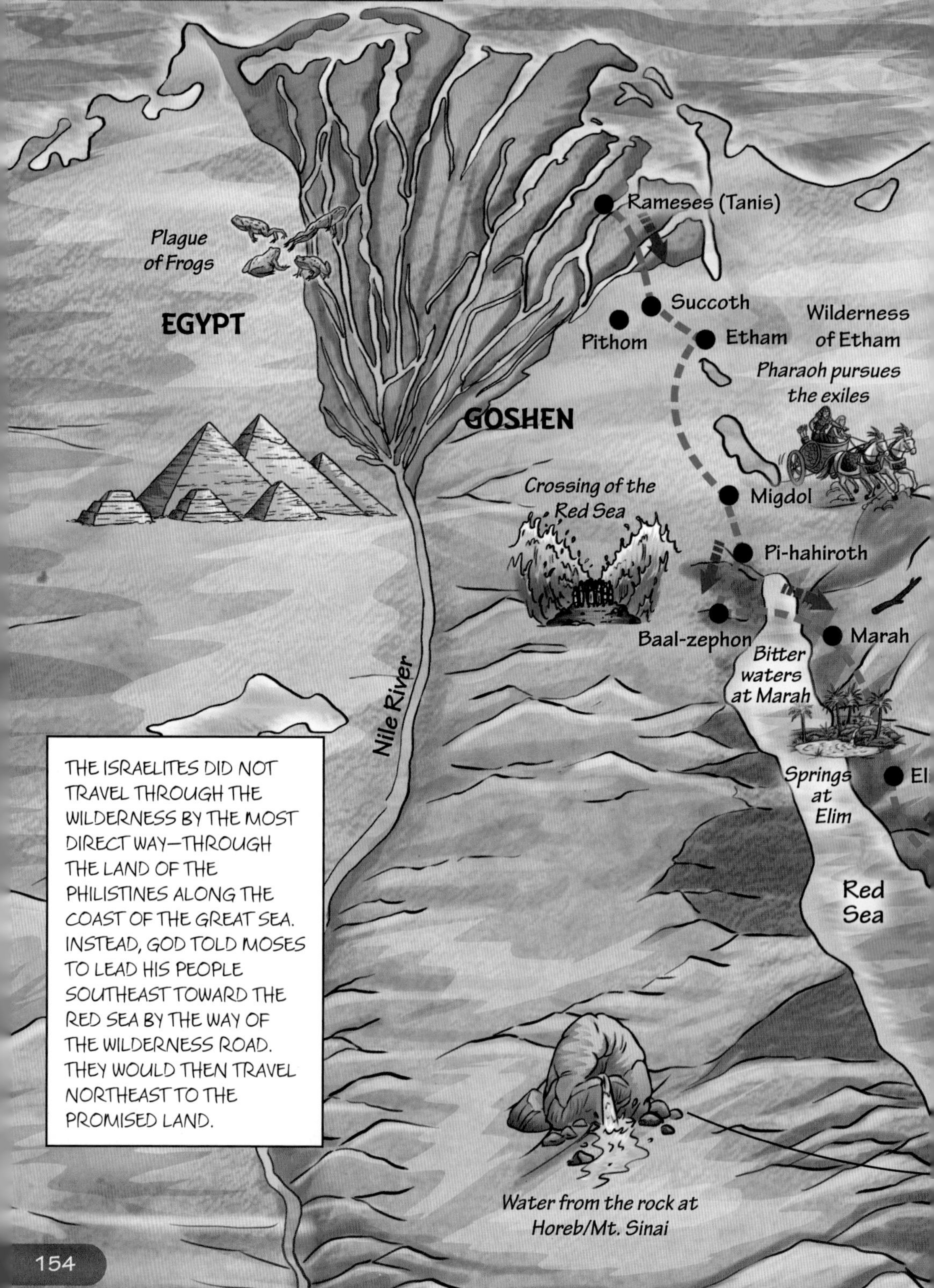

Plague of Frogs

EGYPT

GOSHEN

Rameses (Tanis)

Succoth

Pithom

Etham

Wilderness of Etham

Pharaoh pursues the exiles

Crossing of the Red Sea

Migdol

Pi-hahiroth

Baal-zephon

Marah

Bitter waters at Marah

Springs at Elim

El

Red Sea

Nile River

THE ISRAELITES DID NOT TRAVEL THROUGH THE WILDERNESS BY THE MOST DIRECT WAY—THROUGH THE LAND OF THE PHILISTINES ALONG THE COAST OF THE GREAT SEA. INSTEAD, GOD TOLD MOSES TO LEAD HIS PEOPLE SOUTHEAST TOWARD THE RED SEA BY THE WAY OF THE WILDERNESS ROAD. THEY WOULD THEN TRAVEL NORTHEAST TO THE PROMISED LAND.

Water from the rock at Horeb/Mt. Sinai

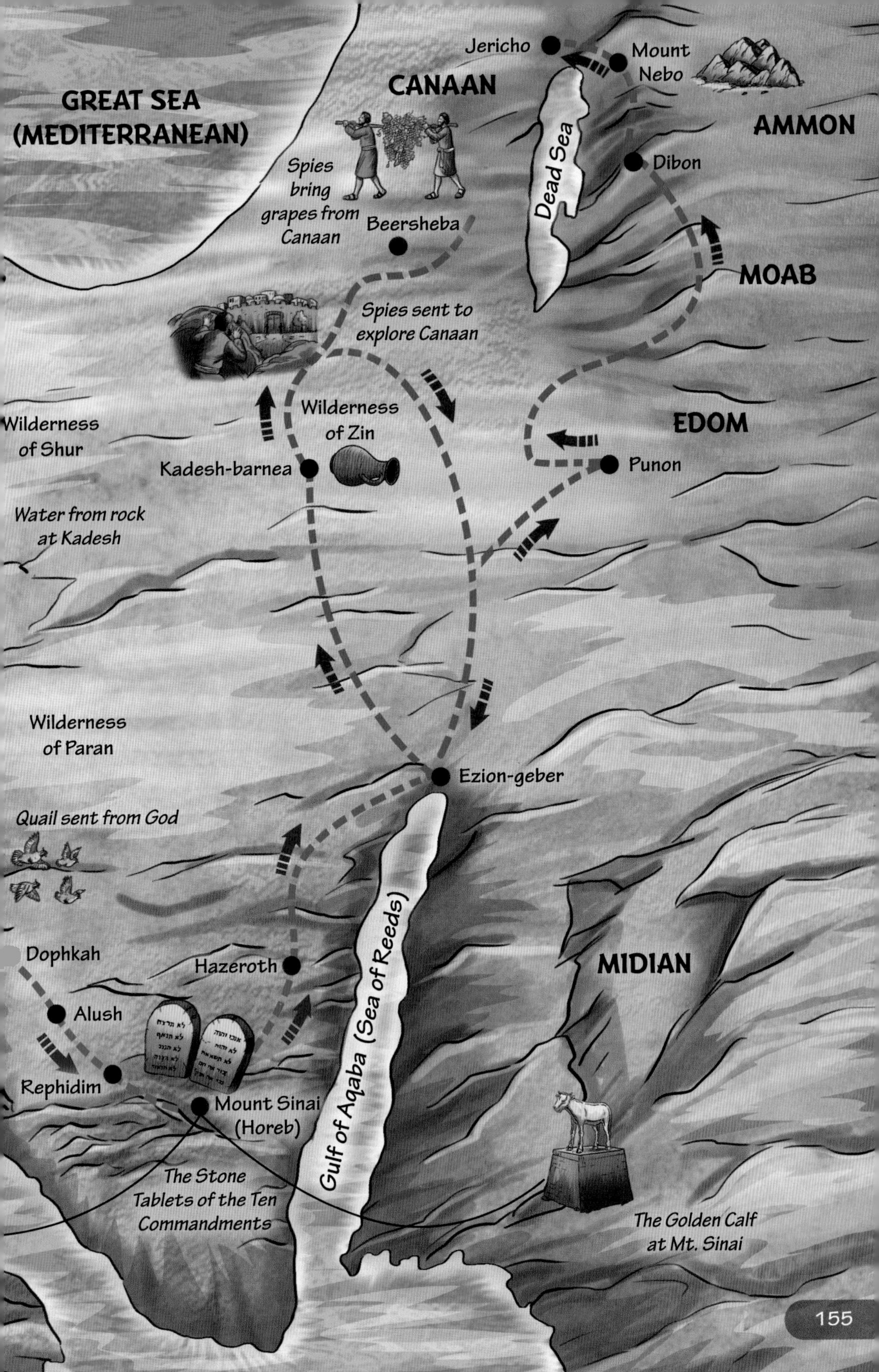
Jericho
Mount Nebo
CANAAN
GREAT SEA (MEDITERRANEAN)
AMMON
Dead Sea
Dibon
Spies bring grapes from Canaan
Beersheba
MOAB
Spies sent to explore Canaan
Wilderness of Zin
EDOM
Wilderness of Shur
Kadesh-barnea
Punon
Water from rock at Kadesh
Wilderness of Paran
Ezion-geber
Quail sent from God
Gulf of Aqaba (Sea of Reeds)
Dophkah
Hazeroth
MIDIAN
Alush
Rephidim
Mount Sinai (Horeb)
The Stone Tablets of the Ten Commandments
The Golden Calf at Mt. Sinai

Crossing the Red Sea

Exodus 14

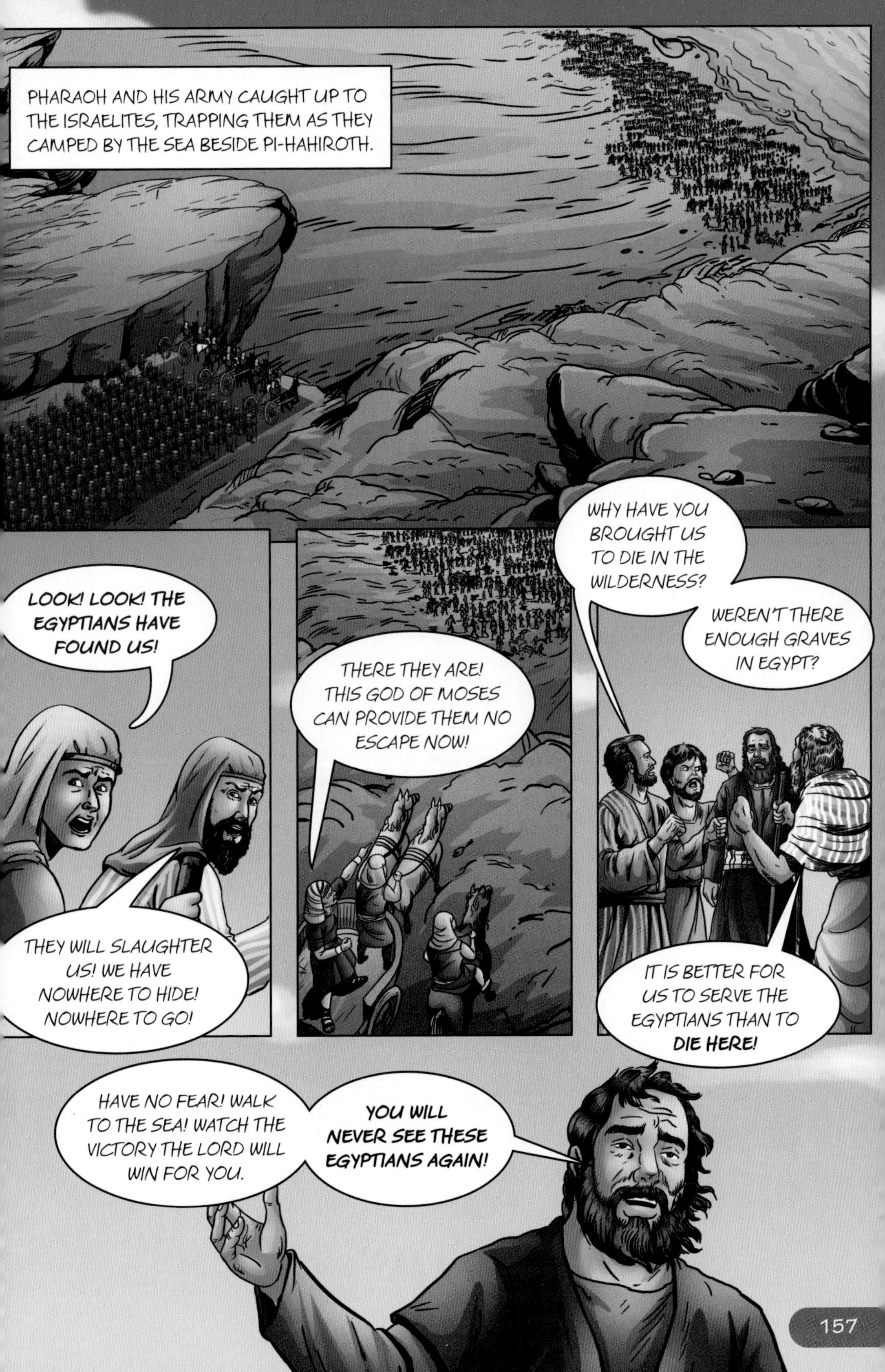
PHARAOH AND HIS ARMY CAUGHT UP TO THE ISRAELITES, TRAPPING THEM AS THEY CAMPED BY THE SEA BESIDE PI-HAHIROTH.
LOOK! LOOK! THE EGYPTIANS HAVE FOUND US!
THEY WILL SLAUGHTER US! WE HAVE NOWHERE TO HIDE! NOWHERE TO GO!
THERE THEY ARE! THIS GOD OF MOSES CAN PROVIDE THEM NO ESCAPE NOW!
WHY HAVE YOU BROUGHT US TO DIE IN THE WILDERNESS?
WEREN'T THERE ENOUGH GRAVES IN EGYPT?
IT IS BETTER FOR US TO SERVE THE EGYPTIANS THAN TO DIE HERE!
HAVE NO FEAR! WALK TO THE SEA! WATCH THE VICTORY THE LORD WILL WIN FOR YOU.
YOU WILL NEVER SEE THESE EGYPTIANS AGAIN!

THE ISRAELITES FOLLOWED MOSES' INSTRUCTIONS AND CONTINUED MOVING TOWARD THE RED SEA...
...AS THE EGYPTIANS READIED FOR THE ATTACK.
GOD THEN MOVED THE PILLAR OF CLOUD BETWEEN THE ISRAELITES AND THE EGYPTIANS, HALTING THEIR ADVANCE.

MOSES STRETCHED HIS STAFF OVER THE WATERS OF THE SEA...
...AND THE WATERS PARTED.

THE ISRAELITES WERE ASTONISHED BY GOD'S MIRACLE.
THE ISRAELITES THEN WALKED THROUGH THE PATH IN THE SEA CREATED BY GOD.
I CANNOT BELIEVE MY EYES!
THE LORD'S POWER TRULY COMES TO US THROUGH MOSES!
HOW LONG CAN HE HOLD UP THE SEA WATER, FATHER?
TRUST GOD! HE SAYS WE WILL BE SAFE.

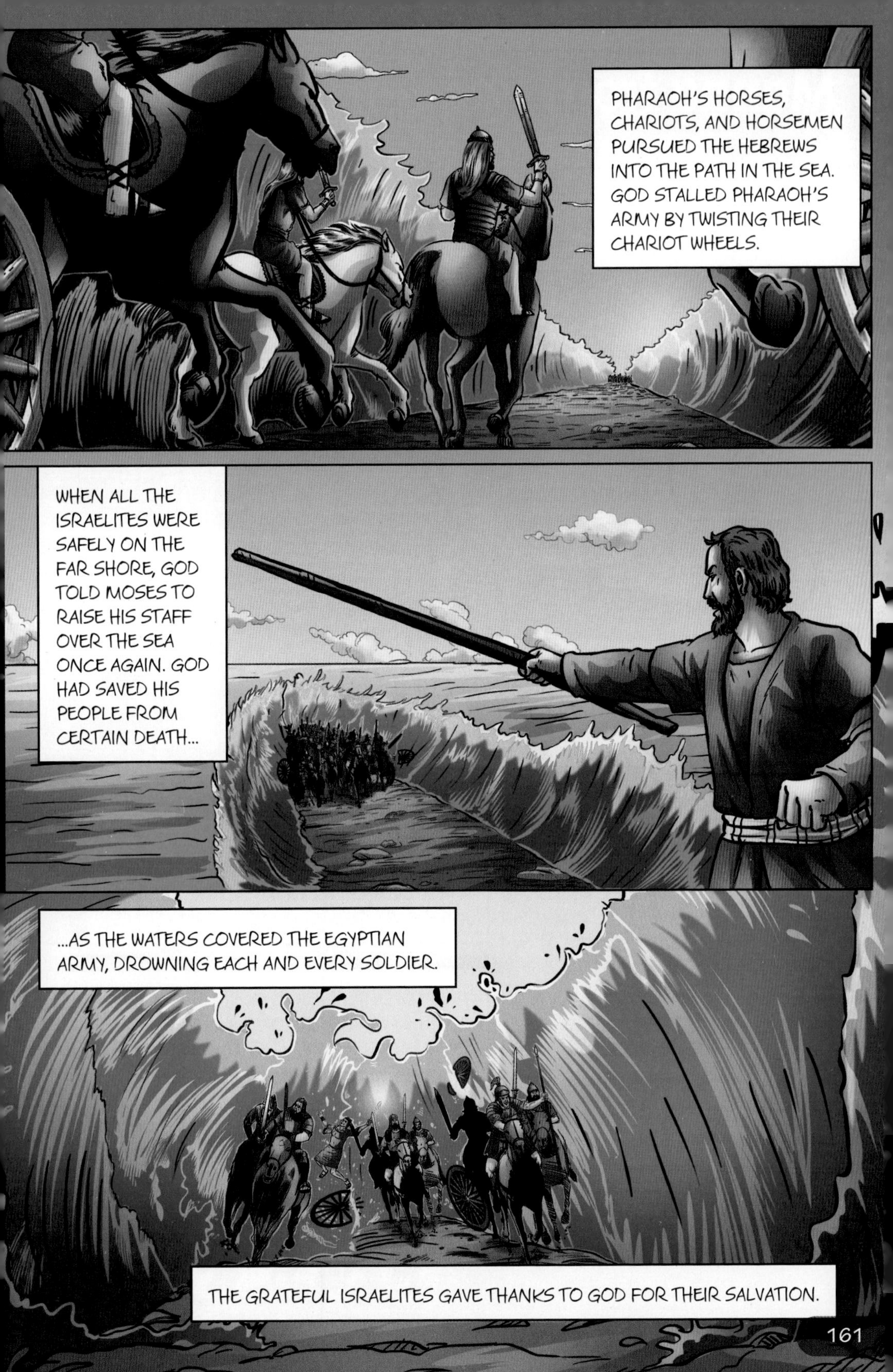

PHARAOH'S HORSES, CHARIOTS, AND HORSEMEN PURSUED THE HEBREWS INTO THE PATH IN THE SEA. GOD STALLED PHARAOH'S ARMY BY TWISTING THEIR CHARIOT WHEELS.

...AS THE WATERS COVERED THE EGYPTIAN ARMY, DROWNING EACH AND EVERY SOLDIER.

THE GRATEFUL ISRAELITES GAVE THANKS TO GOD FOR THEIR SALVATION.

Manna from Heaven

Exodus 15–17

MOSES PROMISED THE ISRAELITES THEY WOULD HAVE MEAT AND BREAD TO EAT. THAT EVENING, QUAIL FLEW IN AND COVERED THEIR CAMP.

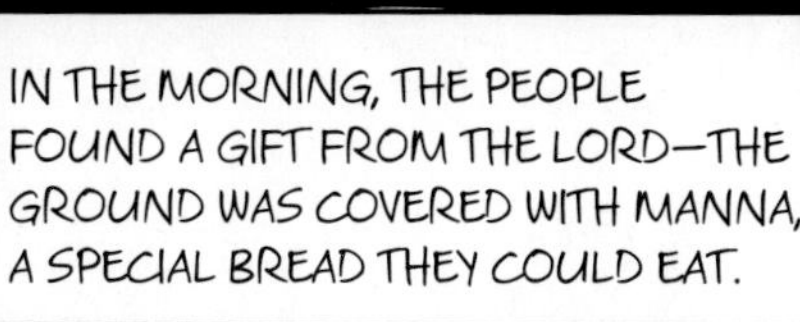

EVERY MORNING WHILE THE ISRAELITES WERE IN THE WILDERNESS, GOD PROVIDED ENOUGH MANNA FOR THEM FOR THAT DAY. ON THE DAY BEFORE THE SABBATH, HE PROVIDED EXTRA MANNA SO THAT THEY COULD REST AND GIVE THANKS ON THE SABBATH.

AGAIN THE ISRAELITES COMPLAINED ABOUT HAVING NO WATER.

GOD TOLD MOSES TO STRIKE A ROCK AT MOUNT SINAI WITH HIS STAFF. WHEN MOSES STRUCK THE ROCK, WATER GUSHED OUT.

The Ten Commandments

Exodus 19–20

TWO MONTHS AFTER LEAVING EGYPT, THE ISRAELITES CAMPED AT MOUNT SINAI—THE SAME PLACE WHERE MOSES HAD FIRST ENCOUNTERED GOD.

MOSES! YOU HAVE SEEN WHAT I DID TO THE EGYPTIANS AND HOW I CARRIED YOU ON EAGLES' WINGS AND BROUGHT YOU TO MYSELF.
NOW, IF YOU WILL OBEY ME AND KEEP MY COVENANT, YOU WILL BE MY OWN SPECIAL TREASURE FROM AMONG ALL THE PEOPLES ON EARTH... MY KINGDOM OF PRIESTS, MY HOLY NATION.
PREPARE THE PEOPLE FOR MY ARRIVAL. HAVE THEM WASH THEIR CLOTHING.
BE SURE THEY ARE READY ON THE THIRD DAY.
WARN THE PEOPLE NOT TO TOUCH THE MOUNTAIN!

MOSES TOLD THE PEOPLE ALL OF GOD'S COMMANDS.
NO OTHER MAN WOULD BE BRAVE ENOUGH TO FACE GOD AS YOU DID, MOSES!
...AND YOU MUST REMAIN PURE FOR THREE DAYS. THEN HE WILL CALL FOR US!
THANK YOU, MOSES!
WE WILL OBEY GOD!
FOR THE NEXT THREE DAYS, THE PEOPLE CLEANSED THEMSELVES AND STAYED PURE. ON THE THIRD DAY, A LOUD BLAST SUMMONED THEM TO MOUNT SINAI.
MOSES LED THE PEOPLE TO THE FOOT OF MOUNT SINAI. THERE, HE WENT UP THE MOUNTAIN PATH...
...TO HEAR THE WORD OF GOD ONCE AGAIN.

GOD TOLD MOSES:
I AM THE LORD YOUR GOD, WHO RESCUED YOU FROM THE LAND OF EGYPT, THE PLACE OF YOUR SLAVERY.
1. YOU MUST NOT HAVE ANY OTHER GOD BUT ME.
2. YOU MUST NOT MAKE FOR YOURSELF AN IDOL OF ANY KIND OR AN IMAGE OF ANYTHING IN THE HEAVENS OR EARTH OR SEA. YOU MUST NOT BOW DOWN TO THEM OR WORSHIP THEM.
3. YOU MUST NOT MISUSE THE NAME OF THE LORD YOUR GOD.
4. REMEMBER TO OBSERVE THE SABBATH DAY BY KEEPING IT HOLY, A DAY OF REST DEDICATED TO THE LORD.
5. HONOR YOUR FATHER AND MOTHER.
6. YOU MUST NOT MURDER.
7. YOU MUST NOT COMMIT ADULTERY.
8. YOU MUST NOT STEAL.
9. YOU MUST NOT TESTIFY FALSELY AGAINST YOUR NEIGHBOR (LIE).
10. YOU MUST NOT COVET.

The Gold Calf

Exodus 32

MOSES STAYED ON SINAI FOR A LONG TIME. THE ISRAELITES FEARED HE MIGHT NEVER RETURN. A GROUP WENT TO TALK WITH AARON, WHO WAS ALSO CONCERNED ABOUT HIS BROTHER.

MOSES HAS BEEN UP ON THE MOUNTAIN TOO LONG!

WE FEAR SOMETHING BAD HAS HAPPENED.

AARON AGREED WITH THEM AND TOLD THE PEOPLE TO TAKE OFF ALL THEIR GOLD JEWELRY...

...AND HE MELTED IT DOWN.

AARON THEN MOLDED THE GOLD INTO A CALF—AN IDOL FOR THE PEOPLE.

THIS IS YOUR GOD, ISRAEL, WHO BROUGHT YOU UP FROM THE LAND OF EGYPT!
REJOICE IN YOUR FREEDOM AND IN YOUR GOD!
THE NEXT DAY THE PEOPLE HAD A FEAST. THEY OFFERED SACRIFICES AND HAD A WILD PARTY.

MOSES REMAINED ON THE MOUNTAIN FOR MANY DAYS AND NIGHTS. GOD GAVE MANY OTHER INSTRUCTIONS TO MOSES. BUT AT THE END OF THESE DAYS, GOD BECAME ANGRY BECAUSE OF THE SINS OF HIS PEOPLE.

I HAVE SEEN HOW STUBBORN AND REBELLIOUS THESE PEOPLE ARE.

I WILL DESTROY THEM!

LORD! DO NOT LET YOUR ANGER GROW HOT AGAINST THE PEOPLE YOU HAVE DELIVERED FROM SLAVERY!

IF YOU KILL THEM NOW, THE EGYPTIANS WILL SAY YOU FREED THEM WITH EVIL INTENT— TO DESTROY THEM IN THE WILDNERNESS!

LORD, DON'T BE ANGRY, **I BEG YOU!**

REMEMBER YOUR SERVANTS: ABRAHAM, ISAAC, AND JACOB!

YOU TOLD THEM YOU WOULD MAKE THEIR DESCENDANTS AS NUMEROUS AS STARS. LORD, **SPARE** THESE PEOPLE!

FINALLY, MOSES DESCENDED THE MOUNTAIN CARRYING GOD'S COMMANDMENTS. THEY WERE WRITTEN BY GOD HIMSELF ON TWO STONE TABLETS.
AS HE CAME DOWN THE MOUNTAIN, MOSES COULD HEAR THE SOUND OF CELEBRATION. WHEN HE SAW WHAT HIS FELLOW ISRAELITES HAD BEEN UP TO IN HIS ABSENCE, HE WAS FURIOUS AND SMASHED THE TABLETS ON THE GROUND.
WHO IS RESPONSIBLE FOR THIS???

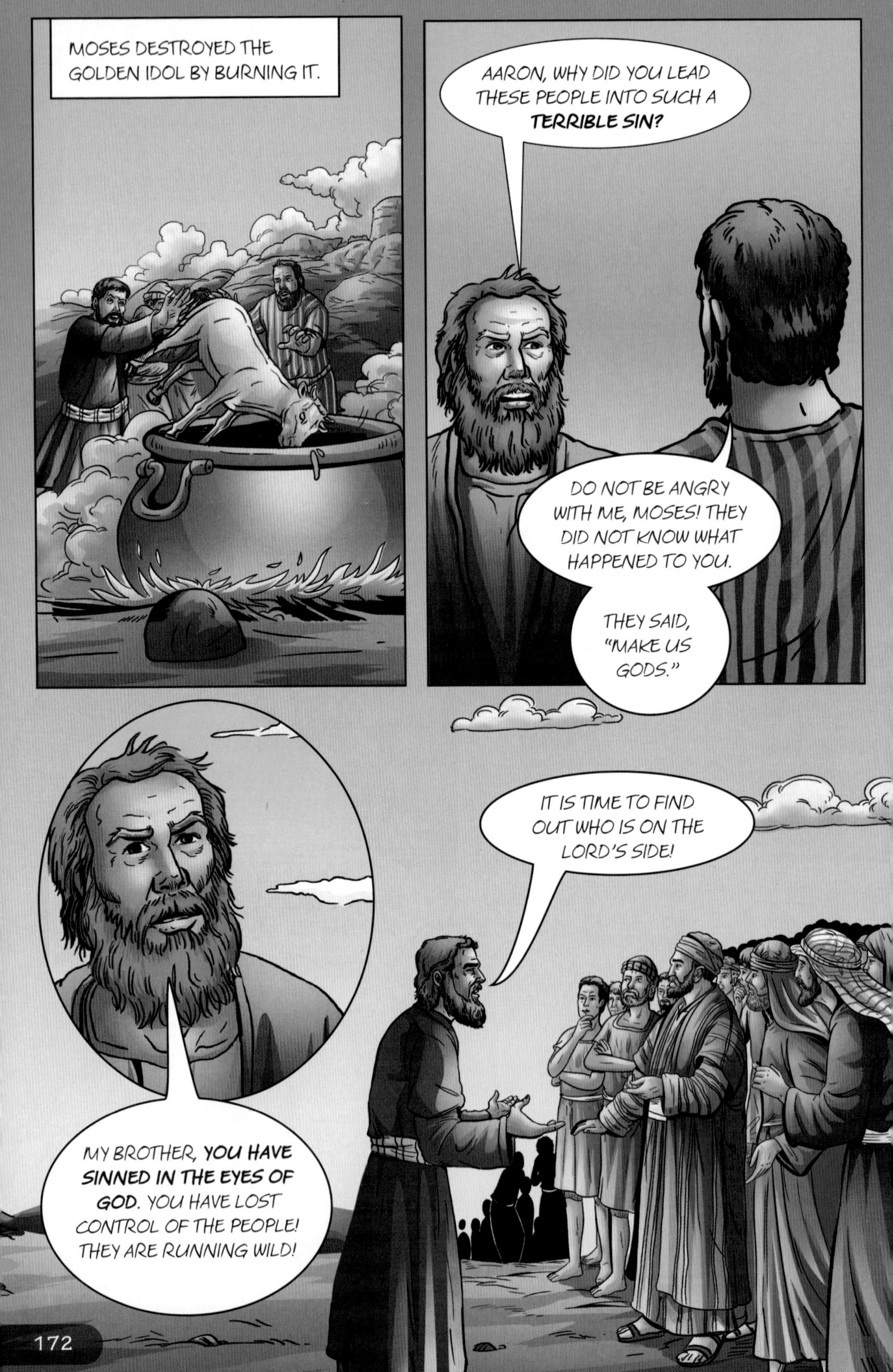
MOSES DESTROYED THE GOLDEN IDOL BY BURNING IT.
AARON, WHY DID YOU LEAD THESE PEOPLE INTO SUCH A **TERRIBLE SIN?**
DO NOT BE ANGRY WITH ME, MOSES! THEY DID NOT KNOW WHAT HAPPENED TO YOU.
THEY SAID, "MAKE US GODS."
MY BROTHER, **YOU HAVE SINNED IN THE EYES OF GOD**. YOU HAVE LOST CONTROL OF THE PEOPLE! THEY ARE RUNNING WILD!
IT IS TIME TO FIND OUT WHO IS ON THE LORD'S SIDE!

WHOEVER IS FOR THE LORD, **COME HERE!**
THIS IS GOD'S COMMAND. YOU MUST GO THROUGH THE CAMP AND KILL BROTHER, NEIGHBOR, FRIEND—THOSE WHO HAVE SINNED AGAINST GOD!
THE FOLLOWERS OF THE LORD DID AS MOSES COMMANDED AND KILLED THE SINNERS.
THE NEXT DAY GOD SPOKE TO MOSES.
I WILL ERASE THE NAME OF EVERYONE WHO HAS SINNED AGAINST ME. NOW, GO LEAD THE PEOPLE TO THE PLACE I TOLD YOU ABOUT. MY ANGEL WILL LEAD THE WAY.

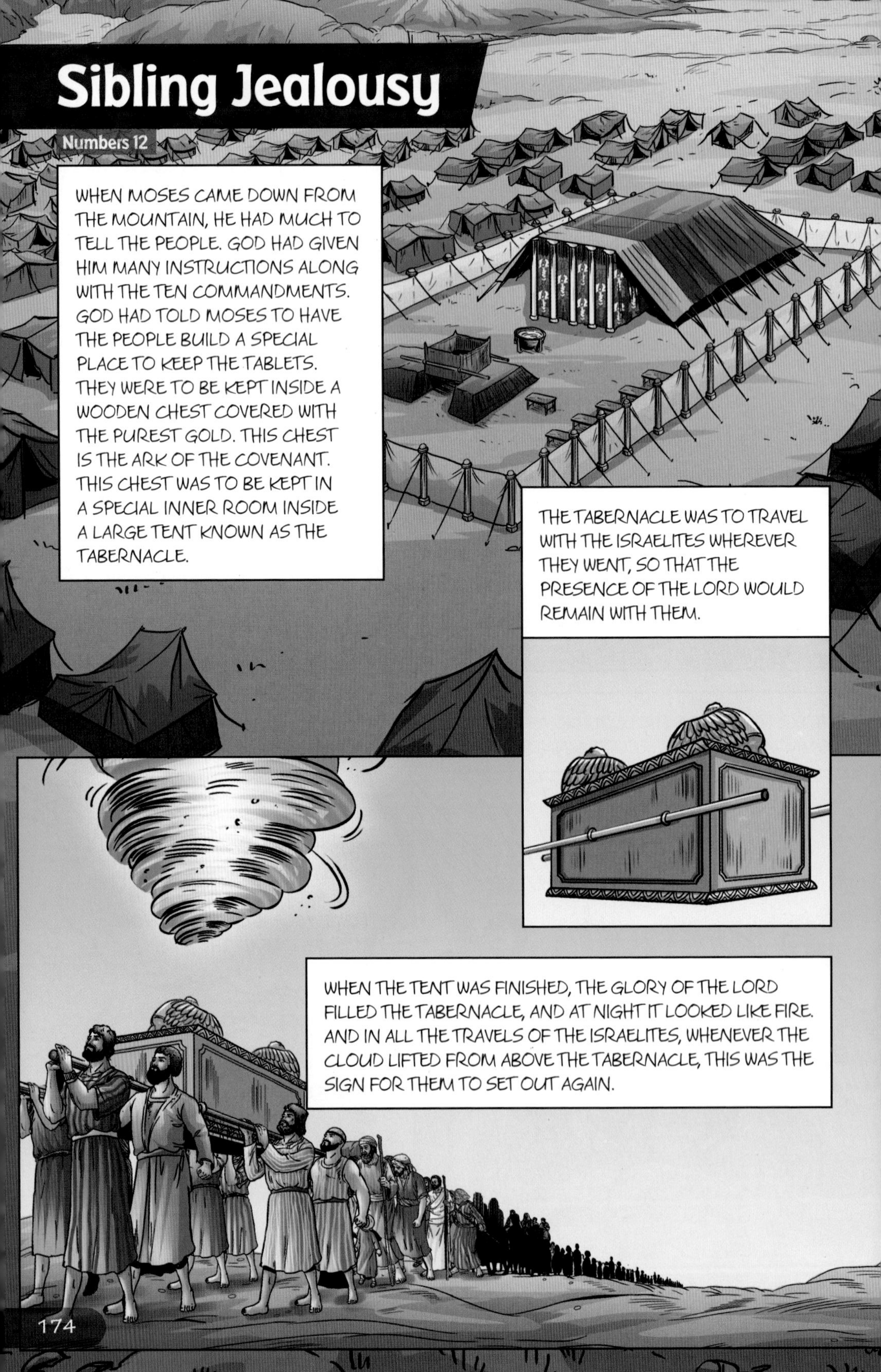
Sibling Jealousy
Numbers 12
WHEN MOSES CAME DOWN FROM THE MOUNTAIN, HE HAD MUCH TO TELL THE PEOPLE. GOD HAD GIVEN HIM MANY INSTRUCTIONS ALONG WITH THE TEN COMMANDMENTS. GOD HAD TOLD MOSES TO HAVE THE PEOPLE BUILD A SPECIAL PLACE TO KEEP THE TABLETS. THEY WERE TO BE KEPT INSIDE A WOODEN CHEST COVERED WITH THE PUREST GOLD. THIS CHEST IS THE ARK OF THE COVENANT. THIS CHEST WAS TO BE KEPT IN A SPECIAL INNER ROOM INSIDE A LARGE TENT KNOWN AS THE TABERNACLE.
THE TABERNACLE WAS TO TRAVEL WITH THE ISRAELITES WHEREVER THEY WENT, SO THAT THE PRESENCE OF THE LORD WOULD REMAIN WITH THEM.
WHEN THE TENT WAS FINISHED, THE GLORY OF THE LORD FILLED THE TABERNACLE, AND AT NIGHT IT LOOKED LIKE FIRE. AND IN ALL THE TRAVELS OF THE ISRAELITES, WHENEVER THE CLOUD LIFTED FROM ABOVE THE TABERNACLE, THIS WAS THE SIGN FOR THEM TO SET OUT AGAIN.

AARON AND MIRIAM GREW JEALOUS OF THEIR BROTHER, MOSES.

GOD HEARD AARON AND MIRIAM'S COMPLAINT AND CAME TO SPEAK TO THEM IN A PILLAR OF CLOUD.

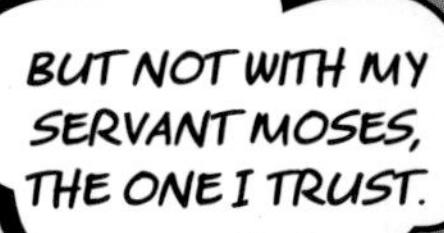

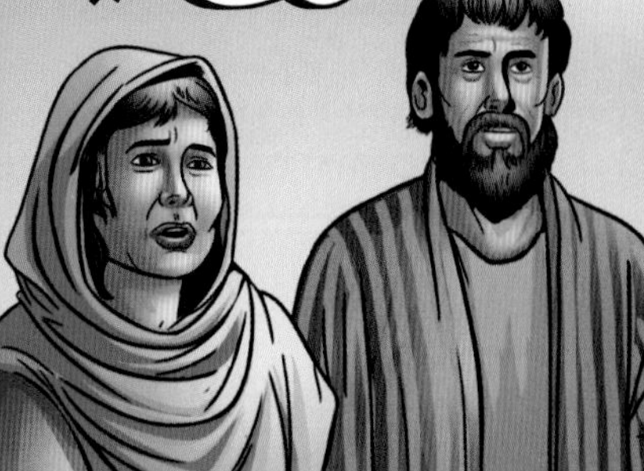

THE LORD INFLICTED MIRIAM WITH LEPROSY THAT RAVAGED HER BODY.

MOSES PLEADED WITH GOD TO HEAL HIS SISTER. SEVEN DAYS LATER, MIRIAM WAS HEALED, AND THE ISRAELITES CONTINUED ON THEIR JOURNEY.

Moses and His Spies

Numbers 13–14

TWO OF THE MEN, CALEB AND JOSHUA, WERE EXCITED BY WHAT THEY SAW.
CANAAN IS TRULY A LAND OF **MILK AND HONEY!**
LET'S GO AT ONCE TO TAKE THE LAND!
THE LORD WILL BRING US SAFELY INTO THE LAND!
BUT THE OTHER SPIES WERE NOT SO OPTIMISTIC.
YES, THE LAND IS FERTILE, BUT THEIR ARMIES ARE STRONG.
THEIR CITIES ARE FORTIFIED.
I SAY WE ATTACK AND SEIZE THE LAND FOR OURSELVES!
WE WOULD BE FOOLISH TO ATTACK.
THE LAND IS FULL OF GIANTS!
WE SHOULD NOT BE AFRAID TO MOVE AGAINST THEM!
THE LORD IS WITH US! **HE IS OUR STRENGTH!**

GOD HAD PROMISED THIS LAND TO HIS PEOPLE, BUT THEY WERE SCARED. THEY DIDN'T PUT THEIR FAITH IN GOD EVEN THOUGH HE HAD BROUGHT THEM OUT OF EGYPT, ACROSS THE RED SEA, AND THROUGH THE WILDERNESS. GOD THREATENED TO KILL THEM ALL, BUT MOSES AGAIN PRAYED AND ASKED THE LORD TO SPARE THEM.
GOD CONDEMNED THE ISRAELITES TO WANDER IN THE DESERT FOR 40 YEARS- ONE YEAR FOR EACH OF THE DAYS THAT THE MEN HAD EXPLORED THE PROMISED LAND.
YOU WILL ALL DROP DEAD IN THIS WILDERNESS! YOU WILL NOT ENTER THE LAND I SWORE TO GIVE YOU. THE ONLY EXCEPTIONS WILL BE CALEB AND JOSHUA.

Water from a Rock

Numbers 20

GOD HAD COMMANDED MOSES AND AARON TO SPEAK TO THE ROCK AND IT WOULD POUR OUT WATER.
LISTEN, YOU REBELLIOUS PEOPLE! MUST WE BRING YOU WATER OUT OF THIS ROCK?
BUT MOSES AND AARON DID NOT SPEAK TO THE ROCK AS GOD HAD COMMANDED. INSTEAD, MOSES STRUCK THE ROCK WITH HIS STAFF. BECAUSE THEY DISOBEYED, GOD TOLD THEM THAT THEY WOULD NOT LEAD THE ISRAELITES INTO THE PROMISED LAND.

Hero Profile
Joshua—Israelite Warrior

BORN: EGYPT

FATHER: NUN, OF THE TRIBE OF EPHRAIM

DIED: CANAAN, THE PROMISED LAND

AGE AT TIME OF DEATH: 110

BEST KNOWN FOR: BEING A LEADER AND MIGHTY WARRIOR FOR GOD

RUINED WALLS

JOSHUA'S GREATEST VICTORY WAS THE DESTRUCTION OF JERICHO. ARCHAEOLOGISTS HAVE UNCOVERED MUD-BRICK WALLS THAT WERE VIOLENTLY DESTROYED.

WHAT'S IN A NAME?

JOSHUA AND JESUS SHARE THE SAME NAME. "JESUS" IS A GREEK FORM OF THE HEBREW NAME. BOTH MEAN "GOD SAVES."

A New Leader Emerges

Deuteronomy 31–34

MOSES TOLD JOSHUA THAT GOD HAD CHOSEN HIM AS THE NEW LEADER OF THE ISRAELITES.
BE STRONG, JOSHUA. BE BRAVE. GOD IS WITH YOU.
YOU WILL LEAD THE PEOPLE TO THE PROMISED LAND.
THEN MOSES WALKED UP MOUNT NEBO, WHERE GOD SHOWED HIM THE PROMISED LAND.
MOSES DIED ON THE MOUNTAIN. HE WAS 120 YEARS OLD. THE ISRAELITES MOURNED FOR A MONTH. THERE WOULD NEVER BE ANOTHER PROPHET LIKE MOSES—A MAN WHO HAD SPOKEN FACE-TO-FACE WITH GOD.

Joshua's Spies
Joshua 1–2
GOD CALLED JOSHUA TO TAKE CHARGE. HE MARCHED THE ISRAELITES TO THE BORDER OF THE PROMISED LAND.
JOSHUA ORDERED TWO OF HIS MEN TO SPY ON THE WALLED CITY OF JERICHO. THEY SNUCK INTO THE CITY AND LOOKED AROUND. THEY ALSO WENT TO THE HOUSE OF A WOMAN NAMED RAHAB.
SOLDIERS CAME LOOKING FOR THEM.
WE ARE LOOKING FOR TWO ISRAELITE SPIES.
WE THINK THEY ARE HERE. SHOW THEM TO US, WOMAN!
THE MEN YOU SEEK CAME TO ME.
BUT I DID NOT KNOW WHERE THEY CAME FROM.

THEY LEFT AT DUSK JUST BEFORE THE GATES CLOSED.
I DON'T KNOW WHERE THEY WENT.
LITTLE DID THE KING'S MEN KNOW THAT RAHAB HAD HIDDEN THE TWO SPIES ON THE ROOF OF HER BUILDING UNDER BUNDLES OF FLAX.
I KNOW THE LORD HAS GIVEN YOU THIS LAND.
PROMISE ME THAT WHEN YOU RETURN, YOU WILL REPAY MY KINDNESS.
WHEN WE COME, HANG A SCARLET ROPE FROM YOUR WINDOW. WE WILL SAVE YOU AND YOUR FAMILY.
THE MEN ESCAPED THROUGH A WINDOW, FOR RAHAB'S HOME WAS BUILT INTO THE CITY WALL.

The River Stops Flowing

Joshua 3–4

WHILE THE PRIESTS STOOD WITH THE ARK OF THE COVENANT IN THE MIDDLE OF THE RIVER, THE PEOPLE OF ISRAEL CROSSED THE RIVER IN SAFETY. WHEN EVERYONE HAD CROSSED, JOSHUA TOLD ONE MAN FROM EACH OF THE TWELVE TRIBES TO COLLECT A STONE FROM THE MIDDLE OF THE RIVERBED, WHERE THE PRIESTS WERE STANDING. THE STONES WERE USED TO BUILD A MEMORIAL SO THE PEOPLE WOULD NEVER FORGET WHAT GOD HAD DONE FOR THEM.
FROM THAT DAY ON, THE ISRAELITES ACCEPTED JOSHUA AS THEIR LEADER.

The Crumbling Walls of Jericho

Joshua 5–6

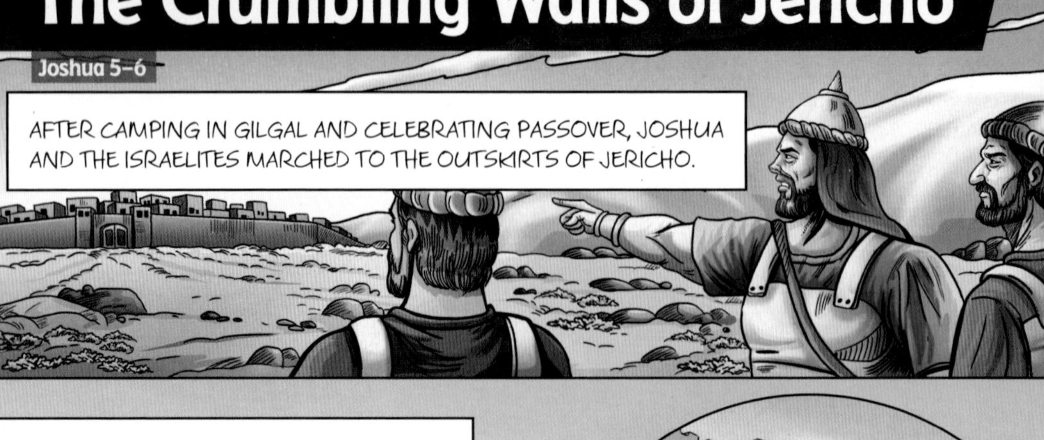

NEAR JERICHO, JOSHUA SAW A MAN WITH A SWORD IN HIS HAND. HE WAS THE COMMANDER OF THE ARMY OF THE LORD.

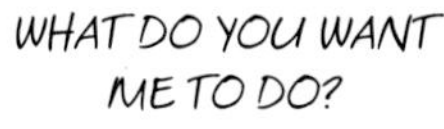

I HAVE GIVEN YOU JERICHO, ITS KING, AND ALL ITS STRONG WARRIORS.

MARCH AROUND THE CITY ONCE FOR SIX DAYS. ON THE SEVENTH DAY, MARCH AROUND THE CITY SEVEN TIMES, WITH THE PRIESTS BLOWING TRUMPETS. THE WALL OF THE CITY WILL COLLAPSE.

THE RESIDENTS OF JERICHO WERE FRIGHTENED AS THE ISRAELITES CAME CLOSER. NO ONE CAME IN, AND NO ONE LEFT THE CITY.
BEHIND CLOSED GATES, THE MEN PREPARED THEIR WEAPONS FOR A FIGHT.
DON'T WORRY, SISTER!
THEY WILL WILL NEVER FIND US HERE!
ONLY RAHAB AND HER FAMILY HAD NOTHING TO FEAR, FOR THEY WOULD BE SPARED.
DON'T WORRY FAMILY, THE ISRAELITES WILL SAVE US.
HAVE YOUR MEN WALK AROUND THE CITY AS THE PRIESTS BLOW THEIR HORNS.
HAVE THEM CARRY THE ARK AS THEY WALK.

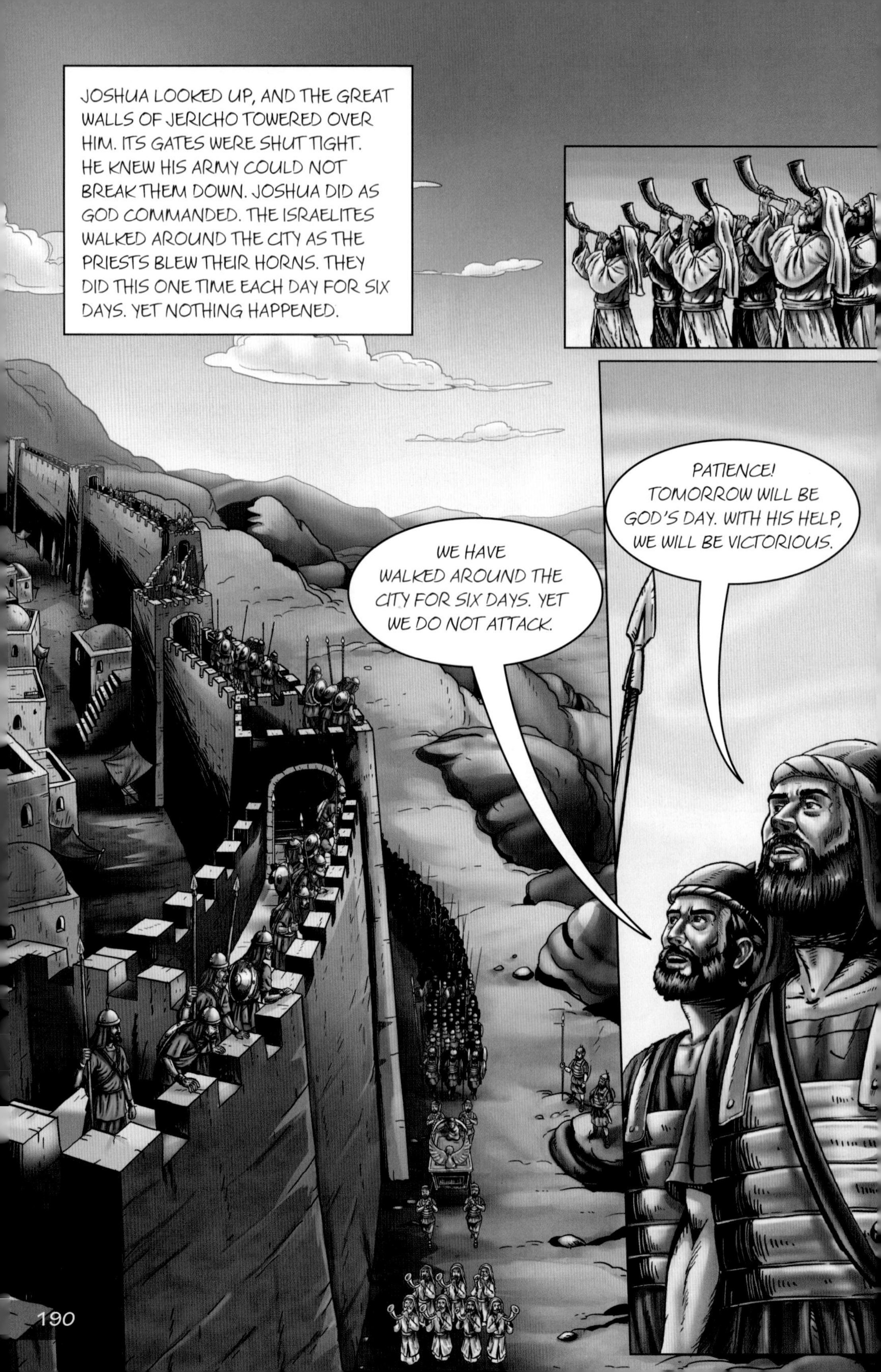
JOSHUA LOOKED UP, AND THE GREAT WALLS OF JERICHO TOWERED OVER HIM. ITS GATES WERE SHUT TIGHT. HE KNEW HIS ARMY COULD NOT BREAK THEM DOWN. JOSHUA DID AS GOD COMMANDED. THE ISRAELITES WALKED AROUND THE CITY AS THE PRIESTS BLEW THEIR HORNS. THEY DID THIS ONE TIME EACH DAY FOR SIX DAYS. YET NOTHING HAPPENED.
WE HAVE WALKED AROUND THE CITY FOR SIX DAYS. YET WE DO NOT ATTACK.
PATIENCE! TOMORROW WILL BE GOD'S DAY. WITH HIS HELP, WE WILL BE VICTORIOUS.

AS DAWN BROKE ON THE SEVENTH DAY, JOSHUA'S ARMY WALKED YET AGAIN AROUND THE MASSIVE CITY. THEY MARCHED SEVEN TIMES, JERICHO'S WALLS TAUNTING THEM AT EVERY STEP.
I'M TIRED OF WALKING. IT'S TIME TO ATTACK!
I HOPE JOSHUA KNOWS WHAT HE IS DOING.
THEN THE PRIESTS BLEW THEIR TRUMPETS LOUDLY, AND ON JOSHUA'S COMMAND, ALL THE ISRAELITES SHOUTED AT THE TOP OF THEIR VOICES. SUDDENLY, THE WALLS OF THE GREAT CITY TUMBLED TO THE GROUND IN A CLOUD OF DUST AND ROCK.
SHOUT! FOR THE LORD HAS GIVEN YOU THE CITY.
THE ISRAELITES DREW THEIR SWORDS AND GRABBED THEIR SPEARS. THE CITY WAS NOW OPEN.
THE ISRAELITES OBEYED GOD'S COMMANDS. THEY CHARGED INTO THE CITY AND DESTROYED EVERYTHING AND EVERYONE IN IT EXCEPT RAHAB AND HER FAMILY, ACCORDING TO GOD'S INSTRUCTIONS. NEWS OF THE VICTORY SPREAD QUICKLY. JOSHUA WAS FAMOUS, AND EVERYONE KNEW THE LORD WAS WITH HIM.

The Defeat at Ai

Joshua 7–8

JOSHUA'S ARMY WAS BEATEN BY AI'S DEFENDERS. THE ISRAELITES RETREATED IN DEFEAT, BLOODY AND BATTERED.
LORD, WHY DID YOU ALLOW US TO CROSS THE JORDAN JUST TO BE DEFEATED?
NEWS OF OUR DEFEAT WILL SPREAD ACROSS THE LAND.
OUR ENEMIES WILL COME AFTER US.

GOD SPOKE TO JOSHUA:
ISRAEL HAS SINNED AND BROKEN MY COVENANT! THEY HAVE STOLEN AND LIED.
I WILL NOT BE WITH YOU ANYMORE UNLESS YOU DESTROY WHATEVER AMONG YOU IS DEVOTED TO DESTRUCTION.
WHOEVER IS CAUGHT SHALL BE DESTROYED!
JOSHUA, HERE IS ACHAN. HE IS THE MAN WHO SINNED.
WHAT SHALL WE DO WITH HIM?
THE ISRAELITES PUNISHED HIM ACCORDING TO GOD'S WILL.

THE ISRAELITES ATTACKED AI ONCE AGAIN, AND ONCE AGAIN THEY RETREATED. BUT THIS TIME IT WAS A PLOY...
LOOK AT THESE COWARDS RUN!
JUST LIKE THEY DID THE LAST TIME.
AS THE ISRAELITES FLED, ANOTHER GROUP AMBUSHED THE ENEMY.
ATTACK! ATTACK!
AFTER THE AMBUSH, JOSHUA'S MEN ATTACKED AI AND BURNED IT TO THE GROUND.

Sun Stopper
Joshua 9–10
JOSHUA'S FAME SPREAD THROUGHOUT THE LAND. ALL THE KINGS WEST OF THE JORDAN RIVER BEGAN TO PLOT TO ATTACK THE ISRAELITES TOGETHER.
WE CANNOT LET THE HEBREWS TAKE OVER OUR LAND!
WE MUST BAND TOGETHER AND DESTROY THEM.
IT IS TIME TO **FIGHT JOSHUA** AND PROTECT OUR PEOPLE AND LANDS!

JOSHUA DID NOT ASK GOD WHAT TO DO. HE LATER DISCOVERED THAT THE TRAVELERS WERE NATIVES OF THE LAND TO BE CONQUERED. BY THE TIME THE TRUTH CAME OUT, IT WAS TOO LATE—JOSHUA HAD MADE THE TREATY. GOD WASN'T HAPPY WITH JOSHUA, BUT HE WAS PLEASED THAT JOSHUA HONORED HIS VOW AND SPARED THEIR LIVES.

THE KING OF JERUSALEM HEARD OF JOSHUA'S GREAT VICTORIES. HE GATHERED SEVERAL OTHER KINGS AND THEIR ARMIES TOGETHER AND MARCHED AGAINST GIBEON.
JOSHUA, YOU MUST HELP US GIBEONITES!
THE FIVE AMORITE KINGS OF THE MOUNTAINS ARE READY TO ATTACK!
THE LORD SAID TO JOSHUA, "DO NOT BE AFRAID OF THEM!" JOSHUA WAS CONFIDENT THEY WOULD WIN.
DON'T WORRY! I WILL STAND BESIDE YOU!

JOSHUA AND HIS SOLDIERS MARCHED ALL NIGHT AND CAUGHT THE ENEMY BY SURPRISE. THE ISRAELITES FOUGHT FURIOUSLY, AND WHEN THE ENEMY SOLDIERS TRIED TO FLEE, THEY WERE STRUCK DOWN BY HUGE HAILSTONES SENT BY GOD. THE HAILSTONES KILLED MORE MEN THAN THE SWORDS OF JOSHUA'S ARMY.
BUT JOSHUA KNEW THAT NIGHT WAS COMING AND THAT MANY OF HIS ENEMIES WOULD BE ABLE TO ESCAPE UNDER COVER OF DARKNESS. HE PRAYED TO GOD AND SAID...
LORD, LET THE SUN STAND STILL OVER GIBEON AND THE MOON OVER THE VALLEY OF AIJALON.
THE LORD LISTENED TO JOSHUA. THE SUN STOPPED IN THE MIDDLE OF THE SKY UNTIL ALL THE FIGHTING WAS OVER. AND EVERYONE SAW THAT THE LORD WAS FIGHTING FOR ISRAEL.

Conquest of Canaan

Joshua 11–12

THE KING OF HAZOR MOBILIZED THE ARMIES OF SEVERAL KINGDOMS IN THE MOUNTAINS TO ATTACK THE ISRAELITES, INCLUDING...

...THE AMORITES, HITTITES, PERIZZITES, JEBUSITES, AND HIVITES.

THEY MARCHED TO THE WATER NEAR MEROM, WHERE THEY CAMPED. THERE THEY WAITED TO FIGHT AGAINST ISRAEL.

THE COMBINED ARMIES WERE AS NUMEROUS AS GRAINS OF SANDS ON A SEASHORE.

BUT IN SPITE OF THEIR ENEMY'S NUMBERS, THE ISRAELITES DEFEATED ALL THEIR FOES. JOSHUA CAPTURED THE CITY OF HAZOR AND KILLED ITS KING...
...AND BURNED THE CITY.
IN ALL THE CAPTURED LANDS, THE ISRAELITES TOOK TREASURES AND LIVESTOCK. JOSHUA WAS PLEASED WITH HIS VICTORY.

Hero Profile
Gideon—God's Soldier

FATHER: JOASH

SONS: GIDEON HAD 70 SONS. ONE, ABIMELECH, KILLED ALL THE OTHERS EXCEPT THE YOUNGEST, JOTHAM.

ORIGINAL OCCUPATION: FARMER

AGAINST ALL ODDS

GIDEON ASSEMBLED A MILITARY FORCE OF 32,000 MEN TO DEFEAT THE MIDIANITES. THE ARMY WAS THEN PARED DOWN TO 10,000, AND THEN TO 300. GIDEON WAS OFFERED A CHANCE TO BE KING AFTER HIS VICTORY, BUT HE REFUSED.

TRUMPET CALL

GIDEON'S MEN BLEW TRUMPETS IN THEIR FIGHT AGAINST THE MIDIANITES. SCHOLARS BELIEVE THEY PROBABLY USED HOLLOWED-OUT RAMS' HORNS. THIS TRUMPET IS SIMILAR TO THE SHOFAR THAT IS BLOWN IN TODAY'S JEWISH SYNAGOGUES TO SIGNAL THE START OF THE JEWISH NEW YEAR, ROSH HASHANAH.

Gideon the Warrior

Judges 6–7

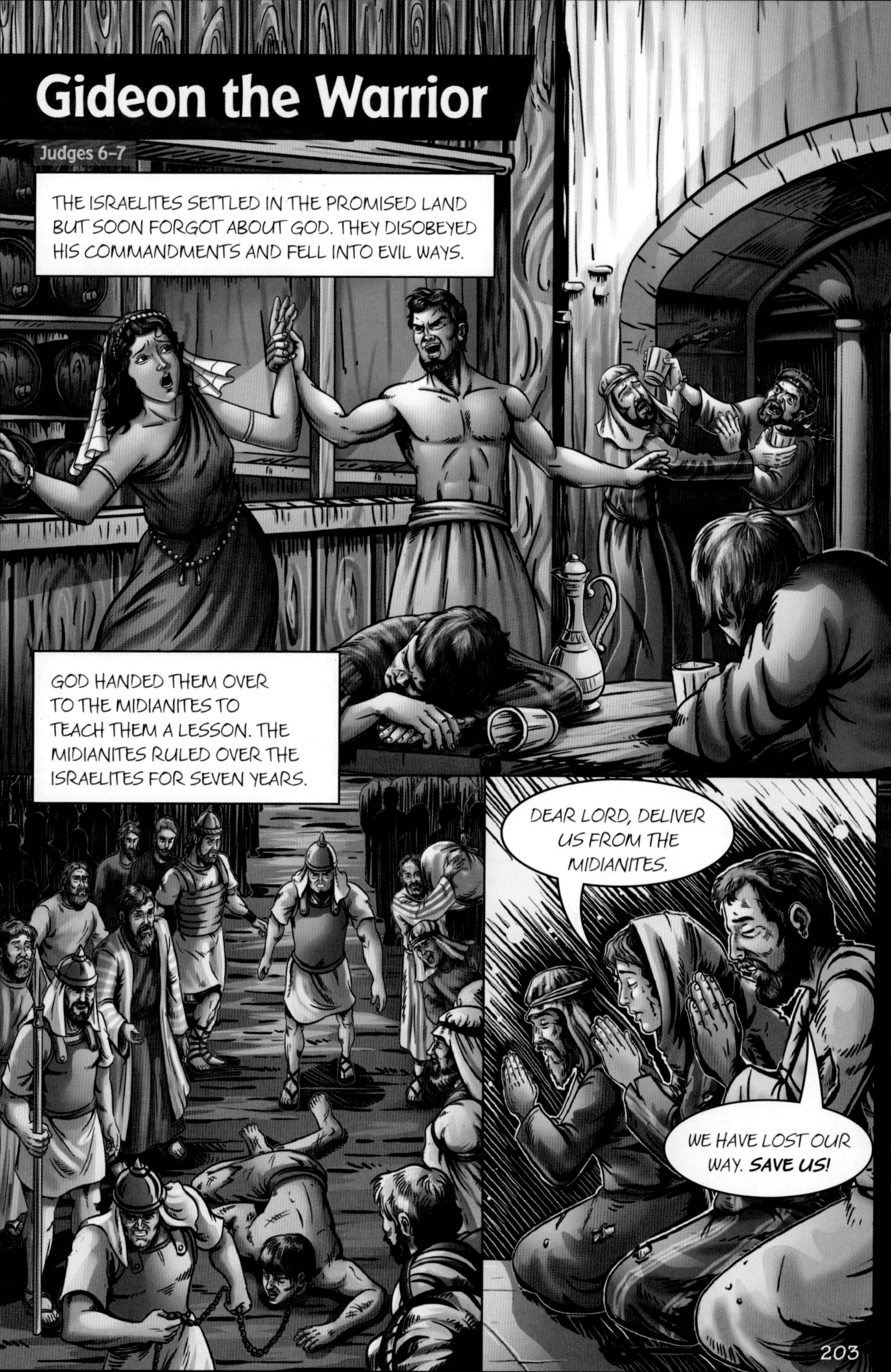

GOD HEARD THE ISRAELITES' PRAYERS AND SENT AN ANGEL TO A MAN CALLED GIDEON.
GOD HAS CHOSEN YOU TO RESCUE ISRAEL FROM THE MIDIANITES.
WHY ME, LORD? I AM FROM A WEAK FAMILY.
GIDEON WAS HUMBLED THAT GOD HAD CHOSEN HIM FOR SUCH A DANGEROUS TASK. HE PLACED AN OFFERING OF MEAT AND BREAD ON A ROCK FOR THE ANGEL.
THE OFFERING BURST INTO FLAMES AS SOON AS THE ANGEL TOUCHED IT WITH HIS STAFF.
OH NO! I HAVE SEEN THE ANGEL OF THE LORD FACE-TO-FACE. I WILL SURELY DIE!
GOD ASSURED GIDEON THAT HIS LIFE WAS NOT IN DANGER AND SENT GIDEON ON HIS MISSION.
GOD TOLD GIDEON TO DESTROY THE PEOPLE'S ALTAR TO BAAL, A PAGAN GOD OF THE CANAANITES. HE ALSO TOLD GIDEON TO CUT DOWN A SACRED POLE. A MOB CONFRONTED GIDEON'S FATHER.
LOOK WHAT YOUR SON HAS DONE!
GIDEON MUST DIE!
WHY ARE YOU DEFENDING BAAL?
IF BAAL IS **REALL** A GOD, **HE** WILL KILL GIDEON.

THE BATTLE BETWEEN ISRAEL AND ITS ENEMIES GREW CLOSER. THE MIDIANITES AND THEIR ALLIES CAMPED IN THE VALLEY OF JEZREEL ON THE BANKS OF THE JORDAN RIVER. THERE THEY PREPARED TO ATTACK.
GIDEON BLEW A HORN TO SUMMON HIS SOLDIERS TO BATTLE. HE ALSO SENT OUT MESSENGERS TO DISTANT LANDS TO RALLY MORE TROOPS.
BUT DESPITE THIS, GIDEON STRUGGLED TO BELIEVE HE WAS THE RIGHT MAN FOR THE JOB. HE ASKED GOD FOR A SIGN.
IF TOMORROW THIS FLEECE IS WET WITH DEW, THEN I KNOW GOD WILL SAVE ISRAEL.
THE NEXT MORNING, THE FLEECE WAS WET BUT THE GROUND WAS DRY.
STILL, GIDEON ASKED FOR ONE MORE SIGN.
GIDEON AGAIN PUT THE FLEECE ON THE GROUND. IF ISRAEL WERE TO TRIUMPH IN BATTLE THE NEXT DAY, THE GROUND WOULD BE WET AND THE WOOL DRY.
THIS IS EXACTLY WHAT HAPPENED. NOW GIDEON WAS CONVINCED!

TENS OF THOUSANDS OF SOLDIERS ANSWERED GIDEON'S CALL. BUT GOD WARNED GIDEON THAT THERE WERE TOO MANY. GOD WANTED THE WORLD TO KNOW THAT IT WAS NOT BY THE MIGHT OF MEN BUT BY THE MIGHT OF GOD THAT VICTORY WOULD BE ACHIEVED.
ANYONE WHO IS AFRAID MUST LEAVE NOW.
THOUSANDS LEFT. GOD THEN TOLD GIDEON TO TAKE THOSE WHO REMAINED DOWN TO THE RIVERBANK.
GOD SAID THOSE WHO DRANK FROM THE RIVER WITH CUPPED HANDS COULD REMAIN AND FIGHT. THOSE WHO KNELT DOWN TO DRINK HAD TO LEAVE. IN THE END, GIDEON WENT TO WAR WITH 300 SOLDIERS.

THAT NIGHT GIDEON FELT SCARED. GOD TOLD HIM TO GO DOWN TO THE MIDIANITES' CAMP. THERE HE OVERHEARD SOME SOLDIERS TALKING ABOUT ONE OF THEIR DREAMS THAT FORETOLD A VICTORY FOR GIDEON. THEY WERE EVEN MORE SCARED THAN HE WAS!
GIDEON'S CONFIDENCE GREW AS HE RETURNED TO HIS CAMP. HE GAVE EACH OF HIS MEN A TRUMPET AND A TORCH INSIDE A JAR. THEY STOOD AROUND THE ENEMY'S CAMP.
THEY LIT THEIR TORCHES...
...AND THEY BLEW THEIR TRUMPETS AND BROKE THEIR JARS. THE MIDIANITES THOUGHT THEY WERE SURROUNDED. THEY WERE TERRIFIED AND FLED IN CONFUSION. GIDEON HAD RESCUED ISRAEL.

Hero Profile
Samson—God's Strong Man

FATHER: MANOAH

NOTABLE WOMEN IN SAMSON'S LIFE: HIS WIFE, A PHILISTINE WOMAN FROM TIMNAH (A CITY IN CANAAN) AND DELILAH, A BEAUTIFUL WOMAN FROM THE VALLEY OF SOREK

NAZIRITE STRENGTH

SAMSON WAS A NAZIRITE. A NAZIRITE WAS A HEBREW MAN WHO WAS DEDICATED TO GOD. NAZIRITES MADE VOWS TO SERVE GOD AND FOLLOW SPECIAL RULES. SAMSON HAD TREMENDOUS STRENGTH, WHICH WAS REPRESENTED BY HIS UNCUT HAIR.

SAMSON AND DELILAH

SAMSON AND DELILAH HAVE LONG BEEN THE SUBJECT OF MANY POPULAR POEMS, BOOKS, AND MOVIES. PERHAPS THE RELATIONSHIP IS SO FASCINATING BECAUSE OF THE MYSTERIOUS STRENGTH OF SAMSON AND DELILAH'S DECEIT TO FIND OUT THE SOURCE OF HIS STRENGTH. SHE BETRAYED HIM, BUT GOD STILL PROVED HIS POWER IN THE END!

Samson Kills a Lion

Judges 13–15

THE ISRAELITES ONCE AGAIN FELL OUT OF GOD'S FAVOR, AND FOR 40 YEARS THEY WERE OPPRESSED BY THE PHILISTINES. ONE DAY AN ANGEL APPEARED TO A MAN NAMED MANOAH AND HIS WIFE. THEY HAD BEEN TRYING FOR YEARS TO HAVE A CHILD.

THEY SOON HAD A SON, WHOM THEY NAMED SAMSON. HE DID NOT CUT HIS HAIR AND GREW UP TO BE VERY STRONG.

SAMSON MET A BEAUTIFUL PHILISTINE WOMAN, AND HE WANTED TO MARRY HER. HE TOLD HIS PARENTS.

SAMSON TRAVELED WITH HIS PARENTS TO SEE THE WOMAN HE WANTED TO MARRY.
AS THEY NEARED SOME VINEYARDS, A LION ATTACKED SAMSON.
THE SPIRIT OF THE LORD CAME UPON SAMSON, AND HE KILLED THE LION WITH HIS BARE HANDS.

SOMETIME LATER, WHEN SAMSON WAS TRAVELING TO MARRY THE WOMAN, HE PASSED BY THE LION HE HAD KILLED. BEES HAD NESTED INSIDE AND MADE DELICIOUS HONEY, WHICH SAMSON SCOOPED OUT AND ATE.
DURING HIS WEDDING CELEBRATION, SAMSON TOLD HIS GUESTS A RIDDLE BASED ON THE HONEY HE HAD EATEN.
I WILL GIVE YOU SEVEN DAYS TO SOLVE THIS RIDDLE.
OUT OF THE ONE WHO EATS CAME SOMETHING TO EAT; OUT OF THE STRONG CAME SOMETHING SWEET.
UNABLE TO SOLVE IT, THE MEN CONFRONTED SAMSON'S WIFE.
TELL US THE ANSWER TO THE RIDDLE OR WE WILL KILL YOU!
SAMSON'S WIFE WEPT AND CONVINCED HIM TO GIVE THE ANSWER, WHICH SHE THEN TOLD THE MEN. WHEN THE MEN ANSWERED HIS RIDDLE, SAMSON BECAME ANGRY.
SAMSON KILLED THIRTY MEN AND WENT HOME. HIS WIFE WAS GIVEN TO ANOTHER MAN.
ANGRY THAT HIS WIFE WAS GIVEN AWAY, SAMSON BURNED THE PHILISTINES' GRAIN FIELDS. SO THE PHILISTINES MURDERED SAMSON'S WIFE. SAMSON THEN VOWED TO KILL EVERY PHILISTINE IN HIS SIGHT. HE USED THE JAWBONE OF A DONKEY TO KILL 1,000 PHILISTINES.
I WILL NOT STOP UNTIL I HAVE MY REVENGE!
SAMSON RETURNED TO THE ISRAELITES AND BECAME THEIR LEADER. MEANWHILE, THE PHILISTINES HUNTED THE LEGENDARY STRONG MAN FOR YEARS.

Samson and Delilah

Judges 16

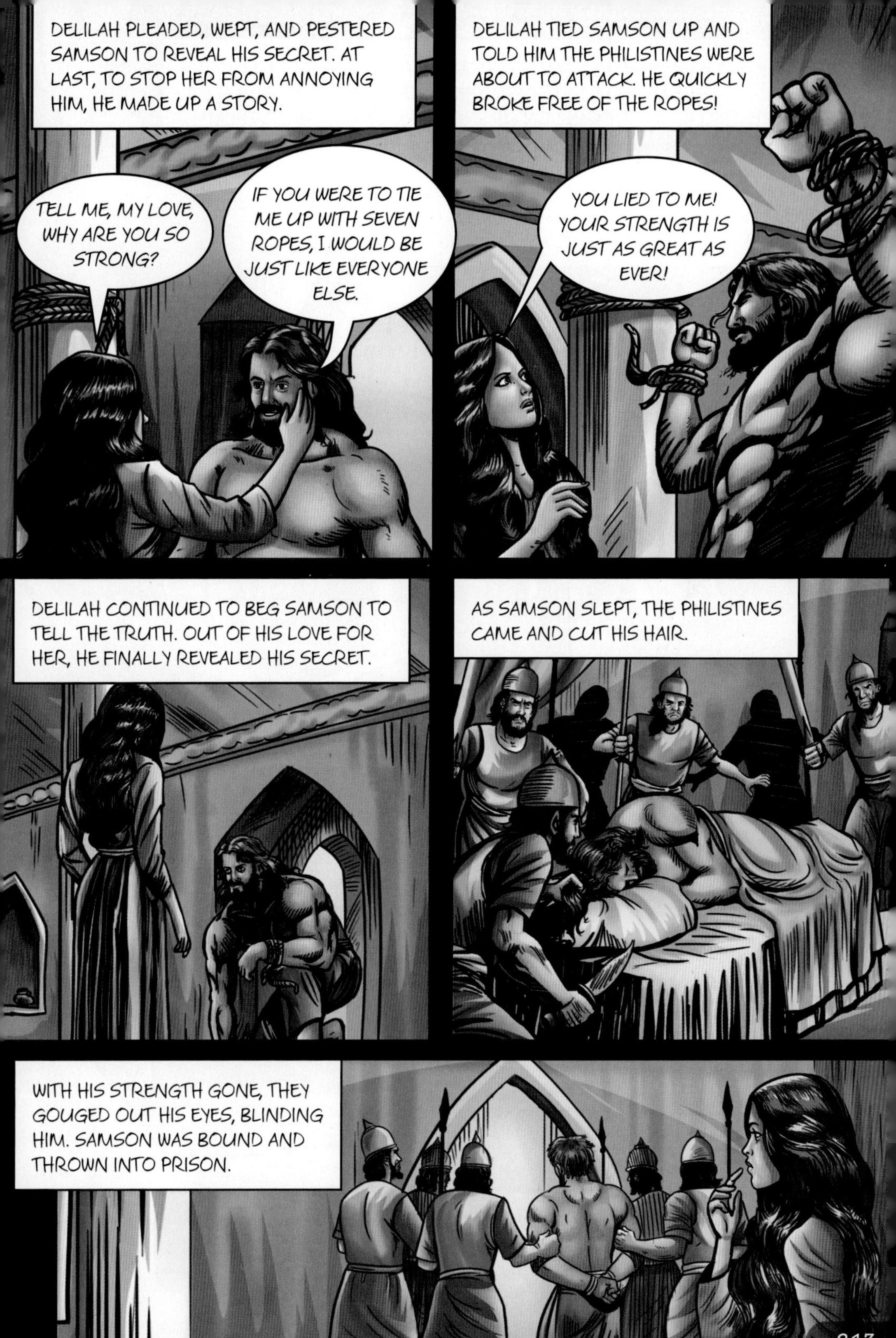

DELILAH PLEADED, WEPT, AND PESTERED SAMSON TO REVEAL HIS SECRET. AT LAST, TO STOP HER FROM ANNOYING HIM, HE MADE UP A STORY.

TELL ME, MY LOVE, WHY ARE YOU SO STRONG?

IF YOU WERE TO TIE ME UP WITH SEVEN ROPES, I WOULD BE JUST LIKE EVERYONE ELSE.

DELILAH TIED SAMSON UP AND TOLD HIM THE PHILISTINES WERE ABOUT TO ATTACK. HE QUICKLY BROKE FREE OF THE ROPES!

YOU LIED TO ME! YOUR STRENGTH IS JUST AS GREAT AS EVER!

DELILAH CONTINUED TO BEG SAMSON TO TELL THE TRUTH. OUT OF HIS LOVE FOR HER, HE FINALLY REVEALED HIS SECRET.

AS SAMSON SLEPT, THE PHILISTINES CAME AND CUT HIS HAIR.

OVER TIME, SAMSON'S HAIR BEGAN TO GROW BACK. THE PHILISTINE LEADERS GATHERED AT A GREAT FEAST TO HONOR THEIR GOD. THE TEMPLE WAS FULL OF PEOPLE. THEY BROUGHT SAMSON UP FROM PRISON TO AMUSE THEM.
SAMSON CAME INTO THE ROOM AND STOOD CHAINED BETWEEN TWO MASSIVE COLUMNS THAT HELD UP THE CEILING. HE ASKED GOD TO MAKE HIM STRONG AGAIN.
LET ME DIE WITH THE PHILISTINES!
SAMSON PUSHED AGAINST THE COLUMNS WITH ALL HIS STRENGTH. THE TEMPLE FELL TO THE GROUND IN AN AVALANCHE OF ROCK AND DEBRIS, KILLING EVERYONE INSIDE—INCLUDING SAMSON. GOD HAD GIVEN SAMSON ONE FINAL VICTORY.

Hero Profile
Ruth—A Faithful Daughter-in-Law

HUSBANDS: MAHLON, BOAZ

SON: OBED (GRANDFATHER OF DAVID)

MEANING OF NAME: HEBREW NAME MEANING "COMPANION, FRIEND"

TOO FORWARD?

WHEN RUTH PUT ON HER FINEST CLOTHES AND WENT TO SEE BOAZ, HER FUTURE HUSBAND, SHE WAS NOT BEING TOO FORWARD. AT THAT TIME, A CHILDLESS WIDOW COULD ASK A RELATIVE TO MARRY HER.

A FOREIGNER

BOAZ MARRYING RUTH, THE MOABITE, MIGHT SEEM AT ODDS WITH THE TEACHINGS OF EZRA AND NEHEMIAH THAT FORBID JEWISH MEN FROM MARRYING NON-JEWISH WOMEN. BUT MUST REMEMBER THAT WHEN RUTH VOLUNTEERED TO STAY WITH NAOMI, SHE ALSO SAID, "YOUR PEOPLE WILL BE MY PEOPLE, AND YOUR GOD WILL BE MY GOD." SHE REJECTED HER PAGAN HERITAGE AND EMBRACED HER MOTHER-IN-LAW'S RELIGION AND NATIONALITY.

BOAZ RECOGNIZED THE WORTH OF HER ACTIONS. HE SAW THAT SHE WAS A GOOD WOMAN AND CHOSE TO MARRY HER.

GOD REWARDED RUTH'S LOVE AND LOYALTY TO NAOMI BY MAKING IT POSSIBLE FOR HER TO BE A GREAT-GRANDMOTHER OF DAVID AND AN ANCESTOR OF JESUS!

A Loyal Woman

Ruth 1

THREE GENERATIONS BEFORE KING DAVID WAS BORN, A FAMINE SPREAD ACROSS JUDAH, INCLUDING THE TOWN OF BETHLEHEM. PEOPLE HAD LITTLE TO EAT. SOME BECAME SICK AND DIED. OTHERS, LIKE ELIMELECH AND HIS FAMILY, DECIDED TO LEAVE.

THIS IS THE LAST OF OUR FOOD, HUSBAND. THERE IS NO MORE.

YOU ARE A GOOD WIFE, NAOMI. YOU'VE DONE A LOT WITH SO LITTLE. IT'S TIME WE LEFT THIS PLACE FOR THE LAND OF MOAB.

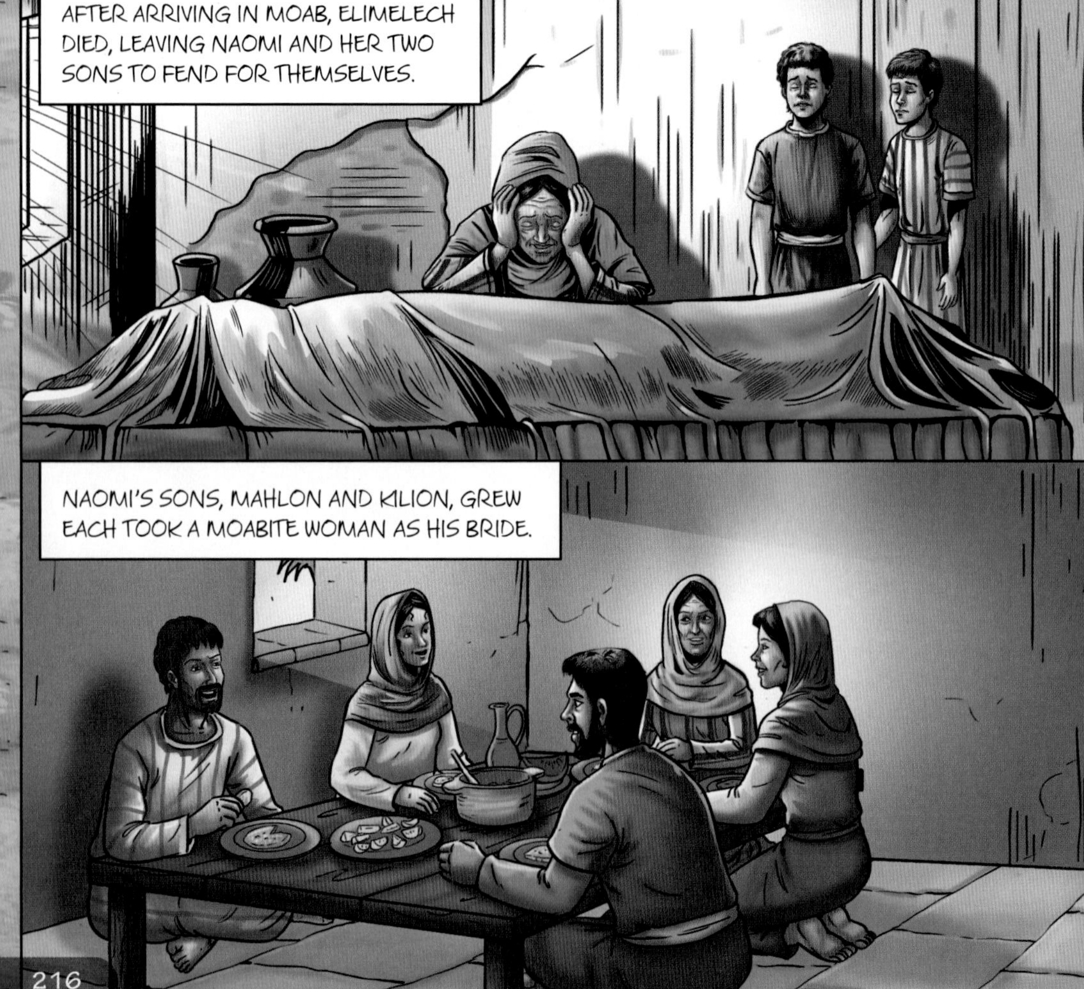

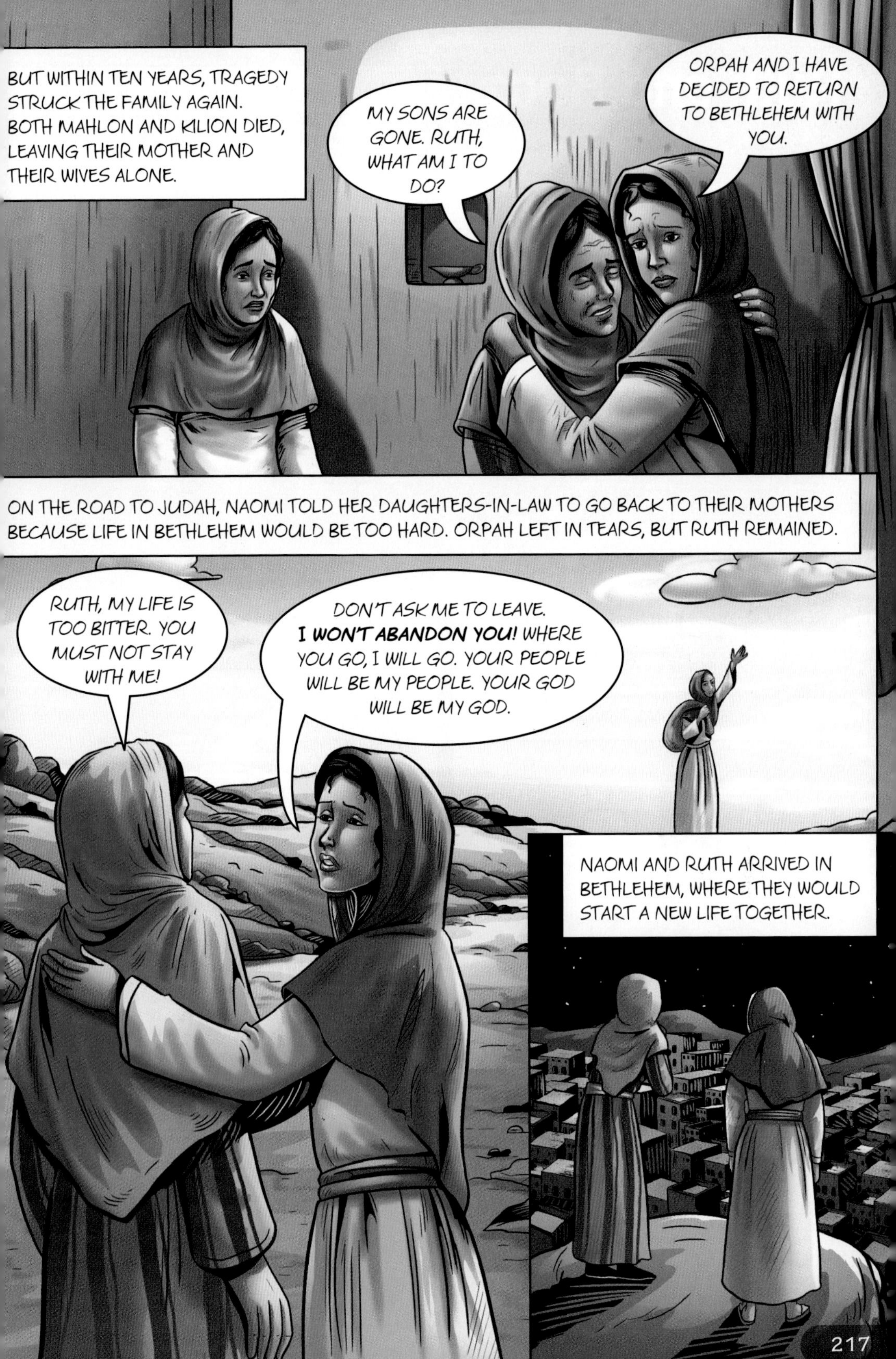
BUT WITHIN TEN YEARS, TRAGEDY STRUCK THE FAMILY AGAIN. BOTH MAHLON AND KILION DIED, LEAVING THEIR MOTHER AND THEIR WIVES ALONE.
MY SONS ARE GONE. RUTH, WHAT AM I TO DO?
ORPAH AND I HAVE DECIDED TO RETURN TO BETHLEHEM WITH YOU.
ON THE ROAD TO JUDAH, NAOMI TOLD HER DAUGHTERS-IN-LAW TO GO BACK TO THEIR MOTHERS BECAUSE LIFE IN BETHLEHEM WOULD BE TOO HARD. ORPAH LEFT IN TEARS, BUT RUTH REMAINED.
RUTH, MY LIFE IS TOO BITTER. YOU MUST NOT STAY WITH ME!
DON'T ASK ME TO LEAVE. **I WON'T ABANDON YOU!** WHERE YOU GO, I WILL GO. YOUR PEOPLE WILL BE MY PEOPLE. YOUR GOD WILL BE MY GOD.
NAOMI AND RUTH ARRIVED IN BETHLEHEM, WHERE THEY WOULD START A NEW LIFE TOGETHER.

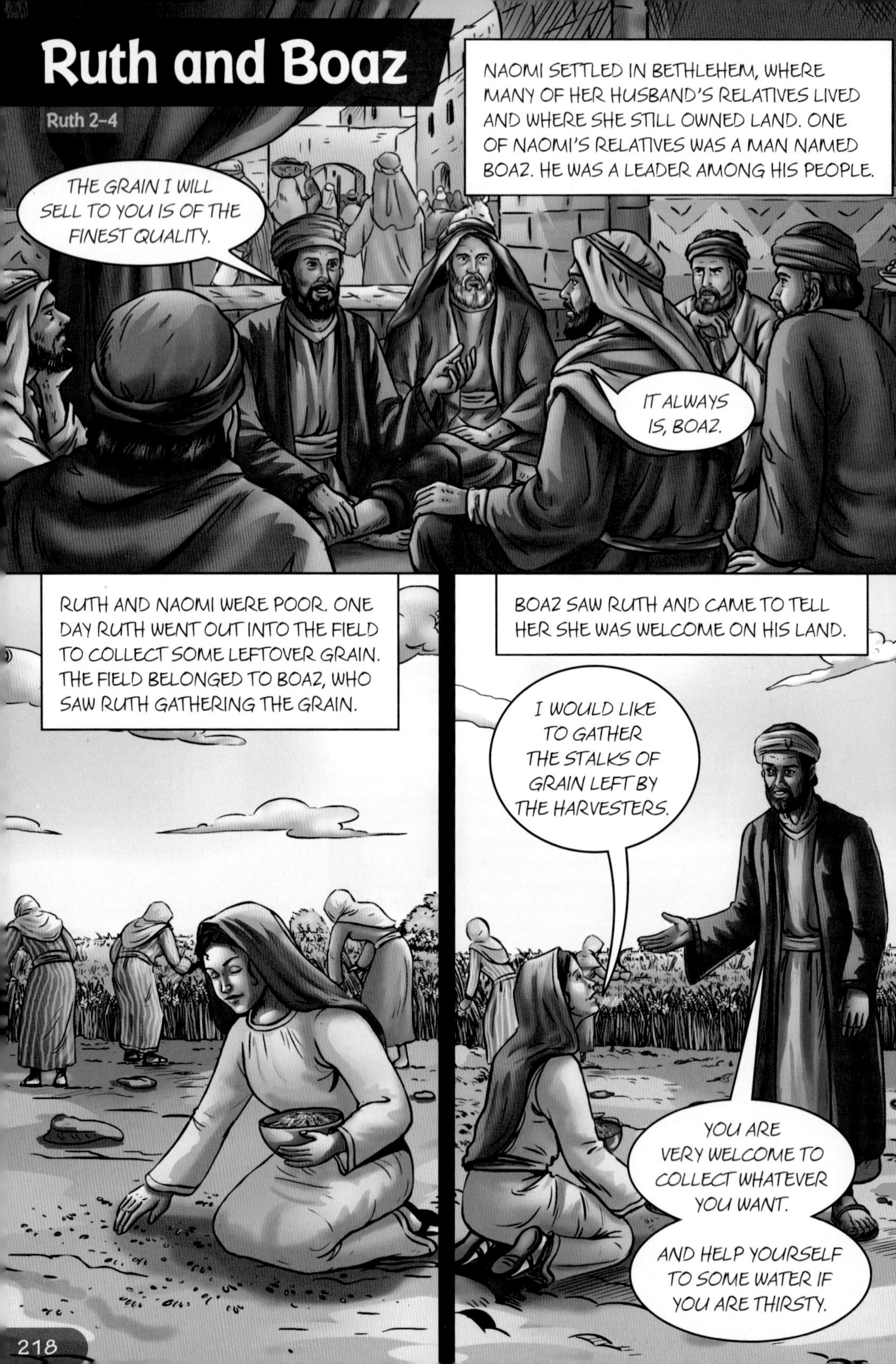
Ruth and Boaz
Ruth 2–4
NAOMI SETTLED IN BETHLEHEM, WHERE MANY OF HER HUSBAND'S RELATIVES LIVED AND WHERE SHE STILL OWNED LAND. ONE OF NAOMI'S RELATIVES WAS A MAN NAMED BOAZ. HE WAS A LEADER AMONG HIS PEOPLE.
THE GRAIN I WILL SELL TO YOU IS OF THE FINEST QUALITY.
IT ALWAYS IS, BOAZ.
RUTH AND NAOMI WERE POOR. ONE DAY RUTH WENT OUT INTO THE FIELD TO COLLECT SOME LEFTOVER GRAIN. THE FIELD BELONGED TO BOAZ, WHO SAW RUTH GATHERING THE GRAIN.
BOAZ SAW RUTH AND CAME TO TELL HER SHE WAS WELCOME ON HIS LAND.
I WOULD LIKE TO GATHER THE STALKS OF GRAIN LEFT BY THE HARVESTERS.
YOU ARE VERY WELCOME TO COLLECT WHATEVER YOU WANT.
AND HELP YOURSELF TO SOME WATER IF YOU ARE THIRSTY.

WHY ARE YOU SO KIND TO ME? I'M A FOREIGNER IN YOUR LAND.
I KNOW WHAT YOU HAVE DONE FOR YOUR MOTHER-IN-LAW.
YOU HAVE LEFT YOUR FATHER AND MOTHER TO STAY WITH HER.
MAY THE GOD OF ISRAEL REWARD YOU. YOU ARE A LOYAL SERVANT.
MAY I CONTINUE TO PLEASE YOU, SIR.
YOU HAVE COMFORTED ME WITH YOUR KIND WORDS.

WHEN IT WAS TIME TO EAT, BOAZ ASKED RUTH TO SIT DOWN AND SHARE SOME ROASTED GRAIN.
RUTH WORKED COLLECTING GRAIN UNTIL EVENING. SHE CAME HOME AND TOLD NAOMI ABOUT HER DAY.
HE WAS SO KIND TO ME.
HE IS A RELATIVE OF MY HUSBAND. HE IS A GOOD MAN.
NAOMI THEN TOLD RUTH TO PUT ON HER BEST CLOTHES AND GO TO BOAZ ONE NIGHT AFTER HIS MEAL.

BOAZ TOOK RUTH AS HIS WIFE, AND THEY PROCLAIMED THEIR HAPPINESS IN FRONT OF NAOMI AND THE TOWN'S ELDERS.
THE COUPLE SOON HAD A CHILD, A SON NAMED OBED, WHO WOULD BECOME THE GRANDFATHER OF ISRAEL'S GREAT KING—DAVID.

Hero Profile
Samuel—The King Maker

MOTHER: HANNAH

FATHER: ELKANAH

LITERAL MEANING OF "SAMUEL" IN HEBREW: "NAME OF GOD"

A MOTHER'S ANSWERED PRAYER

IN BIBLE TIMES GREAT VALUE WAS PLACED ON HAVING CHILDREN. HANNAH LONGED FOR A BABY. SHE PRAYED TO GOD AND PROMISED HER CHILD WOULD LEAD A LIFE OF SERVICE TO GOD.

THE BUILDING OF A NATION

WHILE THE BIBLE TELLS US MUCH ABOUT THE EARLY LIFE OF THE PROPHET SAMUEL, IT DOES NOT OFFER MANY DETAILS ABOUT THE LIFE OF SAUL, ISRAEL'S FIRST KING. THIS SHOWS HOW IMPORTANT SAMUEL WAS TO THE FOUNDING OF ISRAEL AS A NATION. BEFORE SAMUEL, ISRAEL WAS A COLLECTION OF TRIBES, BUT SAMUEL PLAYED AN IMPORTANT ROLE IN ISRAEL BECOMING A NATION.

A Son for Hannah

1 Samuel 1–3

IN THE HILL COUNTRY LIVED A MAN NAMED ELKANAH WITH HIS TWO WIVES, PENINNAH AND HANNAH. PENINNAH HAD CHILDREN, BUT HANNAH DID NOT HAVE ANY. PENINNAH TAUNTED HANNAH AND MADE FUN OF HER. YET ELKANAH LOVED HANNAH VERY MUCH.

HERE IS A CUP OF WATER, HUSBAND.

THANK YOU, HANNAH. YOU TAKE WONDERFUL CARE OF ME.

ONE DAY HANNAH WENT TO THE TEMPLE TO PRAY.

DEAR LORD, LOOK AT MY SADNESS AND ANSWER MY PRAYER. IF YOU GIVE ME A SON, I WILL MAKE SURE HE SERVES YOU HIS ENTIRE LIFE.

ELI, THE PRIEST, OVERHEARD HER PRAYING.

DO NOT WORRY. GO IN PEACE. MAY GOD GRANT YOUR REQUEST.

NOT LONG AFTER, HANNAH HAD A SON AND NAMED HIM SAMUEL. AS SHE HAD PROMISED, SHE TOOK SAMUEL TO THE TEMPLE AND PRESENTED HIM AS GOD'S SERVANT.

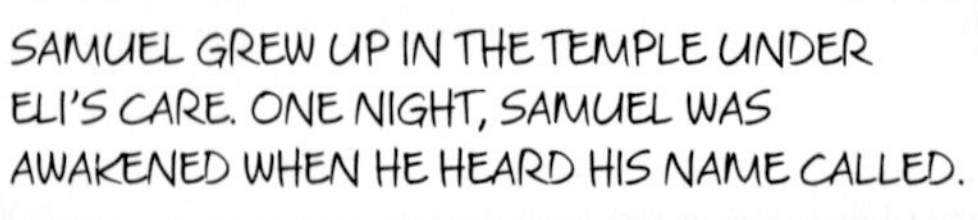

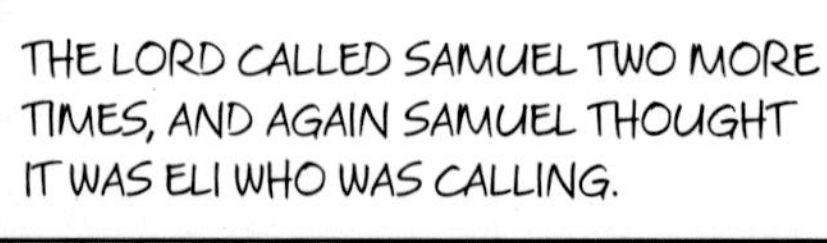

GOD TOLD SAMUEL THAT HE WOULD SOON PUNISH ELI AND HIS TWO SONS, FOR ELI DID NOT DISCIPLINE HIS SONS FOR THEIR SINS. AND GOD WAS WITH SAMUEL AS HE GREW UP. EVENTUALLY, ALL OF ISRAEL RECOGNIZED SAMUEL AS A PROPHET OF THE LORD.

Seizing the Ark
1 Samuel 3–6
THE PHILISTINES AND THE ISRAELITES WERE ONCE AGAIN AT WAR. THE PHILISTINES KILLED MANY ISRAELITES IN BATTLE.
AT THE TIME OF THE WAR, THE LORD APPEARED TO SAMUEL. SOON WORD SPREAD THAT THE SON OF HANNAH WAS A PROPHET WHO COMMUNICATED WITH GOD.
AFTER THE DEFEAT, THE HEBREWS RETREATED. IN DESPERATION, THEY BROUGHT THE ARK OF THE COVENANT TO THEIR CAMP. THEY HOPED IT WOULD BRING THEM VICTORY IN THE BATTLE.
A WILD CHEER AROSE FROM THE ISRAELITE CAMP WHEN THE ARK APPEARED.
NO ONE WILL DEFEAT US NOW!
THE ARK IS TOO POWERFUL. GOD IS TOO POWERFUL!

STILL, THE PHILISTINES DEFEATED THE ISRAELITES BECAUSE THEY HAD NOT SHOWN TRUE FAITH IN GOD. THE PHILISTINES CAPTURED THE ARK.
THE PHILISTINES PUT THE ARK IN THE TEMPLE OF DAGON, THEIR GOD. BUT THE STATUE OF DAGON TUMBLED AND SHATTERED.
GOD THEN AFFLICTED THOSE LIVING IN THE PHILISTINE TOWN OF ASHDOD WITH TUMORS. WHEN THEY MOVED THE ARK TO THE CITY OF GATH, GOD DID THE SAME THING.
THE HEBREW GOD HAS PLAGUED US WITH THESE SORES!
WE MUST GET RID OF THEIR ARK!
AFTER SEVEN MONTHS, THE PHILISTINES SENT THE ARK BACK TO THE ISRAELITES ON A CART DRAWN BY COWS. INSIDE THE ARK THE PHILISTINES PUT GIFTS FOR THE ISRAELITES. THE COWS STOPPED NEAR A WHEAT FIELD OUTSIDE THE TOWN OF BETH-SHEMESH, WHERE PEOPLE REJOICED.
LOOK! THE ARK OF GOD HAS RETURNED TO US.
LET US GIVE THANKS TO GOD!

The Miracle at Mizpah

1 Samuel 7

SAMUEL HEARD THEIR PLEAS AND MADE A SACRIFICE TO GOD.
ON THE BATTLEFIELD OF MIZPAH, GOD SENT THUNDER, WHICH CONFUSED THE ENEMY. THE ISRAELITES RUSHED THE PHILISTINES AND STRUCK THEM DOWN.
THE BATTLE WAS A TURNING POINT. GOD WAS NOW WITH SAMUEL AND THE ISRAELITES IN THEIR FIGHT AGAINST THE PHILISTINES. SAMUEL PLACED A STONE AT THE SITE OF THE BATTLE AS A REMINDER OF GOD'S HELP.
I PLACE THIS STONE HERE. ITS NAME IS EBENEZER, "STONE OF HELP"
THE PHILISTINES WOULD NEVER BOTHER ISRAEL AGAIN ON ISRAEL'S TERRITORY.

Searching for a King

1 Samuel 8–10

WHEN HE BECAME AN OLD MAN, SAMUEL ASKED HIS TWO SONS TO RULE ISRAEL. BUT THE SONS WERE GREEDY. THEY TOOK BRIBES AND DID NOT FOLLOW THEIR FATHER'S EXAMPLE. THE ELDERS MET WITH SAMUEL AND ASKED HIM TO APPOINT A KING.

SAMUEL DESPAIRED WHEN THE ELDERS IGNORED HIS ADVICE AND INSISTED THEY WANTED A KING. GOD TOLD SAMUEL TO DO WHAT THE ELDERS SAID. THEY WERE REJECTING GOD, NOT SAMUEL.

GOD TOLD SAMUEL HE WOULD GUIDE HIM IN SELECTING A MAN TO BE THE ISRAELITES' FIRST KING.
SAUL, GOD HAS CHOSEN YOU TO BE KING.
WITH THIS OIL I ANOINT YOU.
SAMUEL SOON MET A YOUNG WARRIOR NAMED SAUL, WHO WAS LOOKING FOR THE DONKEYS HIS FATHER HAD LOST. GOD TOLD SAMUEL THAT THIS WAS THE MAN WHO SHOULD BE KING.
LATER AFTER SAUL HAD GONE BACK TO HIS PEOPLE, SAMUEL GATHERED THE TRIBES TOGETHER. HE TOLD THEM SAUL WAS THE KING GOD CHOSE. THEY LOOKED FOR HIM AND FOUND HIM BEHIND SOME BAGGAGE.
LONG LIVE THE KING!
SO JUST AS THE LORD HAD TOLD SAMUEL, SAUL BECAME THE KING.

Saul's Disobedience

1 Samuel 11–14

THE PHILISTINES WERE STILL ENEMIES OF ISRAEL. THEIR VAST ARMY HAD ENCAMPED AT A TOWN CALLED MICMASH AND THREATENED THE ISRAELITES. SAMUEL TOLD SAUL TO WAIT FOR HIM BEFORE LAUNCHING THE ATTACK.
MY LORD, MANY OF OUR SOLDIERS ARE FLEEING OUR ARMY.
THEY ARE AFRAID OF THE PHILISTINES.
NOT TO WORRY. SAMUEL WILL BE HERE SOON AND OFFER A SACRIFICE TO GOD. WE WILL WIN WITH THE MEN WE HAVE.
A WEEK PASSED AND SAMUEL HAD NOT ARRIVED. SAUL GREW INCREASINGLY CONCERNED, SO HE MADE A SACRIFICE IN GOD'S NAME.
WHEN SAMUEL ARRIVED, HE WAS ANGRY.
I TOLD YOU TO WAIT! YOU HAVE DONE A FOOLISH THING.
ALL MY SOLDIERS WERE LEAVING! I HAD TO SEEK GOD'S FAVOR.
YOUR KINGDOM ON EARTH IS NO MORE. NO ONE ELSE IN YOUR FAMILY SHALL BE KING!
GOD WAS ANGRY WITH SAUL FOR HIS DISOBEDIENCE. NOW GOD WOULD CHOOSE SOMEONE ELSE TO RULE ISRAEL AFTER SAUL—SOMEONE WHO WOULD OBEY HIM.

Hero Profile
David—From Shepherd to King

FATHER: JESSE

WIVES: MANY, INCLUDING MICHAL, ABIGAIL, AND THE MOST FAMOUS OF ALL, BATHSHEBA

SIBLINGS: SEVEN BROTHERS AND TWO SISTERS

DIRECT ANCESTOR: RUTH, THE MOABITE

ORIGINAL OCCUPATION: SHEPHERD

ROYAL FAMILY

ALL THE KINGS OF ISRAEL WHO CAME AFTER DAVID ARE HIS DESCENDANTS. ALTOGETHER THEY RULED FOR 500 YEARS. YET GOD HAD PROMISED DAVID THAT ONE OF HIS RELATIVES WOULD ALWAYS BE KING, WHICH WAS THE BEGINNING OF THE ANTICIPATION OF A MESSIAH.

DAVID'S OWN CITY

JERUSALEM IS KNOWN AS THE CITY OF DAVID. HE CONQUERED THE CITY AND MADE IT THE CENTER OF HIS KINGDOM. HE EVEN BROUGHT THE ARK OF THE COVENANT THERE.

God Calls David

1 Samuel 16

SAMUEL ASKED JESSE IF HE HAD ANY OTHER SONS. JESSE SAID THERE WAS ONE—DAVID. HE WAS IN THE FIELDS WATCHING SHEEP AND GOATS. SAMUEL ASKED JESSE TO BRING DAVID TO HIM. WHEN SAMUEL SAW DAVID, HE KNEW DAVID WOULD BE ISRAEL'S NEW KING BECAUSE GOD TOLD HIM SO.
MAY GOD'S LIGHT SHINE UPON YOU AND PROTECT YOU, FOR ISRAEL IS YOURS.

David and Goliath
1 Samuel 16–17
THE SPIRIT OF THE LORD LEFT SAUL. AN EVIL SPIRIT CONTINUALLY TORMENTED THE KING. SAUL'S SERVANTS OFFERED TO FIND A MUSICIAN TO PLAY THE HARP FOR HIM. THEY THOUGHT THE MUSIC WOULD HELP SAUL FEEL BETTER.
SAUL HEARD ABOUT DAVID AND SENT FOR HIM. SAUL LIKED THE BOY VERY MUCH. WHENEVER THE TORMENTING SPIRIT WOULD COME UPON THE KING, DAVID WOULD PLAY THE HARP AND THE SPIRIT WOULD GO AWAY.
YOU PLAY THE HARP WELL.
BUT CAN YOU CARRY MY ARMOR AND WEAPONS IN BATTLE?
I WILL TRY, MY KING.
THE PHILISTINES WERE AT WAR AGAINST THE ISRAELITES. THE ARMIES GATHERED ON SEPARATE HILLS DIVIDED BY A WIDE VALLEY.
I HEAR THE PHILISTINES HAVE A GREAT CHAMPION.
I HEAR HIS NAME IS GOLIATH. HE IS SO LARGE THAT HE **BLOTS OUT THE SUN!**

GOLIATH WAS INDEED AN IMPOSING SOLDIER. HE HAD A BRONZE HELMET AND BRONZE LEG ARMOR. THE SHAFT OF HIS SPEAR WAS AS TALL AS HE WAS—OVER NINE FEET!
CHOOSE YOUR BEST MAN! THE TWO OF US WILL **BATTLE!**
IF HE BEATS ME, MY PEOPLE WILL BE YOUR SLAVES.
IF I BEAT YOUR MAN, **YOU WILL BE OUR SLAVES!**
ONLY A **FOOL** WOULD DUEL WITH THAT GIANT.
I'M NOT GOING ANYWHERE NEAR HIM!

DAVID'S FATHER SENT HIM WITH FOOD FOR HIS BROTHERS, WHO WERE IN SAUL'S ARMY. DAVID WAS SHOCKED THAT NOBODY WOULD STEP FORWARD TO FIGHT GOLIATH.
HAVE YOU SEEN THE GIANT? THE KING HAS OFFERED A HUGE REWARD TO THE PERSON WHO KILLS HIM.
WHAT IS THE REWARD FOR KILLING THIS PHILISTINE WHO DEFIES THE ARMIES OF THE LIVING GOD?
DAVID WENT TO KING SAUL AND OFFERED TO FIGHT GOLIATH.
I ADMIRE YOU FOR YOUR COURAGE, YOUNG DAVID. IF YOU MUST FIGHT, PLEASE USE MY ARMOR.
NO, MY KING. I WILL FEEL UNCOMFORTABLE IN YOUR ARMOR. I HAVE ANOTHER IDEA.
INSTEAD OF A SWORD OR A SPEAR, DAVID ARMED HIMSELF WITH A SIMPLE SLING AND FIVE STONES.

DAVID ANSWERED GOLIATH'S CHALLENGE ON THE BATTLEFIELD AS BOTH ARMIES WATCHED.
YOU? YOU ARE THE BEST OF THE HEBREW SOLDIERS? AM I A DOG, THAT YOU COME AT ME WITH A STICK?
YOU HAVE A SWORD IN YOUR HANDS, BUT I HAVE THE LORD ON MY SIDE!
COME OVER HERE, AND I'LL GIVE YOUR FLESH TO THE BIRDS AND WILD ANIMALS!
TODAY THE LORD WILL CONQUER YOU. I WILL KILL YOU AND GIVE THE DEAD BODIES OF YOUR MEN TO THE BIRDS AND WILD ANIMALS!

GOLIATH CHARGED AT DAVID...
...BUT DAVID NEVER WAVERED. HE PLACED A SMOOTH STONE IN HIS SLING...
...HURLED A STONE AT THE MIGHTY WARRIOR...
...AND STRUCK THE GIANT WITH ONE SHOT.
DAVID CUT OFF GOLIATH'S HEAD TO CLAIM HIS VICTORY. THE ISRAELITE ARMY CHASED THE PHILISTINES OUT OF THE VALLEY AND PLUNDERED THE ENEMY'S CAMP.

Saul's Jealousy

1 Samuel 18–24

DAVID'S FAME GREW RAPIDLY. THE PEOPLE CHEERED FOR HIM EVERYWHERE HE WENT.

BUT EVERY CHEER FOR DAVID CUT TO THE HEART OF SAUL.

SAUL BECAME ANGRY AND UPSET BECAUSE THE PEOPLE SEEMED TO LOVE AND RESPECT DAVID MORE THAN HIM. DAVID WOULD OFTEN PLAY HIS HARP TO SOOTHE THE KING. ONE DAY A TORMENTING SPIRIT CONSUMED SAUL AND HE THREW A SPEAR AT DAVID. HE MISSED BUT WAS SO JEALOUS OF DAVID THAT HE DECIDED TO SEND HIM AWAY INTO BATTLE TO GET RID OF HIM.

DAVID WAS VERY SUCCESSFUL AS A MILITARY COMMANDER, WHICH ANGERED SAUL EVEN MORE. HE VOWED TO KILL DAVID.

SAUL TOLD DAVID HE WOULD GIVE HIS DAUGHTER MICHAL TO HIM AS A BRIDE IF DAVID KILLED 100 PHILISTINES. SAUL HOPED DAVID WOULD DIE IN BATTLE.

DAVID KILLED 200 PHILISTINES. THEN HE MARRIED MICHAL.

SAUL BECAME MORE JEALOUS AND FEARFUL OF DAVID. IN HIS ANGER HE TOLD HIS SERVANTS AND HIS SON JONATHAN TO KILL DAVID, BUT JONATHAN WAS DAVID'S GOOD FRIEND. HE TOLD DAVID TO STAY AWAY WHILE HE SPOKE TO HIS FATHER.
KILL HIM!
JONATHAN REMINDED HIS FATHER HOW MUCH DAVID HAD DONE FOR THE COUNTRY AND THAT HE HAD DONE NOTHING WRONG.
VERY WELL, I PROMISE NOT TO HARM HIM.
BUT IT WAS NOT LONG BEFORE A TORMENTING SPIRIT CAME UPON SAUL AGAIN. HE TRIED TO KILL DAVID AS HE WAS PLAYING HIS HARP.
BUT GOD WAS WITH DAVID, AND THE SPEAR MISSED ITS TARGET. DAVID KNEW HE HAD TO LEAVE THE PALACE.

SAUL'S SOLDIERS CAME TO DAVID'S HOUSE ONLY TO FIND THAT HE HAD LEFT.
GO, MY HUSBAND! LEAVE NOW!
MY FATHER, THE KING, HAS SENT HIS MEN FOR YOU.
HE'S NOT HERE! IT'S JUST A DISGUISE TO TRICK US!
ALERT THE KING! DAVID IS GONE!

DAVID SPOKE TO JONATHAN IN SECRET.
JONATHAN, WHY DOES YOUR FATHER HATE ME SO MUCH?
MY FATHER TELLS ME EVERYTHING HE'S GOING TO DO. SURELY HE WOULDN'T HIDE THIS FROM ME!.
TOMORROW IS THE NEW MOON FESTIVAL. I WILL NOT GO.
IF THE KING BECOMES ANGRY AT MY ABSENCE, YOU WILL KNOW HE PLANS TO HARM ME.
YOU'RE MY FRIEND, DAVID.
IF MY FATHER WANTS TO HARM YOU, I'LL LET YOU KNOW BY SHOOTING ARROWS OUT IN THE FIELD.
AT THE FEAST...
WHERE IS DAVID? WHY IS HE NOT HERE?
DAVID BEGGED ME TO LET HIM GO TO BETHLEHEM FOR A FAMILY GATHERING.
REBELLIOUS SON! YOU ARE MORE LOYAL TO DAVID THAN TO ME! AS LONG AS HE IS ALIVE, YOU WILL NEVER BE KING!

JONATHAN WAS CONVINCED THAT HIS FATHER WANTED TO KILL DAVID. JONATHAN AND HIS SERVANT BOY WENT INTO THE FIELD WHERE DAVID WAS HIDING. JONATHAN SHOT HIS ARROWS AS HE AND DAVID HAD PLANNED.
DAVID KNEW HE WAS IN MORTAL DANGER. JONATHAN SENT HIS SERVANT BACK TO THE CITY, AND HE AND DAVID EMBRACED SADLY. THEN DAVID FLED FOR GOOD.

SAUL AND HIS ARMY PURSUED DAVID AND HIS MEN INTO THE WILDERNESS. ONE DAY SAUL CAME CLOSE TO CAPTURING DAVID WHEN HE WAS HIDING IN A CAVE.

WHEN SAUL'S BACK WAS TURNED, DAVID CUT OFF A BIT OF HIS ROBE, ALTHOUGH HE COULD HAVE KILLED SAUL INSTEAD.

KING SAUL! MY MEN TOLD ME TO KILL YOU, BUT I TOOK PITY ON YOU INSTEAD.

HERE IS A PIECE OF YOUR ROBE THAT I SLICED WHILE YOUR BACK WAS TURNED. THIS PROVES I WILL NOT HARM YOU.

SAUL WAS OVERCOME WITH EMOTION. HE REALIZED DAVID HAD BEEN AMAZINGLY KIND TO HIM. HE ASKED DAVID NOT TO HARM HIS FAMILY WHEN DAVID BECAME KING.

David and Abigail

1 Samuel 25

SAMUEL DIED, AND ALL ISRAEL GATHERED TO MOURN HIM. THEY BURIED THE GREAT PROPHET AT HIS HOME IN RAMAH, NORTH OF BETHLEHEM. DAVID THEN TOOK HIS ARMY INTO THE WILDERNESS.

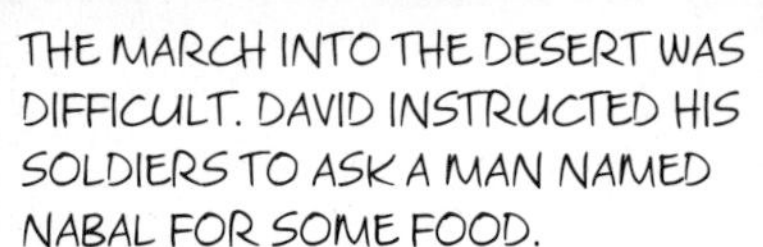

THE MARCH INTO THE DESERT WAS DIFFICULT. DAVID INSTRUCTED HIS SOLDIERS TO ASK A MAN NAMED NABAL FOR SOME FOOD.

OUR MASTER DAVID PROTECTED YOUR MEN AND YOUR ANIMALS.

HE ASKS IF YOU CAN SUPPLY US WITH FOOD.

WHO IS THIS DAVID?

WHY SHOULD I GIVE HIM MY MEAT AND BREAD?

GET OUT OF HERE!

DAVID WAS FURIOUS BECAUSE HE AND HIS MEN HAD BEEN PROTECTING NABAL'S SHEPHERDS AND SHEEP IN THE WILDERNESS. DAVID ORDERED HIS SOLDIERS TO GET THEIR SWORDS.

A SERVANT WARNED NABAL'S WIFE, ABIGAIL.

MY LADY, YOUR HUSBAND HAS INSULTED DAVID, WHO WAS KIND TO US.

ABIGAIL PREPARED FOOD FOR DAVID AND RUSHED OUT TO MEET HIM BEFORE HIS SOLDIERS KILLED NABAL.
KIND SIR, DO NOT PAY ATTENTION TO THAT SCOUNDREL, NABAL! HIS NAME MEANS **FOOL**...
...AND FOOL HE IS! PLEASE ACCEPT THESE GIFTS AND FORGIVE ME IF I HAVE OFFENDED YOU.
DAVID WAS THANKFUL FOR ABIGAIL'S KINDNESS. HE AND HIS ARMY RETURNED TO CAMP.
SOON AFTERWARD, NABAL DIED. DAVID REMEMBERED ABIGAIL'S KINDNESS AND SENT HIS MEN TO ASK HER IF SHE WOULD MARRY DAVID.
MY MASTER HEARD ABOUT YOUR HUSBAND'S DEATH.
HE WOULD LIKE TO MARRY YOU.
ABIGAIL AGREED TO MARRY DAVID.

The Fall of Saul

1 Samuel 28—2 Samuel 1

SAUL HAD BANISHED ALL MEDIUMS AND MAGICIANS FROM ISRAEL. SO HE DISGUISED HIMSELF SO THE MEDIUM WOULD NOT RECOGNIZE HIM.
I NEED YOU TO SUMMON ME A SPIRIT, WOMAN.
ARE YOU MAD? THE KING WILL HAVE MY HEAD!
WHY ARE YOU TRYING TO GET ME KILLED!!!?
DON'T BE AFRAID.
SUMMON SAMUEL!
IT IS SAMUEL!
I SEE AN OLD MAN WRAPPED IN A ROBE.
I'M IN DEEP TROUBLE! THE PHILISTINES ARE AT WAR WITH ME. GOD HAS ABANDONED ME!

WHY HAVE YOU DONE THIS? WHY HAVE YOU DISTURBED ME?
I HAVE CALLED FOR YOU TO TELL ME WHAT TO DO.
TOMORROW YOU AND YOUR SONS WILL DIE.
DAVID WILL SOON BE KING!
YOU DISOBEYED THE LORD.
HE WILL GIVE YOU AND ISRAEL INTO THE HANDS OF THE PHILISTINES.
SAUL COLLAPSED TO THE GROUND IN A FRIGHTENED HEAP.

VERY SOON SAMUEL'S WORDS CAME TRUE. THE PHILISTINES DEFEATED ISRAEL.
THREE OF SAUL'S SONS WERE DEAD, INCLUDING JONATHAN. THE KING WAS WOUNDED, AND HIS REMAINING TROOPS WERE ABOUT TO BE OVERRUN. KNOWING HE WOULD BE KILLED BY HIS ENEMIES, SAUL BEGGED A SERVANT TO END HIS LIFE.
KEEP ME FROM MY ENEMIES— END MY LIFE!
I CAN'T! I CAN'T!
WHEN THE SERVANT REFUSED, SAUL PURPOSELY FELL ON HIS OWN SWORD AND DIED.
DAVID WEPT WHEN HE LEARNED OF THE DEATH OF SAUL AND JONATHAN.
WOMEN OF ISRAEL, WEEP FOR SAUL.
I WEEP FOR YOU, MY BROTHER JONATHAN!

King David

2 Samuel 2–6

AFTER SAUL'S DEATH, TWO PEOPLE CLAIMED THE THRONE OF ISRAEL. THERE WAS DAVID...

...AND ISHBOSHETH, ANOTHER OF SAUL'S SONS.

NOT LONG AFTER SAUL DIED, THE TWO MEN AND THEIR ARMIES BATTLED EACH OTHER. THE WAR OVER WHO WOULD RULE ISRAEL LASTED A LONG TIME. MANY WERE KILLED.

ISHBOSHETH LOST HIS COURAGE. AS HE SLEPT, TWO OF HIS SOLDIERS KILLED HIM.
DAVID DID NOT APPROVE OF THE MURDER OF ISHBOSHETH, AND HE SENTENCED THE MURDERERS TO DEATH.
WITH THE LAND RUNNING RED WITH BLOOD, THE ELDERS FROM EACH TRIBE MET WITH DAVID TO PUT A STOP TO THE WAR.
THIS BLOODSHED MUST END.
GOD SAID YOU WOULD BECOME KING WHEN SAUL DIED.
NOW IS THE TIME.
DAVID AGREED TO BECOME KING, AND THE ELDERS OF ISRAEL ANOINTED HIM WITH OIL. HE WAS THIRTY YEARS OLD WHEN HE TOOK THE THRONE.

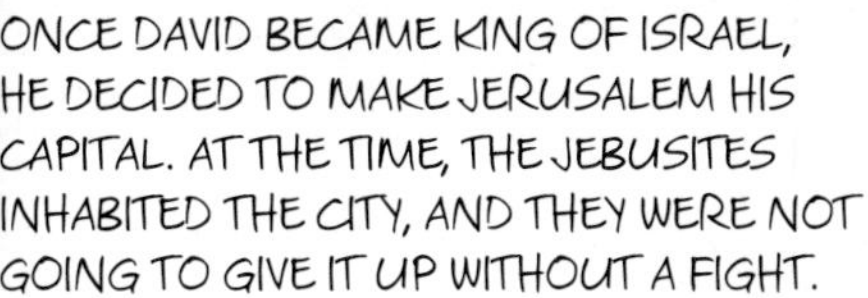

THE ISRAELITES ROUTED THE JEBUSITES AND SEIZED CONTROL OF JERUSALEM, WHICH BECAME KNOWN AS THE CITY OF DAVID.

DAVID GATHERED 30,000 MEN TO BRING THE SACRED ARK OF THE COVENANT TO JERUSALEM.

The Wars of David

2 Samuel 5–10; 1 Chronicles 14–20

DAVID WAS GOD'S WARRIOR.

HE BATTLED THE PHILISTINES AND DEFEATED THEM SEVERAL TIMES.

HE MADE THE MOABITES PAY TRIBUTE TO HIM.

HE DEFEATED THE ARAMEANS, THE EDOMITES, AND OTHER ENEMIES. DAVID FOUGHT BACK HADADEZER, KING OF ZOBAH, AND TOOK THE GOLDEN SHIELDS OF HIS GUARDS.

THE LORD MADE DAVID VICTORIOUS WHEREVER HE WENT.

David and Bathsheba

2 Samuel 11–12

DAVID THOUGHT OF A WAY TO GET BATHSHEBA'S HUSBAND, URIAH, OUT OF HIS WAY. DAVID WROTE TO JOAB, HIS GENERAL, AND SAID...
I WANT YOU TO PUT URIAH ON THE FRONT LINE IN YOUR NEXT BATTLE.
PUT HIM WHERE THE FIGHTING IS FIERCEST. THEN PULL BACK FROM HIM.
JOAB FOLLOWED HIS KING'S COMMAND. URIAH WAS PROMPTLY KILLED IN BATTLE.
WITH URIAH DEAD, DAVID COULD MARRY BATHSHEBA.

AFTER A PERIOD OF MOURNING HAD PASSED, DAVID AND BATHSHEBA WERE MARRIED.
BUT GOD WAS DISPLEASED WITH DAVID. THE KING HAD DONE AN EVIL THING. GOD SENT A PROPHET NAMED NATHAN TO TALK WITH DAVID.
THE LORD HAS SENT ME TO YOU, DAVID.
I HAVE A STORY TO TELL YOU.
ONCE THERE WERE TWO MEN— A RICH MAN...
...AND A POOR MAN.
THE RICH MAN HAD MANY ANIMALS.
THE POOR MAN ONLY HAD A LITTLE LAMB, WHICH HE FED AND TOOK CARE OF.

A VISITOR CAME TO VISIT THE RICH MAN. THE RICH MAN PREPARED A MEAL BUT DIDN'T USE ANY OF HIS ANIMALS. HE SLAUGHTERED THE POOR MAN'S LAMB INSTEAD!
THAT MAN IS TERRIBLE! HE DESERVES TO DIE!
MY KING, **YOU ARE THAT MAN!**
YES, YES, I UNDERSTAND! **I HAVE SINNED! FORGIVE ME, LORD! PLEASE FORGIVE ME!**
THE LORD FORGAVE DAVID, BUT DAVID AND BATHSHEBA'S BABY DIED AS PUNISHMENT.

Hero Profile
Solomon—The Wise One

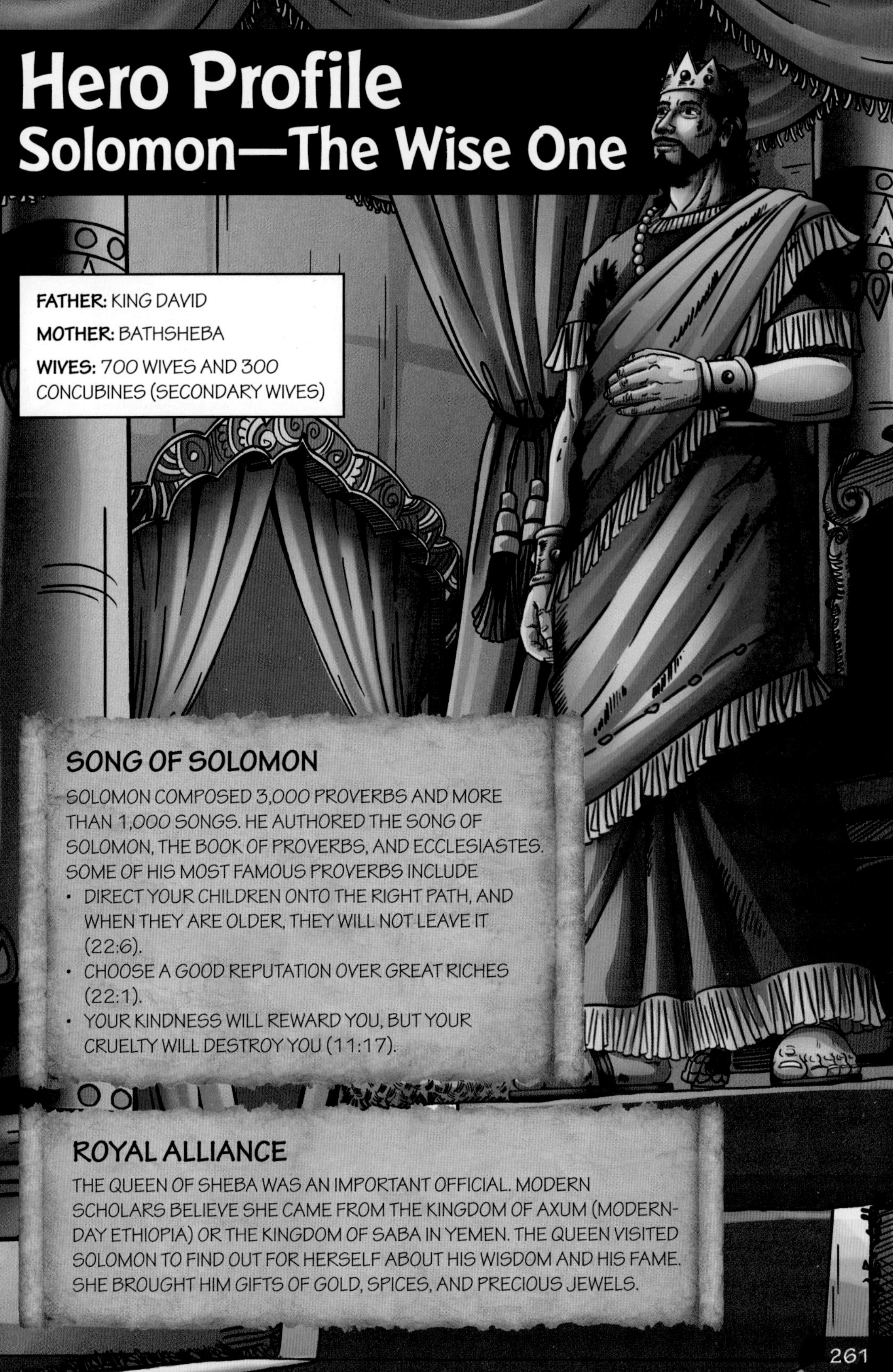

FATHER: KING DAVID

MOTHER: BATHSHEBA

WIVES: 700 WIVES AND 300 CONCUBINES (SECONDARY WIVES)

SONG OF SOLOMON

SOLOMON COMPOSED 3,000 PROVERBS AND MORE THAN 1,000 SONGS. HE AUTHORED THE SONG OF SOLOMON, THE BOOK OF PROVERBS, AND ECCLESIASTES. SOME OF HIS MOST FAMOUS PROVERBS INCLUDE

- DIRECT YOUR CHILDREN ONTO THE RIGHT PATH, AND WHEN THEY ARE OLDER, THEY WILL NOT LEAVE IT (22:6).
- CHOOSE A GOOD REPUTATION OVER GREAT RICHES (22:1).
- YOUR KINDNESS WILL REWARD YOU, BUT YOUR CRUELTY WILL DESTROY YOU (11:17).

ROYAL ALLIANCE

THE QUEEN OF SHEBA WAS AN IMPORTANT OFFICIAL. MODERN SCHOLARS BELIEVE SHE CAME FROM THE KINGDOM OF AXUM (MODERN-DAY ETHIOPIA) OR THE KINGDOM OF SABA IN YEMEN. THE QUEEN VISITED SOLOMON TO FIND OUT FOR HERSELF ABOUT HIS WISDOM AND HIS FAME. SHE BROUGHT HIM GIFTS OF GOLD, SPICES, AND PRECIOUS JEWELS.

Solomon Is Called
1 Kings 1
DAVID RULED FOR MANY YEARS. HE WAS OLD AND FRAIL.
DAVID'S FOURTH SON, ADONIJAH, BOASTED THAT HE SHOULD BE KING UPON HIS FATHER'S DEATH.
IF YOU SUPPORT ME, PLEDGE YOUR LOYALTY.
MY LORD, SURELY YOU REMEMBER THAT YOU PROMISED THAT OUR SON SOLOMON WOULD BE KING.
THAT WRETCHED ADONIJAH IS SCHEMING TO TAKE THE THRONE FROM HIM!
NOT TO WORRY, BATHSHEBA, **SOLOMON** WILL SIT ON THE THRONE.

DAVID ORDERED THE PROPHET NATHAN AND THE PRIEST ZADOK TO ANOINT SOLOMON AS KING. WHEN THE OIL WAS POURED, THE CROWD CHEERED.
WITH THIS OIL I ANOINT YOU KING OF ISRAEL.
LONG LIVE KING SOLOMON!!!
WHEN ADONIJAH HEARD SOLOMON WAS NOW KING, HE HID, FEARING SOLOMON WOULD KILL HIM. SOLOMON THEN ORDERED HIS MEN TO BRING HIS BROTHER TO HIM.
ADONIJAH, MY BROTHER, IF YOU ARE LOYAL TO ME, NOT A HAIR ON YOUR HEAD WILL BE HARMED.

The Wisdom of Solomon

1 Kings 2–3

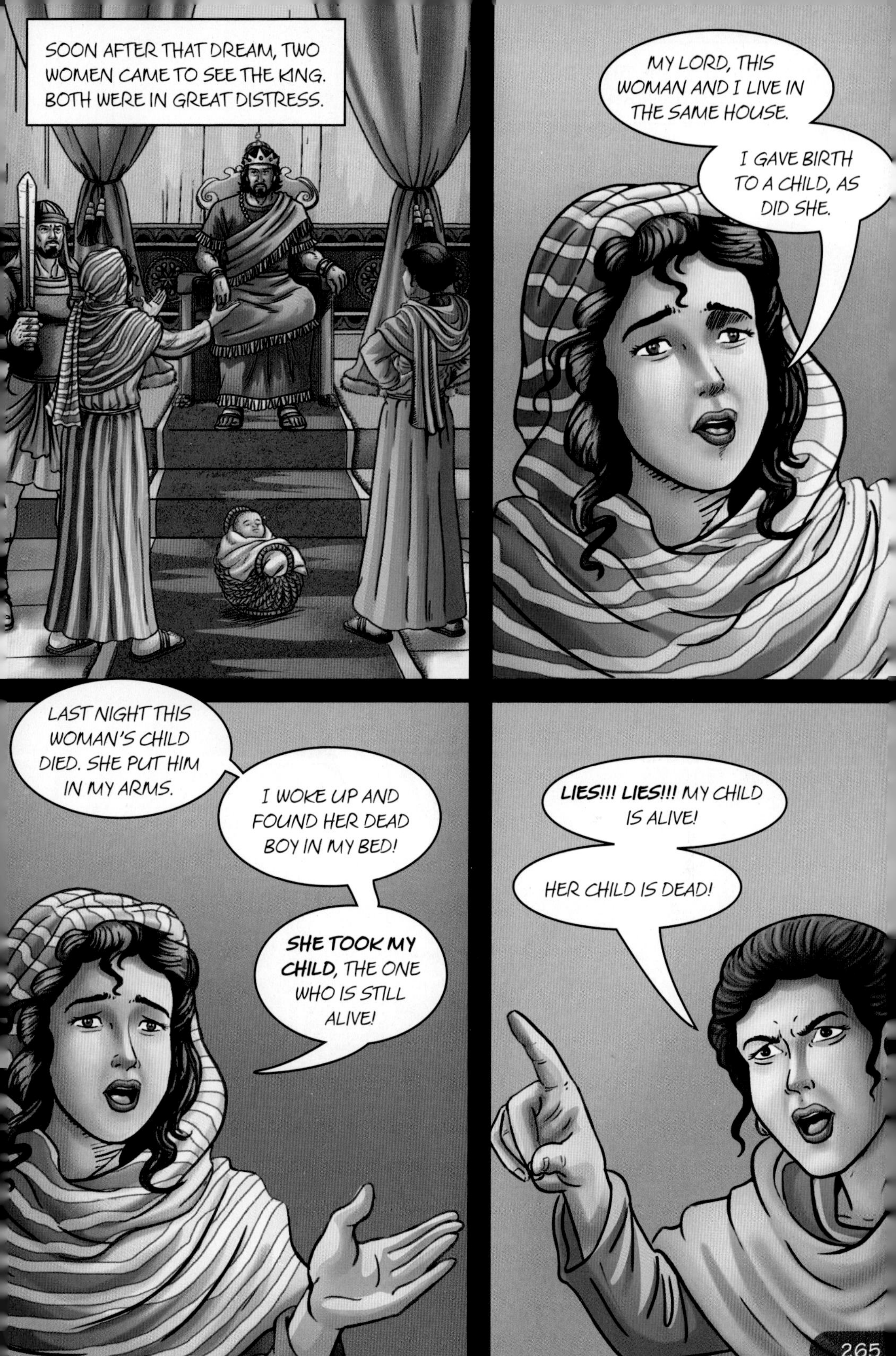

SOON AFTER THAT DREAM, TWO WOMEN CAME TO SEE THE KING. BOTH WERE IN GREAT DISTRESS.

MY LORD, THIS WOMAN AND I LIVE IN THE SAME HOUSE.

I GAVE BIRTH TO A CHILD, AS DID SHE.

SOLOMON LISTENED TO THE TWO WOMEN ARGUE. HE OBSERVED THEIR BEHAVIOR.
SILENCE!

GUARD! DRAW YOUR SWORD!
CUT THE BABY IN TWO AND GIVE EACH WOMAN HALF.
THE GUARD DREW HIS SWORD AND WAS ABOUT TO CUT THE BABY IN TWO.
NOOOOOO!!! SPARE THE CHILD!!!
SHE CAN HAVE HIM!!! DO NOT KILL HIM!!!
GO AHEAD! CUT THE THING IN TWO. NEITHER OF US SHALL HAVE HIM!
SOLOMON SAW HOW EACH WOMAN REACTED. HE KNEW WHO WAS TELLING THE TRUTH.
SOLOMON KNEW THE REAL MOTHER WOULD HAVE RATHER GIVEN UP HER CHILD THAN SEE HIM KILLED. HE GAVE THE CHILD TO HER!
ALL OF ISRAEL SOON HEARD HOW WISE THE NEW KING WAS.

Building the Great Temple

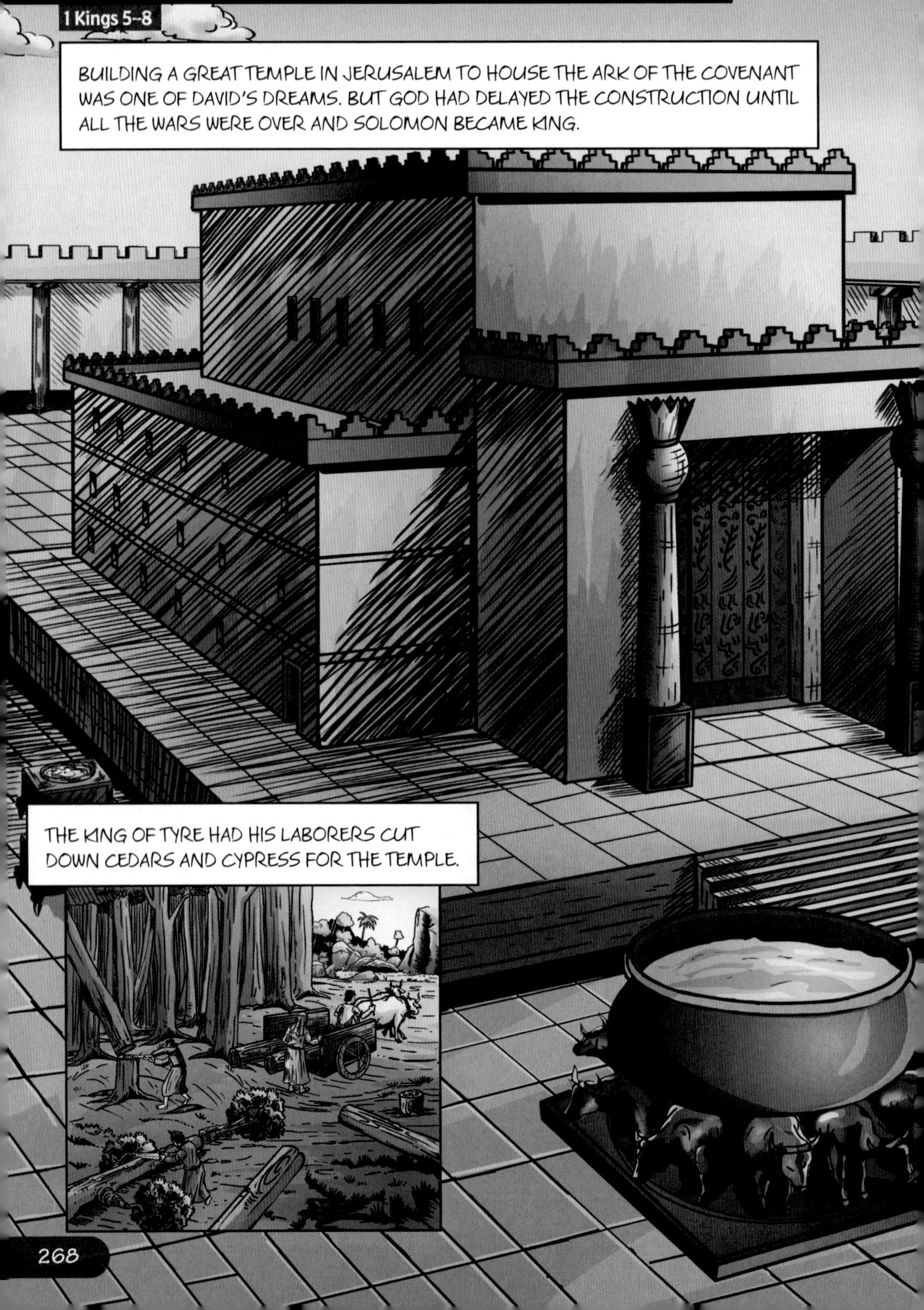

STONECUTTERS CHISELED WALLS OUT OF ROCK.
WHEN THE TEMPLE WAS FINISHED, THE INSIDE WAS MAGNIFICENT. THE INTERIOR WAS COVERED IN WOOD FROM FLOOR TO CEILING. IT WAS DECORATED WITH CARVINGS OF GOURDS AND FLOWERS.
THE ARK OF THE COVENANT WAS PLACED INSIDE THE MOST HOLY PLACE. KING DAVID'S DREAM HAD FINALLY BEEN REALIZED.

God Appears to Solomon Again

1 Kings 9

...I SHALL UPROOT ISRAEL FROM THE LAND I HAVE GIVEN THEM...
...AND I WILL REJECT THIS TEMPLE.
AND WHEN PEOPLE ARE APPALLED AND ASK WHY THIS HAS HAPPENED...
...IT WILL BE BECAUSE THEY ABANDONED ME AND WORSHIPED OTHER GODS.

The Queen of Sheba

1 Kings 10

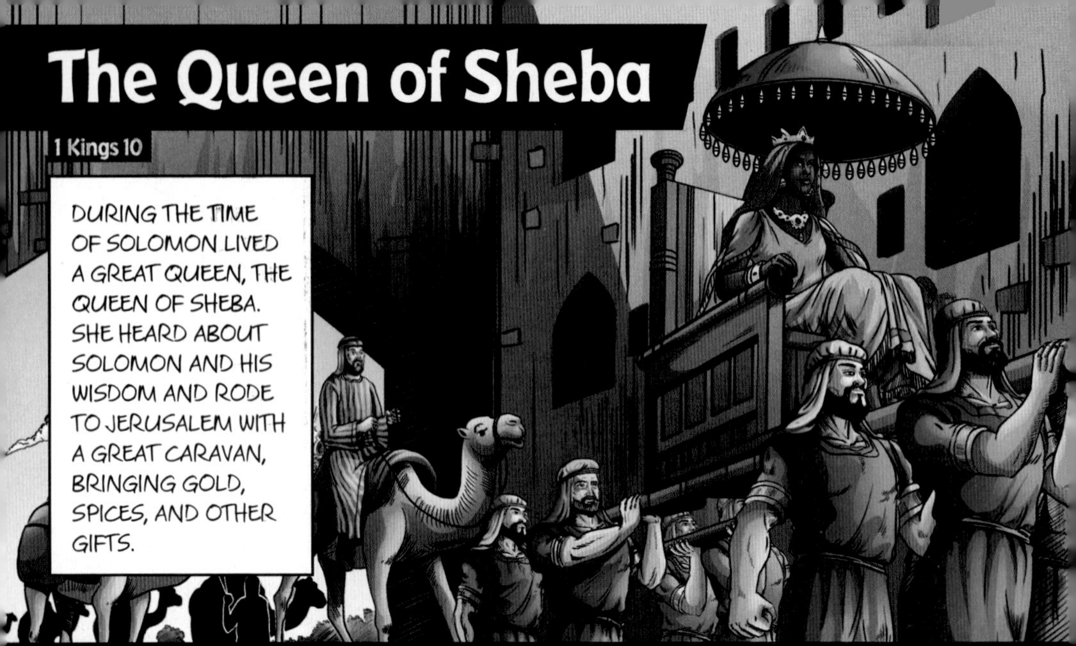

DURING THE TIME OF SOLOMON LIVED A GREAT QUEEN, THE QUEEN OF SHEBA. SHE HEARD ABOUT SOLOMON AND HIS WISDOM AND RODE TO JERUSALEM WITH A GREAT CARAVAN, BRINGING GOLD, SPICES, AND OTHER GIFTS.

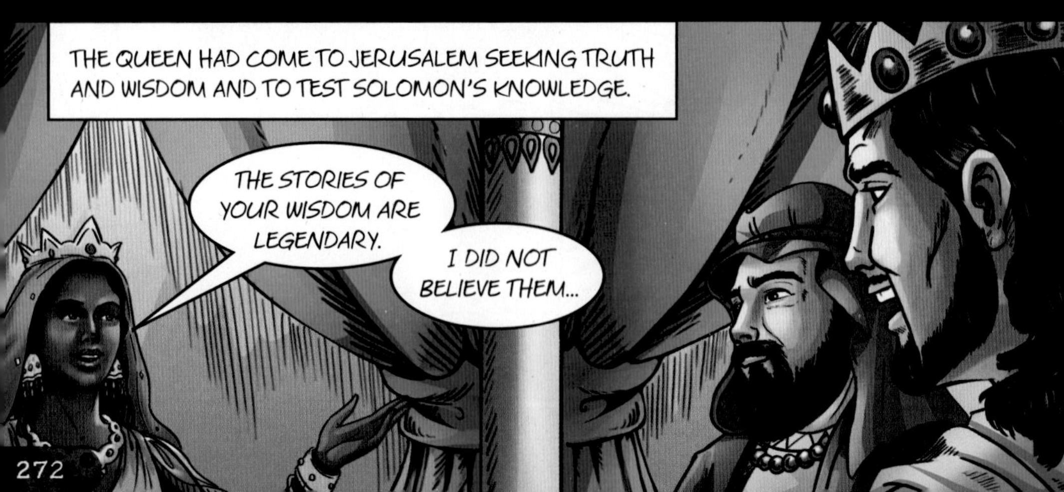

...UNTIL I SAW WITH MY OWN EYES.
YOUR SERVANTS ARE HAPPY.
YOUR OFFICIALS ARE HAPPY.
YOUR PEOPLE ARE HAPPY.
EVERYTHING HERE IS FAR BETTER THAN I IMAGINED.
YOUR PEOPLE ARE FORTUNATE TO HAVE YOU AS THEIR KING.
I OFFER YOU THESE AND MANY MORE GIFTS.
THE QUEEN THEN RETURNED TO HER OWN COUNTRY BUT NOT BEFORE SOLOMON HAD GIVEN HER EVERYTHING SHE ASKED FOR.

Solomon's Reign Ends

1 Kings 11–12

KING SOLOMON GREW OLD AND LOVED MANY FOREIGN WOMEN. HE MARRIED THE DAUGHTER OF AN EGYPTIAN PHARAOH, A MOABITE, AN AMMONITE, AND OTHERS.

SOLOMON'S WIVES TURNED HIS HEART AWAY FROM GOD. HE BEGAN TO WORSHIP THEIR FALSE GODS.

GOD THEN RAISED UP MEN WHO OPPOSED SOLOMON. THEY PLOTTED AGAINST THE KING.

AMONG SOLOMON'S ENEMIES WAS A MAN NAMED JEROBOAM, WHO WAS IN CHARGE OF SOLOMON'S LABOR FORCE.
ONE DAY, JEROBOAM MET THE PROPHET AHIJAH IN A FIELD. THE PROPHET TOOK OFF HIS CLOAK AND TORE IT INTO TWELVE PIECES.
JEROBOAM, TAKE TEN PIECES OF THIS CLOAK.
GOD WILL TEAR THE KINGDOM FROM SOLOMON AND GIVE YOU TEN TRIBES. FOLLOW GOD'S WAYS!
I WILL DO AS YOU SAY, PROPHET!
SOLOMON HEARD ALL ABOUT JEROBOAM. THE KING ORDERED THE MAN KILLED. JEROBOAM FLED TO EGYPT.
WHEN SOLOMON DIED, JEROBOAM RETURNED TO ISRAEL. SOLOMON'S SON REHOBOAM THEN BECAME KING.

Hero Profile
Elijah—Slayer of Idols

MEANING OF NAME: "MY GOD IS YAHWEH"

HOMETOWN: TISHBE, LOCATED IN UPPER GALILEE

FATHER: UNKNOWN

ELIJAH AND THE PROPHETS OF BAAL

ISRAEL'S EVIL KING AHAB HAD FORGOTTEN ABOUT GOD AND WORSHIPED A FAKE GOD NAMED BAAL. GOD SENT A BOLD PROPHET, ELIJAH, TO CHALLENGE THE PROPHETS OF BAAL. GOD GAVE ELIJAH AMAZING POWER TO PERFORM MIRACLES AND BRING THE HEARTS OF THE PEOPLE BACK TO HIM.

WHO TOOK THE ARK?

WHEN BABYLONIAN RULER NEBUCHADNEZZAR DESTROYED SOLOMON'S GRAND TEMPLE, THE ARK OF THE COVENANT VANISHED. SOME PEOPLE BELIEVE IT WAS REMOVED AND TAKEN SOMEWHERE ELSE BEFORE THE TEMPLE WAS DESTROYED. OTHERS SAY NEBUCHADNEZZAR BROUGHT IT TO BABYLON.

The Wicked King and Queen

1 Kings 12, 16–19

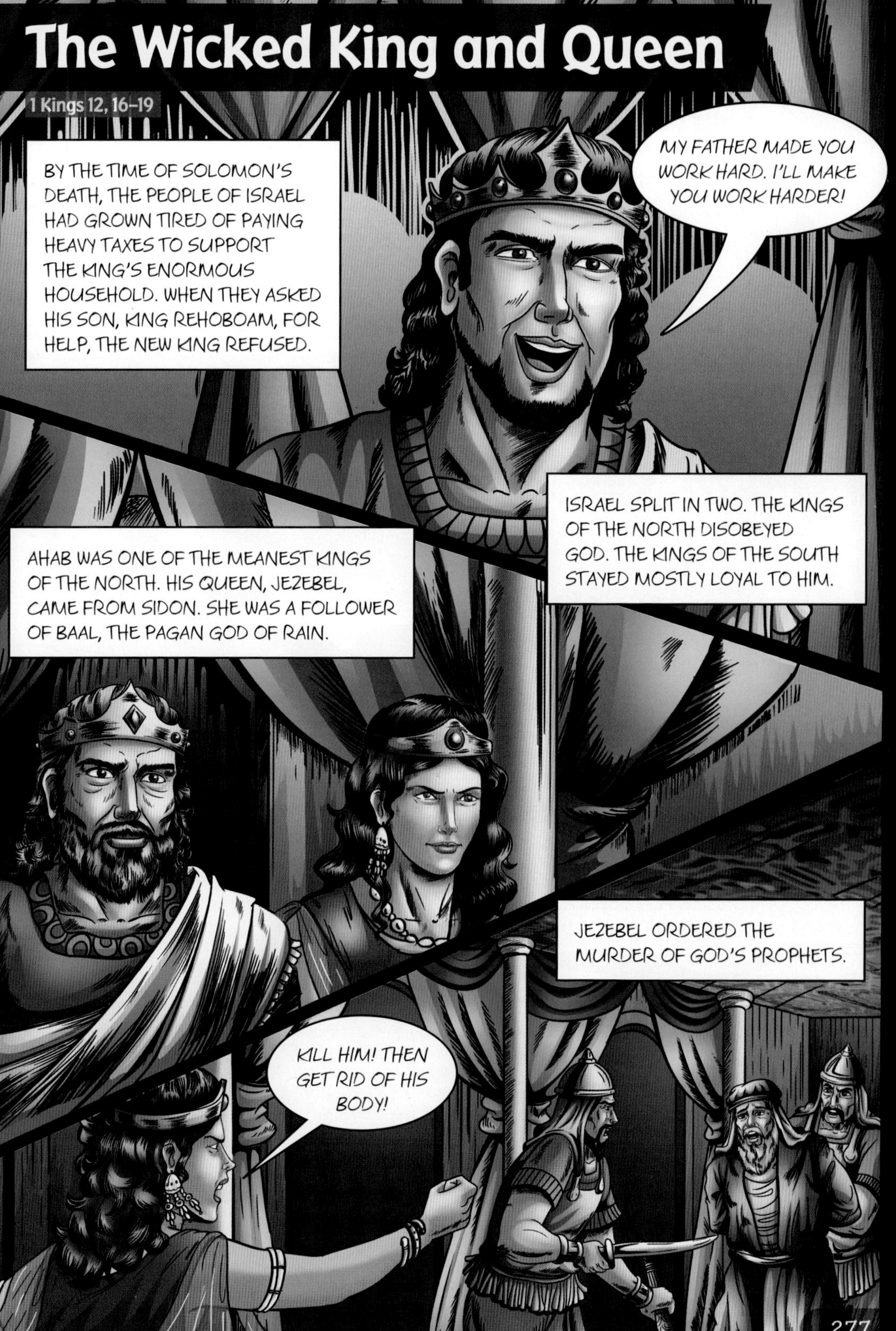

A TERRIBLE DROUGHT SPREAD THROUGHOUT THE LAND.
WILL THIS DROUGHT EVER END?
GOD IS PUNISHING US FOR OUR KING AND QUEEN'S WICKEDNESS.
A PROPHET NAMED ELIJAH WENT TO AHAB. HE SAID THE LORD WOULD NOT SEND RAIN OR DEW FOR SEVERAL YEARS UNTIL HE GAVE THE WORD.
THE LORD THEN LED ELIJAH TO A BROOK EAST OF THE JORDAN RIVER. RAVENS BROUGHT ELIJAH BREAD AND MEAT, AND HE DRANK FROM THE BROOK.

Elijah and the Widow

1 Kings 17

...FOR I HAVE ONLY HANDFUL OF FLOUR LEFT...
...AND A BIT OF OIL.
DON'T BE AFRAID. PLEASE BAKE ME SOME BREAD.
YOUR JUG OF OIL AND JAR OF FLOUR WILL NOT RUN OUT UNTIL THE LORD SENDS RAIN.

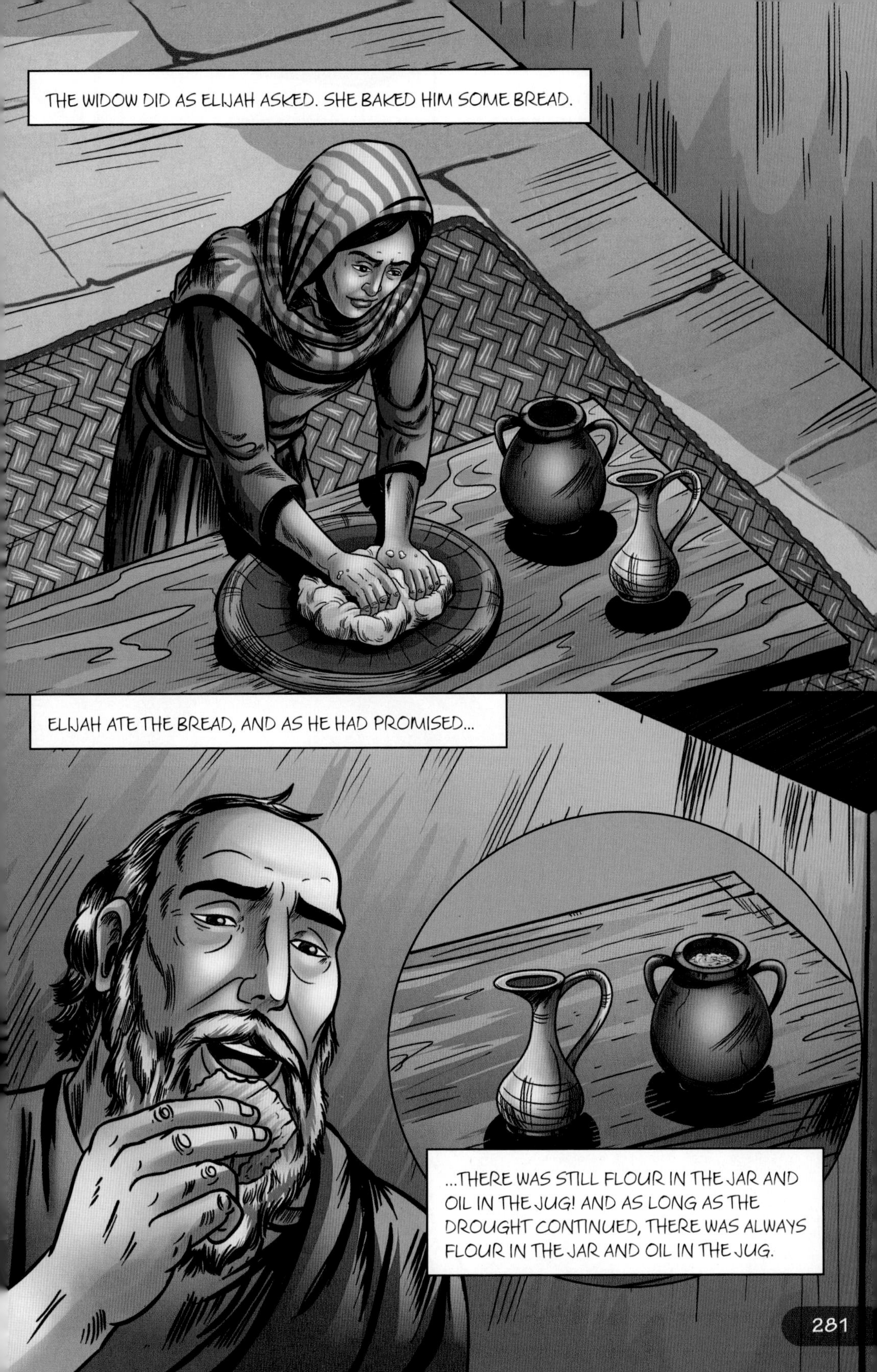
THE WIDOW DID AS ELIJAH ASKED. SHE BAKED HIM SOME BREAD.
ELIJAH ATE THE BREAD, AND AS HE HAD PROMISED...
...THERE WAS STILL FLOUR IN THE JAR AND OIL IN THE JUG! AND AS LONG AS THE DROUGHT CONTINUED, THERE WAS ALWAYS FLOUR IN THE JAR AND OIL IN THE JUG.

SOME TIME PASSED, AND THE SON OF THE WIDOW BECAME SO SICK THAT HE DIED.
WHAT HAVE YOU DONE TO ME, MAN OF GOD?

GOD HEARD ELIJAH'S PRAYER, AND THE BOY WAS REVIVED.
LORD, MY GOD, PLEASE DO NOT TAKE THIS WIDOW'S CHILD.
MY SON?
NOW I KNOW YOU TRULY ARE A MAN OF GOD!

Elijah and the Prophets of Baal

1 Kings 18

...AND THE PROPHETS OF BAAL WILL BUILD AN ALTAR TO THEIR GOD. WE WILL THEN SEE WHOSE GOD IS REAL.
AHAB DID AS ELIJAH ASKED AND ASSEMBLED EVERYONE ON MOUNT CARMEL.
ELIJAH TALKED TO THE PEOPLE.
HOW MUCH LONGER WILL YOU WAVER BETWEEN THE LORD GOD AND FALSE GODS?
A HUSH FELL OVER THE CROWD AS THE ISRAELITES LISTENED TO ELIJAH. NO ONE SAID A WORD.

I AM THE PROPHET OF THE LORD.
FETCH ONE BULL AND PUT IT ON THE ALTAR TO THE LORD GOD.
THEN PUT A SECOND BULL ON THE ALTAR TO BAAL.
WE WILL CALL UPON OUR GODS. WHICHEVER SENDS FIRE FROM HEAVEN IS THE **TRUE GOD!**
THE PROPHETS OF BAAL PRAYED TO THEIR GOD FROM MORNING TO NOON. NOTHING HAPPENED.
BAAL, ANSWER US!
HA! CALL LOUDER. IF BAAL IS A GOD.
MAYBE HE IS ON A TRIP OR RELIEVING HIMSELF...
...OR HE MIGHT BE ASLEEP!

ELIJAH PREPARED HIS ALTAR. HE PUT TWELVE STONES AROUND IT AND SOAKED EVERYTHING THREE TIMES WITH FOUR LARGE JUGS OF WATER.
LORD GOD, PROVE TO THESE PEOPLE THAT YOU ARE THE **TRUE GOD!**
FIRE FLASHED DOWN FROM HEAVEN. IT ENGULFED THE ALTAR AND SET THE SACRIFICE ABLAZE. ELIJAH ORDERED THE PEOPLE TO SEIZE THE FALSE PROPHETS. THEN HE KILLED THEM.
SOON THE SKY BECAME DARK WITH CLOUDS.. IT STARTED TO RAIN. THE DROUGHT WAS OVER!

Elijah Goes to Heaven
2 Kings 2
FOR MANY YEARS ELIJAH PROCLAIMED THE WORD OF GOD. WHEN THE END OF HIS TIME HAD COME, ELIJAH WALKED ALONG A DUSTY ROAD WITH HIS YOUNG DISCIPLE, ELISHA.
STAY HERE, ELISHA. THE LORD WANTS ME TO GO TO BETHEL.
NO, I WILL NOT LEAVE YOU. WE WILL GO TOGETHER.
DID YOU KNOW THAT TODAY GOD WILL TAKE YOUR MASTER AWAY FROM YOU?
YES, I KNOW. DON'T TALK ABOUT IT!
THE LORD HAS SENT ME TO THE JORDAN RIVER. STAY HERE.
I WILL NOT LEAVE YOU, ELIJAH!

ELIJAH AND ELISHA CAME TO THE BANK OF THE JORDAN RIVER. ELIJAH TOOK OFF HIS CLOAK, FOLDED IT, AND STRUCK THE WATER WITH IT.
THE RIVER PARTED, AND THE TWO MEN CROSSED TO THE OTHER SIDE.
GOD WILL SOON TAKE ME UP TO HEAVEN.
WHAT CAN I DO FOR YOU BEFORE I LEAVE?
I WOULD LIKE TO RECEIVE A DOUBLE PORTION OF YOUR SPIRIT.
THAT'S A DIFFICULT REQUEST. IF YOU SEE ME WHEN I AM TAKEN FROM YOU, YOU WILL GET WHAT YOU ASKED FOR.

SUDDENLY, A CHARIOT OF FIRE DRAWN BY FIERY HORSES APPEARED AND TOOK ELIJAH UP TO HEAVEN IN A WHIRLWIND. "MY FATHER, MY FATHER!" ELISHA CRIED OUT, AS THE CHARIOT TOOK ELIJAH TO GOD.
ELISHA PICKED UP ELIJAH'S CLOAK FROM WHERE IT LAY ON THE GROUND. HE STRUCK THE RIVER WITH IT. THE WATER PARTED, AND HE WALKED ACROSS.
THE ELDERS WATCHED AND BOWED TO ELISHA. "ELIJAH'S SPIRIT RESTS UPON ELISHA," THEY SAID.

Jerusalem Is Destroyed

2 Kings 24–25

NEBUCHADNEZZAR, THE GREAT BABYLONIAN KING, INVADED THE LAND OF JUDAH. HE ATTACKED JERUSALEM SEVERAL TIMES. EACH TIME, HE TOOK GROUPS OF CAPTIVES AND SENT THEM TO BABYLON.

DURING ONE ATTACK, JUDAH'S 18-YEAR-OLD KING, JEHOIACHIN, ALONG WITH HIS MOTHER AND OFFICIALS, SURRENDERED TO THE BABYLONIANS.

AS MORE JUDEANS WERE FORCED TO LEAVE JERUSALEM, NEBUCHADNEZZAR'S SOLDIERS LOOTED THE CITY, INCLUDING SOLOMON'S GRAND TEMPLE.

THE GREAT CITY WAS IN A SHAMBLES. ONLY THE POOR AND UNSKILLED WERE ALLOWED TO STAY.

NEBUCHADNEZZAR THEN INSTALLED ZEDEKIAH AS JUDAH'S KING AND MADE HIM SWEAR AN OATH OF ALLEGIANCE. HE WAS 21 YEARS OLD WHEN HE CAME TO THE THRONE. ZEDEKIAH RESTORED THE CITY, BUT AS THE YEARS PASSED, HE BECAME INCREASINGLY DISCONTENT WITH THE KING OF BABYLON.

LIKE JEHOIACHIN BEFORE HIM, ZEDEKIAH DID NOT PLACE HIS FAITH IN THE LORD. HE LED A REBELLION AGAINST BABYLONIA. NEBUCHADNEZZAR'S ARMY SURROUNDED JERUSALEM.

BUILD SIEGE RAMPS AGAINST THE CITY.
SEE TO IT THAT FOOD DOES NOT ENTER AND THAT NO ONE LEAVES.
AS YOU WISH, KING NEBUCHADNEZZAR!
THE WAR CAUSED A GREAT FAMINE IN THE CITY.
PEOPLE STARVED TO DEATH.

FINALLY, NEBUCHADNEZZAR'S SOLDIERS BREACHED THE CITY'S WALLS.
THEY CAPTURED ZEDEKIAH AND KILLED HIS SONS BEFORE HIS EYES.
THEY CARRIED OFF TREASURES FROM SOLOMON'S TEMPLE.
THE BABYLONIANS THEN SET THE CITY ABLAZE, REDUCING THE TEMPLE TO RUBBLE. AS FOR ZEDEKIAH, THE SOLDIERS BOUND HIM WITH SHACKLES, BLINDED HIM, AND TOOK HIM TO BABYLON, WHERE HE DIED IN PRISON.

Hero Profile
Isaiah—Prophet of Deliverance

MEANING OF NAME: "THE LORD HAS SAVED"

PLACE OF BIRTH: JUDAH

SONS: SHEAR-JASHUB, MAHER-SHALAL-HASH-BAZ

FATHER: AMOZ

MENTIONING THE MESSIAH

IF YOU READ THE BOOK OF ISAIAH, YOU'LL SEE THAT THE MESSIAH IS MENTIONED MORE IN THIS BOOK THAN IN ANY OTHER OLD TESTAMENT BOOK. ISAIAH RECORDED VIVID DESCRIPTIONS OF JESUS' BIRTH IN BETHLEHEM, ALONG WITH HIS CRUCIFIXION AND RESURRECTION.

BIBLE FACT

EVEN THOUGH ISAIAH LIVED OVER 700 YEARS BEFORE THE BIRTH OF CHRIST, HE WAS A PROPHET WHO GOD INSPIRED TO BOTH WARN THE PEOPLE OF ISRAEL ABOUT THE COMING JUDGMENT OF GOD (CHAPTERS 1–39) AND TELL OF THE PROMISE OF A MESSIAH AND SALVATION (CHAPTERS 40–66).

God Calls Isaiah

Isaiah 6

ABOUT 700 YEARS BEFORE JESUS WAS BORN, GOD CALLED ONE OF HIS GREATEST PROPHETS TO SPEAK FOR HIM. HIS NAME WAS ISAIAH. AT THE TIME, THE ASSYRIAN EMPIRE WAS BEGINNING TO MOVE WEST, THREATENING THE NORTHERN NATION OF ISRAEL AND THE SOUTHERN NATION OF JUDAH, WHERE ISAIAH LIVED.

ONE DAY ISAIAH SAW THE LORD SEATED ON A LOFTY THRONE IN THE TEMPLE. HE WAS SURROUNDED BY ANGELS WHOSE SIX WINGS COVERED THEIR FACES AND FEET. THE BUILDING WAS FILLED WITH SMOKE.

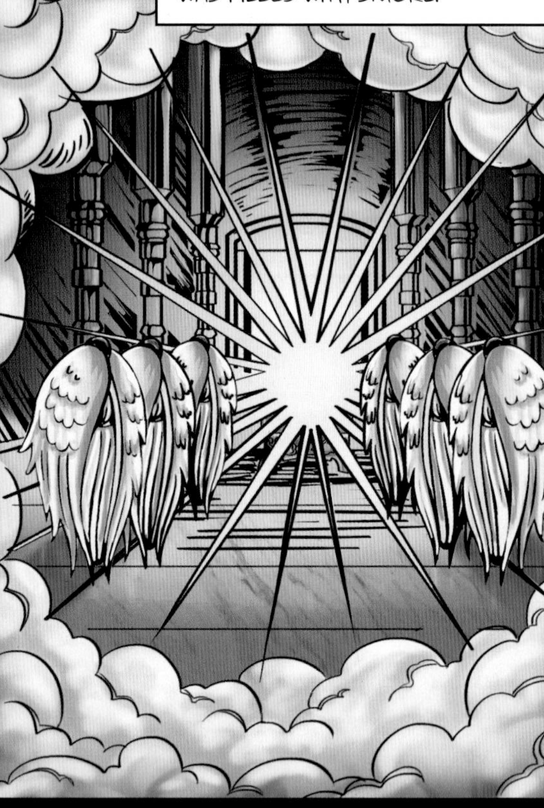

AN ANGEL FLEW ABOVE ISAIAH HOLDING A BURNING COAL IN ITS HANDS. THE ANGEL TOUCHED THE BLAZING EMBER TO ISAIAH'S LIPS.
YOUR GUILT IS REMOVED. YOUR SINS ARE FORGIVEN.
WHOM SHOULD I SEND AS A MESSENGER?
HERE I AM. SEND ME!
GO AND GIVE THE PEOPLE THIS MESSAGE: "YOU LISTEN BUT DO NOT UNDERSTAND. YOU WATCH CLOSELY BUT LEARN NOTHING."
"HARDEN THE HEARTS OF THESE PEOPLE UNTIL THEIR TOWNS ARE EMPTY AND THE ENTIRE LAND OF ISRAEL LIES DESERTED."

Crisis in Judah

Isaiah 7–8

IN THOSE DAYS, SYRIA AND NORTHERN ISRAEL JOINED FORCES AGAINST THE ASSYRIANS TO TRY TO STOP THEIR EXPANSION.

THE KING OF ISRAEL AND THE KING OF SYRIA WANTED JUDAH TO ENTER INTO AN ALLIANCE AGAINST THE ASSYRIANS. KING AHAZ OF JUDAH REFUSED, AND A FORCE OF NORTHERN ISRAEL AND SYRIAN SOLDIERS MARCHED ON HIS KINGDOM.

ISAIAH COUNSELED THE KING.

THE TWO KINGS FROM THE NORTH ARE APPROACHING. ALL IS NOT WELL IN MY KINGDOM.

TAKE CARE. BE CALM. HAVE NO FEAR. GOD IS WITH YOU.

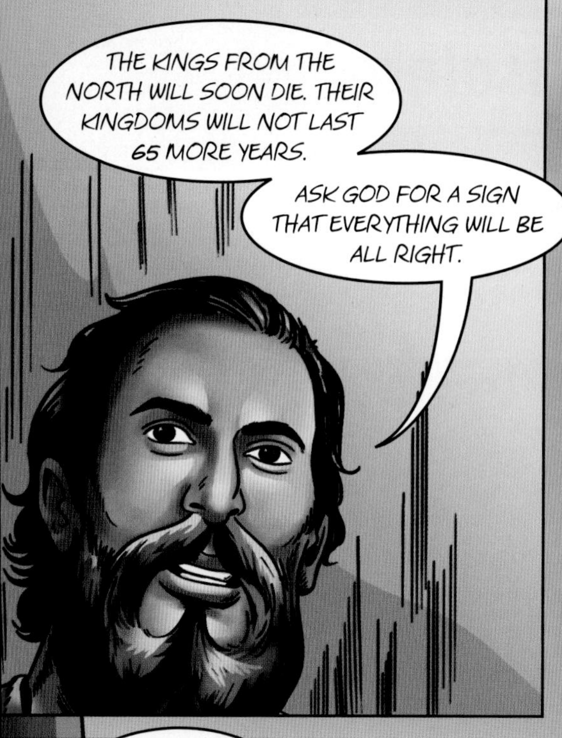

NO! GOD WILL SEND YOU A SIGN!

A YOUNG WOMAN SHALL BEAR A SON AND WILL NAME HIM IMMANUEL. THIS MEANS "GOD IS WITH US."

BY THE TIME THE BOY KNOWS RIGHT FROM WRONG, GOD WILL DEFEAT THE KINGS OF THE NORTH.

BUT AHAZ DID NOT WAIT FOR ISAIAH'S PROPHECY TO COME TRUE. KING AHAZ MADE AN ALLIANCE OF HIS KINGDOM, JUDAH, WITH ASSYRIA.

THE ASSYRIANS CONQUERED SYRIA, AND TEN YEARS LATER THEY RETURNED TO DESTROY ISRAEL. THE INVADERS SENT THOUSANDS OF HEBREWS TO LIVE ELSEWHERE. JUDAH PAID DEARLY FOR ITS ALLIANCE WITH THE ASSYRIANS INSTEAD OF TRUSTING IN GOD.

The Siege of Jerusalem

2 Kings 18–20; 2 Chronicles 32

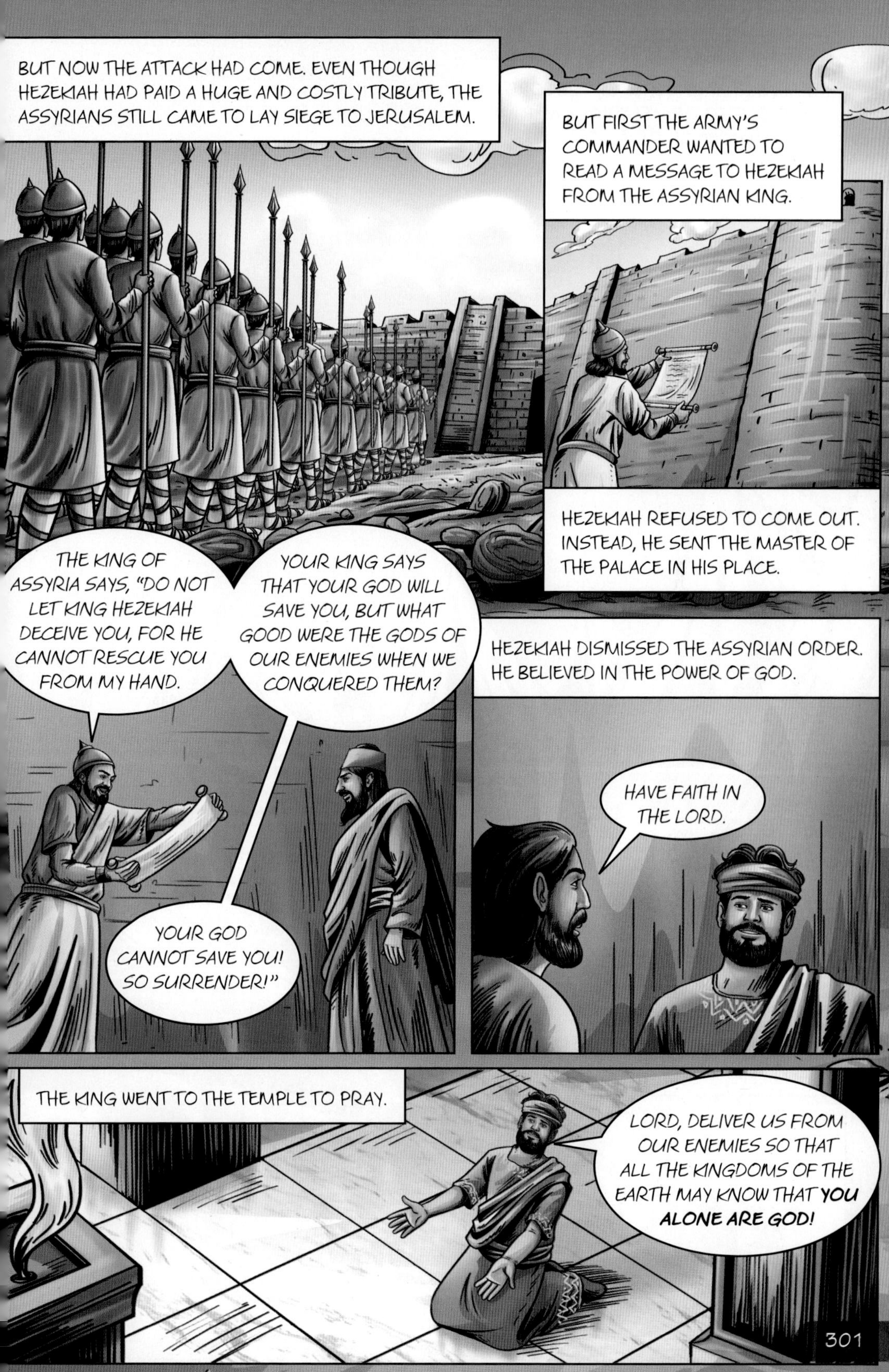
BUT NOW THE ATTACK HAD COME. EVEN THOUGH HEZEKIAH HAD PAID A HUGE AND COSTLY TRIBUTE, THE ASSYRIANS STILL CAME TO LAY SIEGE TO JERUSALEM.
BUT FIRST THE ARMY'S COMMANDER WANTED TO READ A MESSAGE TO HEZEKIAH FROM THE ASSYRIAN KING.
HEZEKIAH REFUSED TO COME OUT. INSTEAD, HE SENT THE MASTER OF THE PALACE IN HIS PLACE.
THE KING OF ASSYRIA SAYS, "DO NOT LET KING HEZEKIAH DECEIVE YOU, FOR HE CANNOT RESCUE YOU FROM MY HAND.
YOUR KING SAYS THAT YOUR GOD WILL SAVE YOU, BUT WHAT GOOD WERE THE GODS OF OUR ENEMIES WHEN WE CONQUERED THEM?
YOUR GOD CANNOT SAVE YOU! SO SURRENDER!"
HEZEKIAH DISMISSED THE ASSYRIAN ORDER. HE BELIEVED IN THE POWER OF GOD.
HAVE FAITH IN THE LORD.
THE KING WENT TO THE TEMPLE TO PRAY.
LORD, DELIVER US FROM OUR ENEMIES SO THAT ALL THE KINGDOMS OF THE EARTH MAY KNOW THAT **YOU ALONE ARE GOD!**

THAT NIGHT THE ANGEL OF THE LORD WENT OUT TO THE ASSYRIAN CAMP AND KILLED 185,000 OF THEIR SOLDIERS.
THE ASSYRIANS RETREATED IN DEFEAT, AND JERUSALEM WAS SPARED.

Hezekiah Cries

Isaiah 38

KING HEZEKIAH, GOD SAYS YOU WILL NOT RECOVER.
YOU WILL DIE SOON.
YOU MUST PUT YOUR HOUSE IN ORDER.
DESPERATE TO ENSURE HIS COUNTRY'S SURVIVAL, HEZEKIAH PRAYED.
OH, LORD, REMEMBER HOW FAITHFUL I WAS.
I HAVE ALWAYS DONE WHAT PLEASES YOU.
I HAVE LOVED YOU. OH, LORD, **HELP ME!**
THE LORD SENT ISAIAH BACK TO SEE THE KING.
THE LORD HAS HEARD YOUR PRAYER.
YOU WILL LIVE. GOD WILL DEFEND JERUSALEM.
GOD WILL SEND A SIGN TO PROVE HE WILL KEEP THIS PROMISE.

GOD MADE THE SUNDIAL MOVE TEN STEPS BACKWARD. HEZEKIAH GAVE THANKS.
ISAIAH THEN TOLD THE KING TO PUT A MIXTURE OF FIGS ON HIS SORES. HEZEKIAH WAS SOON CURED.
I FEEL BETTER. THE LORD HAS SMILED ON ME.
HE HAS GRANTED ME MORE TIME TO LOOK AFTER MY PEOPLE AND MY CITY.

Hero Profile
Jeremiah—Prophet of Doom

PLACE OF BIRTH: ANATHOTH

FATHER: HILKIAH, A HIGH PRIEST

TIME AS A PROPHET: 40 YEARS

PLACE OF DEATH: EGYPT

THE WEEPING PROPHET

JEREMIAH'S NAME MEANS "THE LORD LIFTS UP." SOMETIMES HE IS CALLED THE WEEPING PROPHET BECAUSE OF HIS SADNESS FOR THE PEOPLE OF ISRAEL. JEREMIAH BECAME A MESSENGER OF GOD TO WARN THE PEOPLE OF ISRAEL. HE TOLD THEM TO TURN AWAY FROM THEIR SINS OR FACE SUFFERING FROM THEIR ENEMIES.

IN EXILE!

WHEN THE BABYLONIANS TOOK OVER AN AREA, THEY FORCED PEOPLE TO RESETTLE ELSEWHERE. IT WAS ONE WAY OF DEMONSTRATING THEIR POWER. IT WAS ALSO A WAY TO KEEP REBELLIOUS COMMUNITY LEADERS SEPARATE SO THEY DID NOT STAGE A REVOLT. THESE EXILES WERE FORCED TO WORK AS SOLDIERS, WORKERS, OR FARMERS IN SERVICE TO BABYLON.

The Potter's Wheel

Jeremiah 18–24

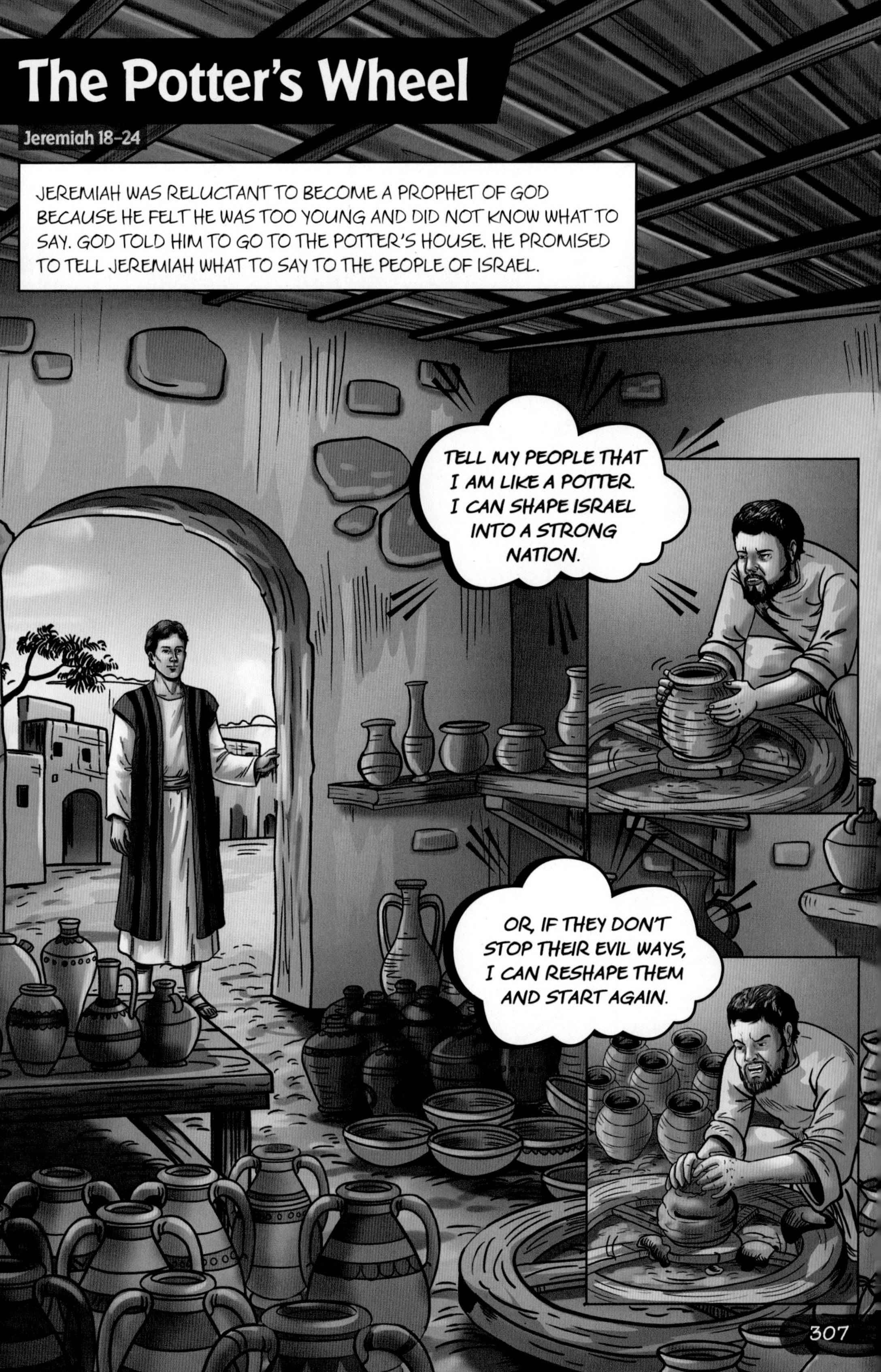

GOD TOLD JEREMIAH TO BUY A CLAY JAR AND GATHER TOGETHER JUDAH'S ELDERS.
LISTEN TO THE WORD OF THE LORD, KINGS OF JUDAH.
YOU HAVE DISOBEYED GOD AND **WORSHIPED FALSE GODS!**
GOD WILL DESTROY JUDAH AND JERUSALEM...
...AND SHATTER THEM AS I SHATTER THIS JAR!
CRASH!!!
THE ELDERS DIDN'T LIKE WHAT JEREMIAH TOLD THEM, BUT THAT DID NOT STOP HIM.

The Baskets of Figs

Jeremiah 24

JEREMIAH KEPT DELIVERING HIS WARNINGS FROM GOD. HE PREDICTED THAT NEBUCHADNEZZAR WOULD DOMINATE JERUSALEM AND EXILE THE CITY'S OFFICIALS, CRAFTSMEN, AND ARTISANS TO BABYLON.

ELDERS OF JUDAH, THE LORD SHOWED ME WHAT WOULD HAPPEN TO THOSE WHO WERE TAKEN AWAY AND TO THOSE WHO WERE SPARED.

GOD SHOWED ME TWO BASKETS OF FIGS.

ONE BASKET HAD RIPE AND EDIBLE FRUIT.

IT REPRESENTS THOSE IN EXILE IN BABYLON.

THE OTHER BASKET WAS FULL OF ROTTING FIGS.

IT REPRESENTS ZEDEKIAH AND THOSE WHO STAYED BEHIND.

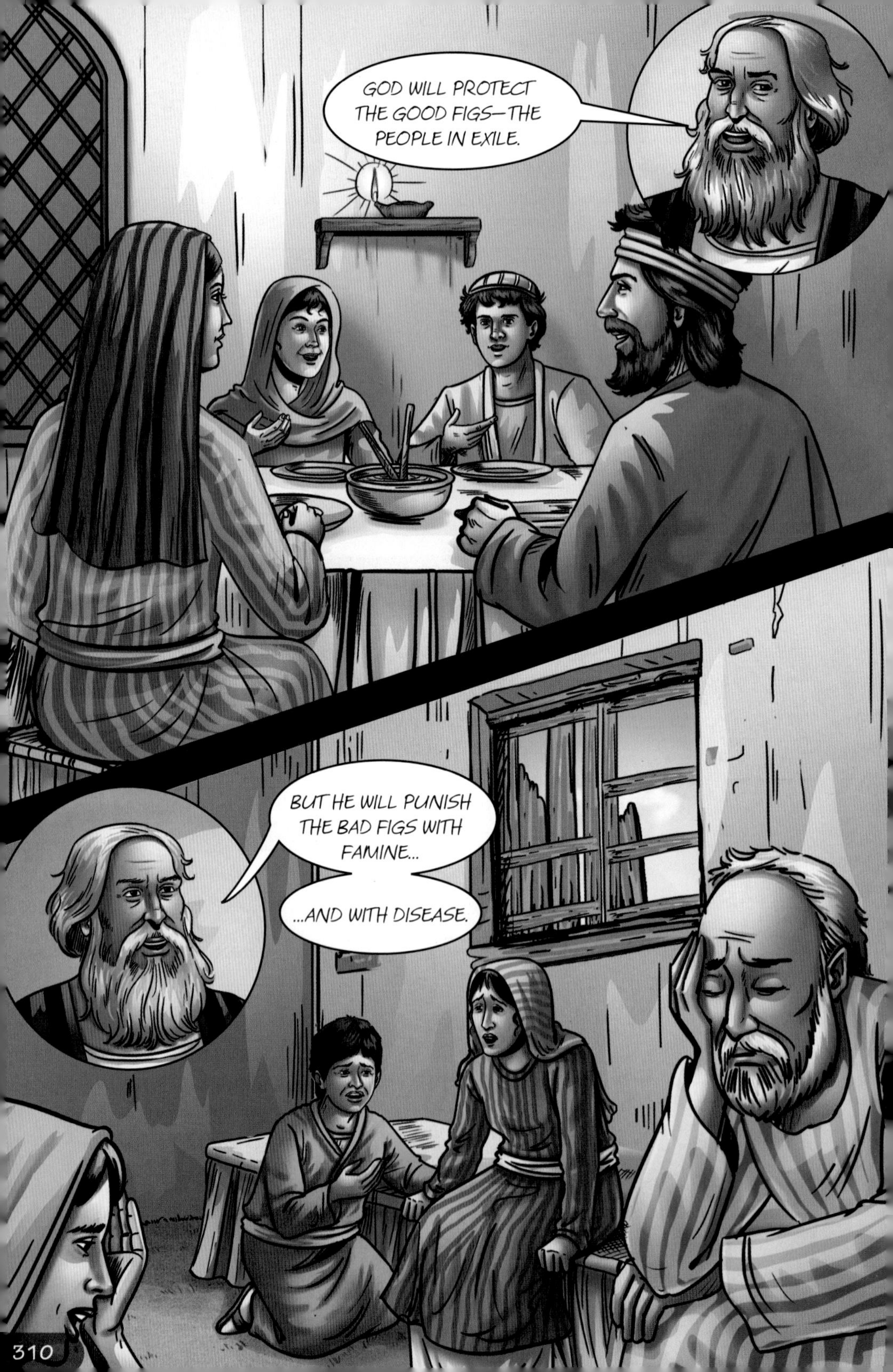
GOD WILL PROTECT THE GOOD FIGS—THE PEOPLE IN EXILE.
BUT HE WILL PUNISH THE BAD FIGS WITH FAMINE...
...AND WITH DISEASE.

Thrown into a Well
Jeremiah 37–38
ZEDEKIAH, NEBUCHADNEZZAR'S PUPPET KING, DID NOT PAY MUCH ATTENTION TO JEREMIAH'S PROPHECIES, YET SECRETLY HE RESPECTED HIM.
WILL YOU PRAY FOR ME, JEREMIAH?
I WILL, BUT THE BABYLONIANS WILL DESTROY JERUSALEM.
ONLY THOSE WHO SURRENDER WILL BE SAVED.
ONE DAY AS JEREMIAH LEFT THE CITY, HE WAS ARRESTED BY THE CAPTAIN OF THE KING'S GUARD BECAUSE HE BELIEVED JEREMIAH WAS DESERTING TO THE BABYLONIANS.
WHAT HAVE I DONE WRONG? I AM INNOCENT.
WHY SHOULD I BE PUNISHED FOR TELLING THE TRUTH?
IN TIME, THE KING RELEASED JEREMIAH FROM PRISON, BUT HE DIDN'T STAY FREE FOR LONG.

THIS MAN, JEREMIAH, IS A TRAITOR. HE DARES TO ENCOURAGE PEOPLE TO SURRENDER TO THE BABYLONIANS. HE IS SCARING THE PEOPLE! HE MUST BE KILLED!
DO AS YOU WILL.
THE KING'S MEN LOWERED JEREMIAH INTO A WELL AND LEFT HIM TO DIE A SLOW DEATH.
BUT GOD SENT A ROYAL OFFICIAL TO ASK ZEDEKIAH TO SPARE JEREMIAH. ZEDEKIAH AGREED. LATER, THE BABYLONIANS DESTROYED JERUSALEM, JUST AS JEREMIAH HAD WARNED.

Hero Profile
Ezekiel—Prophet of Hope

MEANING OF NAME: "GOD WILL STRENGTHEN"

FATHER: BUZI

SENT TO BABYLONIA: AROUND 597 BC

A MAN OF VISIONS: EZEKIEL EXPERIENCED MANY VISIONS OF GOD'S GLORY THROUGHOUT HIS LIFE.

DON'T WORRY

WHEN HE WAS IN EXILE, EZEKIEL BECAME THE COMFORTER OF JEWISH EXILES. THEY LISTENED TO HIM AND TOOK HIS ADVICE.

IN A LAND FAR AWAY

EZEKIEL WAS THE ONLY PROPHET TO MINISTER TO HIS PEOPLE OUTSIDE ISRAEL. HE DID SO IN BABYLONIA, A GREAT KINGDOM IN MESOPOTAMIA. THE RUINS OF THE KINGDOM'S GREATEST CITY, BABYLON, CAN STILL BE SEEN TODAY IN MODERN-DAY IRAQ, SOUTHWEST OF BAGHDAD.

God's Warning

Ezekiel 4–5

WHAT WILL HAPPEN TO THOSE IN JERUSALEM?
THEY ARE LIKE THESE STRANDS OF HAIR.
A THIRD WILL DIE BY THE SWORD OUTSIDE THE CITY.
A THIRD WILL DIE OF ILLNESS OR FAMINE. AND A THIRD WILL BLOW ACROSS THE LAND ON THE WIND AND BE PURSUED BY THOSE WITH SWORDS.
ONLY A VERY FEW SHALL BE SAVED.

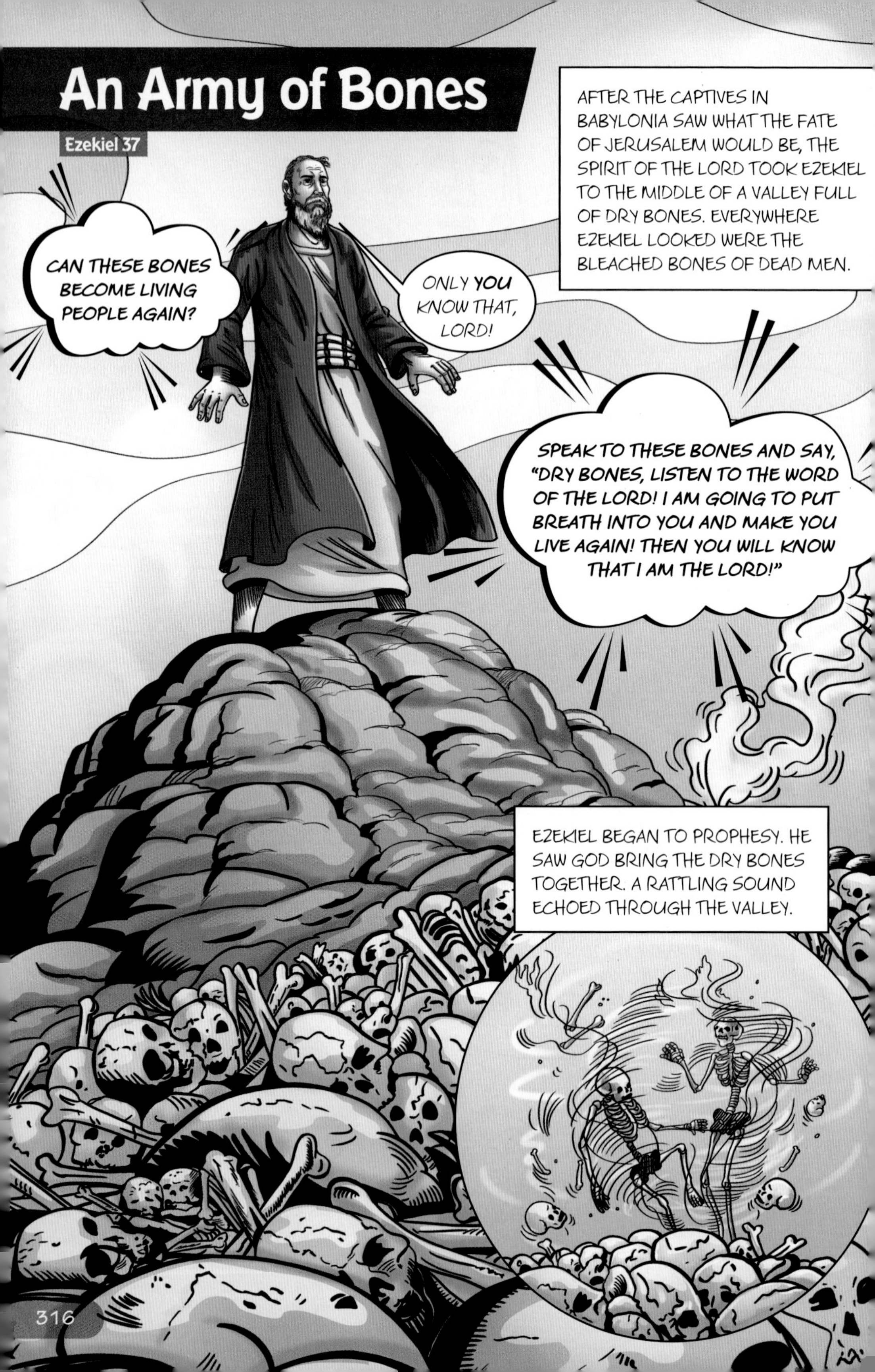
An Army of Bones
Ezekiel 37
AFTER THE CAPTIVES IN BABYLONIA SAW WHAT THE FATE OF JERUSALEM WOULD BE, THE SPIRIT OF THE LORD TOOK EZEKIEL TO THE MIDDLE OF A VALLEY FULL OF DRY BONES. EVERYWHERE EZEKIEL LOOKED WERE THE BLEACHED BONES OF DEAD MEN.
CAN THESE BONES BECOME LIVING PEOPLE AGAIN?
ONLY YOU KNOW THAT, LORD!
SPEAK TO THESE BONES AND SAY, "DRY BONES, LISTEN TO THE WORD OF THE LORD! I AM GOING TO PUT BREATH INTO YOU AND MAKE YOU LIVE AGAIN! THEN YOU WILL KNOW THAT I AM THE LORD!"
EZEKIEL BEGAN TO PROPHESY. HE SAW GOD BRING THE DRY BONES TOGETHER. A RATTLING SOUND ECHOED THROUGH THE VALLEY.

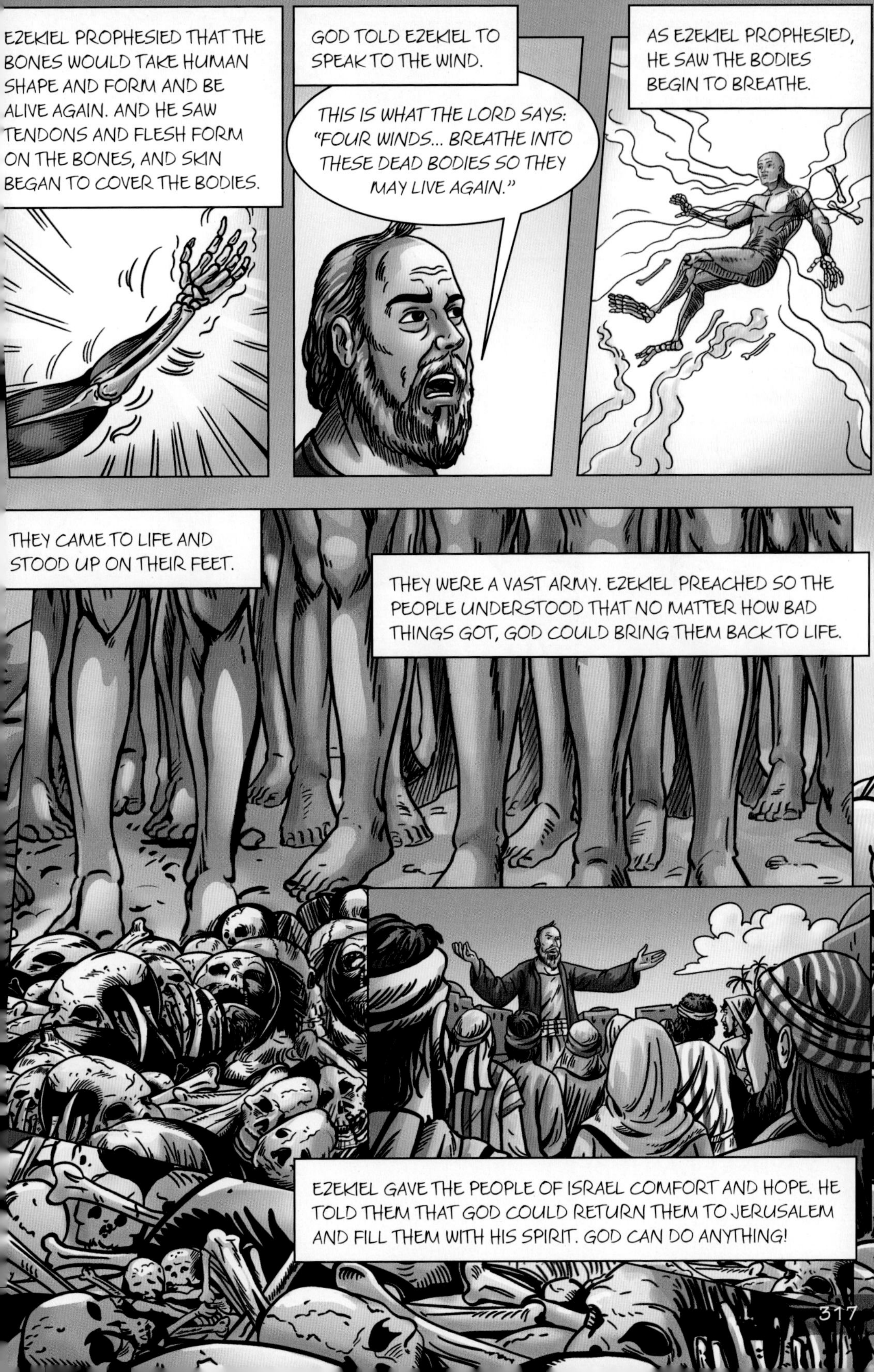

THEY CAME TO LIFE AND STOOD UP ON THEIR FEET.

THEY WERE A VAST ARMY. EZEKIEL PREACHED SO THE PEOPLE UNDERSTOOD THAT NO MATTER HOW BAD THINGS GOT, GOD COULD BRING THEM BACK TO LIFE.

EZEKIEL GAVE THE PEOPLE OF ISRAEL COMFORT AND HOPE. HE TOLD THEM THAT GOD COULD RETURN THEM TO JERUSALEM AND FILL THEM WITH HIS SPIRIT. GOD CAN DO ANYTHING!

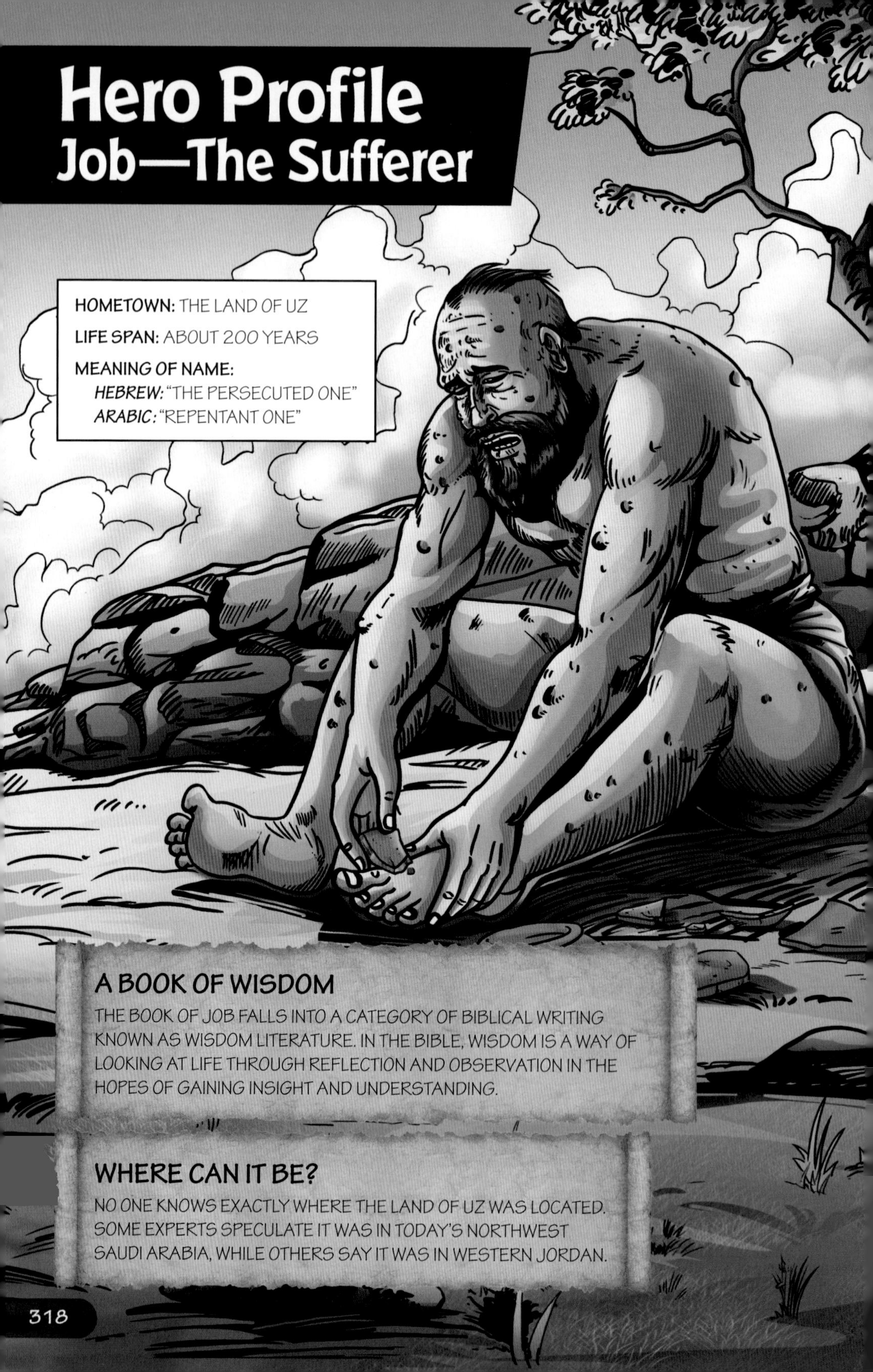
Hero Profile
Job—The Sufferer
HOMETOWN: THE LAND OF UZ
LIFE SPAN: ABOUT 200 YEARS
MEANING OF NAME:
HEBREW: "THE PERSECUTED ONE"
ARABIC: "REPENTANT ONE"
A BOOK OF WISDOM
THE BOOK OF JOB FALLS INTO A CATEGORY OF BIBLICAL WRITING KNOWN AS WISDOM LITERATURE. IN THE BIBLE, WISDOM IS A WAY OF LOOKING AT LIFE THROUGH REFLECTION AND OBSERVATION IN THE HOPES OF GAINING INSIGHT AND UNDERSTANDING.
WHERE CAN IT BE?
NO ONE KNOWS EXACTLY WHERE THE LAND OF UZ WAS LOCATED. SOME EXPERTS SPECULATE IT WAS IN TODAY'S NORTHWEST SAUDI ARABIA, WHILE OTHERS SAY IT WAS IN WESTERN JORDAN.

Satan Tests Job
Job 1–37
JOB WAS A GOOD MAN WHO FEARED GOD AND AVOIDED EVIL. HE WAS RICH AND BLESSED. HE HAD SEVEN SONS AND THREE DAUGHTERS.
HE OWNED MANY SHEEP...
...MANY HERDS OF CATTLE...
...THOUSANDS OF CAMELS, AND HUNDREDS OF OXEN.

GOD SPOKE TO SATAN, THE ACCUSER, ABOUT JOB.
HE IS THE FINEST MAN IN ALL THE EARTH.
JOB IS A MAN OF INTEGRITY.
REACH OUT AND TAKE AWAY EVERYTHING HE HAS...
...AND HE WILL SURELY CURSE YOU TO YOUR FACE!
YOU MAY TEST HIM, BUT DON'T HARM HIM PHYSICALLY.
SATAN QUICKLY WENT TO WORK. RAIDERS RAN OFF WITH JOB'S OXEN AND DONKEYS. THEY KILLED HIS SERVANTS...
...AND STOLE HIS CAMELS. YET JOB WOULD NOT TURN AWAY FROM THE LORD.

THEN A TERRIBLE STORM KILLED ALL HIS SONS AND DAUGHTERS.
AFTER THIS, JOB TORE HIS ROBE...
...SHAVED HIS HEAD, AND FELL TO HIS KNEES.
THE LORD GAVE, AND THE LORD HAS TAKEN AWAY.
BUT HE STILL TRUSTED GOD.

SATAN SPOKE TO GOD AGAIN. THE DEVIL SAID THAT JOB'S TRIALS HAD BEEN TOO EASY—JOB HAD NOT HAD TO SUFFER HIMSELF. GOD ALLOWED SATAN TO TEST JOB FURTHER BUT SAID THAT HE MUST NOT KILL JOB.
WHEN I GET DONE WITH HIM, HE WILL SURELY CURSE GOD.
SATAN AFFLICTED JOB WITH PAINFUL SORES FROM HIS FEET TO HIS HEAD. ALTHOUGH JOB WAS IN PAIN, HE KNEW THAT LIFE OFFERED BOTH BLESSINGS AND TRIALS. HE STILL RESPECTED GOD.
HUSBAND, ARE YOU STILL HOLDING TO YOUR INTEGRITY? **CURSE GOD AND DIE!**
YOU'RE FOOLISH, WOMAN! WE ACCEPT GOOD THINGS FROM GOD. SHOULD WE NOT ACCEPT BAD THINGS TOO?
THREE OF JOB'S FRIENDS, ELIPHAZ, BILDAD, AND ZOPHAR TRIED TO CONSOLE HIM. THEY SAT IN SILENCE FOR SEVEN DAYS UNTIL JOB SPOKE.
CURSED BE THE DAY I WAS BORN!!!

GOD HAS STRUCK ME WITH HIS ARROW.
THE PAIN LASTS. IT IS AS IF THE NIGHT GOES ON FOREVER.
WHY DOES GOD JUDGE PEOPLE BY WHAT THEY DO, WHEN HE CAN FORGIVE THEM?
WHY DOESN'T HE SEND ME TO THE GRAVE? **WHY, OH WHY, DOES GOD DO THIS TO ME???**
JOB'S FRIENDS TRIED TO OFFER HIM ADVICE.
PAIN HELPS A MAN REALIZE GOD'S LOVE AND FORGIVENESS WHEN HE IS WELL AGAIN.
GOD IS PUNISHING YOU FOR SOME HIDDEN SIN.
REPENT AND ALL WILL BE WELL.
YOU MUST HAVE DONE SOMETHING TO DESERVE THIS, JOB. JUST TELL GOD YOU ARE SORRY!
BUT I KNOW I HAVEN'T DONE ANYTHING WRONG!
NONE OF YOU KNOW WHAT YOU ARE TALKING ABOUT! YOU MIGHT BE OLDER THAN ME, BUT YOU DON'T SEEM ANY WISER! JOB, HOW CAN YOU BEGIN TO JUDGE GOD'S ACTIONS OR TRY TO JUSTIFY YOURSELF BEFORE HIM? HOW CAN YOU EVER UNDERSTAND HIS WAYS?

God Speaks to Job
Job 38–42
GOD SPOKE TO JOB FROM A WHIRLWIND, REVEALING HIS POWER AND MAJESTY.
DO YOU KNOW WHEN WILD GOATS GIVE BIRTH? HAVE YOU WATCHED AS DEER ARE BORN IN THE WILD?
HAVE YOU EVER CAUSED THE DAWN TO RISE IN THE EAST? DO YOU STILL WANT TO ARGUE WITH THE ALMIGHTY?
YOU ARE GOD'S CRITIC, BUT DO YOU HAVE THE ANSWERS?
I KNOW YOU ARE GREAT AND CAN DO ANYTHING.
I HAVE SPOKEN BUT DID NOT UNDERSTAND.
I HAVE HEARD ABOUT YOU BUT NEVER SEEN YOU.
I TAKE BACK EVERYTHING I SAID. I AM TRULY SORRY.
324

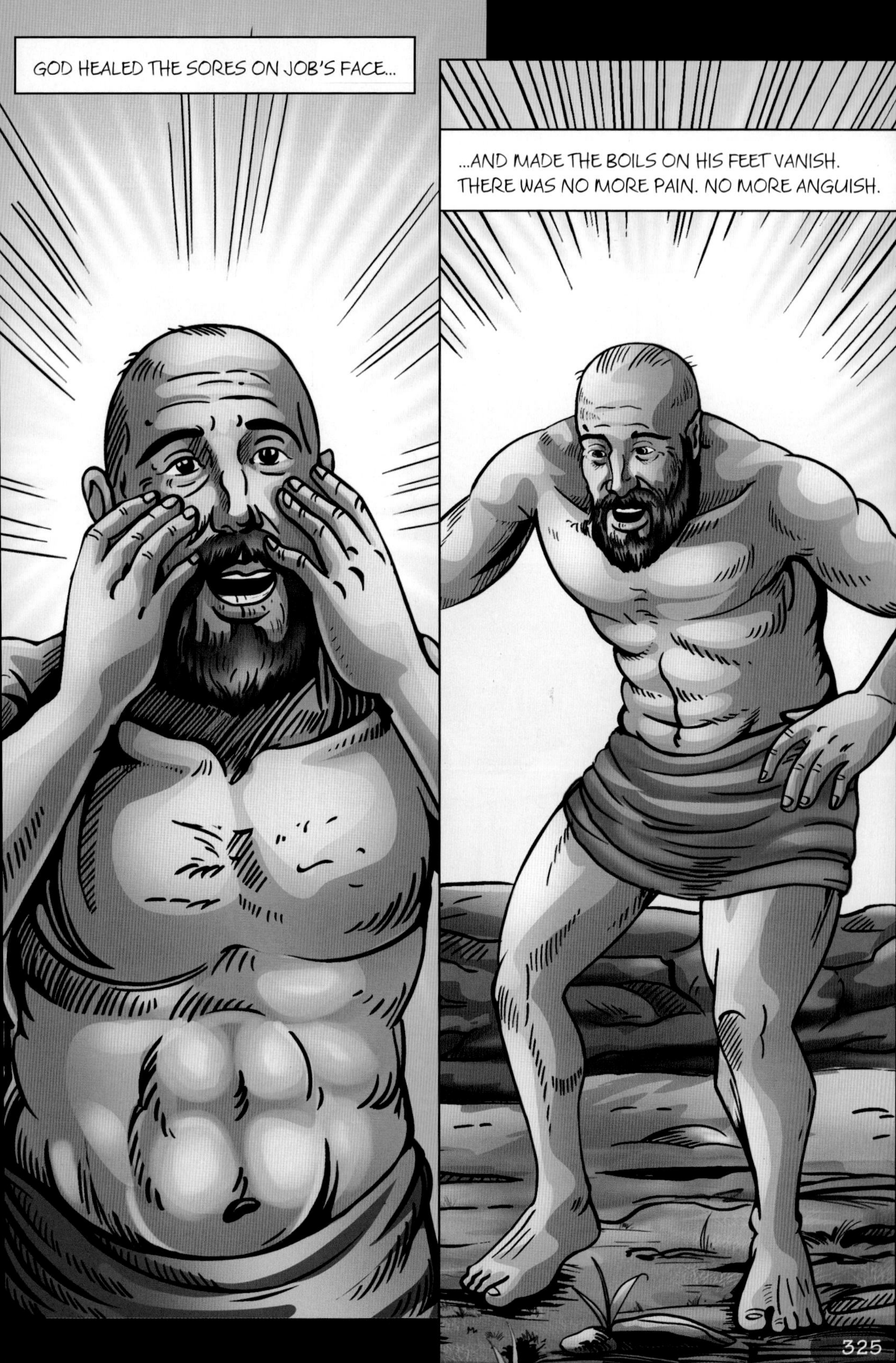
GOD HEALED THE SORES ON JOB'S FACE...
...AND MADE THE BOILS ON HIS FEET VANISH. THERE WAS NO MORE PAIN. NO MORE ANGUISH.

God Blesses Job
Job 42
BECAUSE JOB WAS A GOOD AND FAITHFUL MAN, GOD RESTORED HIS RICHES.
HIS BROTHERS AND SISTER VISITED HIM.
HIS FRIENDS DINED WITH HIM AND COMFORTED HIM BECAUSE OF ALL THE TRIALS HE HAD ENDURED.

AS JOB GREW OLD, GOD BLESSED HIM WITH 14,000 SHEEP....

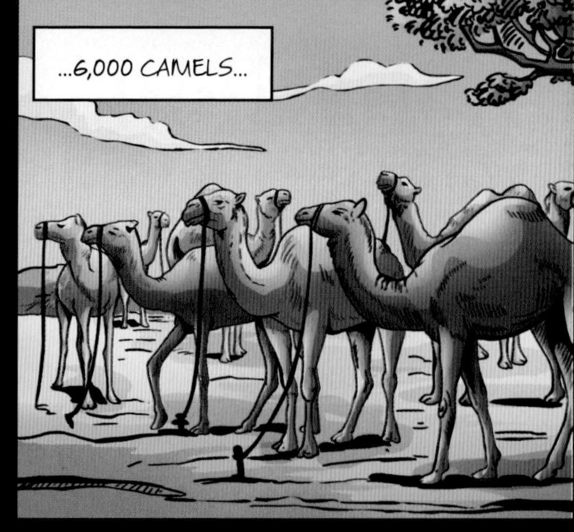
...6,000 CAMELS...

...A THOUSAND TEAMS OF OXEN...

...A THOUSAND DONKEYS...

...AND TEN CHILDREN. HIS THREE DAUGHTERS WERE THE MOST BEAUTIFUL IN THE LAND.

THE LORD BLESSED JOB WITH MANY GRANDCHILDREN AND GREAT-GRANDCHILDREN. JOB DIED OLD, CONTENT, AND TRUSTING AND LOVING THE LORD.

Hero Profile
Daniel—A Noble Prophet

MEANING OF NAME: "GOD IS MY JUDGE"
DANIEL TAKEN CAPTIVE: AROUND 605 BC
DANIEL IN THE LIONS' DEN: AROUND 539 BC

WORD WISE

THE OLD SAYING "I COULD SEE THE WRITING ON THE WALL" COMES FROM THE BOOK OF DANIEL. TERRIFIED KING BELSHAZZAR SAW A MYSTERIOUS HAND WRITING WORDS ON A WALL DURING A FEAST.

TEEN EXILE

DANIEL WAS A TEENAGER WHEN NEBUCHADNEZZAR FORCED HIM INTO EXILE DURING THE FIRST SIEGE OF JERUSALEM IN 605 BC. ACCORDING TO THE BIBLE, DANIEL SPOKE TO TWO OF GOD'S ANGELS, GABRIEL AND MICHAEL.

Daniel and the King's Food

Daniel 1–2

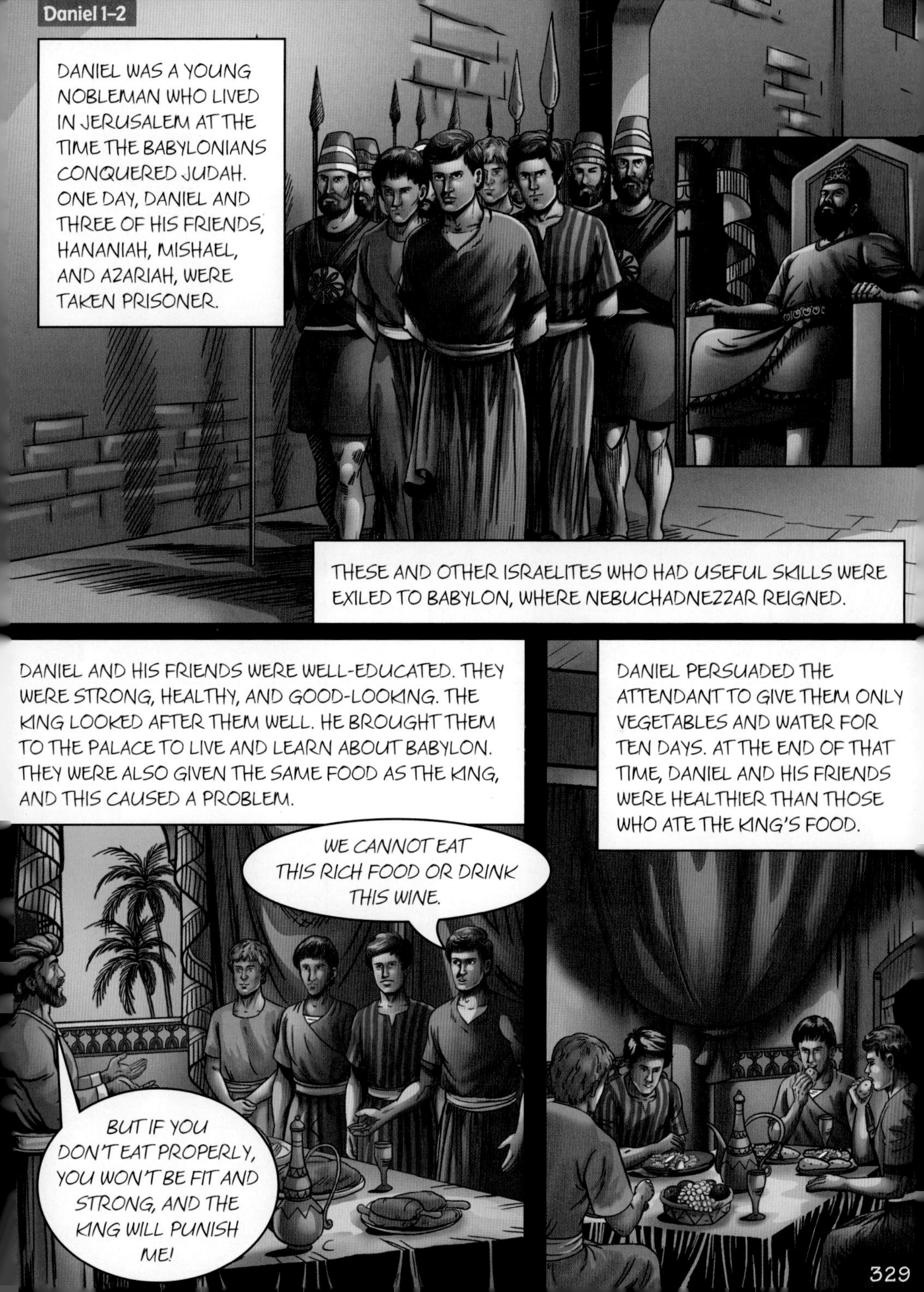

DANIEL WAS A YOUNG NOBLEMAN WHO LIVED IN JERUSALEM AT THE TIME THE BABYLONIANS CONQUERED JUDAH. ONE DAY, DANIEL AND THREE OF HIS FRIENDS, HANANIAH, MISHAEL, AND AZARIAH, WERE TAKEN PRISONER.

THESE AND OTHER ISRAELITES WHO HAD USEFUL SKILLS WERE EXILED TO BABYLON, WHERE NEBUCHADNEZZAR REIGNED.

DANIEL AND HIS FRIENDS WERE WELL-EDUCATED. THEY WERE STRONG, HEALTHY, AND GOOD-LOOKING. THE KING LOOKED AFTER THEM WELL. HE BROUGHT THEM TO THE PALACE TO LIVE AND LEARN ABOUT BABYLON. THEY WERE ALSO GIVEN THE SAME FOOD AS THE KING, AND THIS CAUSED A PROBLEM.

WE CANNOT EAT THIS RICH FOOD OR DRINK THIS WINE.

BUT IF YOU DON'T EAT PROPERLY, YOU WON'T BE FIT AND STRONG, AND THE KING WILL PUNISH ME!

DANIEL PERSUADED THE ATTENDANT TO GIVE THEM ONLY VEGETABLES AND WATER FOR TEN DAYS. AT THE END OF THAT TIME, DANIEL AND HIS FRIENDS WERE HEALTHIER THAN THOSE WHO ATE THE KING'S FOOD.

GOD GAVE THESE FOUR GREAT WISDOM. THEY WERE SELECTED TO ACT AS ADVISORS TO THE KING.
AT THAT TIME, THE KING HAD A STRANGE DREAM. NONE OF NEBUCHADNEZZAR'S MAGICIANS OR WISE MEN COULD TELL THE KING WHAT HE DREAMED OR WHAT IT MEANT. BUT DANIEL PRAYED TO GOD, AND GOD TOLD HIM HOW TO INTERPRET THE DREAM.
DANIEL EXPLAINED TO THE KING THAT HIS DREAM OF A FALLING STATUE TOLD OF THE FUTURE COLLAPSE OF HIS EMPIRE, AND OF THE ONES TO FOLLOW, AND THEN OF THE KINGDOM OF GOD, WHICH WOULD NEVER END.
NEBUCHADNEZZAR WAS IMPRESSED WITH DANIEL AND MADE HIM HIS CHIEF WISE MAN.

The King's Fiery Furnace
Daniel 3
KING NEBUCHADNEZZAR WANTED ALL HIS SUBJECTS TO WORSHIP A HUGE GOLD STATUE HE HAD BUILT. HE INVITED MANY NOBLE PEOPLE TO THE UNVEILING, INCLUDING DANIEL'S FRIENDS, WHO HAD BEEN RENAMED SHADRACH, MESHACH, AND ABEDNEGO.
FALL DOWN ON YOUR KNEES AND WORSHIP THE STATUE.
DANIEL'S FRIENDS WERE AMONG THE CROWD. THEY REFUSED TO BOW DOWN.
WHAT'S THIS? WHOEVER DOES NOT KNEEL WILL BE THROWN INTO A BLAZING FURNACE!
THE FURIOUS KING ORDERED THE MEN INTO HIS FURNACE. THE FLAMES WERE SO HOT THAT THE GUARDS WERE SCORCHED TO DEATH.
THE KING WAS AMAZED.
YOUR GOD IS TRULY GREAT! HE HAS SENT HIS ANGEL TO RESCUE HIS SERVANTS. HE SHOULD BE PRAISED!
NEBUCHADNEZZAR SAW THAT THE MEN WERE MOVING FREELY AND UNHARMED AS THE FLAMES LAPPED AT THEIR BODIES. WITH THEM WAS A FOURTH MAN WHO LOOKED LIKE A GOD.

Writing on the Wall

Daniel 5

I HEAR THAT YOU HAVE THE SPIRIT OF THE GODS IN YOU. TELL ME WHAT THIS MEANS!
MENE MENE TEKEL PARSIN
I WILL GIVE YOU RICHES AND APPOINT YOU AS A RULER!
DANIEL EXPLAINED THE MEANING OF THE WORDS: MENE—NUMBERED; TEKEL—WEIGHED; PARSIN—DIVIDED.
GOD HAS NUMBERED YOUR DAYS. YOU HAVE BEEN WEIGHED AND HAVE NOT MEASURED UP. YOUR KINGDOM WILL BE DIVIDED BETWEEN THE MEDES AND THE PERSIANS.
BECAUSE YOU DRANK OUT OF THE SACRED CUPS AND HAVE WORSHIPED THE FALSE GODS OF SILVER AND GOLD...
...YOUR REIGN OVER BABYLON IS ENDING.
THAT VERY NIGHT, INVADERS UNDER DARIUS THE MEDE KILLED BELSHAZZAR AND CONQUERED HIS KINGDOM.

Daniel in the Lions' Den

Daniel 6

THE KING AGREED TO THE LAW, BUT DANIEL CONTINUED TO PRAY TO GOD THREE TIMES A DAY.
SEE, HE PRAYS TO HIS GOD!
LET'S TELL THE KING AND HAVE HIM ARREST DANIEL.
OFF TO THE LIONS' DEN WITH YOU!
YOU WILL MAKE A DELICIOUS MEAL.

KING DARIUS DID NOT WANT DANIEL TO DIE, BUT HIS HANDS WERE TIED. UNDER MEDE LAW, EVERY ROYAL ORDER WAS FINAL. HIS GUARDS THREW DANIEL INTO THE LIONS' DEN.

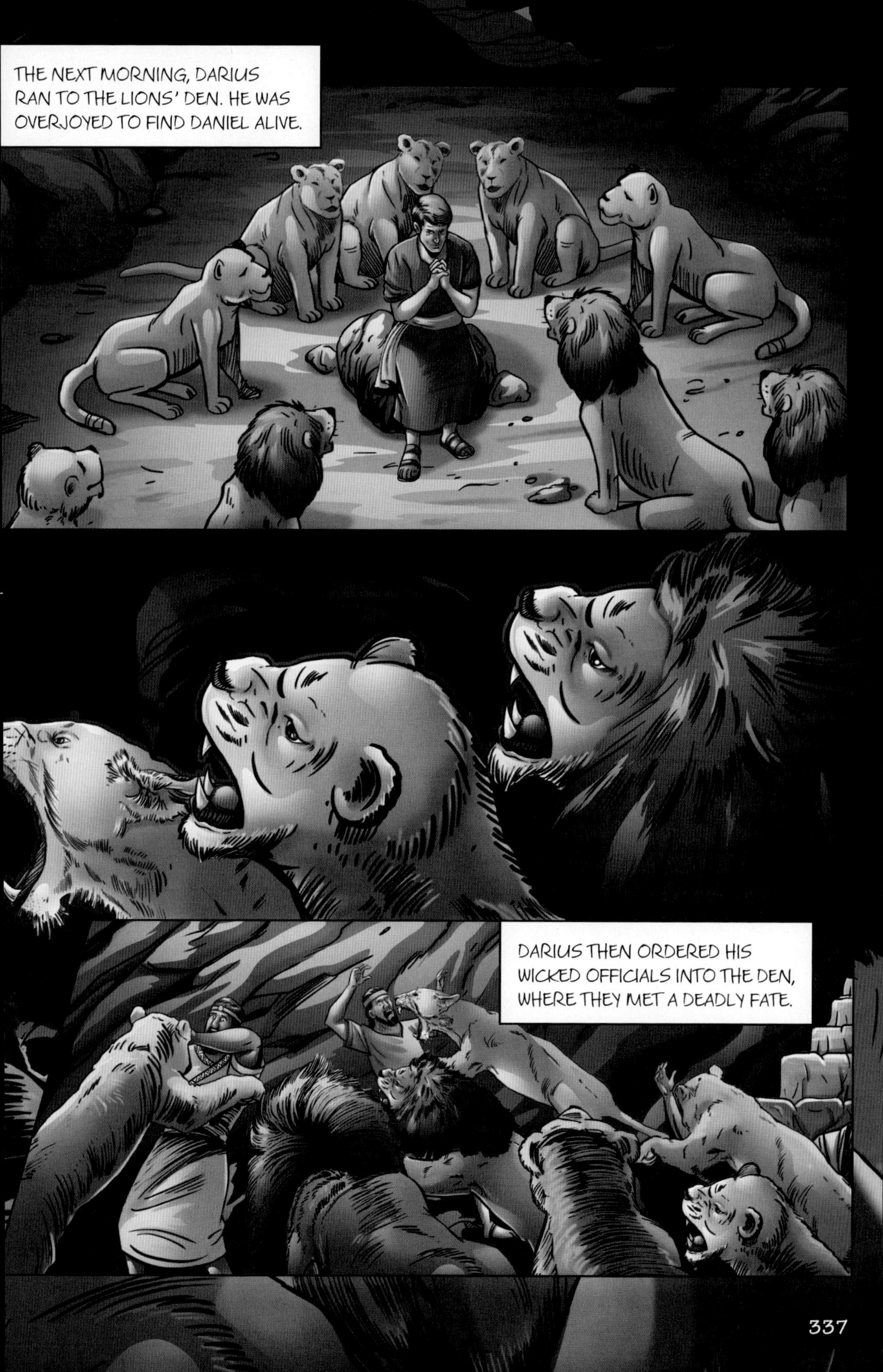
THE NEXT MORNING, DARIUS RAN TO THE LIONS' DEN. HE WAS OVERJOYED TO FIND DANIEL ALIVE.
DARIUS THEN ORDERED HIS WICKED OFFICIALS INTO THE DEN, WHERE THEY MET A DEADLY FATE.

Hero Profile
Esther—A Heroic Queen

MEANING OF NAME: IN PERSIAN, "ESTHER" MEANS "STAR."

JEWISH NAME: HADASSAH, MEANING "MYRTLE"

THE FEAST OF PURIM

THE JEWISH FEAST OF PURIM IS A CELEBRATION TO REMEMBER THE DELIVERANCE OF THE JEWS FROM THE EVIL HANDS OF HAMAN, WHO WANTED TO DESTROY ALL THE JEWS IN BABYLON.

BEAUTY WITH A PURPOSE

LIKE DANIEL, MORDECAI AND ESTHER LIVED FAR AWAY FROM THE HOMELAND OF THEIR ANCESTORS. THEY LIVED IN A FOREIGN COUNTRY RULED BY THE PERSIAN KING XERXES. GOD HAD BIG PLANS FOR THEIR LIVES AND POSITIONED THEM IN THE RIGHT PLACE AT THE RIGHT TIME. THROUGH HER BEAUTY, WISDOM, AND BRAVERY, ESTHER BECAME A PERSON OF AUTHORITY TO HELP SAVE THE FUTURE OF GOD'S PEOPLE.

Esther the Queen

Esther 1–2

WHAT DO YOU MEAN SHE WON'T COME?
HOW DARE SHE REFUSE A ROYAL COMMAND!
WHAT SHALL I DO, ADVISERS? QUEEN VASHTI HAS DISOBEYED ME.
THIS COULD SET A DANGEROUS EXAMPLE. THIS DISOBEDIENCE COULD SPREAD.
ISSUE A ROYAL DECREE THAT SAYS EVERY MAN SHOULD BE LORD IN HIS OWN HOUSE.
YOU SHALL NEVER AGAIN BE IN MY PRESENCE.
LEAVE! BE GONE!
THE KING BANISHED VASHTI. HE THEN SENT HIS OFFICERS TO SEEK OUT ALL THE BEAUTIFUL YOUNG WOMEN IN THE LAND SO HE COULD CHOOSE A NEW QUEEN.

IN SUSA LIVED A JEWISH MAN NAMED MORDECAI. HE WAS THE COUSIN AND GUARDIAN OF HADASSAH, A BEAUTIFUL YOUNG WOMAN WHOSE PARENTS HAD DIED.
SHE RECEIVED AN ORDER TO PRESENT HERSELF TO KING XERXES.
I WARN YOU, HADASSAH. DO NOT TELL THE KING YOU ARE A JEW. DO NOT USE YOUR HEBREW NAME. CALL YOURSELF **ESTHER**.
WHEN XERXES SAW ESTHER, HE FELL IN LOVE. HE MARRIED HER AND MADE HER QUEEN.

SOME TIME LATER, TWO OF THE KING'S MEN BECAME ANGRY AT XERXES AND PLOTTED TO KILL HIM. MORDECAI OVERHEARD THEIR PLANS.
THE TIME HAS COME TO KILL THE KING.
YES! HE MUST DIE!
I MUST TELL THE QUEEN SO SHE CAN WARN KING XERXES.
THE KING IS IN DANGER. THERE IS A PLOT TO **MURDER** HIM!
I SHALL WARN HIM.
ESTHER TOLD THE KING WHAT MORDECAI OVERHEARD. THE TWO CONSPIRATORS WERE ARRESTED AND SENTENCED TO DEATH.
BUT DUE TO AN OVERSIGHT, MORDECAI WAS NOT REWARDED FOR HIS LOYALTY.

Planning the Slaughter

Esther 3–4

BEFORE HAMAN BEGAN THE KILLING, HE HAD TO GET THE KING'S PERMISSION.
THROUGHOUT YOUR KINGDOM THERE IS A RACE OF PEOPLE...
...WHO WORSHIP A DIFFERENT GOD...
...WHO FOLLOW DIFFERENT LAWS.
IT IS NOT PROPER FOR THE KING TO TOLERATE THEM. WITH YOUR PERMISSION, I WILL **KILL THEM ALL!**
DO WHAT YOU WILL TO THEM.
THE KING'S DECREE WAS WRITTEN, AND THE ROYAL STAMP WAS USED. THROUGHOUT THE KINGDOM, THE ORDER WAS GIVEN FOR ALL JEWS TO BE KILLED ON MARCH 7 OF THE NEXT YEAR.

WHEN MORDECAI LEARNED WHAT WAS HAPPENING, HE TORE HIS CLOTHES, PUT ON BURLAP AND ASHES, AND CRIED LOUDLY OUTSIDE THE PALACE GATE.
QUEEN ESTHER HEARD ABOUT MORDECAI. SHE GAVE INSTRUCTIONS TO HER SERVANT.
TAKE THESE CLOTHES TO MORDECAI.
THEN COME BACK AND TELL ME WHAT THIS IS ALL ABOUT.

ESTHER'S SERVANT RETURNED WITH ALARMING NEWS.
HAMAN CONVINCED THE KING TO KILL ALL THE JEWS IN THE KINGDOM.
MORDECAI WANTS YOU TO GO TO THE KING....
...AND BEG HIM TO SPARE YOUR PEOPLE.
TELL MORDECAI THAT IF I SEE THE KING WITHOUT BEING SUMMONED, HE WILL EXECUTE **ME!**
MORDECAI SAYS YOU SHOULD NOT ASSUME YOUR SAFETY JUST BECAUSE YOU ARE QUEEN. YOU ARE ALSO A JEW.
MORDECAI SAYS PERHAPS GOD HAS MADE YOU QUEEN TO STOP THE SLAUGHTER.

Esther Saves Her People

Esther 4–9

ESTHER DRESSED IN HER ROYAL CLOTHES AND WENT TO SEE HER HUSBAND.
I BEG THE KING'S PARDON. I KNOW YOU HAVE NOT SUMMONED ME.
WHAT IS IT ESTHER? WHAT IS YOUR REQUEST?
WHATEVER YOU ASK OF ME SHALL BE GRANTED.
I WOULD LIKE YOU TO COME WITH HAMAN TO A BANQUET I WILL PREPARE.
ESTHER WAS TOO SCARED TO ASK THE KING AT THE BANQUET. INSTEAD SHE MADE A SECOND REQUEST.
PLEASE COME WITH HAMAN TOMORROW FOR A SECOND BANQUET.
THEN I WILL EXPLAIN THINGS TO YOU.
WHATEVER YOU ASK FOR SHALL BE GRANTED.

AFTER THE FIRST BANQUET, HAMAN WAS FEELING PLEASED WITH HIMSELF. BUT THEN HE PASSED MORDECAI, WHO AGAIN REFUSED TO BOW TO HIM.

THAT NIGHT XERXES COULD NOT SLEEP, SO HE READ A REPORT OF RECENT EVENTS. HE DISCOVERED THAT MORDECAI HAD PLAYED A ROLE IN STOPPING THE ATTEMPTED ASSASSINATION.

HAMAN WAS FURIOUS. LATER THAT DAY HE COMPLAINED TO HIS WIFE AND FRIENDS. THEY CONVINCED HIM TO SET UP A SHARPENED POLE ON WHICH TO EXECUTE MORDECAI FOR HIS DISRESPECT.

THAT NIGHT HAMAN VISITED THE KING TO ASK FOR PERMISSION TO KILL MORDECAI. BUT FIRST THE KING ASKED A QUESTION.

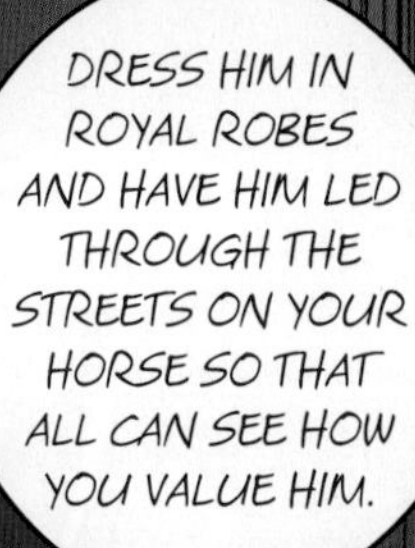

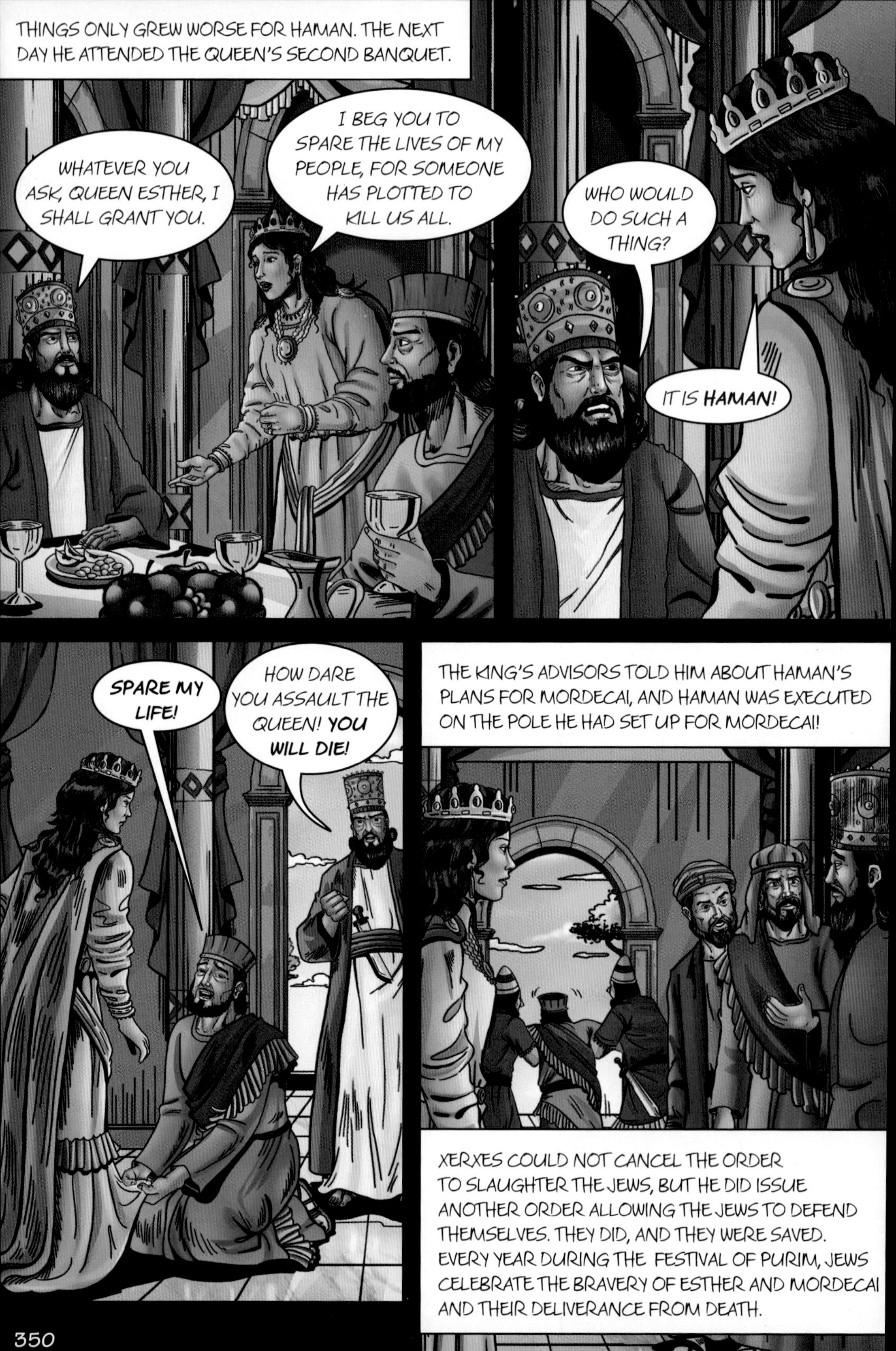

THINGS ONLY GREW WORSE FOR HAMAN. THE NEXT DAY HE ATTENDED THE QUEEN'S SECOND BANQUET.

WHATEVER YOU ASK, QUEEN ESTHER, I SHALL GRANT YOU.

I BEG YOU TO SPARE THE LIVES OF MY PEOPLE, FOR SOMEONE HAS PLOTTED TO KILL US ALL.

WHO WOULD DO SUCH A THING?

IT IS **HAMAN!**

THE KING'S ADVISORS TOLD HIM ABOUT HAMAN'S PLANS FOR MORDECAI, AND HAMAN WAS EXECUTED ON THE POLE HE HAD SET UP FOR MORDECAI!

XERXES COULD NOT CANCEL THE ORDER TO SLAUGHTER THE JEWS, BUT HE DID ISSUE ANOTHER ORDER ALLOWING THE JEWS TO DEFEND THEMSELVES. THEY DID, AND THEY WERE SAVED. EVERY YEAR DURING THE FESTIVAL OF PURIM, JEWS CELEBRATE THE BRAVERY OF ESTHER AND MORDECAI AND THEIR DELIVERANCE FROM DEATH.

Hero Profile
Jonah—A Reluctant Prophet

HOMETOWN: GATH-HEPHER, LOCATED JUST NORTH OF NAZARETH AND WEST OF THE SEA OF GALILEE

FOCAL POINT OF HIS MINISTRY: THE ASSYRIAN CITY OF NINEVEH, A CITY THAT IS NOW IN NORTHERN IRAQ

A FISHY STORY

THE BIBLE MENTIONS A "GREAT FISH" (NOT SPECIFICALLY A WHALE) IN THE WELL-KNOWN STORY OF JONAH. THE MODERN EXPRESSION "IN THE BELLY OF THE BEAST" IS A REFERENCE TO THE BOOK OF JONAH.

NEW TESTAMENT CONNECTION

JONAH IS THE ONLY PROPHET WHOM JESUS COMPARED HIMSELF TO IN THE NEW TESTAMENT. ACCORDING TO MATTHEW 12:40, JESUS SAID, "FOR AS JONAH WAS IN THE BELLY OF THE GREAT FISH FOR THREE DAYS AND THREE NIGHTS, SO WILL THE SON OF MAN BE IN THE HEART OF THE EARTH FOR THREE DAYS AND THREE NIGHTS."

Jonah and the Great Fish

Jonah 1–4

A PROPHET NAMED JONAH PREACHED GOD'S WORD TO THE ISRAELITES.

MY FRIENDS, THE LORD SEES ALL, AND KNOWS ALL.

GOD TOLD JONAH TO GO EAST AND DELIVER A MESSAGE TO THE ASSYRIANS.

GO TO NINEVEH AND ANNOUNCE MY JUDGMENT AGAINST THEM.

ISRAEL'S ENEMIES ARE IN NINEVEH. I WILL NOT GO. I DON'T WANT TO PREACH TO THEM!

JONAH DEFIED GOD AND BOARDED A SHIP FOR TARSHISH, A CITY IN THE OPPOSITE DIRECTION OF NINEVEH.

ARE YOU HEADING OUR WAY? WELCOME ABOARD.

HOWEVER, GOD SAW JONAH BOARD THE VESSEL.

GOD SENT A POWERFUL WIND. THE STORM WAS SO GREAT THAT THE CAPTAIN AND CREW FEARED FOR THEIR SURVIVAL.
LIGHTEN THE LOAD! IT MAY SAVE US!
IT'S NOT WORKING. WE'RE GOING TO DROWN!!!
HOW CAN YOU SLEEP WHILE THE SHIP IS TOSSING ABOUT LIKE THIS?
THE STORM CONTINUED. THE CREW DECIDED THAT THERE MUST BE A MAN ON BOARD WHO HAD BROUGHT THIS STORM UPON THEM. THEY DREW LOTS TO SEE WHO THAT PERSON WAS.
HE'S THE ONE! HE HAS DRAWN THE SHORTEST LOT!
WHERE DO YOU COME FROM? WHY DID YOU BRING THIS EVIL UPON US?

JONAH TOLD THE STORY OF HOW HE CAME TO BE ON THE BOAT AND HOW HE HAD DISOBEYED GOD.
TAKE ME AND **THROW ME IN THE SEA!**
THE STORM WILL SUBSIDE. IT IS THE ONLY WAY TO SAVE YOURSELVES.
AT FIRST THE MEN HESITATED, BUT THEN THEY DID AS JONAH SAID.
GOD FORGIVE US! WE DON'T WANT TO KILL AN INNOCENT MAN, BUT WE WILL DO AS YOU WANT.
AS SOON AS JONAH HIT THE WATER, THE STORM STOPPED, AND THOSE ABOARD THE SHIP WERE FILLED WITH AWE. THEY NOW FEARED AND RESPECTED THE LORD.
AN ENORMOUS FISH THEN APPEARED... **AND SWALLOWED JONAH WHOLE!**

JONAH DID NOT DIE BUT STAYED IN THE FISH'S BELLY FOR THREE DAYS AND NIGHTS.
OH, LORD, YOU THREW ME INTO THE OCEAN DEPTHS, AND I SANK DOWN TO THE HEART OF THE SEA.
I WILL PRAISE AND THANK YOU. SALVATION COMES FROM YOU ALONE.
GOD HEARD JONAH'S PRAYER AND MADE THE FISH SPIT JONAH OUT ONTO THE BEACH.
GET UP AND GO TO NINEVEH, AND DELIVER THE MESSAGE I HAVE GIVEN YOU.
JONAH OBEYED GOD.
GOD WILL DESTROY YOUR CITY IN 40 DAYS!

THE PEOPLE OF NINEVEH HEARD GOD'S WORD. THEY FASTED AND PRAYED. EVERYONE DRESSED IN BURLAP.

JONAH, MEANWHILE, LEFT NINEVEH. HE SAT IN A SPOT OVERLOOKING THE CITY. HE WAS ANGRY WITH GOD.

I KNEW THAT YOU WOULD BE KIND TO THESE ENEMIES OF MY PEOPLE. I WOULD HAVE RATHER SEEN THEM KILLED!

JONAH BUILT A SHELTER AND WAITED TO SEE IF GOD WOULD CHANGE HIS MIND. GOD PROVIDED JONAH WITH THE SHADE OF A PLANT TO KEEP HIM COOL.

THE NEXT MORNING GOD SENT A WORM TO EAT THE PLANT, AND IT WITHERED. JONAH HAD NO SHADE FROM THE SCORCHING SUN. HE WANTED TO DIE.

JONAH, IF YOU CAN GET UPSET OVER A PLANT—A PLANT THAT YOU DID NOTHING TO HELP GROW—THEN SURELY I CAN FEEL THE SAME WAY TOWARD A CITY OF PEOPLE!

DO NOT BE ANGRY WITH ME FOR CARING ABOUT THE GREAT CITY OF NINEVEH. WHY SHOULD THE THOUSANDS OF PEOPLE THERE NOT KNOW THAT I LOVE THEM?

Hero Profile
Nehemiah—The Man behind the Wall
FATHER: HACALIAH
CAME FROM: JERUSALEM
MEANING OF NAME: "JEHOVAH HAS COMFORTED"
NEHEMIAH THE INSPECTOR
UPON ARRIVING IN JERUSALEM, NEHEMIAH UNDERTOOK A SECRET INSPECTION OF THE RUINS. HE THEN ORGANIZED A REBUILDING PARTY OF JEWISH EXILES WHO HAD RETURNED FROM BABYLON.
NEHEMIAH THE GOVERNOR
AFTER NEHEMIAH REBUILT THE WALLS PROTECTING JERUSALEM, HE SERVED AS THE GOVERNOR OF JUDAH FOR MANY YEARS. HE ENFORCED LAWS THAT PROVIDED CHARITY FOR THE POOR AND STRENGTHENED THE PEOPLE'S OBSERVANCE OF THE SABBATH.

Rebuilding Solomon's Temple

Ezra 1–6

FOR MANY YEARS THE JEWS HAD LIVED IN EXILE. BUT AFTER PERSIA DEFEATED BABYLON, PERSIA'S KING CYRUS SAID THE JEWS COULD RETURN TO JERUSALEM. MORE THAN 40,000 PEOPLE EMBARKED ON THE JOURNEY.

WHEN THEY ARRIVED, THEY SAW THAT THE TEMPLE HAD BEEN DESTROYED.

THE PEOPLE WENT TO WORK AND BEGAN REBUILDING THE TEMPLE'S FOUNDATION.

WHEN THE ENEMIES OF JUDAH HEARD THAT THE JEWS WERE REBUILDING THE TEMPLE, THEY CAME TO OFFER THEIR HELP.
LET US HELP REBUILD THE TEMPLE. WE WORSHIP YOUR GOD TOO.
NO, GOD WANTS US TO DO THIS WORK OURSELVES.
THE EXILES KNEW THAT THEIR ENEMIES STILL WORSHIPED FALSE IDOLS AND THAT GOD WOULD NOT WANT THEM TO ACCEPT THEIR HELP.
JUDAH'S ENEMIES BEGAN TO SCARE OFF THE STONECUTTERS AND CARPENTERS. WORK ON THE TEMPLE STOPPED. THE JEWS HAD TO ASK THE NEW KING OF PERSIA, DARIUS, FOR HELP.
DARIUS ORDERED WORK TO BEGIN AGAIN. THE TEMPLE WAS REBUILT AND DEDICATED TO GOD.

Walls in Ruin

Nehemiah 1–7

THE WALLS OF THE CITY OF JERUSALEM WERE STILL IN RUINS. MADE FROM HUGE BLOCKS OF STONE, THE WALLS WERE MEANT TO PROTECT THE CITY FROM ATTACK.

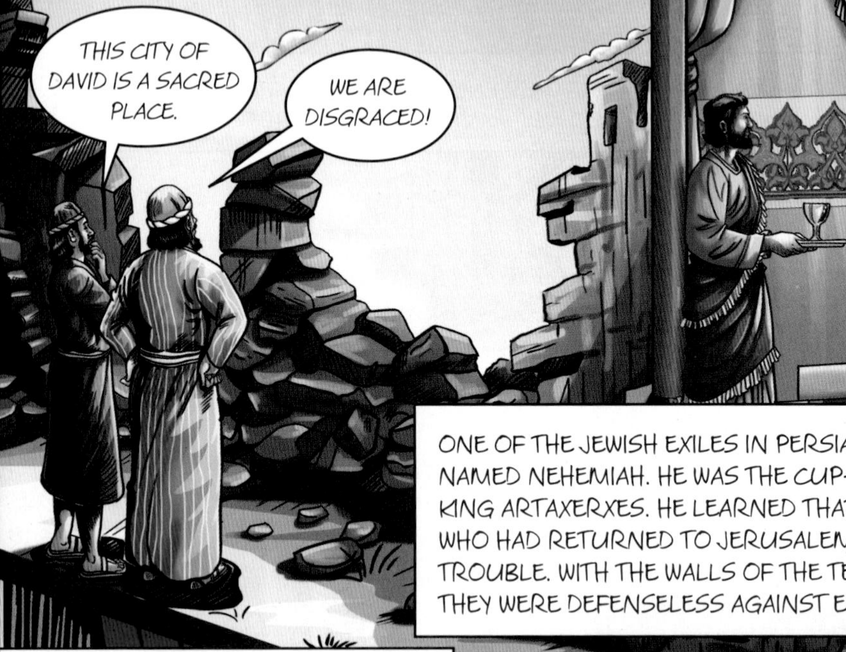

ONE OF THE JEWISH EXILES IN PERSIA WAS A MAN NAMED NEHEMIAH. HE WAS THE CUP-BEARER TO KING ARTAXERXES. HE LEARNED THAT THE EXILES WHO HAD RETURNED TO JERUSALEM WERE IN TROUBLE. WITH THE WALLS OF THE TEMPLE IN RUINS, THEY WERE DEFENSELESS AGAINST ENEMY ATTACK.

NEHEMIAH WAS VERY SAD. HE CRIED WHEN HE LEARNED THE NEWS. HE KNEW HE MUST SPEAK TO THE KING, EVEN THOUGH IT MIGHT MAKE HIM ANGRY.

GREAT AND ALMIGHTY GOD, HEAR MY PRAYER.

I WANT TO HELP REBUILD JERUSALEM'S WALLS. LET ME BE SUCCESSFUL WHEN I SPEAK TO THE KING ABOUT WHAT IS IN MY HEART.

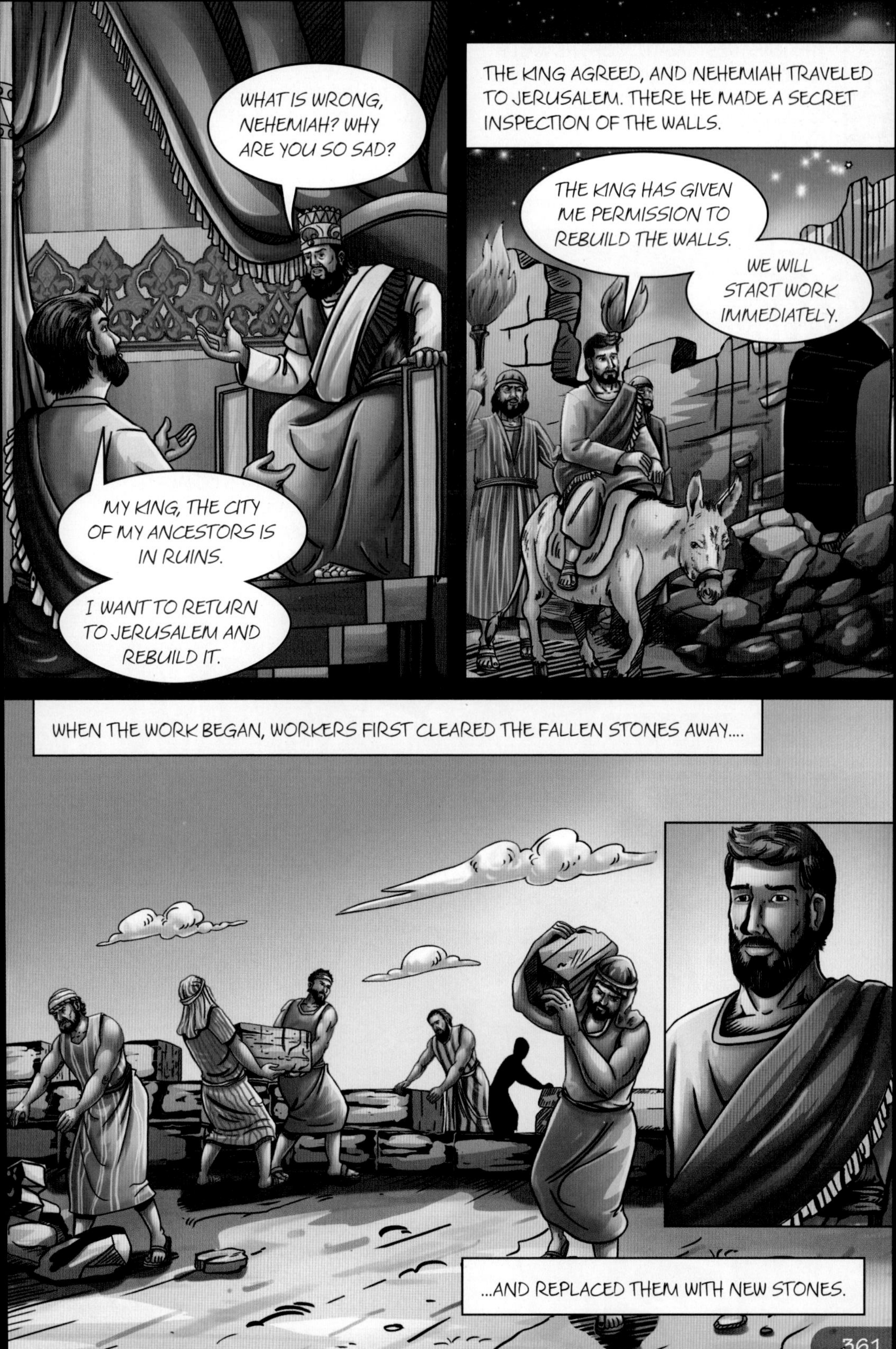

WHAT IS WRONG, NEHEMIAH? WHY ARE YOU SO SAD?

MY KING, THE CITY OF MY ANCESTORS IS IN RUINS.

I WANT TO RETURN TO JERUSALEM AND REBUILD IT.

THE KING AGREED, AND NEHEMIAH TRAVELED TO JERUSALEM. THERE HE MADE A SECRET INSPECTION OF THE WALLS.

THE KING HAS GIVEN ME PERMISSION TO REBUILD THE WALLS.

WE WILL START WORK IMMEDIATELY.

WHEN THE WORK BEGAN, WORKERS FIRST CLEARED THE FALLEN STONES AWAY....

...AND REPLACED THEM WITH NEW STONES.

THE JEWS' RESTORATION OF THE WALLS ANGERED AND WORRIED THEIR ENEMIES. THEY PLANNED AN ATTACK. BUT NEHEMIAH DIVIDED HIS MEN INTO TWO GROUPS. WHILE ONE HALF WORKED ON THE WALL, THE OTHER HALF KEPT GUARD.
BE READY IF OUR ENEMIES ATTACK.
I HAVE STATIONED GUARDS AROUND THE CITY.
CONTINUE WORKING AND DON'T WORRY. TRUST IN GOD.
THE ENEMIES TRIED TO SET A TRAP FOR NEHEMIAH TO HARM HIM. AN ENEMY NAMED SANBALLAT TRIED TO SCHEDULE A MEETING WITH NEHEMIAH FIVE TIMES. BUT EACH TIME, NEHEMIAH REFUSED TO GO.
SANBALLAT WAS GOING TO CAPTURE ME. BUT I SENT MY MESSENGERS TO TELL THEM MY WORK IS TOO IMPORTANT.
WE FINISHED THE WALLS IN 52 DAYS. GOD WAS WITH US!
WHEN THE JEWS' ENEMIES HEARD THE WALLS WERE FINISHED, THEY BECAME VERY DISCOURAGED, FOR THEY KNEW IT WAS WITH GOD'S HELP THAT THE WALLS WERE COMPLETED.

Hero Profile
Ezra—The Priest

FATHER: SERAIAH (DESCENDANT OF AARON, MOSES' BROTHER)

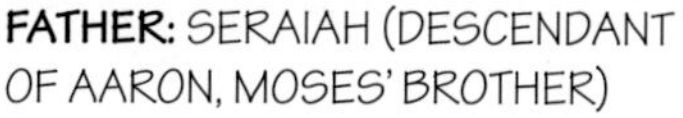

MEANING OF NAME: "HELPER"

JOBS: PRIEST AND SCRIBE (WROTE AND ORGANIZED BIBLICAL TEXTS)

IGNORING GOD'S LAWS

WHEN EZRA ARRIVED IN JERUSALEM, HE DISCOVERED THAT MANY JEWISH MEN WERE IGNORING GOD'S LAWS ABOUT MARRYING FOREIGN WOMEN. HE BELIEVED THAT ASSOCIATING WITH NON-JEWS LED TO IDOLATRY. HE FEARED GOD WOULD PUNISH HIS PEOPLE AS HE HAD DONE BEFORE.

ARAMAIC AND HEBREW

THE BOOK OF EZRA IS ONE OF JUST A FEW PARTS OF THE OLD TESTAMENT THAT WAS WRITTEN PARTLY IN ARAMAIC, THE MIDDLE EASTERN LANGUAGE SPOKEN COMMONLY IN ANCIENT TIMES.

Ezra Reads the Law

Ezra 9–10; Malachi 1–4; Nehemiah 8

BEFORE NEHEMIAH RETURNED TO HELP REBUILD JERUSALEM, A PRIEST IN JERUSALEM LEARNED THAT THE PEOPLE WHO HAD GONE BACK TO JERUSALEM WERE NOT FOLLOWING GOD'S LAW. THIS MAN WAS EZRA.

I HAVE TRAVELED SUCH A GREAT DISTANCE TO JERUSALEM ONLY TO FIND THAT THE PEOPLE HAVE SINNED. MANY OF OUR MEN HAVE MARRIED FOREIGN WOMEN WHO WORSHIP GODS OTHER THAN OURS!

LORD, I AM SORRY! I APOLOGIZE FOR THE PEOPLE OF JERUSALEM! THEY HAVE SINNED AGAINST YOU!

UPON HEARING EZRA'S PRAYER, THE PEOPLE WEPT TOO. THE MEN PROMISED TO FOLLOW GOD'S COMMAND. THEY WOULD SEND THE FOREIGN WOMEN AWAY. AFTER EZRA SPOKE TO THE LEADERS, THIS IS EXACTLY WHAT HAPPENED.

SOME TIME LATER, AFTER NEHEMIAH HAD OVERSEEN THE REBUILDING OF THE WALLS AND THE PEOPLE HAD MOVED BACK INTO THE CITY, EVERYONE CAME TOGETHER IN ONE OF THE CITY SQUARES. THERE, EZRA READ FROM THE BOOK OF LAW OF MOSES. MANY WERE STILL UPSET BY THEIR SINS.

FRIENDS, DO NOT BE SAD! THIS IS A HOLY DAY—A DAY TO REJOICE!

WE MUST HAVE A FEAST AND MAKE SURE THE POOR HAVE PLENTY TO EAT.

SO THE PEOPLE CELEBRATED.

AND FOR SEVEN DAYS EZRA READ FROM THE BOOK OF LAW. BY THE END OF THE FEAST, EVERYONE RECOMMITTED TO HONOR GOD AND TO KEEP THEIR SIDE OF THE COVENANT.

THE JEWS WERE FILLED WITH GOOD INTENTIONS WHEN THEY COMPLETED THE WALLS, AND JERUSALEM WAS WHOLE ONCE AGAIN. BUT AS THE YEARS PASSED, THEY FELL BACK INTO THEIR OLD WAYS. THEN MALACHI CAME ON THE SCENE—THE LAST OF THE OLD TESTAMENT PROPHETS. HE ENCOURAGED THE PEOPLE TO RETURN TO THEIR COVENANT WITH GOD.
MY PEOPLE, YOU MUST WELCOME GOD BACK INTO YOUR HEARTS!
MALACHI TOLD THE PEOPLE THAT GOD WOULD BE SENDING A MESSENGER—A MIGHTY MESSENGER—TO PREPARE THE WAY FOR THE LORD.

ISRAEL DURING THE TIME OF JESUS
Sidon
Zarephath
Damascu
SYRIA
Tyre
Mt Hermon
Caesarea Philippi
Ptolemais
Mediterranean Sea
Capernaum
Bethsaida
GALILEE
Cana
Sea of Galilee
Gennesaret
Tiberias
Nazareth
Caesarea
Salim
Mt Ebal
SAMARIA
Sychar
Mt Gerizim
River Jordan
Joppa
Ephraim
Emmaus
Jericho
Jerusalem
Bethany
JUDAH
Ashkelon
Bethlehem
Wilderness of Judah
Dead Sea
Gaza
Hebron
En-gedi
IDUMEA
Moladah
Zoar
Kadesh-Barnea

The New Testament

"For this is how God loved the world: He gave his one and only Son, so that everyone who believes in him will not perish but have eternal life."

John 3:16

Hero Profile
John the Baptist

RELATION TO JESUS: COUSIN

FATHER: ZECHARIAH

MOTHER: ELIZABETH

LOCUSTS AND HONEY

WHEN JOHN THE BAPTIST WAS IN THE WILDERNESS PREACHING, HE ATE LOCUSTS AND HONEY. PEOPLE STILL EAT LOCUSTS TODAY IN MANY AFRICAN, MIDDLE EASTERN, AND ASIAN COUNTRIES. THE BUGS ARE CONSIDERED A DELICACY.

GOD'S MESSENGERS

ANGELS ARE HEAVENLY BEINGS—GOD'S MESSENGERS ON EARTH. THE WORD "ANGEL" COMES FROM THE GREEK WORD "AGGELOS," WHICH MEANS "MESSENGER." WHEN GOD WANTS TO COMMUNICATE WITH HUMANS, HE OFTEN SENDS HIS ANGELS. THE ANGEL GABRIEL PLAYS AN IMPORTANT ROLE AS THE NEW TESTAMENT BEGINS, AS HE IS THE ONE WHO FORETELLS THE BIRTH OF JOHN THE BAPTIST.

Gabriel Delivers Some News

Luke 1

BUT ZECHARIAH WAS DOUBTFUL. HE COULD NOT BELIEVE WHAT THE ANGEL HAD TOLD HIM.
HOW WILL THIS HAPPEN? I AM AN OLD MAN. ELIZABETH IS AN OLD WOMAN.
I AM GABRIEL! I STAND IN THE PRESENCE OF GOD. IT WAS HE WHO SENT ME.
BECAUSE YOU DID NOT BELIEVE, YOU WILL BE UNABLE TO SPEAK UNTIL YOUR SON IS BORN. BUT IT WILL HAPPEN AS I HAVE SAID.
PEOPLE WERE WAITING OUTSIDE THE TEMPLE. THEY WONDERED WHY ZECHARIAH HAD BEEN IN THE TEMPLE FOR SO LONG. WHEN HE FINALLY EMERGED, HE TRIED TO EXPLAIN WITH SIGNS WHAT HAD HAPPENED. PEOPLE REALIZED THAT HE HAD SEEN A VISION, BUT ZECHARIAH COULDN'T SPEAK A SINGLE WORD!

Gabriel Visits Mary

Luke 1

THE HOLY SPIRIT WILL COME UPON YOU...
...AND THE POWER OF THE MOST HIGH WILL OVERSHADOW YOU.
YOUR RELATIVE ELIZABETH WILL ALSO HAVE A SON.
FOR THE WORD OF GOD WILL NEVER FAIL.
I AM GOD'S SERVANT. MAY EVERYTHING YOU HAVE SAID ABOUT ME COME TRUE.

MARY LEFT HER HOME IN NAZARETH AND WENT TO SEE ELIZABETH. WHEN ELIZABETH GREETED MARY, THE BABY IN ELIZABETH'S WOMB JUMPED. ELIZABETH SMILED AND WAS FILLED WITH THE HOLY SPIRIT.
GOD HAS BLESSED YOU ABOVE ALL WOMEN, AND YOUR CHILD IS BLESSED.
WHEN I HEARD YOUR VOICE, THE BABY IN MY WOMB JUMPED FOR JOY.
GOD IS GREAT. HE SHOWS MERCY TO THOSE WHO HONOR HIM.
ELIZABETH LATER GAVE BIRTH TO A SON, JUST AS GABRIEL HAD PROMISED. WHEN PEOPLE ASKED WHAT THE CHILD WAS TO BE CALLED, ZECHARIAH WROTE ON A SLATE, "HIS NAME IS JOHN." FROM THEN ON, HE COULD SPEAK AGAIN. PEOPLE WERE FILLED WITH WONDER.

John Preaches
Matthew 3; Luke 3
JOHN GREW UP AND BEGAN PREACHING IN THE REGION AROUND THE JORDAN RIVER.
REPENT, FOR THE KINGDOM OF HEAVEN IS NEAR.
OUR SAVIOR IS COMING. AS ISAIAH HAD SAID, "PREPARE THE WAY FOR THE LORD'S COMING!"
AS JOHN PREACHED, CROWDS OF PEOPLE CAME TO HIM TO BE BAPTIZED IN THE JORDAN RIVER.
I BAPTIZE YOU WITH WATER.

THE JEWISH LEADERS DID NOT LIKE WHAT JOHN WAS PREACHING.
YOU BROOD OF SNAKES! YOU NEED TO CHANGE YOUR WAYS!
SOMEONE IS COMING WHO IS GREATER THAN I AM! I BAPTIZE YOU WITH WATER, BUT HE WILL BAPTIZE YOU **WITH THE HOLY SPIRIT!**
WHO IS THIS SAVIOR YOU SPEAK OF?

The Ultimate Hero
Jesus Christ—The Son of God

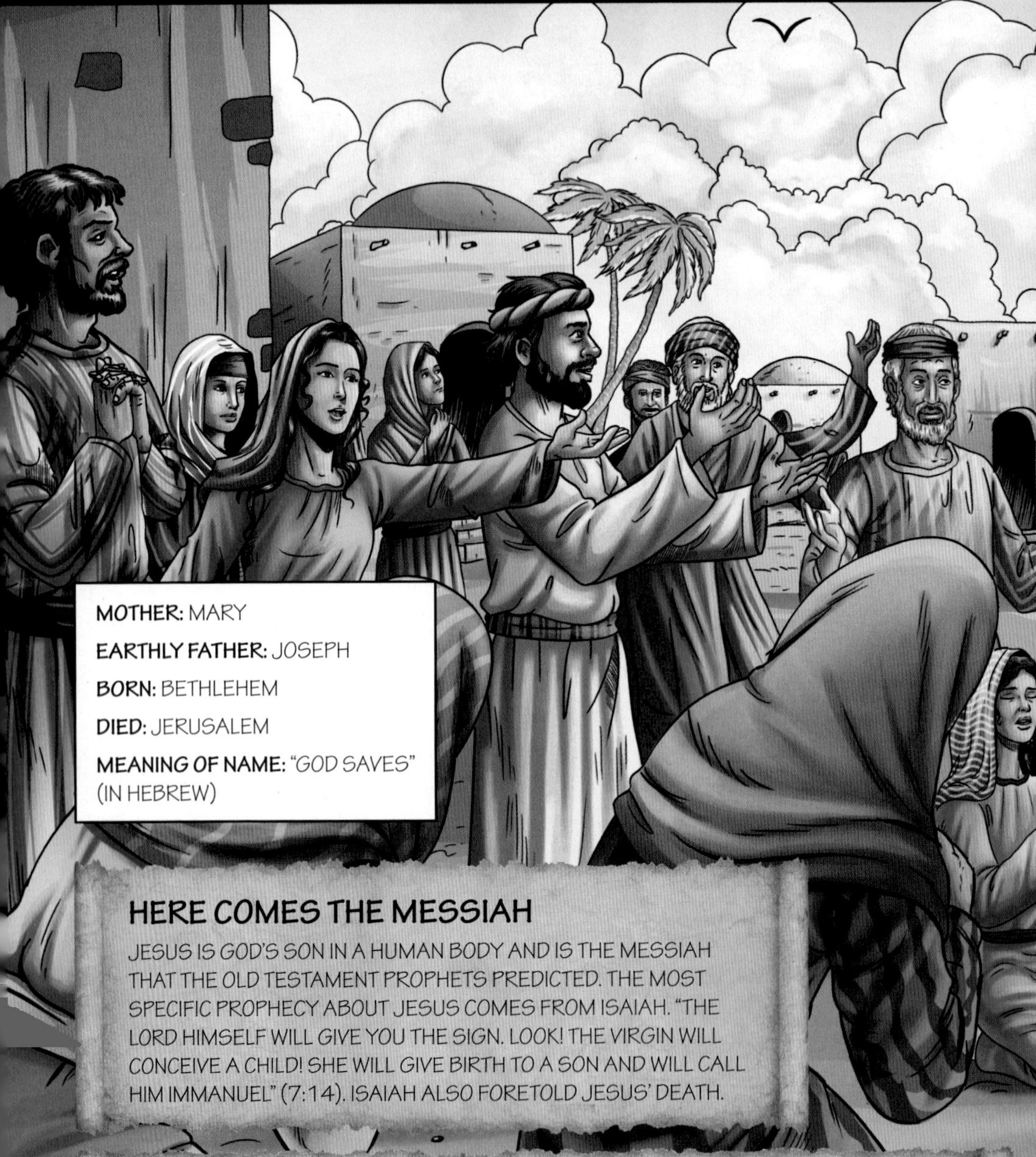

MOTHER: MARY

EARTHLY FATHER: JOSEPH

BORN: BETHLEHEM

DIED: JERUSALEM

MEANING OF NAME: "GOD SAVES" (IN HEBREW)

HERE COMES THE MESSIAH

JESUS IS GOD'S SON IN A HUMAN BODY AND IS THE MESSIAH THAT THE OLD TESTAMENT PROPHETS PREDICTED. THE MOST SPECIFIC PROPHECY ABOUT JESUS COMES FROM ISAIAH. "THE LORD HIMSELF WILL GIVE YOU THE SIGN. LOOK! THE VIRGIN WILL CONCEIVE A CHILD! SHE WILL GIVE BIRTH TO A SON AND WILL CALL HIM IMMANUEL" (7:14). ISAIAH ALSO FORETOLD JESUS' DEATH.

FAMILY MATTERS

JESUS WAS A DESCENDANT OF ABRAHAM AND KING DAVID. HE BEGAN TEACHING WHEN HE WAS ABOUT 30 YEARS OLD AND WAS CRUCIFIED ABOUT THREE YEARS LATER.

The Birth of Christ

BORN IN A STABLE?

THE TRADITIONAL NATIVITY STORY HAS JESUS' BIRTH IN A STABLE BECAUSE THERE WAS NO ROOM AT THE INN. WE DON'T KNOW EXACTLY THE TYPE OF STRUCTURE THAT HE WAS BORN IN, BUT WE KNOW THAT ANIMALS WERE CARED FOR THERE. THE BIBLE SAYS JESUS WAS PLACED IN A MANGER, THE FEEDING BOX WHERE ANIMALS WOULD EAT THEIR FOOD.

OUT OF WEDLOCK

AN UNMARRIED GIRL WHO GAVE BIRTH TO A CHILD MIGHT HAVE BEEN REJECTED BY HER FAMILY OR EVEN FORCED TO LEAVE HER VILLAGE. THE BIBLE TELLS US THAT JOSEPH MARRIED MARY AFTER AN ANGEL OF THE LORD SPOKE TO HIM.

A Special Baby
Matthew 1; Luke 2
WHEN JOSEPH FOUND OUT THAT MARY WAS PREGNANT, HE WAS TROUBLED.
I WILL BREAK OFF OUR ENGAGEMENT QUIETLY SO IT WON'T BRING SHAME ON US.
JOSEPH LATER WENT TO SLEEP. AN ANGEL OF THE LORD APPEARED TO HIM IN A DREAM.
JOSEPH, SON OF DAVID, DO NOT BE AFRAID TO TAKE MARY AS YOUR WIFE.
IT IS THROUGH THE HOLY SPIRIT THAT MARY WILL HAVE THIS CHILD.
SHE WILL HAVE A SON, AND YOU ARE TO NAME HIM JESUS, FOR HE WILL SAVE HIS PEOPLE FROM THEIR SINS.
WHEN JOSEPH AWOKE, HE DID AS THE ANGEL SAID AND TOOK MARY AS HIS WIFE.

IN THOSE DAYS THE ROMANS RULED JUDEA. THE ROMAN EMPEROR, AUGUSTUS, ORDERED THAT A CENSUS OF HIS EMPIRE BE TAKEN. EVERYONE HAD TO GO TO THEIR TOWN OF ORIGIN AND BE COUNTED.
WHAT'S YOUR NAME, AND HOW MANY CHILDREN DO YOU HAVE?
MY NAME IS JOSIAH, AND I HAVE THREE CHILDREN.
MARY AND JOSEPH TRAVELED TO BETHLEHEM, THE CITY OF JOSEPH'S ANCESTOR DAVID.
THEY STOPPED AT AN INN TO REST.
MY WIFE IS ABOUT TO GIVE BIRTH! ARE YOU SURE THERE ARE NO ROOMS?
I AM SORRY, FRIEND. BUT THERE IS A STABLE IN THE BACK.
YOU CAN STAY THERE.

MARY GAVE BIRTH TO A SON. SHE WRAPPED HIM
IN STRIPS OF CLOTH AND LAID HIM IN A MANGER.

THAT NIGHT THERE WERE SHEPHERDS IN THE FIELDS, GUARDING THEIR SHEEP. AN ANGEL APPEARED AND SAID...
DON'T BE AFRAID! I BRING YOU GOOD NEWS THAT WILL BRING GREAT JOY TO ALL PEOPLE.
THE SAVIOR—YES, THE MESSIAH, THE LORD—HAS BEEN BORN TODAY IN BETHLEHEM! YOU WILL FIND A BABY WRAPPED IN STRIPS OF CLOTH, LYING IN A MANGER.

WHEN THE ANGEL FINISHED SPEAKING, THE DARK NIGHT WAS FILLED WITH MANY ANGELS PRAISING GOD.
GLORY TO GOD IN HIGHEST HEAVEN, AND PEACE ON EARTH.
I THINK WE SHOULD GO TO BETHLEHEM!
YES, TO SEE WHAT HAS HAPPENED!

THE SHEPHERDS LEFT THE FIELD AND CAME TO SEE THE NEWBORN BABY.
THE SHEPHERDS FOUND A BABY LYING IN A MANGER, JUST AS THE ANGEL HAD SAID. HE WAS WRAPPED IN STRIPS OF CLOTH. THE SHEPHERDS TOLD EVERYONE ABOUT THE BABY AND WHAT THE ANGEL HAD SAID.
THE SHEPHERDS RETURNED TO THE FIELDS AND WORSHIPED AND PRAISED GOD.

The Wise Men

Matthew 2

THE WISE MEN SET OUT FOR JERUSALEM. THE STAR GUIDED THEM WITH EACH STEP.
WHEN THEY ARRIVED IN JERUSALEM, THE WISE MEN ASKED ABOUT THE NEWBORN KING OF THE JEWS. WHEN HEROD LEARNED OF THIS, HE CALLED FOR THE JEWISH PRIESTS AND TEACHERS.
WHO IS THIS KING? WHERE HAS HE BEEN BORN?
THE PROPHET SAID, "A RULER WILL COME FROM BETHLEHEM WHO WILL BE THE SHEPHERD FOR MY PEOPLE ISRAEL."

BRING THESE WISE MEN TO ME. I WANT TO SPEAK TO THEM!
THE WISE MEN CAME BEFORE HEROD AND TOLD HIM THAT THEY WERE SEARCHING FOR THE PROPHESIED KING.
GO TO BETHLEHEM AND SEARCH CAREFULLY FOR THE CHILD.
WHEN YOU FIND HIM, BRING WORD BACK TO ME AND TELL ME WHERE HE IS...
...SO THAT I MIGHT WORSHIP HIM.

THE WISE MEN LEFT HEROD AND TRAVELED TO BETHLEHEM, GUIDED BY THE STAR.
WE HAVE TRAVELED A LONG WAY TO SEE THIS CHILD.
WE BRING THESE GIFTS FOR HIM.

AS THE WISE MEN SLEPT, GOD WARNED THEM NOT TO RETURN TO HEROD.
SO THEY PACKED UP THEIR BELONGINGS AND LEFT FOR THEIR OWN COUNTRY BY A DIFFERENT ROUTE.

THOSE FOOLISH MEN. **HOW DARE THEY DECEIVE ME!**
GO TO BETHLEHEM AND **KILL EVERY BOY** WHO IS TWO YEARS OLD OR YOUNGER!
STOP! DON'T TAKE MY CHILD!
STEP BACK OR YOU WILL SUFFER THE CONSEQUENCES! WE DO THIS ON THE KING'S ORDERS!
IN A DREAM, AN ANGEL TOLD JOSEPH THAT THEY MUST FLEE.
IT ISN'T SAFE TO STAY HERE!
JOSEPH TOOK HIS FAMILY TO EGYPT. AFTER KING HEROD HAD DIED AND THE DANGER WAS OVER, THEY RETURNED TO ISRAEL.

Jesus in the Temple

Luke 2

MARY AND JOSEPH RETURNED TO JERUSALEM. THEY SEARCHED EVERYWHERE FOR JESUS.
HAVE YOU SEEN MY SON? HE'S TWELVE YEARS OLD, AND WE CANNOT FIND HIM.
NO, I HAVE NOT SEEN YOUR BOY.
MARY AND JOSEPH THEN CAME TO THE TEMPLE.
WHY ARE ALL THOSE PEOPLE LOOKING INSIDE?

AFTER THREE DAYS OF SEARCHING, MARY AND JOSEPH HAD FOUND THEIR SON.
JESUS WAS IN THE TEMPLE SITTING AMONG THE TEACHERS. HE WAS LISTENING TO THEM AND ASKING QUESTIONS. ALL WHO HEARD HIM WERE AMAZED AT HIS UNDERSTANDING AND ANSWERS.

SON, WHY HAVE YOU DONE THIS TO US?
YOUR FATHER AND I WERE WORRIED ABOUT YOU.
WHY WERE YOU LOOKING FOR ME?
DIDN'T YOU KNOW I MUST BE IN MY FATHER'S HOUSE?
MARY AND JOSEPH TOOK JESUS HOME TO NAZARETH, WHERE HE GREW UP INTO A KIND AND WISE YOUNG MAN.

The Ministry of Jesus

POLITICS OF THE TIME

JESUS LIVED IN A TIME OF TERRIBLE POLITICAL STRIFE. CAESAR AUGUSTUS RULED THE REGION FROM ROME. HIS SOLDIERS KEPT ORDER AND UNIFIED THE MEDITERRANEAN WORLD UNDER ONE GOVERNMENT.

THREAT OF THE PHARISEES

JESUS ANGERED THE JEWISH PHARISEES. THEY SAW JESUS AS A THREAT. THE PHARISEES WERE A JEWISH RELIGIOUS GROUP WHO STRICTLY FOLLOWED THE RELIGIOUS LAWS AND CUSTOMS JESUS OFTEN CRITICIZED THEM FOR DISTORTING GOD'S LAW AND NOT UNDERSTANDING THE TRUE MESSAGE OF SCRIPTURE.

The Baptism of Jesus

Matthew 3; Mark 1; Luke 3

JOHN CONTINUED TO BAPTIZE PEOPLE. ONE DAY JESUS CAME TO HIM.
I HAVE COME HERE TO BE BAPTIZED.
MASTER, YOU SHOULD BE BAPTIZING ME!
IT IS WHAT GOD WANTS.

JOHN BAPTIZED JESUS IN THE JORDAN RIVER, AND THE HEAVENS OPENED UP. A VOICE FROM ABOVE SAID, "THIS IS MY DEARLY LOVED SON, WHO BRINGS ME GREAT JOY."

Temptation in the Desert

Matthew 4; Mark 1; Luke 4

SATAN CAME TO JESUS TO TEMPT HIM.
IF YOU ARE THE SON OF GOD, COMMAND THESE STONES TO BECOME BREAD.
PEOPLE DO NOT LIVE BY BREAD ALONE.

SATAN TEMPTED JESUS AGAIN. HE TOOK JESUS TO THE HIGHEST POINT OF THE TEMPLE.
IF YOU ARE THE SON OF GOD, JUMP! THE SCRIPTURES SAY...
...THAT GOD WILL ORDER HIS ANGELS TO PROTECT YOU.
THE SCRIPTURES ALSO SAY, "YOU MUST NOT TEST GOD."

FINALLY, SATAN TOOK JESUS UP TO A HILL AND SHOWED HIM THE KINGDOMS OF THE WORLD.
I WILL GIVE YOU ALL OF THIS POWER...
...AND ALL THIS GLORY IF YOU WORSHIP ME.
THE SCRIPTURES SAY, "WORSHIP THE LORD ONLY."
SATAN VANISHED AFTER HE HAD TEMPTED JESUS.

A Prophet in His Hometown

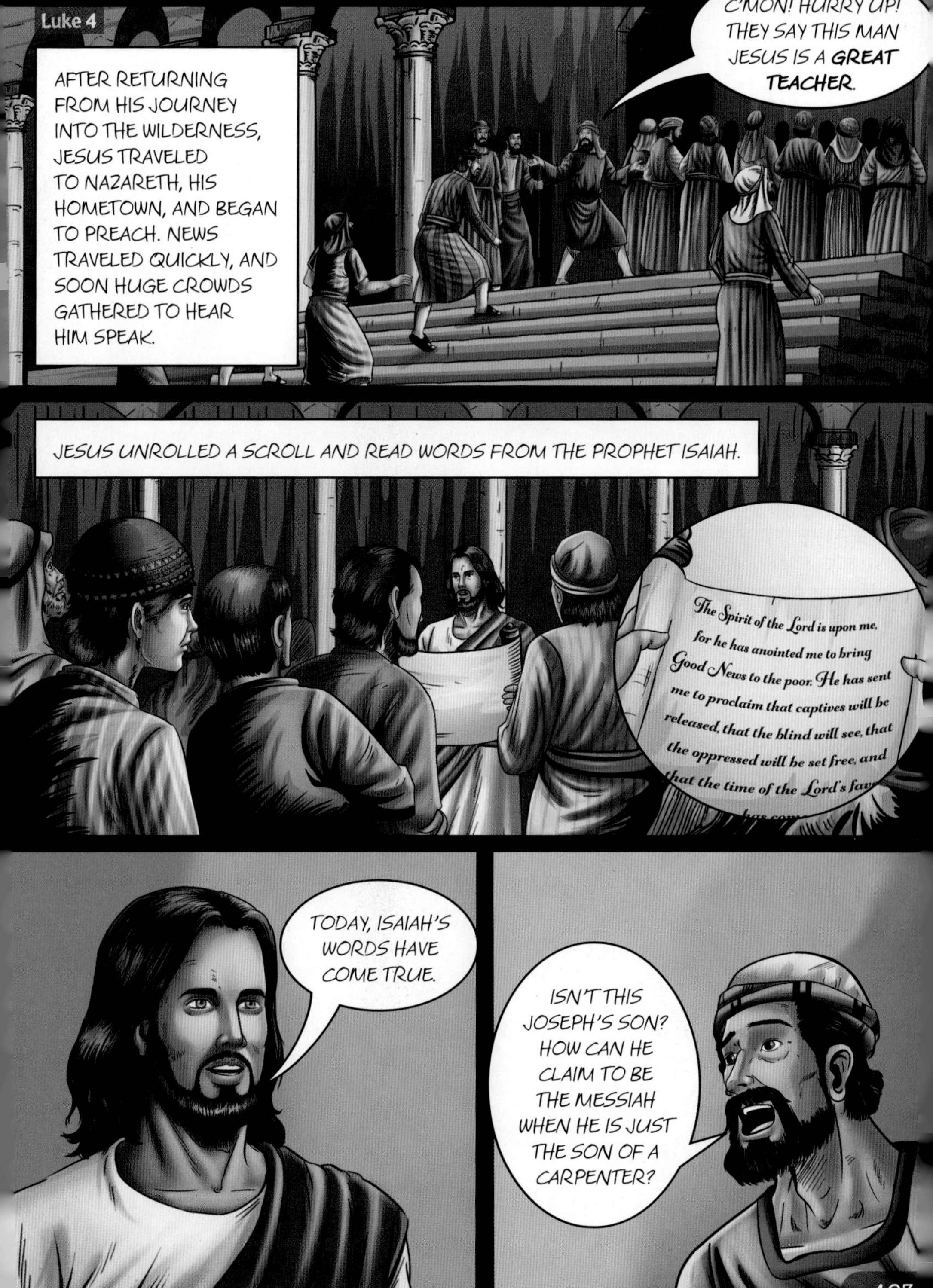

Luke 4

AFTER RETURNING FROM HIS JOURNEY INTO THE WILDERNESS, JESUS TRAVELED TO NAZARETH, HIS HOMETOWN, AND BEGAN TO PREACH. NEWS TRAVELED QUICKLY, AND SOON HUGE CROWDS GATHERED TO HEAR HIM SPEAK.

C'MON! HURRY UP! THEY SAY THIS MAN JESUS IS A **GREAT TEACHER**.

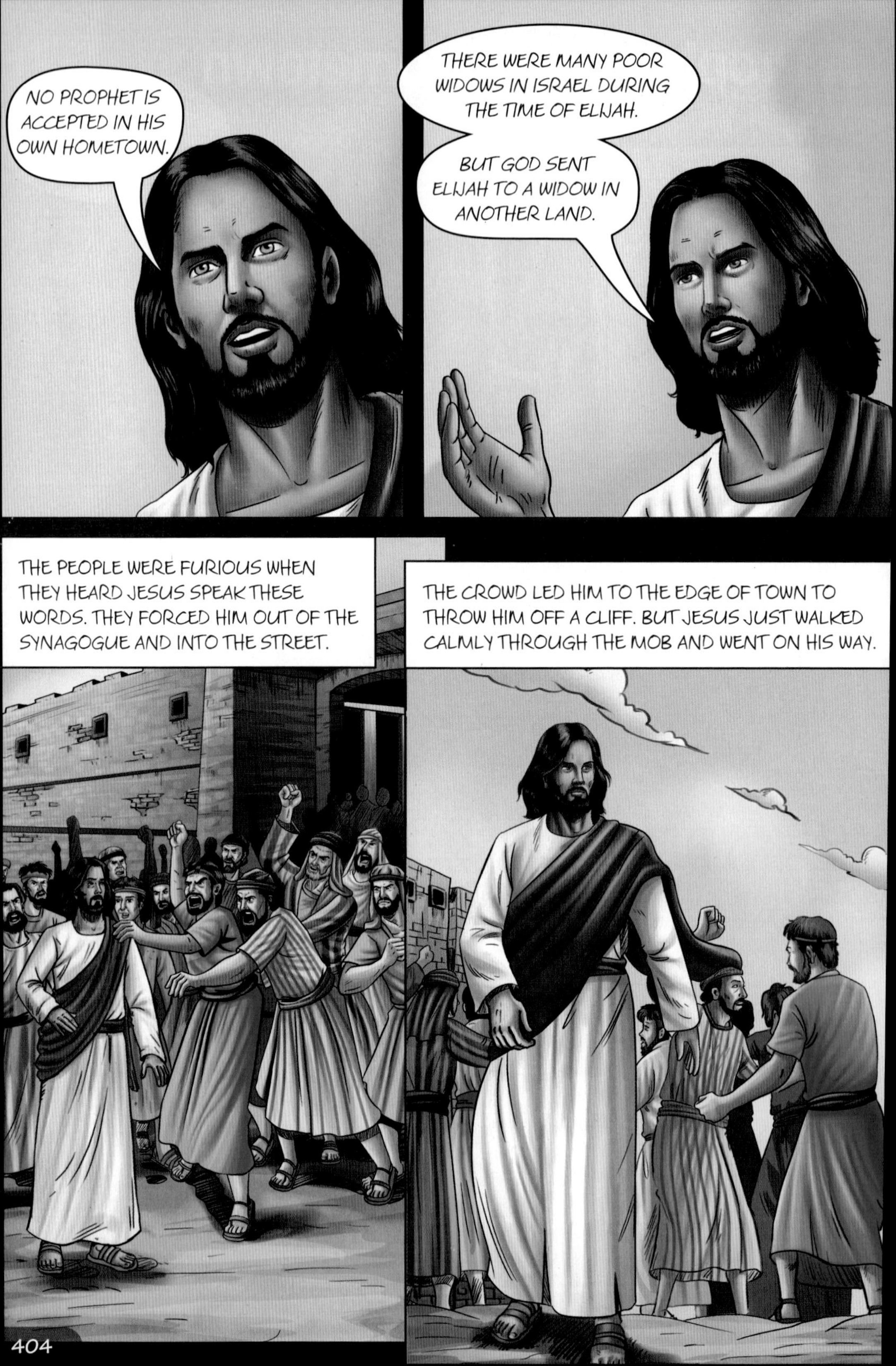

THE PEOPLE WERE FURIOUS WHEN THEY HEARD JESUS SPEAK THESE WORDS. THEY FORCED HIM OUT OF THE SYNAGOGUE AND INTO THE STREET.

THE CROWD LED HIM TO THE EDGE OF TOWN TO THROW HIM OFF A CLIFF. BUT JESUS JUST WALKED CALMLY THROUGH THE MOB AND WENT ON HIS WAY.

Jesus Calls His Disciples
Matthew 4, 9–10; Mark 1–3, 6; Luke 5–6
JESUS LATER SPOKE TO A CROWD OF PEOPLE ON THE BANKS OF THE SEA OF GALILEE.
THERE WERE SO MANY PEOPLE THAT NOT EVERYONE COULD SEE OR HEAR JESUS.
JESUS ASKED ONE OF THE FISHERMEN, A MAN NAMED SIMON, TO TAKE HIM OUT ON HIS BOAT A SHORT WAY SO THAT EVERYONE COULD SEE AND HEAR HIM. THEN HE TAUGHT THE PEOPLE FROM THE BOAT.
WHEN JESUS WAS FINISHED SPEAKING, HE SAID TO SIMON...
SAIL INTO THE DEEPEST PART OF THE LAKE AND LOWER YOUR NETS.
MASTER, WE HAVE BEEN OUT ALL NIGHT.
WE HAVE NOT CAUGHT A SINGLE FISH. BUT IF YOU INSIST...
405

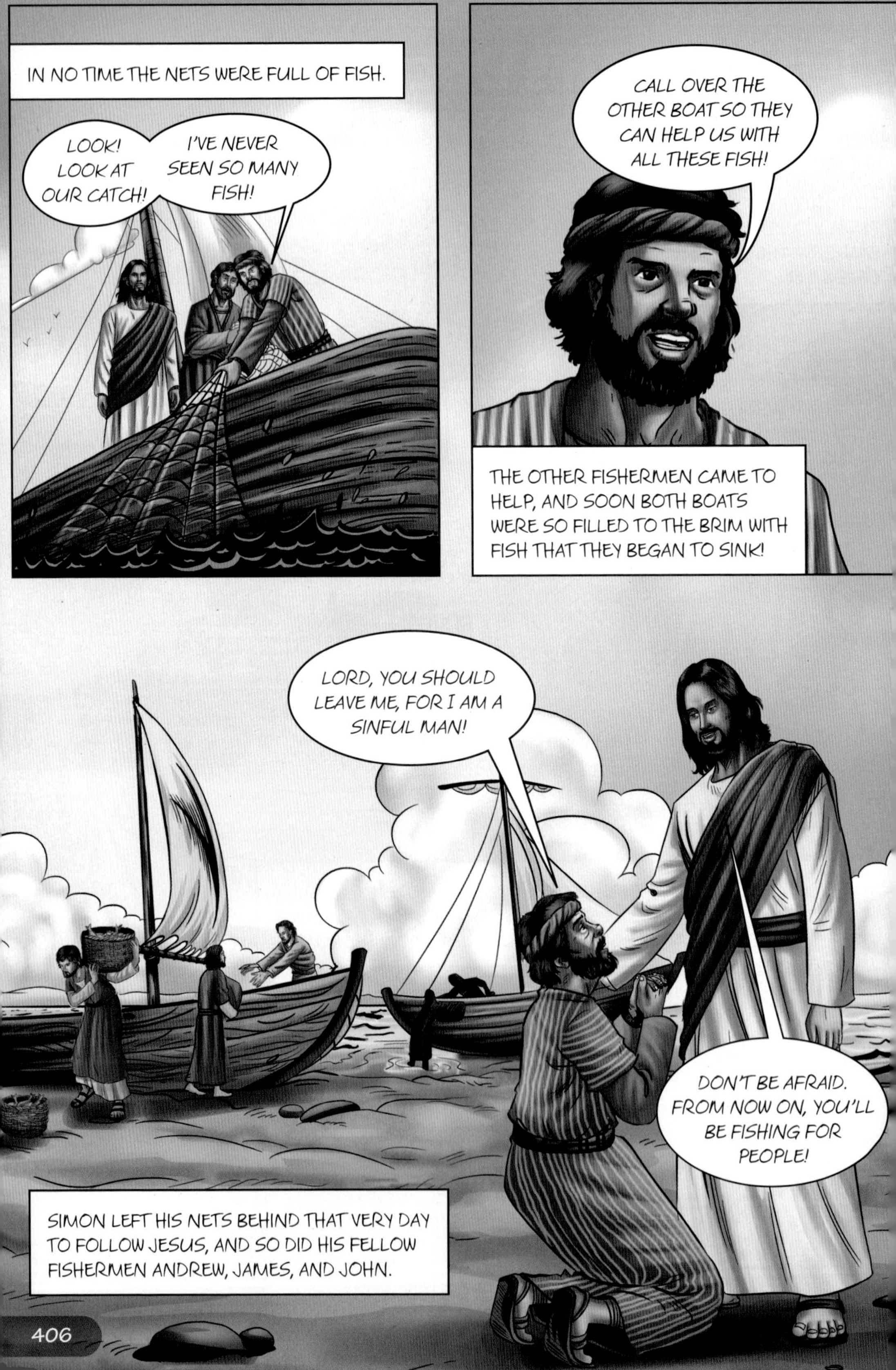

LORD, YOU SHOULD LEAVE ME, FOR I AM A SINFUL MAN!

DON'T BE AFRAID. FROM NOW ON, YOU'LL BE FISHING FOR PEOPLE!

SIMON LEFT HIS NETS BEHIND THAT VERY DAY TO FOLLOW JESUS, AND SO DID HIS FELLOW FISHERMEN ANDREW, JAMES, AND JOHN.

ONE DAY JESUS CAME ACROSS LEVI, A TAX COLLECTOR, WORKING IN HIS TAX BOOTH BY THE HARBOR.
JEWS HATED THE TAX COLLECTORS, WHO WERE ALSO JEWS, BECAUSE THEY WORKED FOR THE ROMANS. THEY OFTEN CHEATED THEIR FELLOW JEWS OUT OF MONEY.
YOU ARE LEVI THE TAX COLLECTOR.
FOLLOW ME AND LEAVE EVERYTHING BEHIND.
I WILL CALL YOU MATTHEW, AND YOU WILL BE **MY DISCIPLE**.
I WILL FOLLOW YOU, LORD.

MATTHEW GAVE A GREAT BANQUET FOR JESUS AND INVITED SEVERAL GUESTS, MANY OF WHOM WERE TAX COLLECTORS.
LEVI, THE MEAL WAS DELICIOUS.
I WANT TO TELL YOU THAT I AM QUITTING MY JOB AND FOLLOWING THIS MAN.
AFTER DINNER, JESUS WALKED OUTSIDE, WHERE A GROUP OF PEOPLE CONFRONTED HIM.
HOW CAN YOU EAT AND DRINK WITH TAX COLLECTORS? THEY ARE **SINNERS!**
HEALTHY PEOPLE DON'T NEED A DOCTOR. SICK PEOPLE DO.
I HAVE COME TO CALL THOSE WHO KNOW THEY ARE SINNERS.

ONE NIGHT JESUS WENT UP TO THE TOP OF A MOUNTAIN TO PRAY. WHEN HE CAME DOWN, HE ASSEMBLED THE MEN WHO BECAME HIS APOSTLES. THEY AGREED TO TRAVEL WITH HIM AND HELP SPREAD THE WORD OF GOD.

MANY PEOPLE BECAME DISCIPLES, OR FOLLOWERS, OF JESUS. HE CHOSE TWELVE OF THEM TO BE HIS APOSTLES. THESE MEN CAME FROM EVERY WALK OF LIFE. TWO OF THE TWELVE—MATTHEW AND JOHN—EACH WROTE A GOSPEL, A RECORDING OF JESUS' TEACHINGS AND THE EVENTS IN HIS LIFE. THE GOSPELS WERE NOT MEANT TO BE MOMENT-BY-MOMENT ACCOUNTS OF JESUS' LIFE. IN FACT, JOHN WROTE, "JESUS ALSO DID MANY OTHER THINGS. IF THEY WERE ALL WRITTEN DOWN...THE WHOLE WORLD COULD NOT CONTAIN THE BOOKS THAT WOULD BE WRITTEN." TWO OTHERS ALSO WROTE GOSPELS: LUKE, A DOCTOR, AND A YOUNG MAN NAMED MARK, WHO IS BELIEVED TO HAVE BEEN A COMPANION AND INTERPRETER OF THE DISCIPLE PETER.

Simon Peter

SIMON WAS A FISHERMAN WHO JESUS NAMED PETER. HE WAS MARRIED. PETER WAS BORN IN GALILEE. HIS FATHER'S NAME WAS JOHN. REFERRING TO PETER, JESUS SAID, "UPON THIS ROCK I WILL BUILD MY CHURCH." IN GREEK, PETER'S NAME WAS "PETROS," AND THE WORD FOR "ROCK" IN GREEK IS "PETRA."

James the Greater
JAMES THE GREATER WAS THE SON OF ZEBEDEE AND SALOME. HE WAS THE BROTHER OF ANOTHER DISCIPLE, JOHN. FISHERMEN BY TRADE, HE AND JOHN WERE SEEMINGLY NEVER APART.
Andrew
ANDREW WAS PETER'S BROTHER. HE WAS ORIGINALLY A DISCIPLE OF JOHN THE BAPTIST, AND ACCORDING TO SOME ACCOUNTS, HE INTRODUCED PETER TO JESUS.
John
JOHN WAS A FISHERMAN FROM GALILEE AND WAS POSSIBLY THE YOUNGER BROTHER OF JAMES THE GREATER. A MEMBER OF JESUS' INNER CIRCLE, JOHN WAS "THE DISCIPLE JESUS LOVED." MANY BELIEVE HE WROTE ONE OF THE GOSPELS, ALTHOUGH SOME EXPERTS DISPUTE THIS. SOME SCHOLARS BELIEVE THE NEW TESTAMENT REFERS TO THREE SEPARATE JOHNS: JOHN THE APOSTLE, JOHN THE EVANGELIST, AND JOHN OF PATMOS (TO WHOM THE BOOK OF REVELATION IS TRADITIONALLY ATTRIBUTED).

Simon the Zealot
NOT MUCH IS KNOWN ABOUT SIMON, ONLY THAT HE WAS A ZEALOT—A FANATIC WHO HATED THE RULING ROMANS.

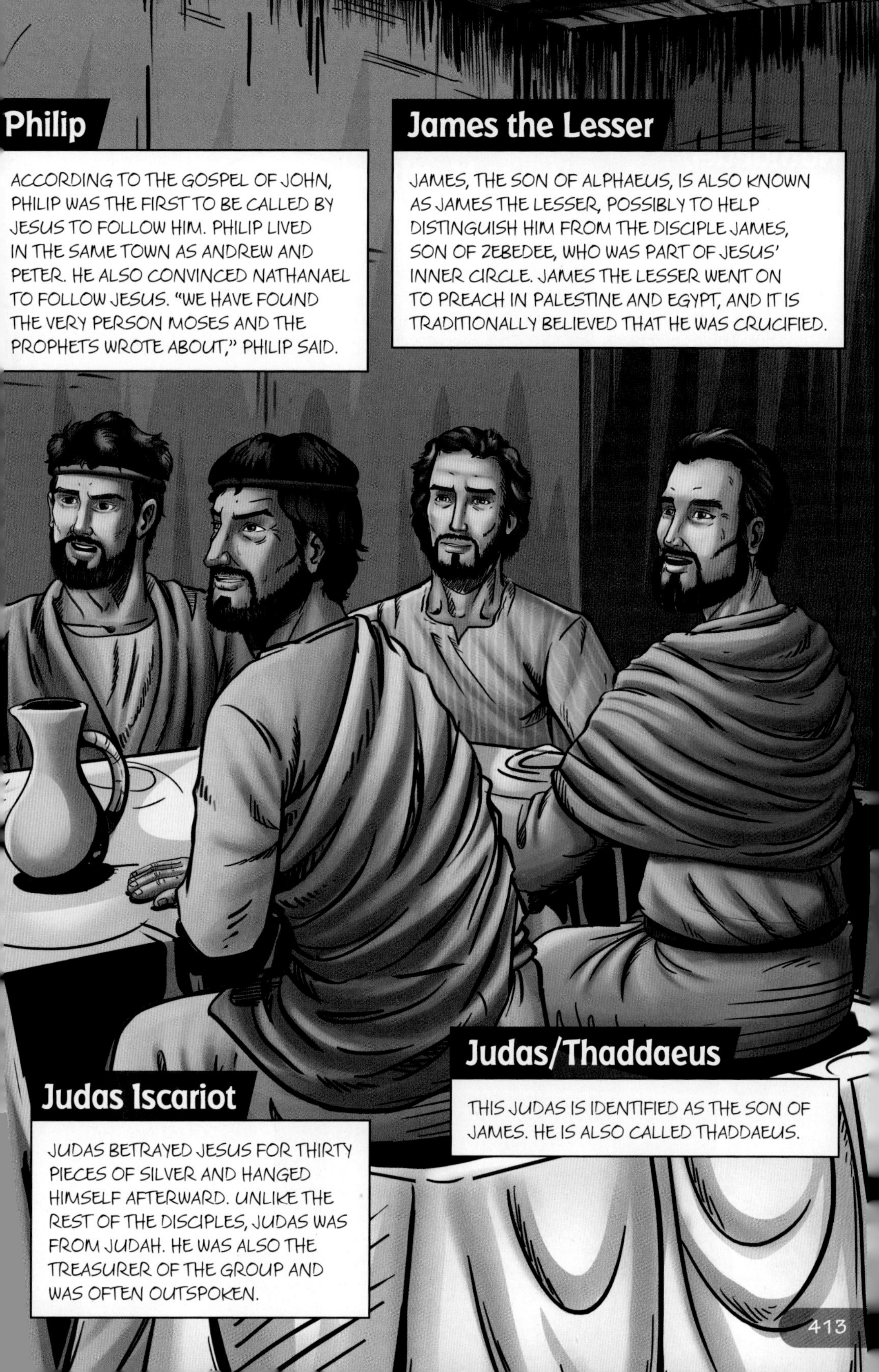
Philip
ACCORDING TO THE GOSPEL OF JOHN, PHILIP WAS THE FIRST TO BE CALLED BY JESUS TO FOLLOW HIM. PHILIP LIVED IN THE SAME TOWN AS ANDREW AND PETER. HE ALSO CONVINCED NATHANAEL TO FOLLOW JESUS. "WE HAVE FOUND THE VERY PERSON MOSES AND THE PROPHETS WROTE ABOUT," PHILIP SAID.
James the Lesser
JAMES, THE SON OF ALPHAEUS, IS ALSO KNOWN AS JAMES THE LESSER, POSSIBLY TO HELP DISTINGUISH HIM FROM THE DISCIPLE JAMES, SON OF ZEBEDEE, WHO WAS PART OF JESUS' INNER CIRCLE. JAMES THE LESSER WENT ON TO PREACH IN PALESTINE AND EGYPT, AND IT IS TRADITIONALLY BELIEVED THAT HE WAS CRUCIFIED.
Judas/Thaddaeus
THIS JUDAS IS IDENTIFIED AS THE SON OF JAMES. HE IS ALSO CALLED THADDAEUS.
Judas Iscariot
JUDAS BETRAYED JESUS FOR THIRTY PIECES OF SILVER AND HANGED HIMSELF AFTERWARD. UNLIKE THE REST OF THE DISCIPLES, JUDAS WAS FROM JUDAH. HE WAS ALSO THE TREASURER OF THE GROUP AND WAS OFTEN OUTSPOKEN.

Nathanael/
Bartholomew
SCRIPTURE DOESN'T SAY MUCH ABOUT NATHANAEL, ALSO KNOWN AS BARTHOLOMEW. HE PREACHED THE GOSPEL IN MANY COUNTRIES, INCLUDING INDIA AND ARMENIA.
Matthew
MATTHEW'S ORIGINAL NAME WAS LEVI. HIS GOSPEL IS THE FIRST BOOK IN THE NEW TESTAMENT. MATTHEW WAS A TAX COLLECTOR, ONE OF THE MOST HATED PROFESSIONS IN THE JEWISH WORLD. AT THE TIME, MOST JEWS BELIEVED THAT ONLY GOD SHOULD BE PAID TRIBUTE.
Thomas
THOMAS SAID HE WAS WILLING TO DIE WITH JESUS. HOWEVER, HIS GREATEST CLAIM TO FAME WAS DOUBTING THAT JESUS HAD RISEN FROM THE DEAD. ONLY WHEN HE TOUCHED JESUS' WOUNDS WAS THOMAS CONVINCED.

Water into Wine
John 2
IN CANA OF GALILEE THERE WAS A WEDDING. PEOPLE CAME FROM ALL OVER TO CELEBRATE.
THIS IS A FINE FEAST, HUSBAND.
THE GUESTS SEEM TO BE HAVING A GOOD TIME.
JESUS AND HIS DISCIPLES WERE INVITED TO THE FEAST, AS WAS JESUS' MOTHER, MARY.
DURING THE CELEBRATION THE WINE RAN OUT.
WE'VE RUN OUT OF WINE! THE WEDDING WILL BE RUINED IF WE DON'T DO SOMETHING!

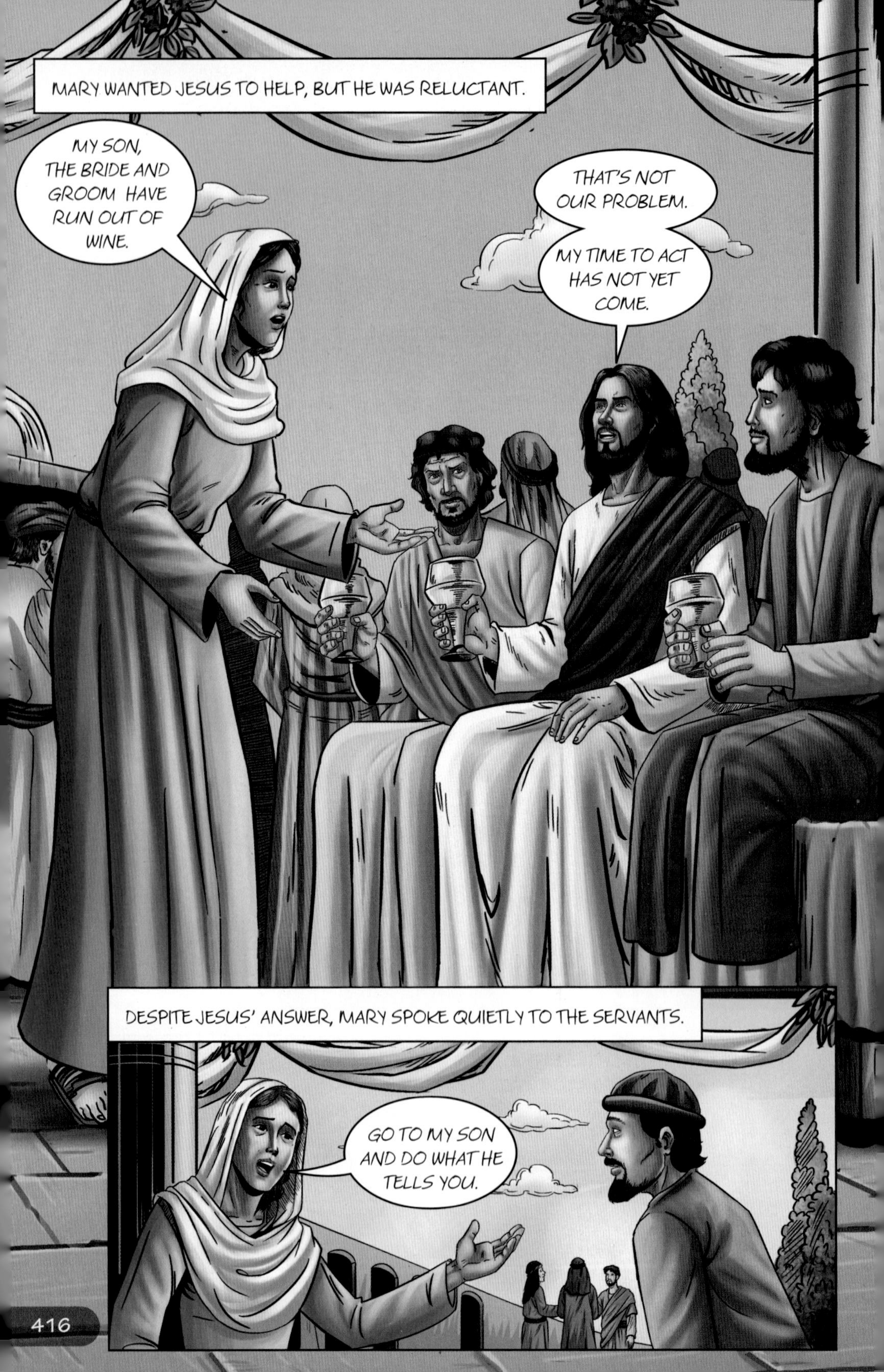
MARY WANTED JESUS TO HELP, BUT HE WAS RELUCTANT.
MY SON, THE BRIDE AND GROOM HAVE RUN OUT OF WINE.
THAT'S NOT OUR PROBLEM.
MY TIME TO ACT HAS NOT YET COME.
DESPITE JESUS' ANSWER, MARY SPOKE QUIETLY TO THE SERVANTS.
GO TO MY SON AND DO WHAT HE TELLS YOU.

THE SERVANTS DID AS MARY ASKED. NEARBY WERE SIX STONE JARS THAT PEOPLE USED TO WASH THEMSELVES DURING CEREMONIES. EACH JAR HELD PERHAPS 20 TO 30 GALLONS OF WATER.
FILL THE JARS WITH WATER.
DIP SOME OUT, AND TAKE IT TO THE MASTER OF CEREMONIES.
THE SERVANTS DID WHAT JESUS WANTED.

THE SERVANTS OFFERED WINE TO THE MASTER OF CEREMONIES. HE TOOK A SIP AND WAS AMAZED.
DURING ALL WEDDINGS, THE GOOD WINE IS SERVED FIRST.
BY THE END OF THE WEDDING, ONLY THE CHEAPER WINE IS LEFT.
BUT YOU HAVE KEPT THE BEST WINE UNTIL NOW.
THIS WAS THE FIRST OF MANY MIRACLES THAT JESUS WOULD PERFORM. HIS DISCIPLES PLACED THEIR TRUST IN HIM.

The Samaritan Woman

John 4

IF YOU ONLY KNEW THE GIFT GOD HAS FOR YOU AND WHO YOU ARE SPEAKING TO, YOU WOULD ASK ME, AND I WOULD GIVE YOU LIVING WATER.

BUT YOU DON'T EVEN HAVE A BUCKET, AND THE WELL IS SO DEEP! WHERE WOULD YOU GET THIS WATER?

ALL WHO DRINK FROM THIS WELL WILL BE THIRSTY AGAIN...
...BUT THOSE WHO DRINK THE WATER THAT I GIVE THEM WILL NEVER BE THIRSTY AGAIN. THE WATER I GIVE IS THE WATER OF **ETERNAL LIFE!**

SIR, GIVE ME THIS WATER, SO THAT I MAY NOT BE THIRSTY.
I KNOW THE MESSIAH IS COMING. WHEN HE COMES, HE WILL TELL US EVERYTHING.
I AM THE MESSIAH!
THE WOMAN LEFT HER WATER JAR AND WENT INTO TOWN TO TELL PEOPLE ABOUT JESUS.
COME SEE THE MAN I HAVE MET. I BELIEVE HE IS THE MESSIAH!
JESUS STAYED IN THE TOWN FOR TWO DAYS, AND MANY PEOPLE CAME TO BELIEVE IN HIM.

Matthew 8; Mark 1; Luke 5

IN JESUS' TIME, THE DISEASE OF LEPROSY WAS BELIEVED TO BE A CURSE FROM GOD. THE DISEASE DISFIGURED PEOPLE'S FACES AND LIMBS.

PEOPLE FEARED AND SCORNED THOSE WITH LEPROSY.

LOOK AT THE LEPER. SOON HIS NOSE WILL FALL OFF!

YOU ARE **CURSED**. GO SOMEWHERE ELSE!

ONE DAY JESUS AND HIS DISCIPLES PASSED BY A MAN WITH LEPROSY.

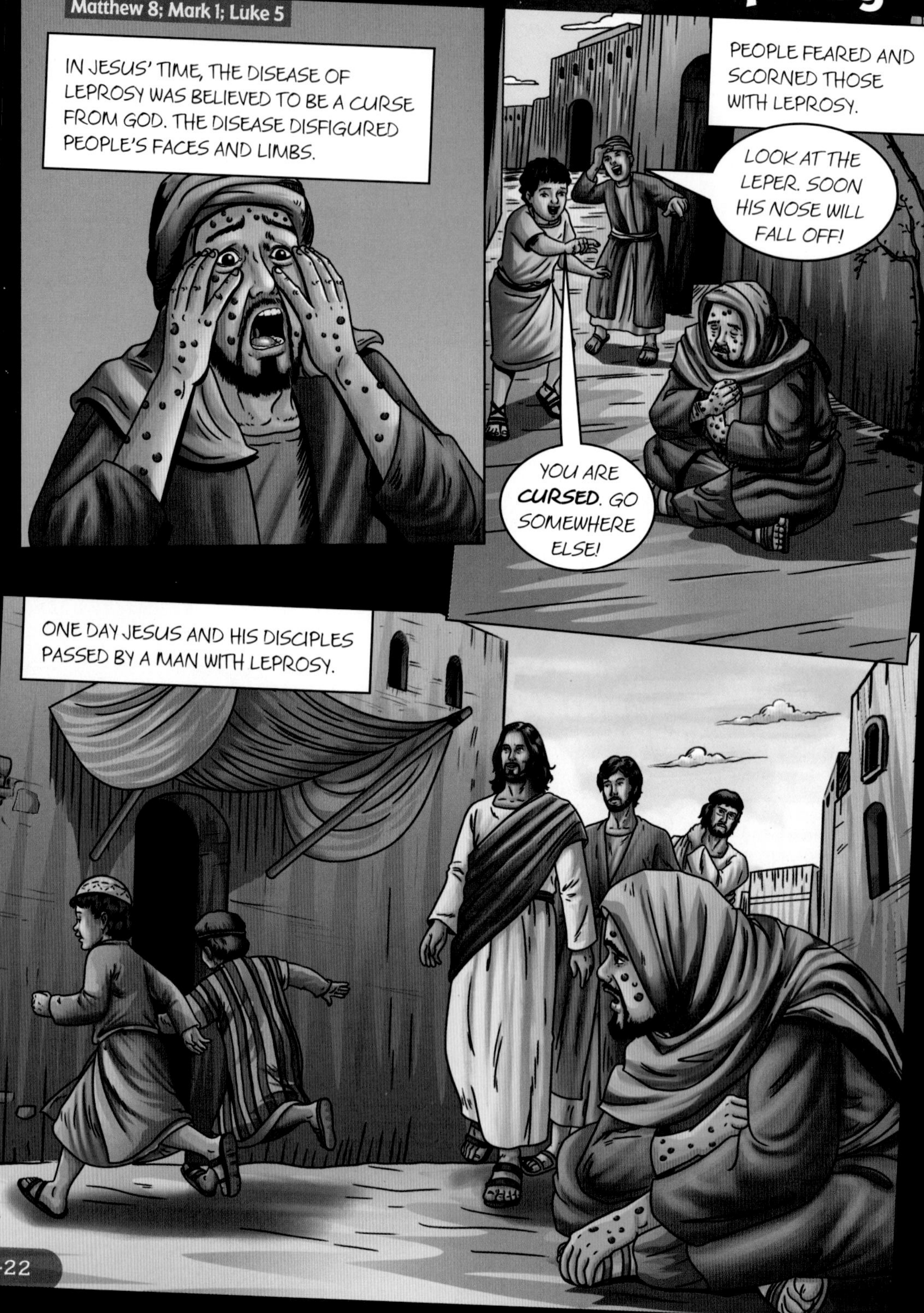

THE LEPER LOOKED AT JESUS AND PLEADED FOR HELP.
IF YOU WISH, YOU CAN MAKE ME CLEAN.
OF COURSE I WILL HEAL YOU. BE MADE CLEAN.
THE CURSE IS GONE. I AM CLEAN! I AM CLEAN!

DO NOT TELL ANYONE WHAT I DID.
INSTEAD, SHOW YOURSELF TO THE PRIEST AND MAKE AN OFFERING JUST AS MOSES INSTRUCTED.
BUT THE MAN SIMPLY COULD NOT KEEP THE WONDERFUL NEWS TO HIMSELF. HE TOLD EVERYONE HE SAW ABOUT THE MIRACLE.
JESUS CLEANSED ME!
GOD HAS SMILED ON ME!
WORD SPREAD QUICKLY. IT WAS IMPOSSIBLE FOR JESUS TO ENTER A TOWN WITHOUT A CROWD GATHERING AROUND HIM. EVEN WHEN HE FOUND A DESERTED PLACE TO BE ALONE, PEOPLE FLOCKED TO SEE HIM.

The Roman Officer
Matthew 8; Luke 7
JESUS ENTERED CAPERNAUM, A TOWN NEAR NAZARETH. A ROMAN OFFICER CAME TO SEE JESUS. HE WAS A FRIEND OF THE JEWS. HE HELPED THEM BUILD THE SYNAGOGUE.
LORD, MY SERVANT IS LYING AT HOME, PARALYZED, SUFFERING DREADFULLY. CAN YOU HELP HIM?
I WILL COME AND HEAL HIM.

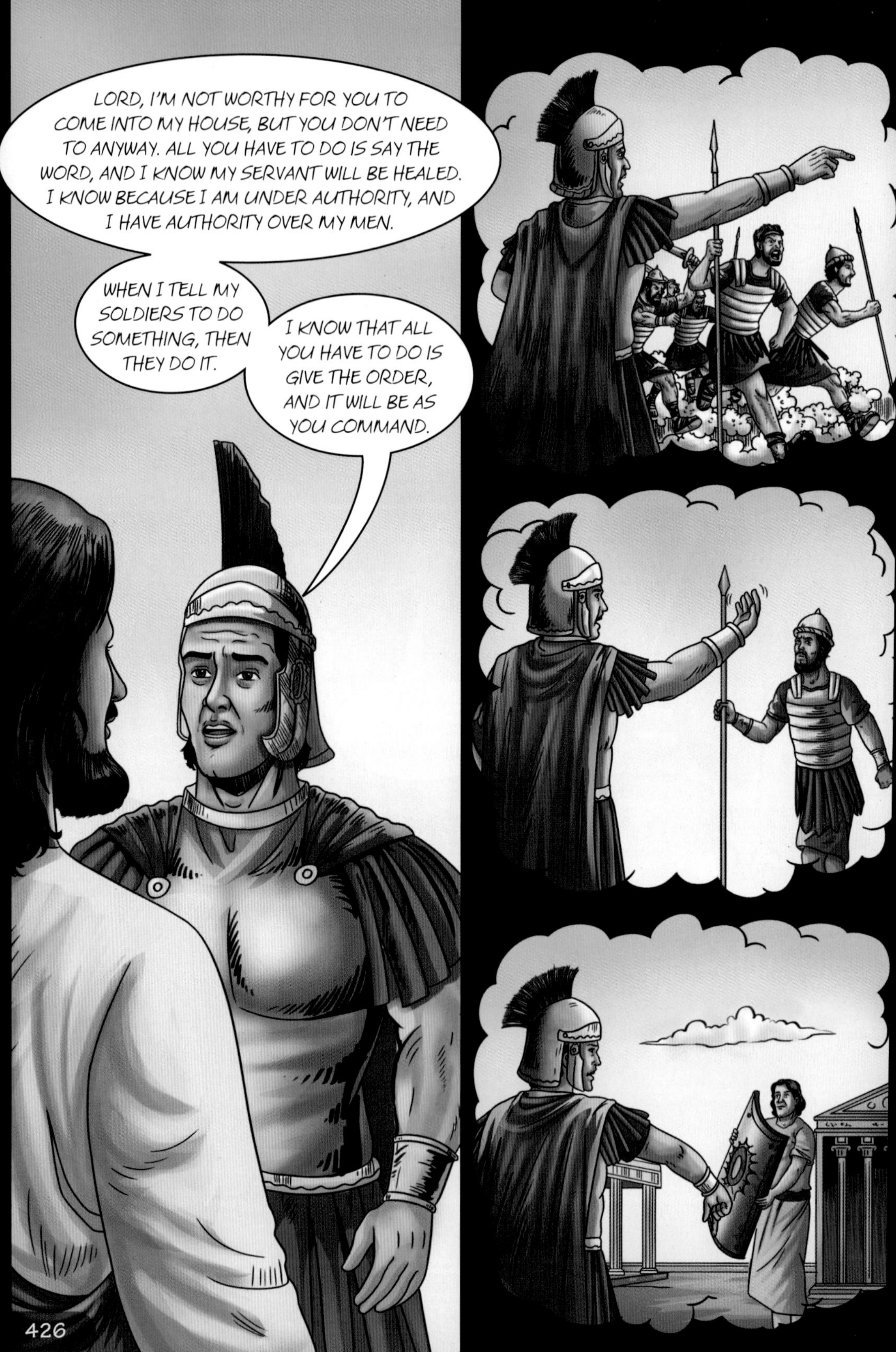
LORD, I'M NOT WORTHY FOR YOU TO COME INTO MY HOUSE, BUT YOU DON'T NEED TO ANYWAY. ALL YOU HAVE TO DO IS SAY THE WORD, AND I KNOW MY SERVANT WILL BE HEALED. I KNOW BECAUSE I AM UNDER AUTHORITY, AND I HAVE AUTHORITY OVER MY MEN.
WHEN I TELL MY SOLDIERS TO DO SOMETHING, THEN THEY DO IT.
I KNOW THAT ALL YOU HAVE TO DO IS GIVE THE ORDER, AND IT WILL BE AS YOU COMMAND.

JESUS LISTENED TO THE OFFICER AND WAS AMAZED AT THE MAN'S FAITH. HE SPOKE TO THE CROWD THAT HAD GATHERED.
I TELL YOU, I HAVE NOT SEEN FAITH LIKE THIS IN ALL ISRAEL!
GO BACK HOME. BECAUSE YOU BELIEVED, IT HAS HAPPENED.
THE OFFICER DID AS JESUS SAID. WHEN THE OFFICER RETURNED HOME, HIS SERVANT WAS HEALED.

Sermon on the Mount

Matthew 5–7; Luke 6, 11

GOD BLESSES THOSE WHO HUNGER AND THIRST FOR **JUSTICE,** FOR THEY WILL BE SATISFIED.
GOD BLESSES THOSE WHO ARE **MERCIFUL,** FOR THEY WILL BE SHOWN MERCY.
GOD BLESSES THOSE WHOSE HEARTS ARE **PURE,** FOR THEY WILL SEE GOD.
GOD BLESSES THOSE WHO WORK FOR **PEACE,** FOR THEY WILL BE CALLED CHILDREN OF GOD.

GOD BLESSES THOSE WHO ARE PERSECUTED FOR DOING RIGHT...
...FOR THE KINGDOM OF HEAVEN IS THEIRS.

YOU ARE THE SALT OF THE EARTH AND THE LIGHT OF THE WORLD.
LET YOUR GOOD DEEDS SHINE OUT FOR ALL TO SEE, SO THAT EVERYONE WILL PRAISE YOUR HEAVENLY FATHER.
I DID NOT COME TO ABOLISH THE LAW OF MOSES OR THE WRITINGS OF THE PROPHETS. I CAME TO ACCOMPLISH THEIR PURPOSE.

HOW COULD YOU DO THIS TO ME?
OUR ANCESTORS WERE TOLD, "YOU MUST NOT MURDER." BUT I SAY, IF YOU ARE EVEN ANGRY WITH SOMEONE, YOU WILL BE JUDGED!
FORGIVE THAT PERSON WHO HAS MADE YOU ANGRY.
YOU'RE MY FRIEND, MY BROTHER. I FORGIVE YOU.

IF SOMEONE SLAPS YOU ON THE RIGHT CHEEK...
...OFFER THE OTHER CHEEK ALSO.
LOVE YOUR ENEMIES.

DON'T DO GOOD DEEDS SO OTHERS MAY SEE THEM. WHEN YOU GIVE TO SOMEONE IN NEED, DO NOT LET YOUR LEFT HAND KNOW WHAT YOUR RIGHT IS DOING.
WHEN YOU PRAY, DO NOT BE LIKE THE HYPOCRITES WHO PRAY SO THAT OTHERS MAY SEE THEM.
INSTEAD GO AWAY BY YOURSELF, SHUT THE DOOR, AND PRAY TO YOUR FATHER.

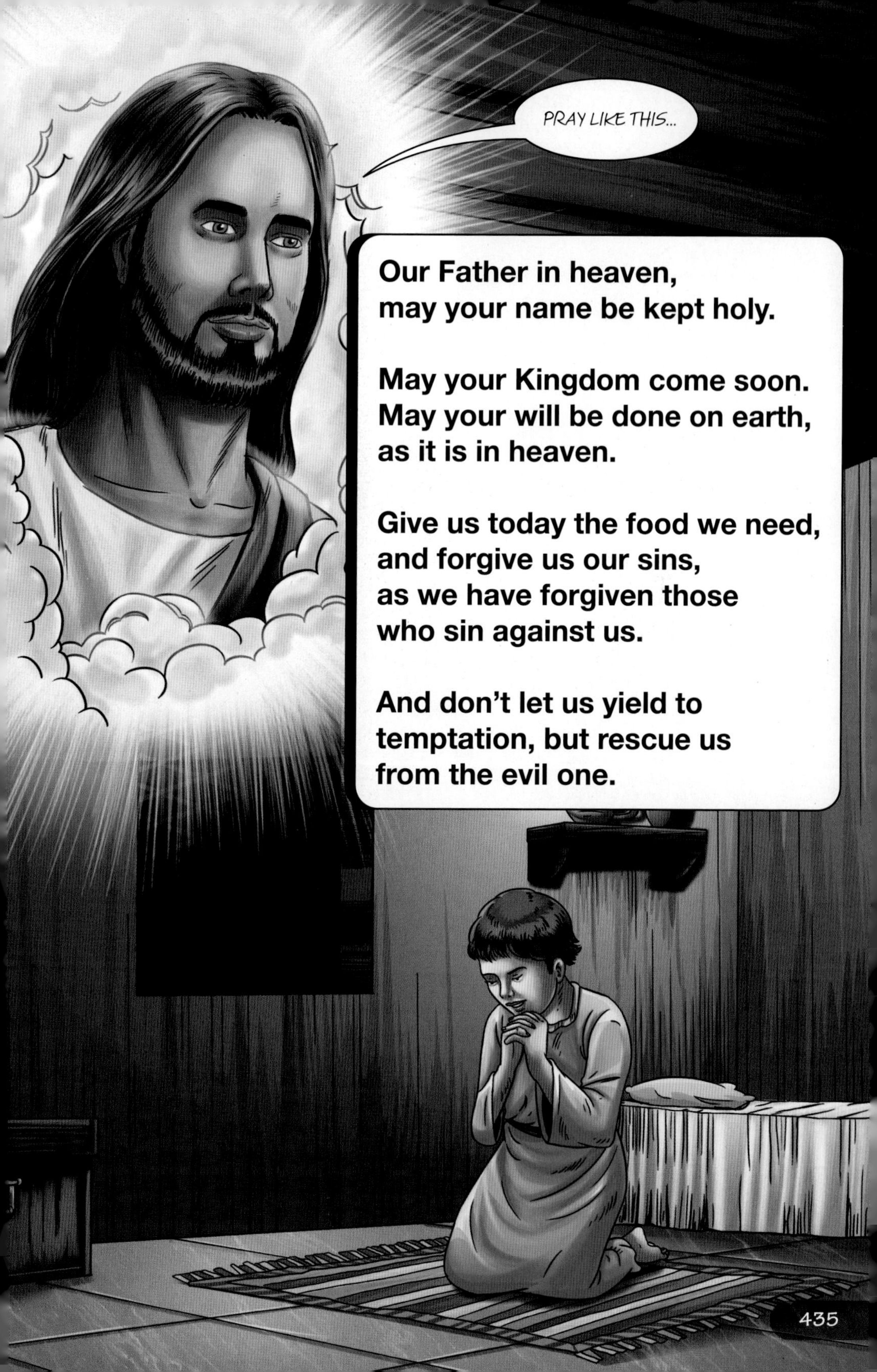
PRAY LIKE THIS...
Our Father in heaven,
may your name be kept holy.
May your Kingdom come soon.
May your will be done on earth,
as it is in heaven.
Give us today the food we need,
and forgive us our sins,
as we have forgiven those
who sin against us.
And don't let us yield to
temptation, but rescue us
from the evil one.

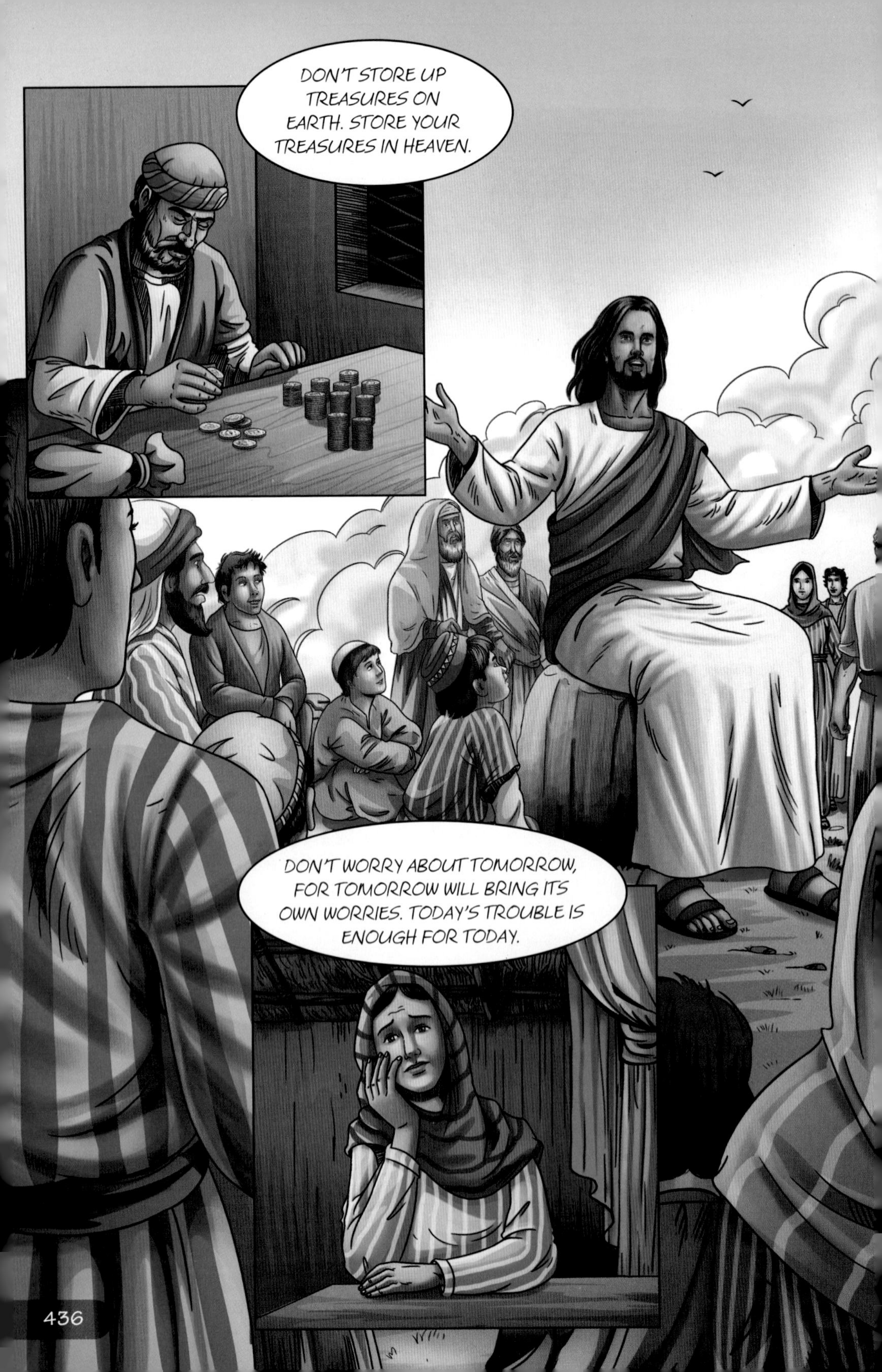
DON'T STORE UP TREASURES ON EARTH. STORE YOUR TREASURES IN HEAVEN.
DON'T WORRY ABOUT TOMORROW, FOR TOMORROW WILL BRING ITS OWN WORRIES. TODAY'S TROUBLE IS ENOUGH FOR TODAY.

STOP JUDGING OTHERS, AND YOU WILL NOT BE JUDGED. TREAT OTHERS AS YOU WOULD HAVE THEM TREAT YOU.
BEWARE OF FALSE PROPHETS WHO COME DISGUISED AS HARMLESS SHEEP. NOT EVERYONE WHO SAYS TO ME, "LORD, LORD" WILL ENTER THE KINGDOM OF HEAVEN. ONLY THOSE WHO DO THE WILL OF MY FATHER IN HEAVEN WILL ENTER.

THEN JESUS SAID, "KEEP ON ASKING, AND YOU WILL RECEIVE WHAT YOU ASK FOR. KEEP ON SEEKING, AND YOU WILL FIND. KEEP ON KNOCKING, AND THE DOOR WILL BE OPENED TO YOU."
ANYONE WHO HEARS THESE WORDS AND PUTS THEM INTO PRACTICE IS LIKE A WISE MAN WHO BUILDS HIS HOUSE ON SOLID ROCK. THE RAIN COMES DOWN, THE FLOODS RISE, AND THE WINDS BEAT AGAINST THAT HOUSE. BUT IT WON'T COLLAPSE BECAUSE IT IS BUILT ON THE ROCK.
BUT ANYONE WHO HEARS THESE WORDS AND DOES NOT OBEY THEM IS LIKE A FOOLISH MAN WHO BUILDS HIS HOUSE ON SAND. THE RAIN COMES DOWN, THE FLOODS RISE, AND THE WINDS BEAT AGAINST THAT HOUSE, AND IT COLLAPSES WITH A GREAT CRASH.
HE FINISHED SPEAKING, AND EVERYONE WAS AMAZED AT HIS WORDS.

Jesus and the Children

Matthew 19; Mark 10; Luke 18

The Parable of the Farmer

Matthew 13; Luke 8

SOME SEEDS FELL AMONG THORNS. BUT THE THORNS GREW AND CHOKED THE PLANT.
SOME SEEDS FELL ON GOOD SOIL AND PRODUCED AN ENORMOUS AMOUNT OF GRAIN.
WHY DO YOU SPEAK TO THE PEOPLE IN PARABLES? SOMETIMES THEY ARE HARD TO UNDERSTAND.
I SPEAK TO THEM IN PARABLES BECAUSE THEY LOOK BUT DO NOT SEE.
THEY LISTEN BUT DO NOT UNDERSTAND.

LISTEN TO THE EXPLANATION OF THE PARABLE ABOUT THE FARMER.
THE SEED ON THE PATH IS LIKE PEOPLE WHO HEAR GOD'S WORD BUT DON'T UNDERSTAND IT. THE DEVIL, THE EVIL ONE, COMES AND TAKES AWAY WHAT WAS PLANTED IN THEIR HEARTS.
THE SEED ON ROCKY SOIL IS LIKE PEOPLE WHO HEAR GOD'S WORD AND RECEIVE IT WITH GREAT JOY. BUT THEIR FAITH HAS NO ROOTS, AND IT LASTS ONLY FOR A SHORT TIME.
THE SEED AMONG THE THORNS IS LIKE PEOPLE WHO HEAR GOD'S WORD, BUT THE WORRIES OF THIS LIFE AND THE LURE OF RICHES CHOKE THEM, AND THEY DON'T BEAR FRUIT.
BUT THE SEED PLANTED IN RICH SOIL IS LIKE PEOPLE WHO HEAR GOD'S WORD, UNDERSTAND IT, AND LET IT GROW AND BEAR FRUIT.

The Parable of Wheat and Weeds

Matthew 13

THE STORY CONFUSED JESUS' DISICIPLES.
PLEASE EXPLAIN WHAT THAT PARABLE MEANS, MASTER.
WE DON'T UNDERSTAND.
JESUS TOLD HIS DISCIPLES, "THE FARMER WHO PLANTS THE SEEDS IS THE SON OF MAN. THE FIELD IS THE WORLD, AND THE SEEDS OF WHEAT ARE THE CHILDREN OF GOD."

THE WEEDS, HOWEVER, ARE THE FOLLOWERS OF THE DEVIL. THE PERSON WHO PLANTS THE WEEDS IS SATAN HIMSELF.
WHEN THE WHEAT GROWS, SO WILL THESE WEEDS. HIS CROPS WILL BE RUINED!
THE HARVEST IS THE END OF TIME, AND THE HARVESTERS ARE ANGELS.
JUST AS THE WEEDS ARE COLLECTED AND BURNED, SO THE SON OF MAN WILL COLLECT THOSE WHO SIN. THE SINNERS WILL BE TOSSED INTO THE FIRE.

The Parable of the Lost Sheep

THE PHARISEES DID NOT LIKE THAT JESUS ASSOCIATED WITH SINNERS.

JESUS HEARD THE PHARISEES TALKING ABOUT HIM. JESUS ASKED WHO AMONG THEM WOULD NOT LEAVE 99 SHEEP IN THE FIELD TO FIND THE ONE SHEEP THAT WAS LOST.

ONCE THE SHEEP WAS FOUND, JESUS SAID, WHO WOULD NOT CALL HIS FRIENDS TO CELEBRATE AND SAY, "I HAVE FOUND MY LOST SHEEP"?

The Parable of the Lost Coin

Luke 15

The Parable of the Good Samaritan

Luke 10

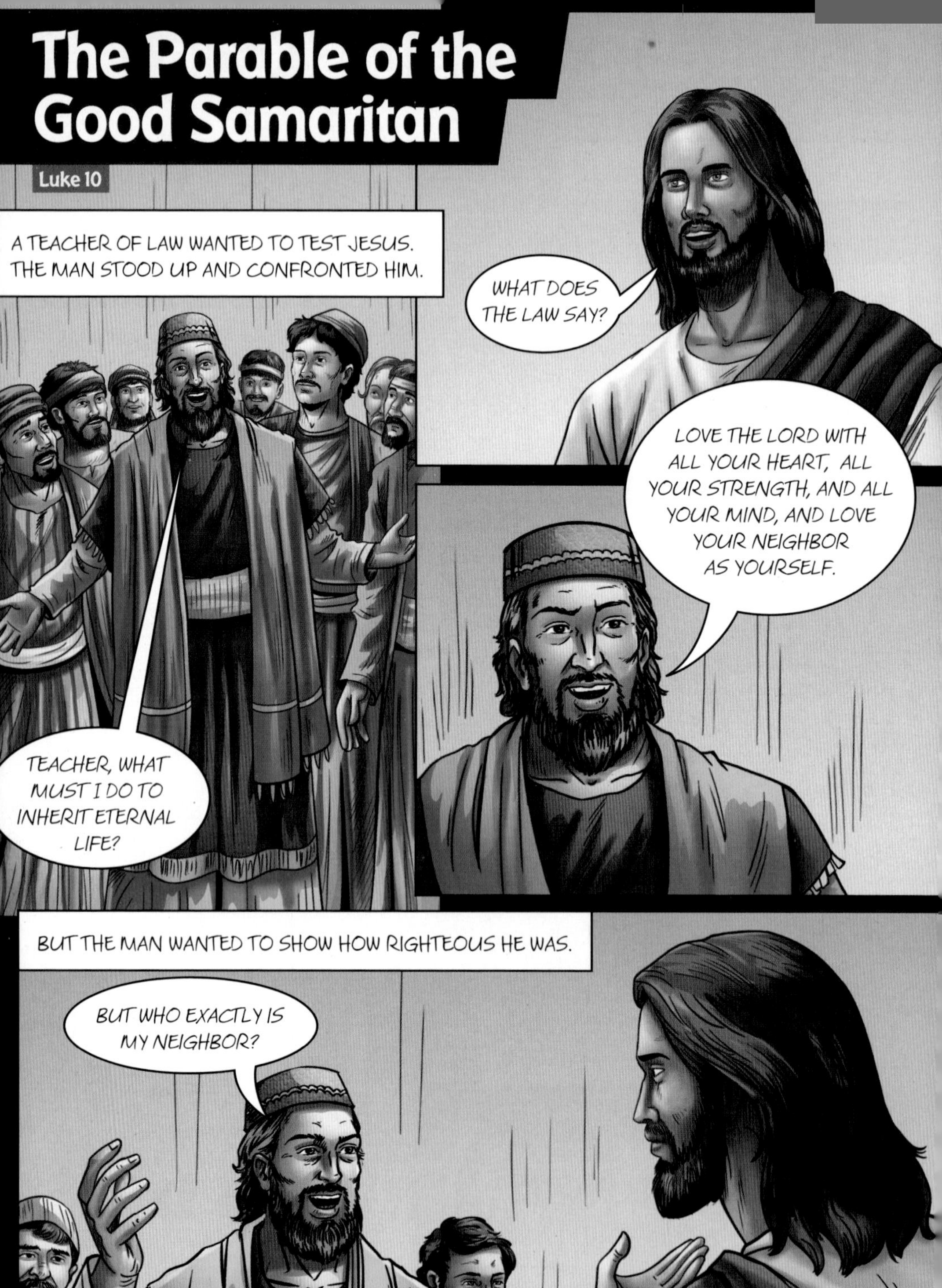

THEN JESUS TOLD THIS PARABLE.
ONCE, A JEWISH MAN WAS TRAVELING FROM JERUSALEM TO JERICHO. AS HE WALKED, A GROUP OF ROBBERS ATTACKED HIM.
THE ROBBERS STRIPPED THE MAN OF HIS CLOTHES...
...AND LEFT HIM ON THE ROAD TO DIE.

A PRIEST WALKED BY, SAW THE MAN, AND DID NOTHING.
A SECOND MAN PASSED THE WOUNDED MAN. HE WAS A LEVITE, WHO WORKED IN THE TEMPLE. HE ALSO DID NOTHING.
A THIRD MAN PASSED BY. HE WAS A SAMARITAN. (SAMARITANS WERE ENEMIES OF THE JEWS.) HE TOOK PITY ON THE STRANGER.

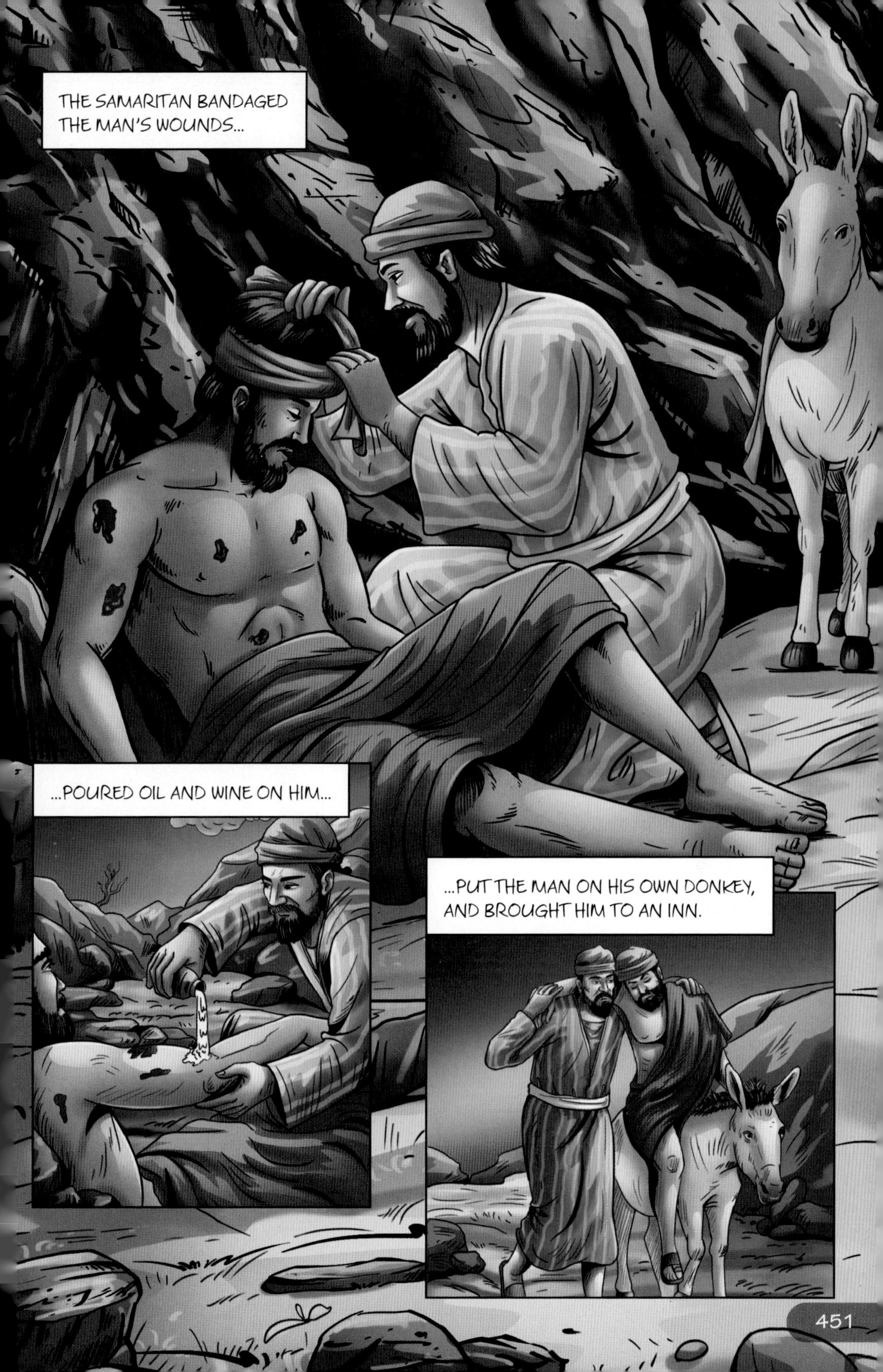
THE SAMARITAN BANDAGED THE MAN'S WOUNDS...
...POURED OIL AND WINE ON HIM...
...PUT THE MAN ON HIS OWN DONKEY, AND BROUGHT HIM TO AN INN.

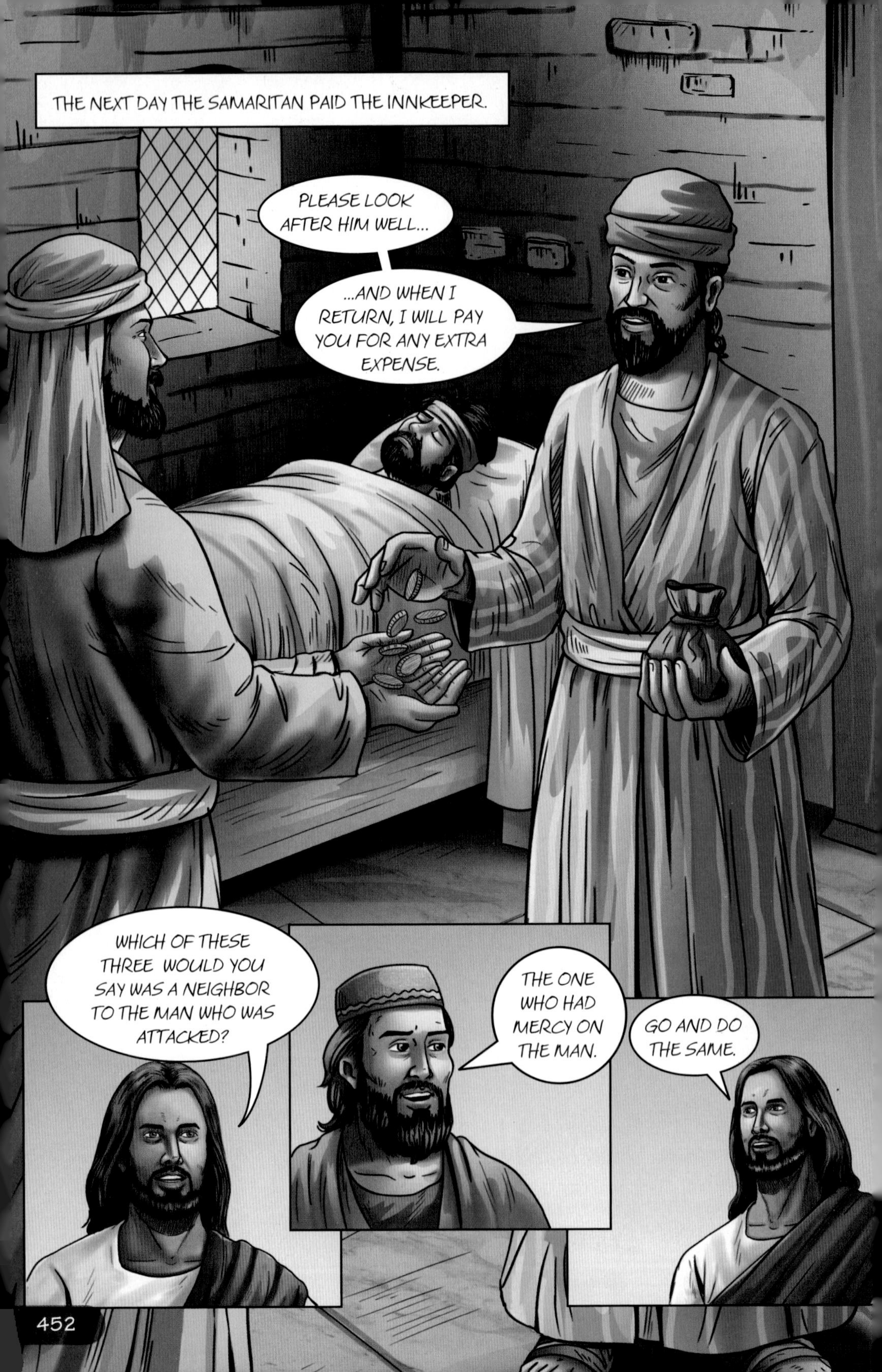
THE NEXT DAY THE SAMARITAN PAID THE INNKEEPER.
PLEASE LOOK AFTER HIM WELL...
...AND WHEN I RETURN, I WILL PAY YOU FOR ANY EXTRA EXPENSE.
WHICH OF THESE THREE WOULD YOU SAY WAS A NEIGHBOR TO THE MAN WHO WAS ATTACKED?
THE ONE WHO HAD MERCY ON THE MAN.
GO AND DO THE SAME.

The Parable of the Wise and Foolish Bridesmaids

Matthew 25

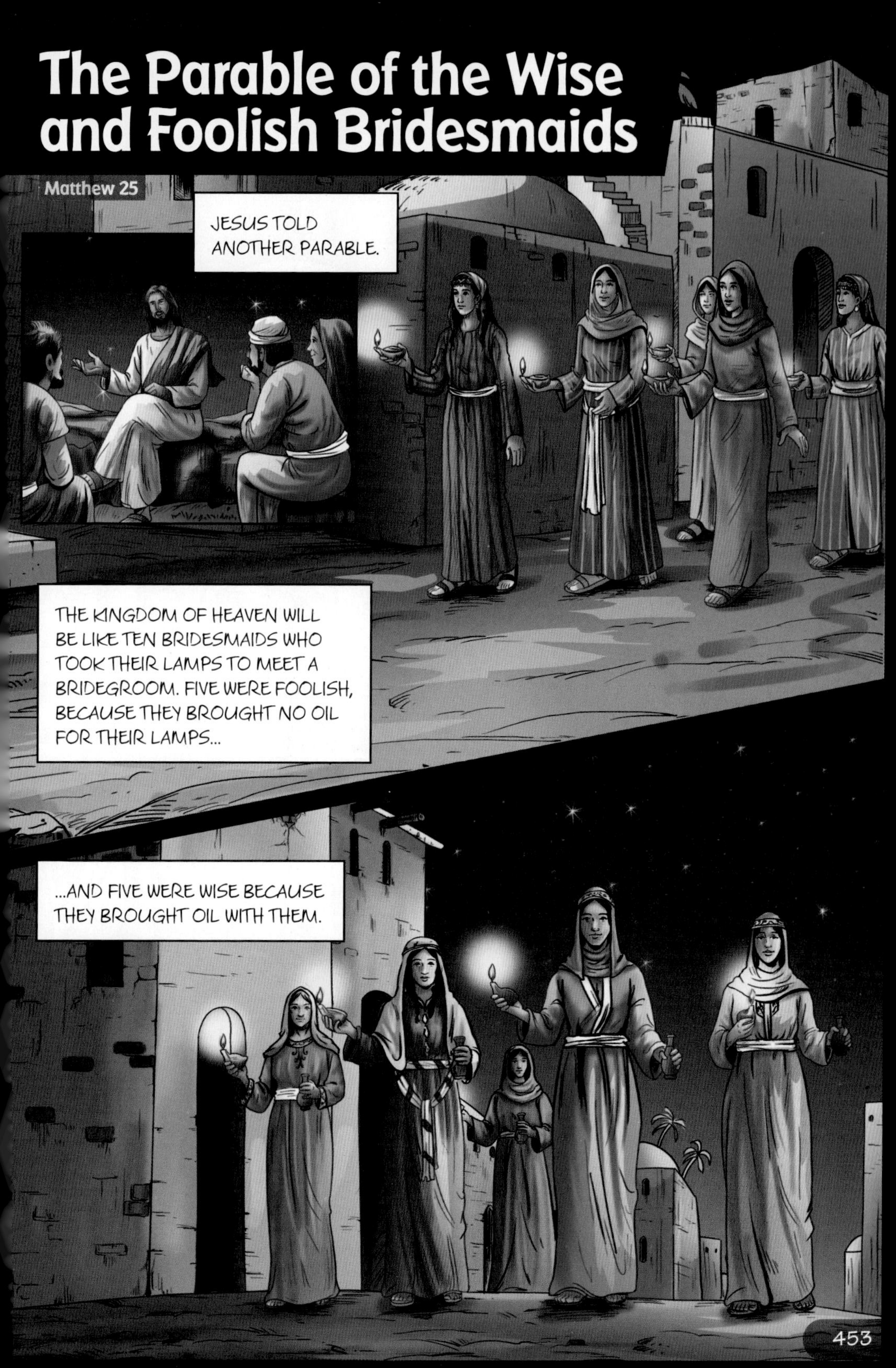

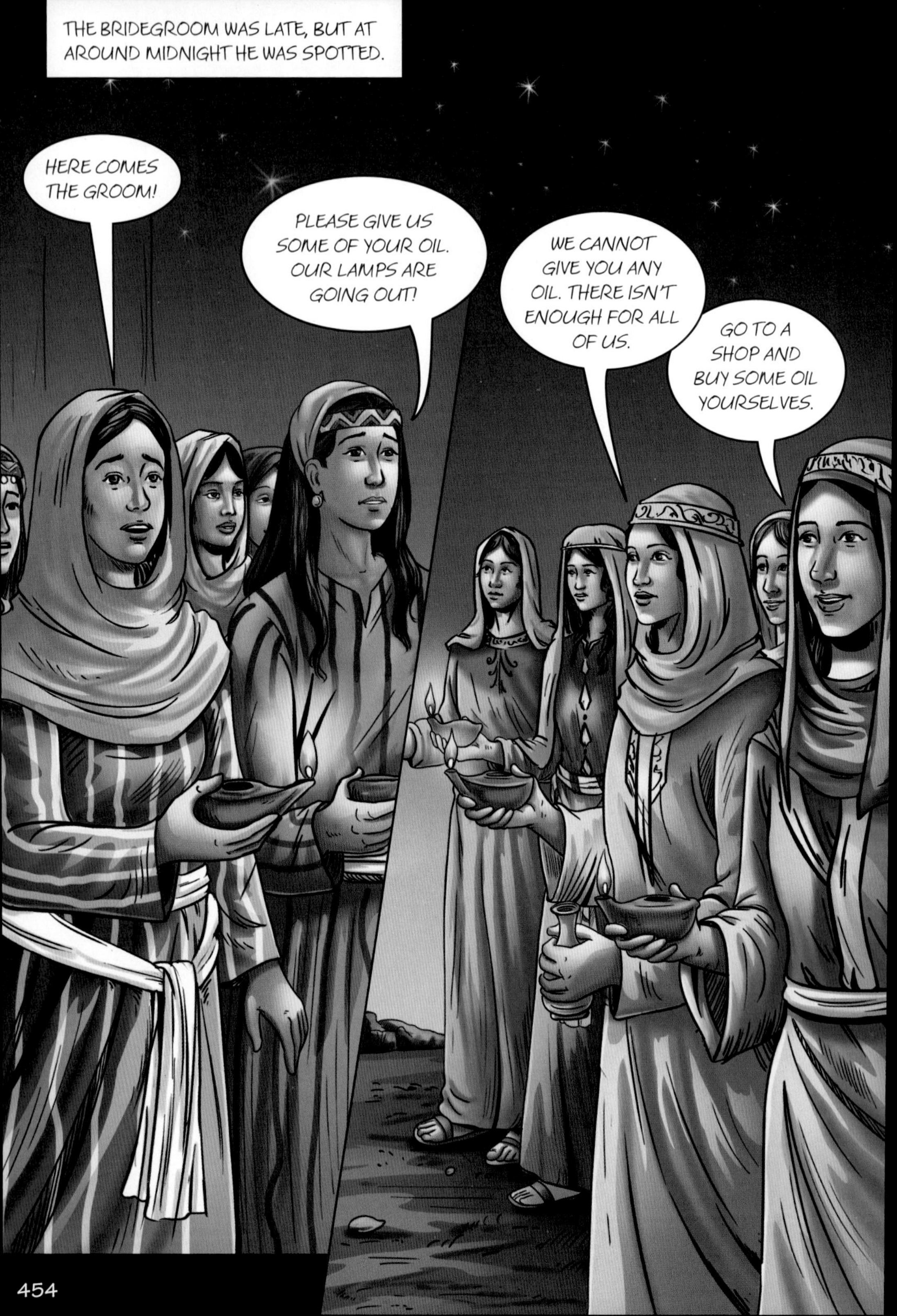

THE BRIDEGROOM WAS LATE, BUT AT AROUND MIDNIGHT HE WAS SPOTTED.

THE BRIDEGROOM FINALLY ARRIVED. THE FIVE WISE GIRLS FOLLOWED HIM INTO THE MARRIAGE FEAST.

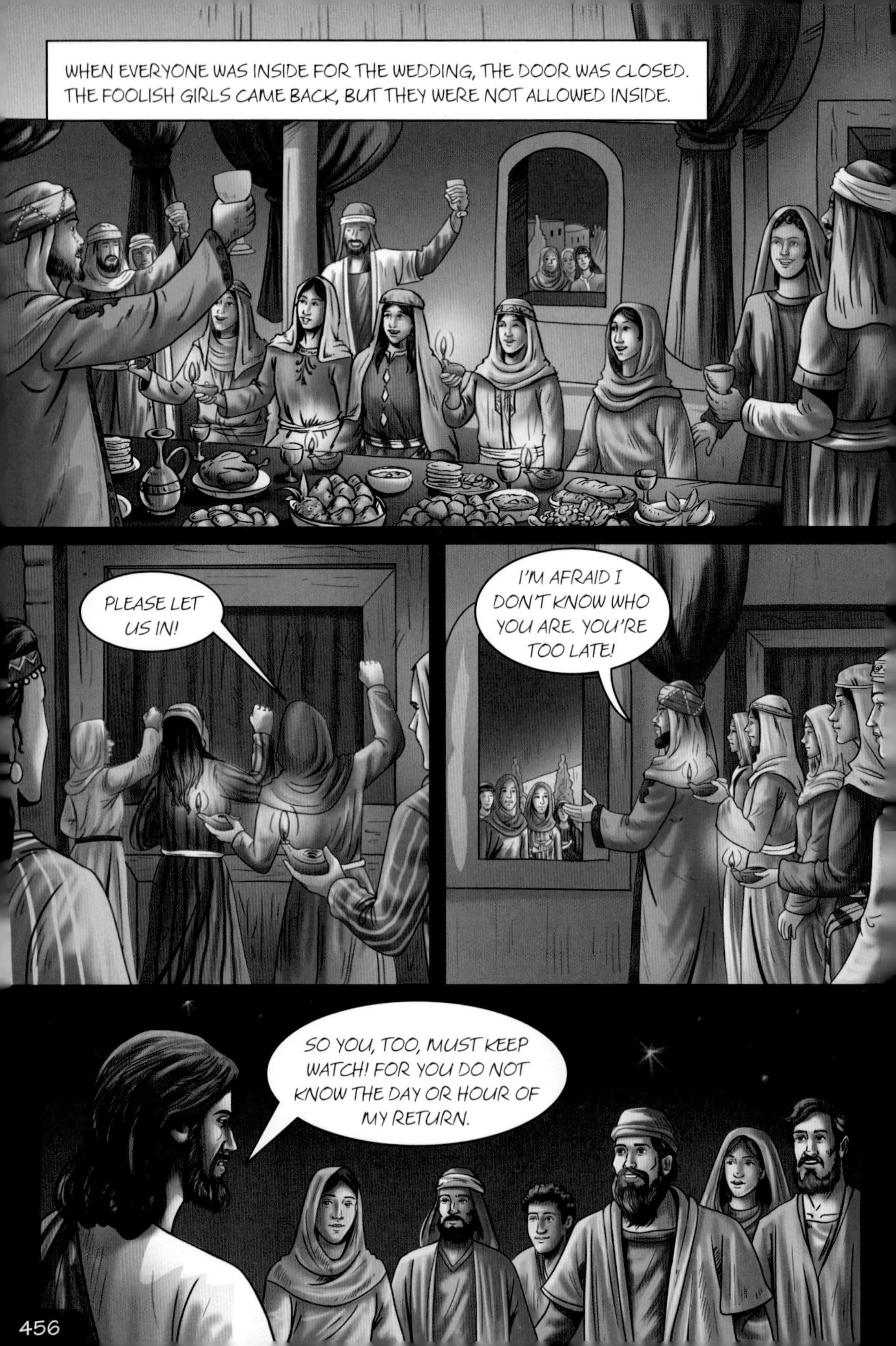

WHEN EVERYONE WAS INSIDE FOR THE WEDDING, THE DOOR WAS CLOSED. THE FOOLISH GIRLS CAME BACK, BUT THEY WERE NOT ALLOWED INSIDE.

The Parable of the Lost Son

Luke 15

JESUS TOLD A STORY OF A MAN WITH TWO SONS.

AFTER A FEW DAYS, THE YOUNGER SON TOOK HIS INHERITANCE AND SET OFF TO A DISTANT COUNTRY.
THE YOUNG MAN HAD A WONDERFUL TIME. HE SPENT HIS MONEY CARELESSLY ON FOOD AND DRINK AND ON PARTIES WITH FRIENDS, AND HE NEVER THOUGHT ABOUT HIS FUTURE.
BUT ALL TOO SOON HIS MONEY RAN OUT. HIS NEW FRIENDS LEFT HIM NOW THAT HE HAD NO MONEY TO SPEND. AND THEN THINGS GOT EVEN WORSE, FOR A FAMINE STRUCK THE LAND.

THE YOUNGER SON WAS POOR AND HUNGRY. HE TOOK CARE OF A HERD OF PIGS FOR ANOTHER MAN. THE PIGS HAD MORE TO EAT THAN HE DID.

I AM DYING FROM HUNGER.

I'LL GO SEE MY FATHER AND TELL HIM I HAVE SINNED.

I'M NOT WORTHY TO BE HIS SON, BUT I'LL BEG HIM TO TREAT ME AS HE WOULD ONE OF HIS WORKERS.

SOME TIME HAD PASSED. THE FATHER LOOKED OUT ACROSS THE FIELD AND SAW HIS YOUNGER SON COMING DOWN THE ROAD.
THE FATHER RAN TO HIS SON AND EMBRACED AND KISSED HIM.
FATHER, I HAVE SINNED AGAINST HEAVEN AND AGAINST YOU. I'M NOT WORTHY TO BE CALLED YOUR SON!

THE FATHER WAS OVERJOYED TO SEE HIS YOUNGER SON. HE BROUGHT HIM INTO THE HOUSE.
QUICKLY, SERVANTS! BRING THE FINEST ROBE AND PUT IT ON MY YOUNGER SON.
PUT A RING ON HIS FINGER AND SHOES ON HIS FEET.
THE FATHER THEN TOLD HIS SERVANTS TO PREPARE A GREAT FEAST WITH A FATTENED CALF.
THIS SON OF MINE WAS DEAD AND IS NOW ALIVE. HE WAS LOST BUT NOW IS FOUND.

THE OLDER BROTHER CAME IN FROM THE FIELDS TO FIND EVERYONE CELEBRATING.
WHY ARE PEOPLE DANCING? WHY ARE PEOPLE FEASTING?
YOUR BROTHER HAS RETURNED, AND YOUR FATHER HAS SLAUGHTERED A CALF FOR HIM!
THE OLDER BROTHER WAS FURIOUS. HE CONFRONTED HIS FATHER.
MY BROTHER LEFT AND WASTED HIS FORTUNE, AND YOU SLAUGHTER A FATTENED CALF FOR HIM!
SON, YOU ARE HERE WITH ME ALWAYS, AND EVERYTHING I HAVE IS YOURS.
BUT LET US CELEBRATE. YOUR BROTHER WAS LOST AND HAS BEEN FOUND.

A Hole in the Roof

Mark 2; Luke 5

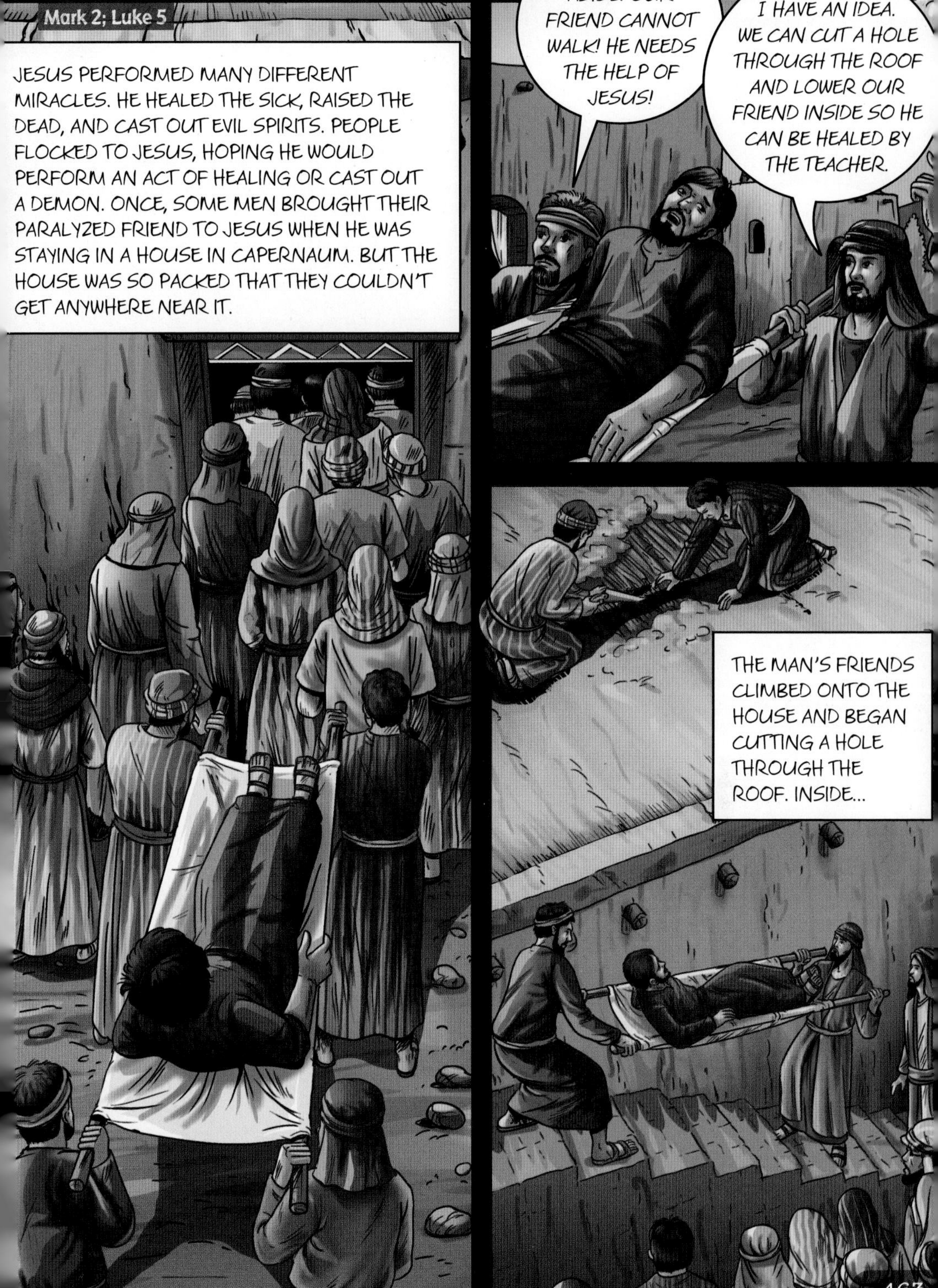

JESUS PERFORMED MANY DIFFERENT MIRACLES. HE HEALED THE SICK, RAISED THE DEAD, AND CAST OUT EVIL SPIRITS. PEOPLE FLOCKED TO JESUS, HOPING HE WOULD PERFORM AN ACT OF HEALING OR CAST OUT A DEMON. ONCE, SOME MEN BROUGHT THEIR PARALYZED FRIEND TO JESUS WHEN HE WAS STAYING IN A HOUSE IN CAPERNAUM. BUT THE HOUSE WAS SO PACKED THAT THEY COULDN'T GET ANYWHERE NEAR IT.

PLEASE MOVE ASIDE! OUR FRIEND CANNOT WALK! HE NEEDS THE HELP OF JESUS!

I HAVE AN IDEA. WE CAN CUT A HOLE THROUGH THE ROOF AND LOWER OUR FRIEND INSIDE SO HE CAN BE HEALED BY THE TEACHER.

THE MAN'S FRIENDS CLIMBED ONTO THE HOUSE AND BEGAN CUTTING A HOLE THROUGH THE ROOF. INSIDE...

...JESUS WAS SITTING AMONG A HUGE CROWD OF PEOPLE.
MY CHILD, YOUR SINS ARE FORGIVEN.
WHY DOES THIS MAN SPEAK THAT WAY? IT IS BLASPHEMY!
WHO BUT GOD ALONE CAN FORGIVE SINS?
JESUS KNEW WHAT THE MEN WERE THINKING.
IS IT EASIER TO SAY TO THIS MAN, "YOUR SINS ARE FORGIVEN"...
...OR "STAND UP, PICK UP YOUR MAT, AND WALK"?
THE SON OF MAN HAS AUTHORITY ON EARTH TO FORGIVE SINS.
STAND UP, PICK UP YOUR MAT, AND GO HOME.
THE MAN DID AS JESUS COMMANDED. EVERYONE WHO WITNESSED THE EVENT WAS AMAZED, FOR THEY HAD NEVER SEEN ANYTHING LIKE THIS BEFORE.

Healing Jairus's Daughter

Mark 5; Luke 8

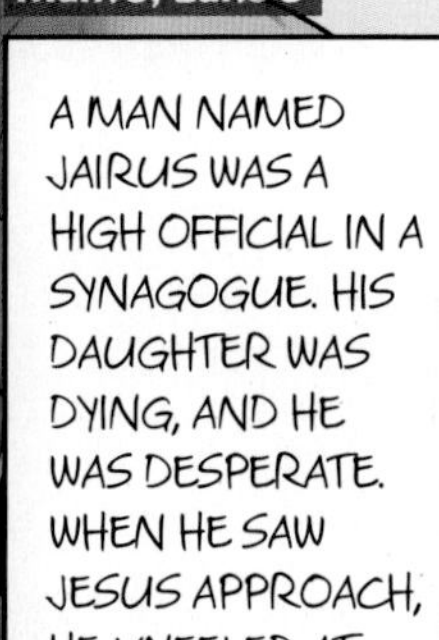

JAIRUS WANTED TO GET HOME AS SOON AS POSSIBLE, BUT JESUS STOPPED WHEN HE FELT SOMEONE TOUCH HIM.

JESUS CONTINUED WALKING UNTIL HE ARRIVED AT THE SICK GIRL'S HOUSE.
MY FRIEND, I HAVE BAD NEWS.
YOUR DAUGHTER HAS DIED.
DO NOT TROUBLE THE TEACHER ANY LONGER.
DON'T BE AFRAID.
HAVE FAITH AND SHE WILL BE HEALED.

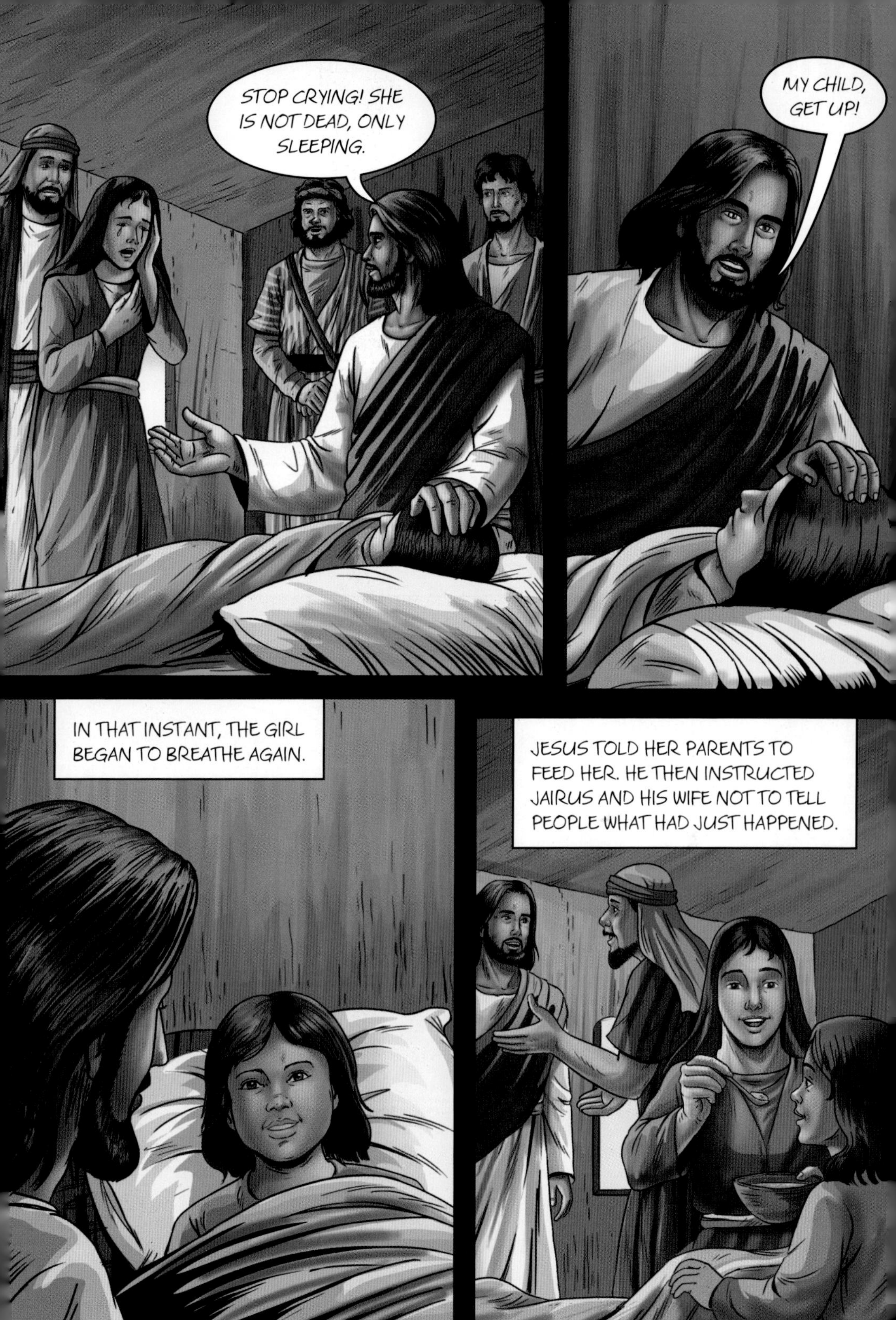

STOP CRYING! SHE IS NOT DEAD, ONLY SLEEPING.

MY CHILD, GET UP!

JESUS TOLD HER PARENTS TO FEED HER. HE THEN INSTRUCTED JAIRUS AND HIS WIFE NOT TO TELL PEOPLE WHAT HAD JUST HAPPENED.

Calming the Storm
Matthew 8; Mark 4; Luke 8
JESUS HEALED SICK AND DEMON-POSSESSED PEOPLE. HE ALSO CONTROLLED THE FORCES OF NATURE. ONE DAY, HE AND HIS DISCIPLES WERE SAILING TO THE OTHER SIDE OF THE LAKE. JESUS LAY SLEEPING WHEN A DREADFUL STORM ROSE UP. THE WINDS HOWLED, AND HUGE WAVES DANGEROUSLY TOSSED THE BOAT.
MASTER, WAKE UP! WE'RE ALL GOING TO DROWN!
THE DISCIPLES WERE TERRIFIED. THEY WOKE JESUS UP AND BEGGED HIM TO SAVE THEM. JESUS STOOD UP CALMLY AND COMMANDED THE WINDS AND WAVES TO BE STILL. AND AT ONCE, ALL WAS CALM.
BE STILL.
WHY ARE YOU SO AFRAID? YOU HAVE SO LITTLE FAITH!
WHO IS THIS MAN?
EVEN THE WINDS AND WAVES OBEY HIM!

The Head of John the Baptist

Matthew 11, 14; Mark 6; Luke 7

HERODIAS HEARD WHAT JOHN HAD SAID ABOUT HER. SHE WAS ANGRY BECAUSE JOHN HAD SHAMED HER IN PUBLIC.
YOU SHOULD EXECUTE THAT VILE MAN! YET HE SITS IN PRISON.
THERE IS NO REASON TO KILL HIM. IT IS NOT THE RIGHT PUNISHMENT.
JOHN SAT IN PRISON AND RECEIVED VISITORS.
GO SEE JESUS. ASK HIM IF HE IS THE MESSIAH OR IF WE SHOULD WAIT FOR ANOTHER.
TELL JOHN ABOUT ALL THE MIRACLES YOU HAVE SEEN.

IT WAS HEROD'S BIRTHDAY, AND A GRAND FEAST WAS UNDERWAY. THE DAUGHTER OF HERODIAS DANCED FOR THEM.
KING HEROD WAS PLEASED BY THE DANCE.
YOU CAN HAVE ANYTHING YOU WISH!
MOTHER, WHAT SHALL I ASK FOR?
I SHALL TELL YOU.

GIVE ME THE HEAD OF JOHN THE BAPTIST ON A TRAY.
HEROD WAS SHOCKED BY HER REQUEST, BUT HE COULD NOT GO BACK ON HIS PROMISE.
HEROD GAVE THE EXECUTIONER THE ORDER...
...AND HE CUT OFF THE HEAD OF JOHN THE BAPTIST.
HIS HEAD WAS BROUGHT ON A TRAY TO THE DAUGHTER, WHO THEN GAVE IT TO HER MOTHER, HERODIAS.
UPON HIS DEATH, JOHN'S FOLLOWERS BURIED HIS BODY.
WHEN JESUS HEARD OF JOHN'S DEATH, HE TOOK A BOAT ON THE SEA OF GALILEE AND SAILED TO A DESERTED PLACE TO BE ALONE.

Feeding the Crowd

Matthew 14; Mark 6; Luke 9; John 6

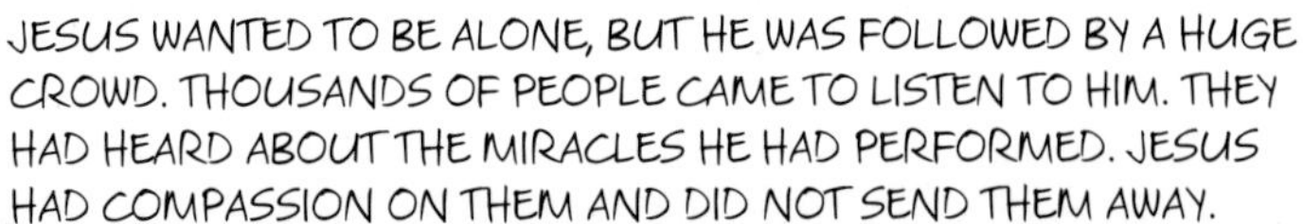

A WHILE LATER, ANDREW, THE BROTHER OF SIMON PETER, BROUGHT A SMALL BOY TO JESUS.
THIS BOY HAS FIVE BARLEY LOAVES AND TWO FISH. BUT I DON'T KNOW HOW MUCH USE THEY WILL BE WITH SO MANY PEOPLE!

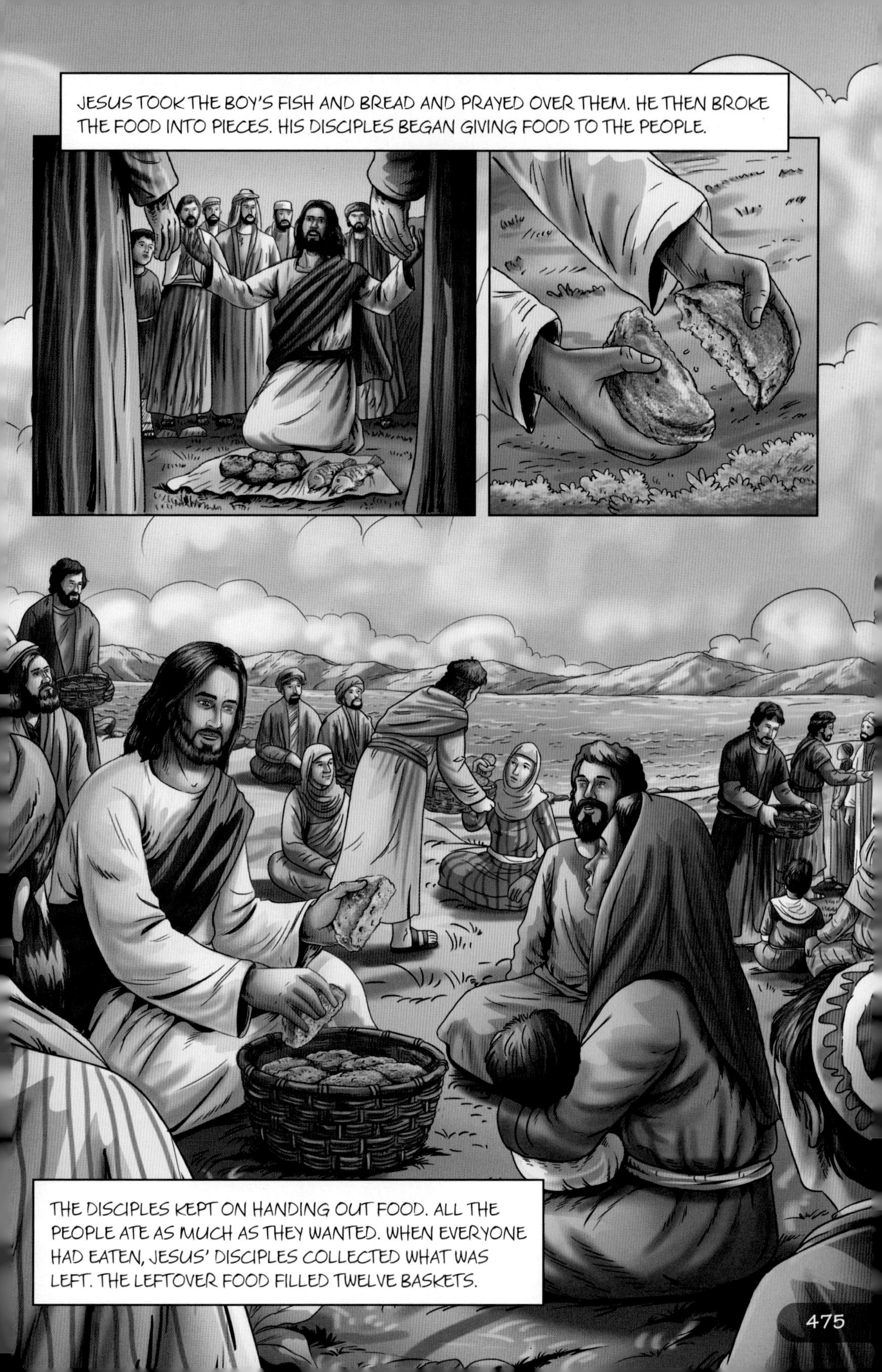

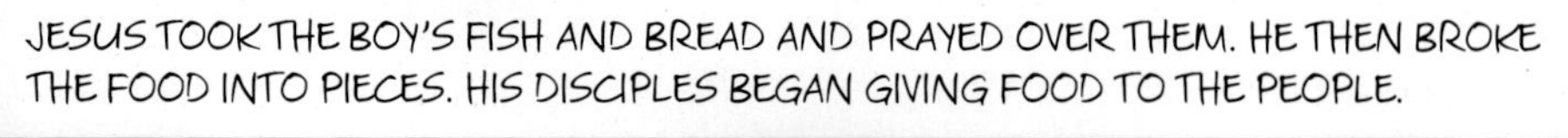

THE DISCIPLES KEPT ON HANDING OUT FOOD. ALL THE PEOPLE ATE AS MUCH AS THEY WANTED. WHEN EVERYONE HAD EATEN, JESUS' DISCIPLES COLLECTED WHAT WAS LEFT. THE LEFTOVER FOOD FILLED TWELVE BASKETS.

Jesus Walks on Water

Matthew 14

AFTER THE CROWD WAS FED, JESUS TOLD HIS DISCIPLES TO GET BACK INTO THEIR BOAT AND SET SAIL FOR THE OTHER SHORE.

JESUS THEN TOLD THE PEOPLE TO GO HOME...

...AND HE WALKED UP THE SIDE OF THE MOUNTAIN TO PRAY.

THE DISCIPLES HAD ROWED VERY FAR OUT ONTO THE LAKE. THE WIND WAS STRONG AGAINST THEM. SUDDENLY, THEY SAW A FIGURE WALKING ON THE WATER TOWARD THEM.

LORD, IF IT IS YOU, TELL ME TO COME TO YOU ON THE WATER.
COME TO ME, PETER!
PETER GOT OUT OF THE BOAT AND BEGAN TO WALK TOWARD JESUS.
BUT WHEN HE LOOKED AROUND HIM AT THE WIND AND THE WAVES, HE BECAME AFRAID AND BEGAN TO SINK. HE CRIED OUT TO JESUS TO SAVE HIM.
YOU HAVE SO LITTLE FAITH. WHY DID YOU DOUBT ME?
ONCE JESUS AND PETER WERE BOTH IN THE BOAT, THE WIND CALMED DOWN. THOSE IN THE BOAT NOW KNEW JESUS WAS TRULY THE SON OF GOD, AND THEY WORSHIPED HIM.

A Woman of Great Faith
Matthew 15; Mark 7
JESUS AND HIS DISCIPLES TRAVELED TO THE AREA OF TYRE AND SIDON. THEY STAYED IN A HOUSE, HOPING TO BE ALONE. ONE DAY, A WOMAN WHO WAS NOT A JEW CAME TO THE DOOR.
HAVE PITY ON ME, LORD, SON OF DAVID! A DEMON TORMENTS MY DAUGHTER!
JESUS DID NOT SAY A WORD, BUT THE WOMAN DIDN'T GO AWAY.
LORD, SEND HER AWAY. SHE KEEPS CRYING OUT AND WON'T LEAVE US ALONE.
I WAS SENT ONLY TO HELP THE LOST SHEEP OF THE HOUSE OF ISRAEL.

FIRST I SHOULD FEED MY OWN FAMILY, THE JEWS. IT ISN'T RIGHT TO TAKE FOOD FROM THE CHILDREN AND THROW IT TO THE DOGS.
LORD, EVEN THE DOGS UNDER THE TABLE EAT THE CHILDREN'S SCRAPS.

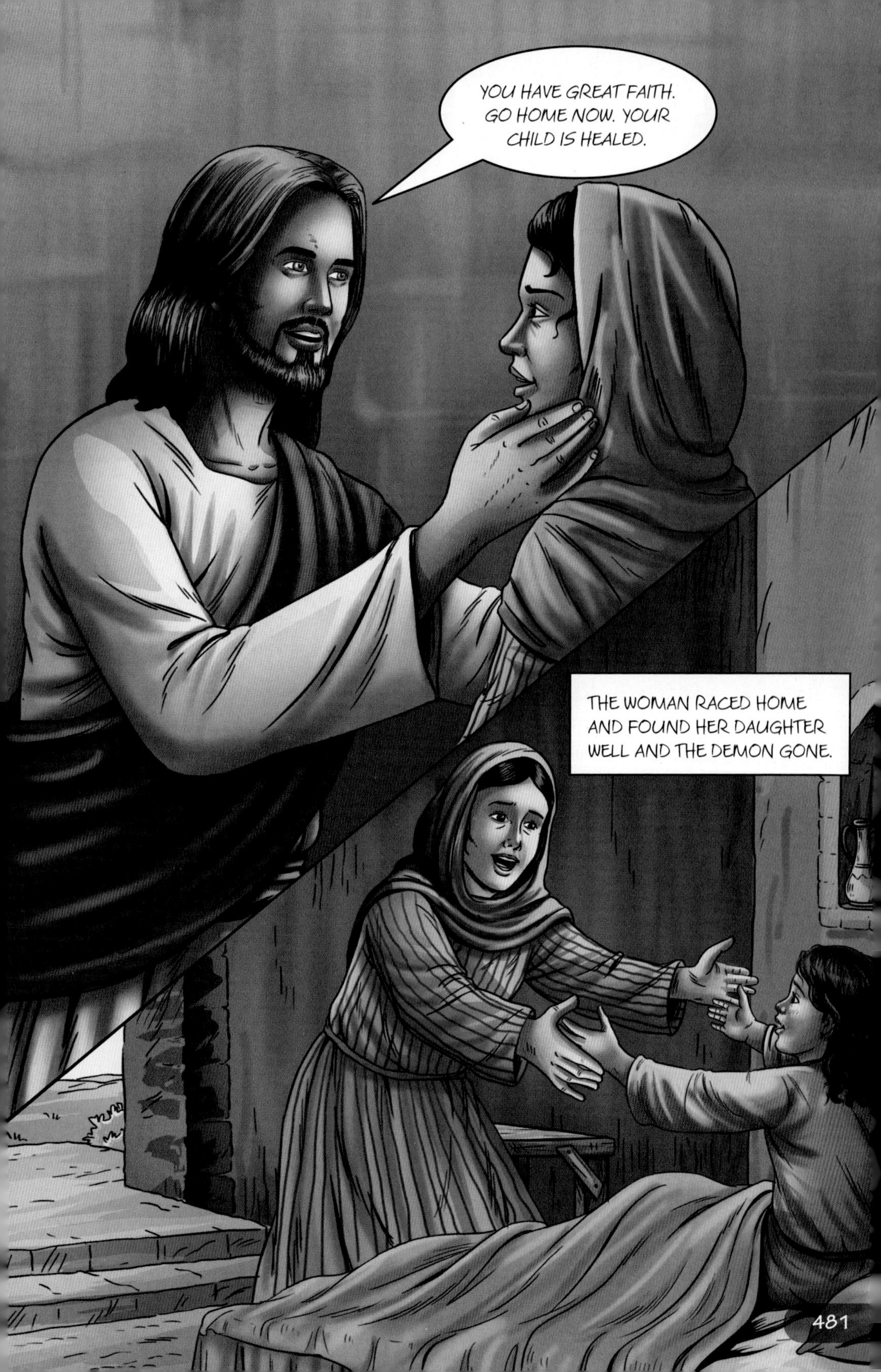
YOU HAVE GREAT FAITH. GO HOME NOW. YOUR CHILD IS HEALED.
THE WOMAN RACED HOME AND FOUND HER DAUGHTER WELL AND THE DEMON GONE.

The Transfiguration of Jesus Christ
Mark 9; Luke 9
ONE DAY JESUS LED PETER, JOHN, AND JAMES UP A HIGH MOUNTAIN.
AS JESUS PRAYED, HIS FACE WAS TRANSFORMED.
HIS CLOTHES BECAME DAZZLING WHITE.

IN THAT INSTANT, MOSES AND ELIJAH APPEARED AND SPOKE WITH JESUS.
PETER, JOHN, AND JAMES HAD FALLEN ASLEEP. WHEN THEY AWOKE, THEY SAW JESUS WITH THE GREAT PROPHETS. THEY WERE AMAZED AT WHAT THEY WERE WITNESSING.

LORD, IT IS GOOD FOR US TO BE HERE.

I WILL PREPARE THREE SHELTERS—ONE FOR YOU, ONE FOR MOSES, AND ONE FOR ELIJAH.

BUT PETER DID NOT KNOW WHAT HE WAS SAYING. AS HE WAS STILL SPEAKING, A CLOUD PASSED OVERHEAD, CASTING A SHADOW OVER THEM. PETER AND THE OTHERS WERE SCARED WHEN THEY ENTERED THE CLOUD. SUDDENLY, FROM THE CLOUD CAME A VOICE.

THIS IS MY DEARLY LOVED SON. LISTEN TO HIM.

JESUS RETURNED.

GET UP. DON'T BE AFRAID.

DON'T TELL ANYONE WHAT YOU HAVE SEEN UNTIL THE SON OF MAN HAS BEEN RAISED FROM THE DEAD.

The Demon-Possessed Boy

Matthew 17; Mark 9; Luke 9

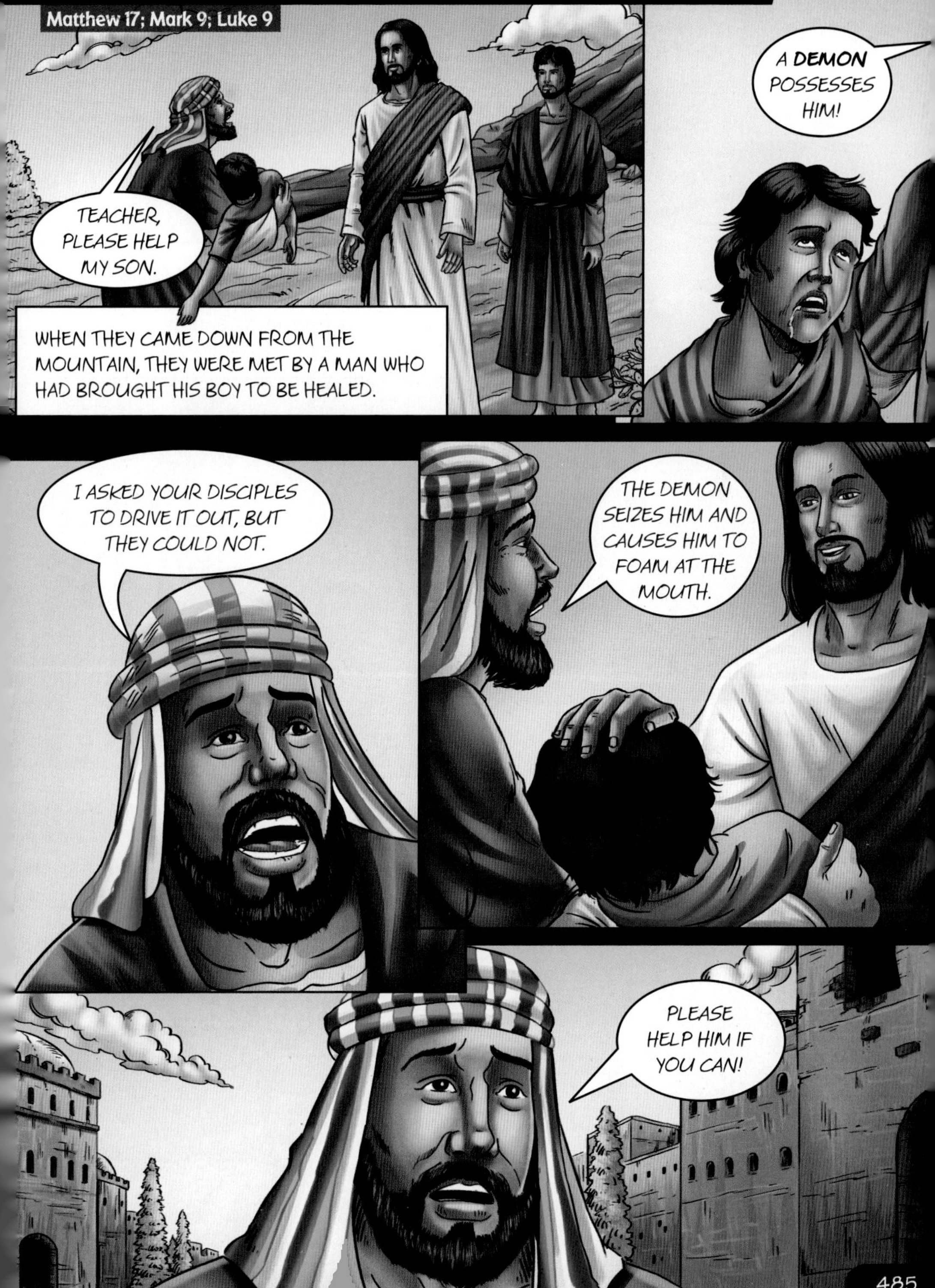

TEACHER, PLEASE HELP MY SON.

WHEN THEY CAME DOWN FROM THE MOUNTAIN, THEY WERE MET BY A MAN WHO HAD BROUGHT HIS BOY TO BE HEALED.

A **DEMON** POSSESSES HIM!

I ASKED YOUR DISCIPLES TO DRIVE IT OUT, BUT THEY COULD NOT.

THE DEMON SEIZES HIM AND CAUSES HIM TO FOAM AT THE MOUTH.

PLEASE HELP HIM IF YOU CAN!

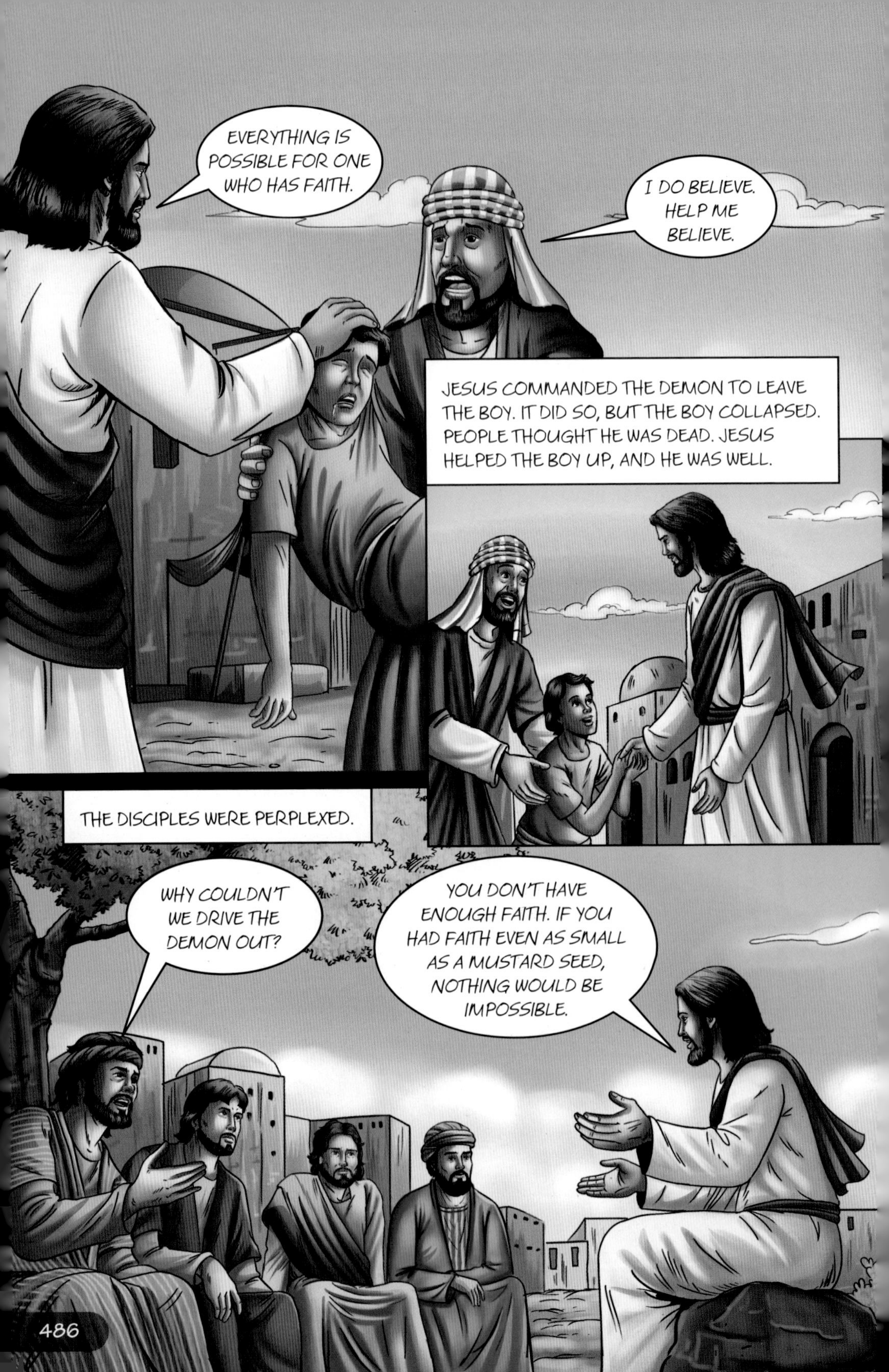
EVERYTHING IS POSSIBLE FOR ONE WHO HAS FAITH.
I DO BELIEVE. HELP ME BELIEVE.
JESUS COMMANDED THE DEMON TO LEAVE THE BOY. IT DID SO, BUT THE BOY COLLAPSED. PEOPLE THOUGHT HE WAS DEAD. JESUS HELPED THE BOY UP, AND HE WAS WELL.
THE DISCIPLES WERE PERPLEXED.
WHY COULDN'T WE DRIVE THE DEMON OUT?
YOU DON'T HAVE ENOUGH FAITH. IF YOU HAD FAITH EVEN AS SMALL AS A MUSTARD SEED, NOTHING WOULD BE IMPOSSIBLE.

Healing Ten Men with Leprosy

Luke 17

THE MEN DID AS JESUS ASKED AND SET OFF TO SEE THE PRIESTS.
SUDDENLY, ALL WERE CLEANSED!
ONE OF THEM, WHO HAPPENED TO BE A SAMARITAN, TURNED AROUND IMMEDIATELY AND RAN BACK TO JESUS TO THANK HIM.
I GIVE PRAISE TO THE LORD! I AM CLEANSED! THANK YOU! THANK YOU!
DIDN'T I HEAL TEN MEN? WHERE ARE THE OTHER NINE?
STAND UP. YOUR **FAITH** HAS HEALED YOU.

The Blind Beggar

Mark 10; Luke 18

JESUS! JESUS!
BRING THAT MAN TO ME.
WHAT DO YOU WANT ME TO DO?
LORD, PLEASE LET ME SEE.

JESUS RESTORED THE BEGGAR'S SIGHT. WHEN THE PEOPLE SAW THIS, THEY GAVE PRAISE TO GOD.
THE MAN THEN FOLLOWED JESUS AS HE CONTINUED ON HIS JOURNEY.

Zacchaeus the Tax Collector

Luke 19

THE IDEA THAT JESUS WAS STAYING AT THE HOUSE OF A TAX COLLECTOR ANGERED MANY IN THE CROWD.
THE TEACHER IS GOING TO STAY AT THE HOME OF A **SINNER?**
AFTER ALL THAT ZACCHAEUS HAS STOLEN FROM US!
ZACCHAEUS HEARD THEIR CONCERNS. HE TURNED TO JESUS AND SPOKE.
LORD, I WILL GIVE HALF MY WEALTH **TO THE POOR**.
IF I HAVE STOLEN FROM ANYONE, I WILL PAY IT BACK **FOUR TIMES**.
TODAY SALVATION HAS COME TO YOU. FOR THE SON OF MAN HAS COME TO SEEK AND SAVE THOSE WHO ARE LOST.

Martha and Mary

Luke 10

JESUS WAS FRIENDS WITH TWO SISTERS, MARTHA AND MARY. ONE DAY JESUS AND HIS DISCIPLES STOPPED TO VISIT THEM.

MARTHA RUSHED AROUND TRYING TO PREPARE THE FOOD FOR ALL THE MEN, BUT MARY DROPPED EVERYTHING TO SIT AT JESUS' FEET AND LISTEN TO HIS EVERY WORD.

WHY SHOULD MARY GET AWAY WITH SITTING AROUND WHILE I DO ALL THE WORK!

MARTHA WAS ANGRY THAT HER SISTER WASN'T HELPING HER.

MY DEAR MARTHA, YOU ARE WORRIED ABOUT ALL THESE DETAILS! ONLY ONE THING IS IMPORTANT. MARY HAS DISCOVERED IT, AND IT WILL NOT BE TAKEN AWAY FROM HER.

Raising Lazarus from the Dead

John 11

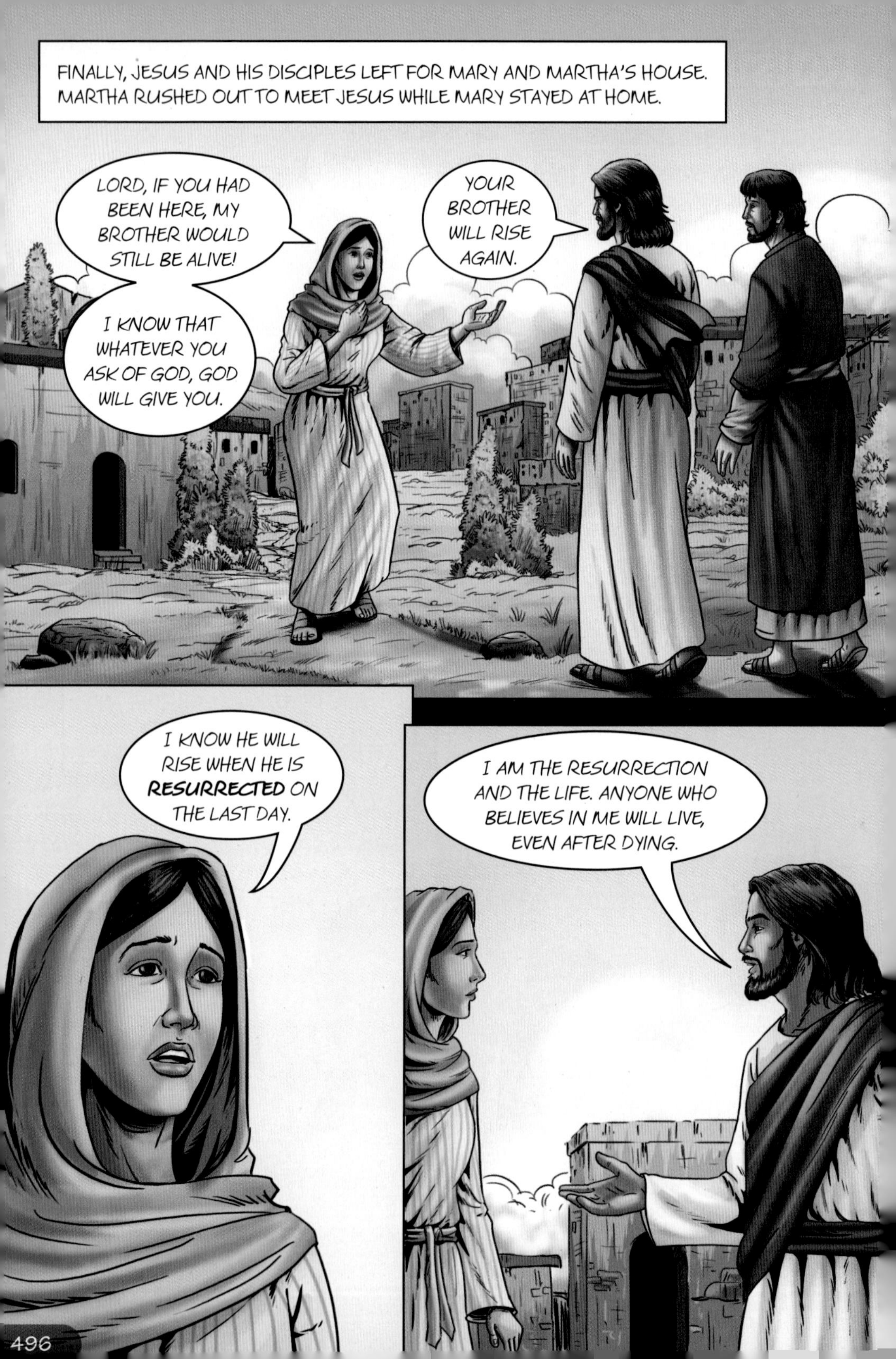

FINALLY, JESUS AND HIS DISCIPLES LEFT FOR MARY AND MARTHA'S HOUSE. MARTHA RUSHED OUT TO MEET JESUS WHILE MARY STAYED AT HOME.

LORD, IF YOU HAD BEEN HERE, MY BROTHER WOULD STILL BE ALIVE!

I KNOW THAT WHATEVER YOU ASK OF GOD, GOD WILL GIVE YOU.

YOUR BROTHER WILL RISE AGAIN.

MARTHA RETURNED HOME AND SENT HER SISTER OUT TO SEE JESUS.
JESUS IS ASKING FOR YOU.
WHEN HE SAW MARY'S TEARS, JESUS WEPT TOO.
LORD, IF YOU HAD BEEN HERE, LAZARUS WOULD NOT HAVE DIED.
WHERE HAVE YOU BURIED YOUR BROTHER?

THE PEOPLE SHOWED JESUS THE TOMB OF LAZARUS.
ROLL THE STONE ASIDE
IF YOU BELIEVE, YOU WILL SEE THE GLORY OF GOD.
BUT LORD, SURELY IT WILL SMELL!
FATHER, THANK YOU FOR HEARING MY PRAYER.
LAZARUS, COME OUT!
LAZARUS WALKED OUT OF THE TOMB, ALIVE AND WELL. JESUS TOLD THE SISTERS TO REMOVE HIS GRAVECLOTHES.

Peter the Rock

Matthew 16

The Last Days of Jesus

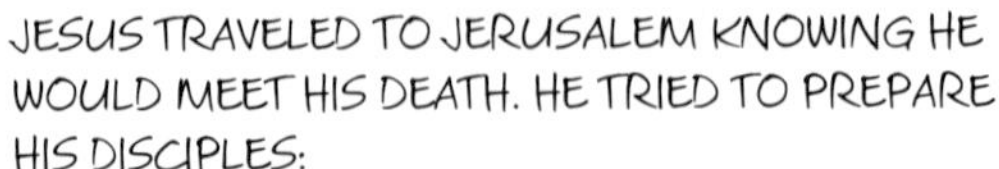

JESUS TRAVELED TO JERUSALEM KNOWING HE WOULD MEET HIS DEATH. HE TRIED TO PREPARE HIS DISCIPLES:

"ALL THE PREDICTIONS OF THE PROPHETS CONCERNING THE SON OF MAN WILL COME TRUE. HE WILL BE HANDED OVER TO THE ROMANS, AND HE WILL BE MOCKED, TREATED SHAMEFULLY, AND SPIT UPON. THEY WILL WHIP AND KILL HIM, BUT ON THE THIRD DAY HE WILL RISE AGAIN."

JERUSALEM AT THE TIME OF JESUS

AT THE TIME OF JESUS, JERUSALEM WAS A BUSTLING CITY OF ABOUT 30,000 PEOPLE AND WAS UNDER ROMAN CONTROL. INSIDE ITS GATES, DUSTY STREETS AND ALLEYWAYS RAN IN EVERY DIRECTION. THE CITY'S ARTISANS, CRAFTSMEN, WEAVERS, BAKERS, AND CARPENTERS WORKED IN OPEN-AIR SHOPS, TRYING TO MAKE A LIVING.

Jesus Arrives in Jerusalem

Matthew 21; Mark 11; Luke 19

A HUGE CROWD GATHERED AS JESUS ENTERED JERUSALEM. SOME WAVED PALM BRANCHES IN THE AIR, WHILE OTHERS PUT THEIR CLOAKS ON THE ROAD AS JESUS PASSED.
PRAISE GOD FOR THE SON OF DAVID!

BLESSINGS ON THE ONE WHO COMES IN THE NAME OF THE LORD!

The Money Changers
Matthew 21; Luke 19
ONCE JESUS ARRIVED IN JERUSALEM, HE MADE HIS WAY TO THE TEMPLE.
THERE HE SAW A GROUP OF PEOPLE BUYING AND SELLING THINGS.
JESUS OVERTURNED THE TABLES OF THE MONEY CHANGERS AND THE CHAIRS OF THOSE SELLING DOVES.
MY TEMPLE WILL BE A HOUSE OF PRAYER...
...BUT YOU HAVE TURNED IT INTO A DEN OF THIEVES!
ONCE JESUS HAD THROWN OUT THE MONEY CHANGERS, BLIND AND LAME PEOPLE LINED UP TO SEE HIM.

THROW AWAY YOUR CRUTCHES. YOU CAN WALK.
OPEN YOUR EYES. YOU CAN SEE.
THE NEXT MORNING, JESUS WAS HUNGRY. HE SAW A FIG TREE WITH NO FRUIT.
MAY NO FRUIT EVER COME FROM YOUR BRANCHES AGAIN!
THE FIG TREE SUDDENLY DIED.
WHY IS THE FIG TREE WITHERED?
IF YOU HAVE FAITH AND DON'T DOUBT, WHATEVER YOU PRAY FOR YOU WILL RECEIVE.

By What Authority?

Matthew 21; Luke 20

DID JOHN'S AUTHORITY TO BAPTIZE COME FROM HEAVEN, OR WAS IT MERELY HUMAN?
IF WE SAY OF HEAVEN, HE WILL SAY, "THEN WHY DID YOU NOT BELIEVE JOHN?"
IF WE SAY OF HUMAN ORIGIN, THE CROWD WILL TURN ON US, FOR THEY SAY JOHN IS A PROPHET.
THE PRIESTS SAID THEY DID NOT KNOW THE ANSWER, AND JESUS REFUSED TO TELL THEM WHERE HIS AUTHORITY CAME FROM.

A Conspiracy Brews
Matthew 22–23; Mark 12–15; Luke 20–22
FOR SEVERAL DAYS JESUS CONTINUED TO TEACH.
HIS WORDS THREATENED THE RELIGIOUS LEADERS. THEY PLOTTED AGAINST HIM, HOPING TO TRAP HIM.
TEACHER, YOU ARE A TRUTHFUL MAN. TELL US...
IS IT LAWFUL OR NOT TO PAY TAX TO CAESAR?
YOU HYPOCRITES! WHY ARE YOU TRYING TO TRAP ME?
WHOSE PICTURE IS THIS?

IT IS CAESAR'S IMAGE!
THEN GIVE CAESAR WHAT IS CAESAR'S...
...AND GIVE GOD WHAT IS GOD'S.

THE PHARISEES CONTINUED TO CHALLENGE JESUS.
TEACHER! WHICH COMMANDMENT IS THE GREATEST?
YOU MUST LOVE THE LORD YOUR GOD WITH ALL YOUR HEART, ALL YOUR SOUL, AND ALL YOUR MIND.
A SECOND IS EQUALLY IMPORTANT: LOVE YOUR NEIGHBOR AS YOURSELF.

JESUS CONTINUED TO CRITICIZE THE RELIGIOUS LEADERS.
OBEY THE PHARISEES, BUT DON'T FOLLOW THEIR EXAMPLE.
FOR THEY DO NOT PRACTICE WHAT THEY TEACH!
THE PHARISEES FELT THREATENED AND DECIDED JESUS MUST BE STOPPED.
SOMETHING MUST BE DONE ABOUT THIS MAN.
HIS TEACHINGS THREATEN US.
BUT THE PEOPLE LOVE AND FOLLOW HIM.

The Coming Persecution

Matthew 24; Mark 13; Luke 21

Two Good Women
Mark 12, 14
ONE TIME JESUS WAS SITTING IN THE TEMPLE WITH SOME OF HIS DISCIPLES. HE WATCHED AS ALL THE RICH PEOPLE PUT GOLD AND SILVER INTO THE TEMPLE COLLECTION. BUT HE ALSO SAW A POOR WIDOW GIVING TWO SMALL COINS.
THIS POOR WIDOW HAS GIVEN MORE THAN ALL THE OTHERS. FOR THEY GAVE A TINY PART OF THEIR SURPLUS, BUT SHE, POOR AS SHE IS, HAS GIVEN EVERYTHING SHE HAD TO LIVE ON.

ONE DAY, WHEN JESUS WAS VISITING THE HOUSE OF SIMON THE LEPER IN BETHANY, A WOMAN CAME WITH A JAR OF PERFUMED OIL AND GENTLY POURED IT ON HIS HEAD.
WHY IS THAT WOMAN WASTING SUCH EXPENSIVE OIL? IT COULD HAVE BEEN SOLD TO FEED THE POOR!
LEAVE HER ALONE. WHY CRITICIZE HER FOR DOING SUCH A GOOD THING TO ME? YOU WILL ALWAYS HAVE THE POOR AMONG YOU, BUT YOU WILL NOT ALWAYS HAVE ME. SHE HAS ANOINTED MY BODY FOR BURIAL.

Planning the Betrayal

Matthew 26; Mark 14

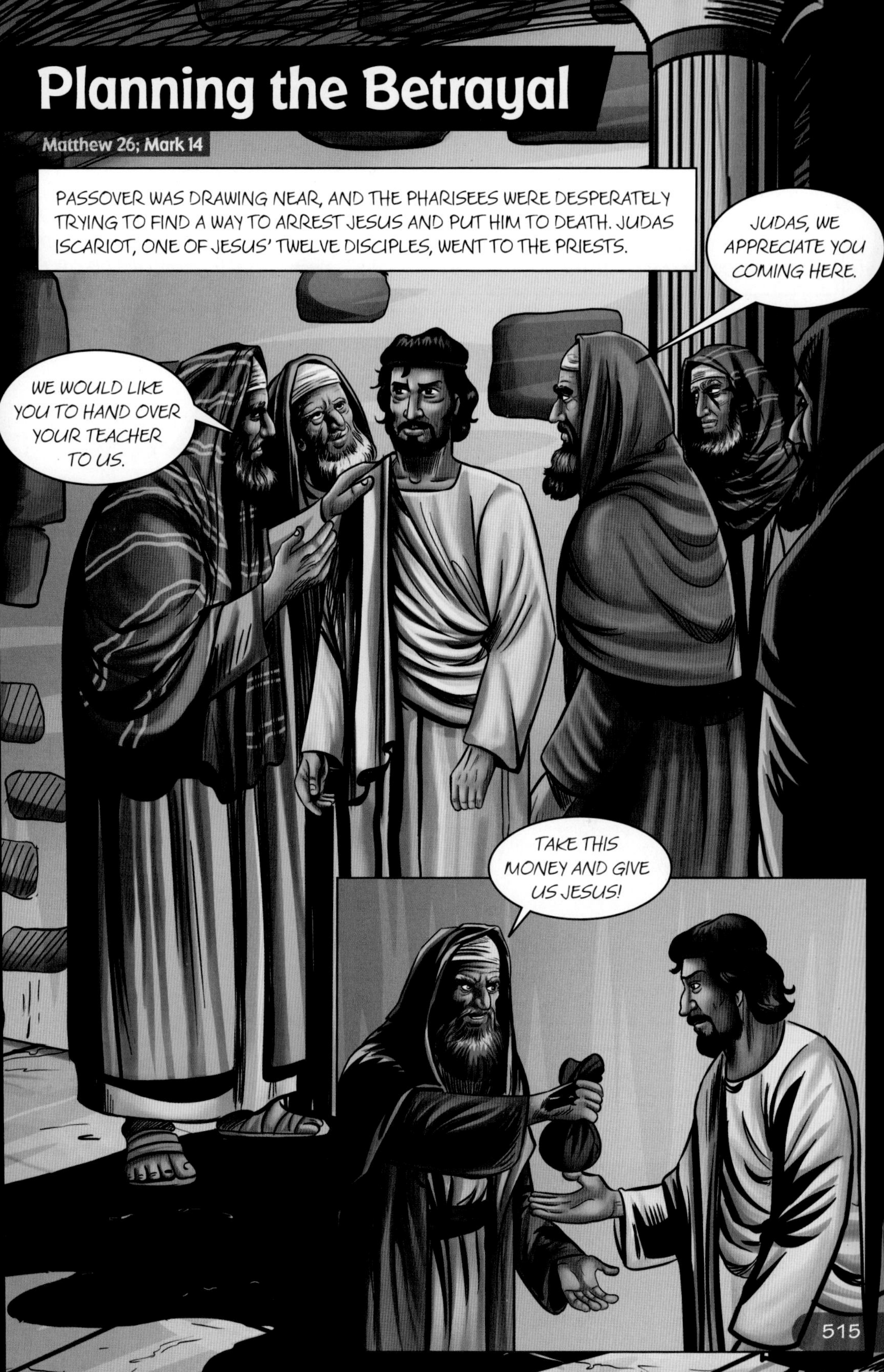

Preparing for Passover

Luke 22

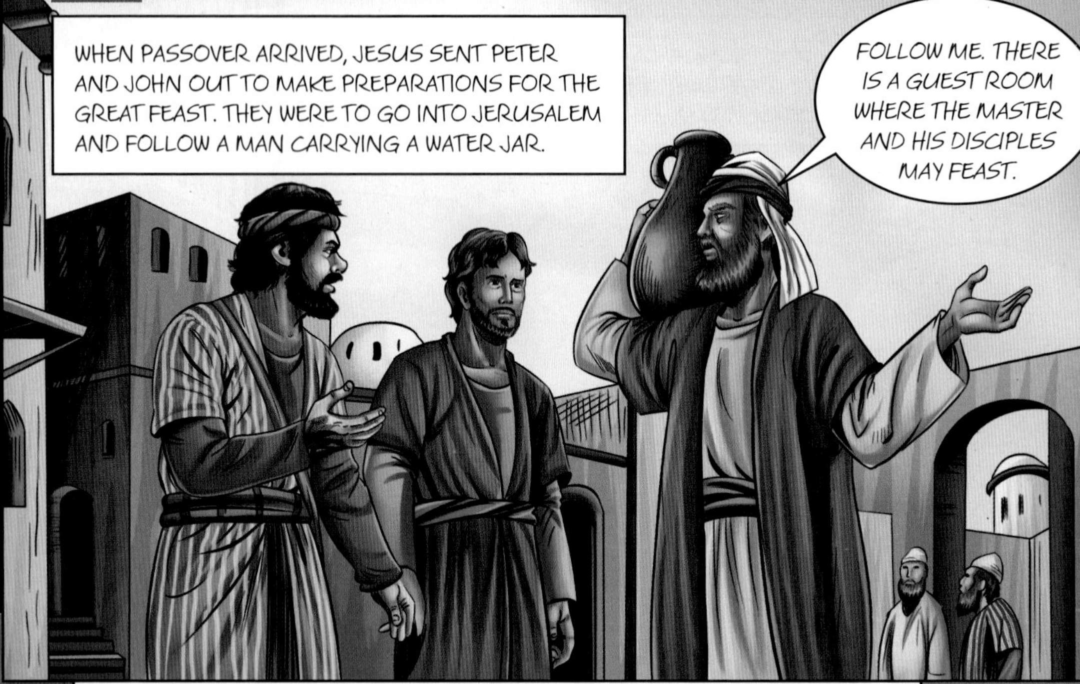

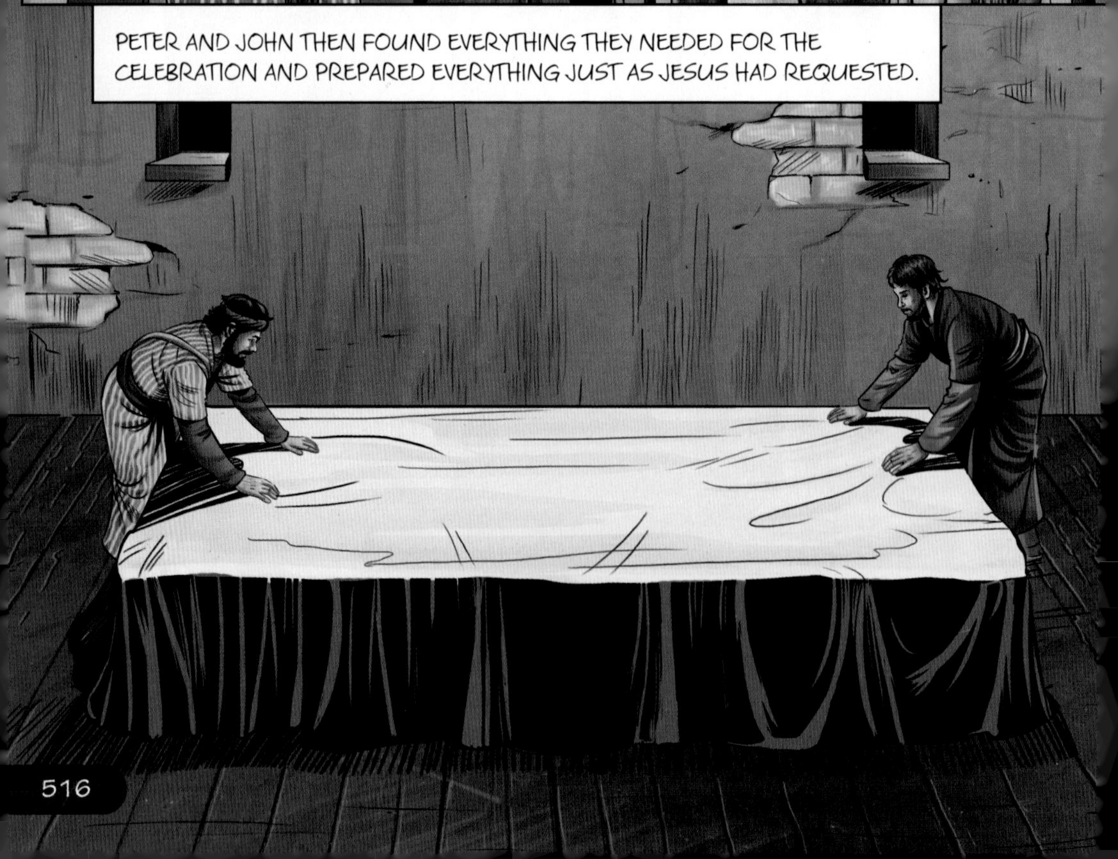

WHEN PASSOVER ARRIVED, JESUS SENT PETER AND JOHN OUT TO MAKE PREPARATIONS FOR THE GREAT FEAST. THEY WERE TO GO INTO JERUSALEM AND FOLLOW A MAN CARRYING A WATER JAR.

PETER AND JOHN THEN FOUND EVERYTHING THEY NEEDED FOR THE CELEBRATION AND PREPARED EVERYTHING JUST AS JESUS HAD REQUESTED.

Servant King

John 13

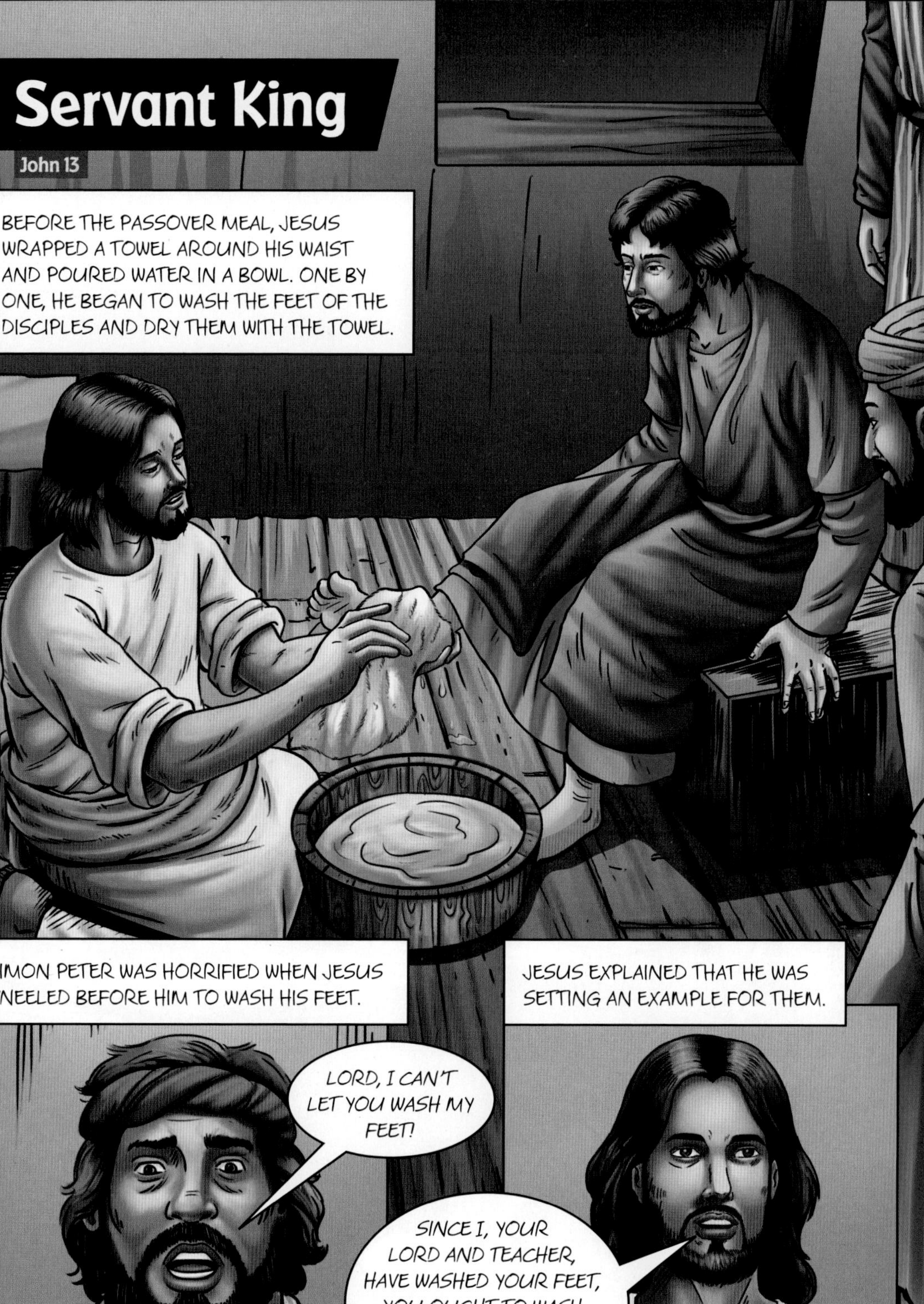

The Last Supper

Matthew 26; Mark 14; Luke 22; John 13

JESUS MADE AN ANNOUNCEMENT THAT SHOCKED HIS FOLLOWERS.

HE WHOM
I GIVE THIS BREAD TO
IS THE ONE WHO WILL
BETRAY ME.

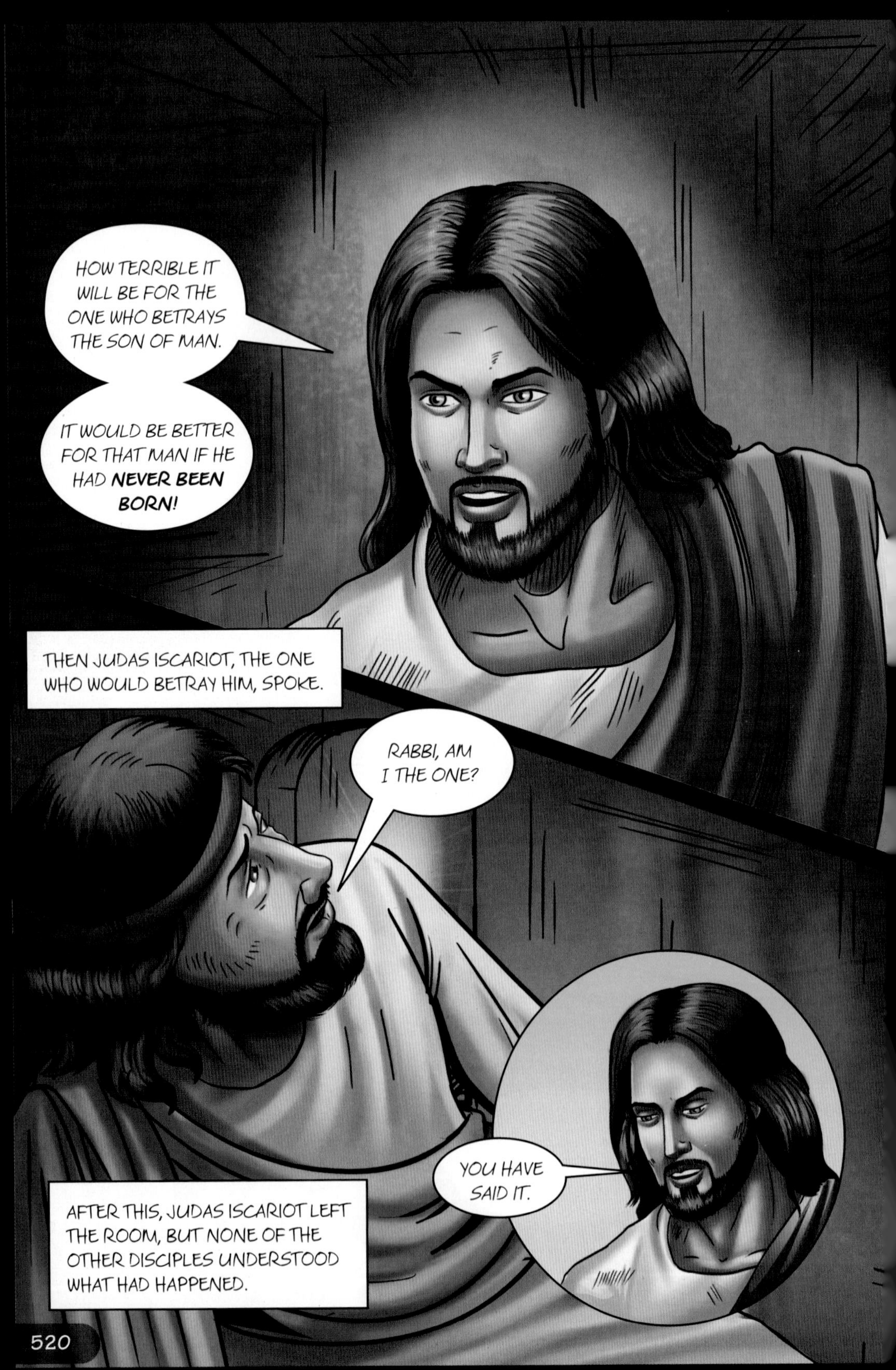
HOW TERRIBLE IT WILL BE FOR THE ONE WHO BETRAYS THE SON OF MAN.
IT WOULD BE BETTER FOR THAT MAN IF HE HAD **NEVER BEEN BORN!**
THEN JUDAS ISCARIOT, THE ONE WHO WOULD BETRAY HIM, SPOKE.
RABBI, AM I THE ONE?
YOU HAVE SAID IT.
AFTER THIS, JUDAS ISCARIOT LEFT THE ROOM, BUT NONE OF THE OTHER DISCIPLES UNDERSTOOD WHAT HAD HAPPENED.

AFTER JESUS MADE HIS STARTLING ANNOUNCEMENT, HE AND HIS DISCIPLES BEGAN TO EAT. JESUS TOOK BREAD...
TAKE AND EAT; THIS IS MY BODY.
...AND A CUP OF WINE.
TAKE THIS CUP, AND DRINK FROM IT, FOR THIS IS MY BLOOD.
MY BLOOD CONFIRMS THE COVENANT BETWEEN GOD AND HIS PEOPLE. IT IS POURED OUT TO FORGIVE THE SINS OF MANY.

Betrayed with a Kiss

Matthew 26; Mark 14; Luke 22

AFTER SUPPER, JESUS AND THE OTHERS WALKED TOWARD THE MOUNT OF OLIVES. HE TOLD HIS FOLLOWERS THAT THEY WOULD HAVE THEIR FAITH TESTED IN THE COMING HOURS.

ALL OF YOU WILL DESERT ME.

LORD, I WOULD NEVER LEAVE YOU. I AM WILLING TO DIE WITH YOU!

I TELL YOU, PETER, BEFORE THE ROOSTER CROWS, YOU WILL DENY THAT YOU KNOW ME THREE TIMES.

EVEN IF I HAVE TO DIE, I WOULD NEVER DENY THAT I KNEW YOU, LORD!

THEN JESUS AND THREE OF HIS DISCIPLES—INCLUDING PETER—WALKED TO THE GARDEN OF GETHSEMANE. JESUS BECAME SAD BECAUSE HE KNEW HE WAS ABOUT TO ENDURE SUFFERING.

SIT HERE WHILE I GO TO PRAY.

KEEP WATCH WITH ME.

MY FATHER! IF IT IS POSSIBLE, LET THIS CUP OF SUFFERING BE TAKEN AWAY FROM ME. YET I WANT YOUR WILL TO BE DONE, NOT MINE.
JESUS RETURNED TO HIS DISCIPLES. HE FOUND THEM ASLEEP.
COULDN'T YOU WATCH WITH ME EVEN ONE HOUR? THE SPIRIT IS WILLING, BUT THE BODY IS WEAK!
JESUS RETURNED TWO MORE TIMES AND FOUND HIS DISCIPLES ASLEEP.
LOOK—THE TIME HAS COME. MY BETRAYER IS HERE!

MOMENTS LATER JUDAS ARRIVED. WITH HIM WERE SOLDIERS AND A LARGE CROWD OF MEN ARMED WITH SWORDS AND CLUBS, SENT FROM THE LEADING PRIESTS AND ELDERS. JUDAS HAD TOLD THEM THAT THE MAN THAT HE KISSED WOULD BE THE ONE THEY WERE TO ARREST.
RABBI...
MY FRIEND, DO WHAT YOU HAVE COME FOR.
THE SOLDIERS MOVED IN TO ARREST JESUS.

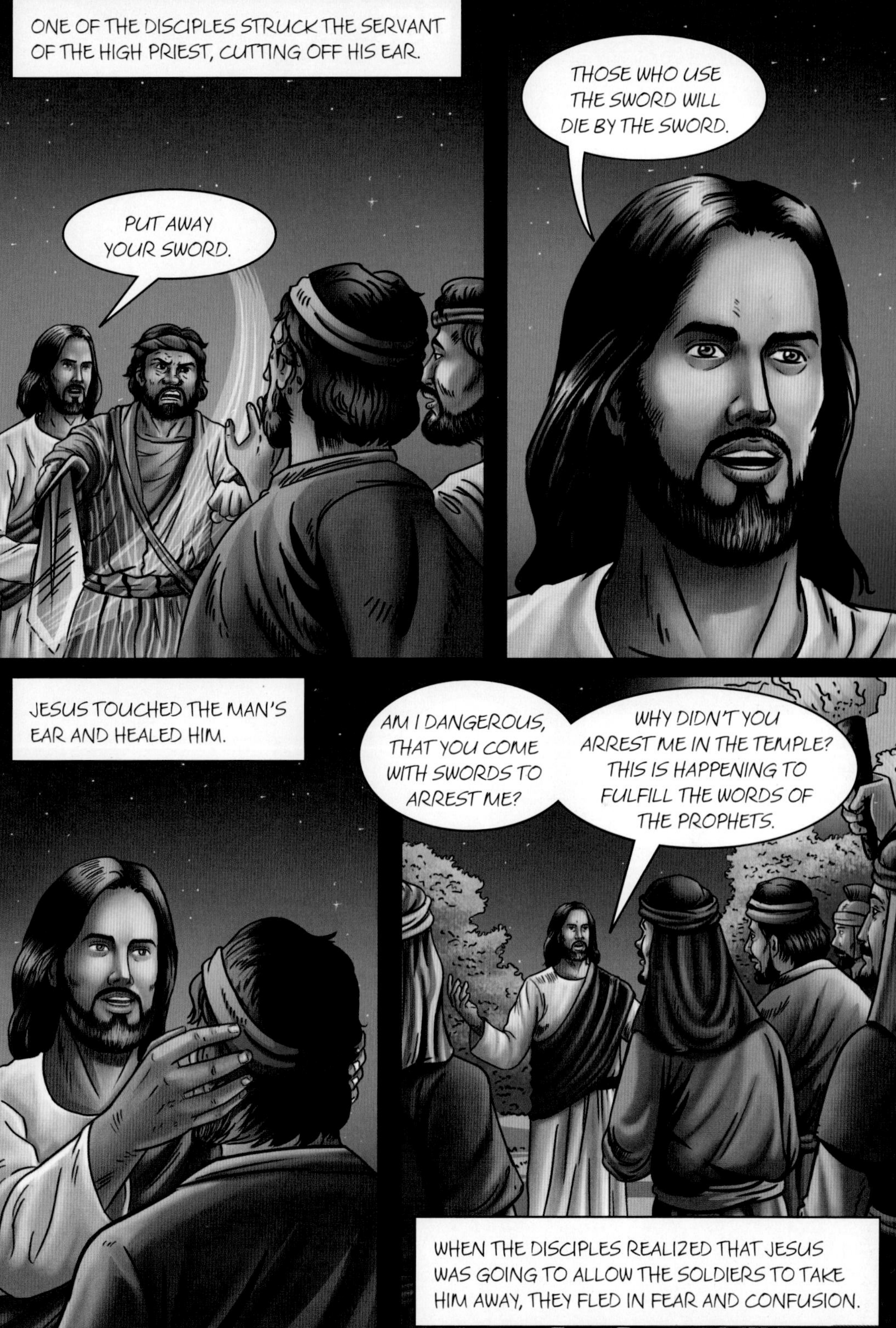
ONE OF THE DISCIPLES STRUCK THE SERVANT OF THE HIGH PRIEST, CUTTING OFF HIS EAR.
PUT AWAY YOUR SWORD.
THOSE WHO USE THE SWORD WILL DIE BY THE SWORD.
JESUS TOUCHED THE MAN'S EAR AND HEALED HIM.
AM I DANGEROUS, THAT YOU COME WITH SWORDS TO ARREST ME?
WHY DIDN'T YOU ARREST ME IN THE TEMPLE? THIS IS HAPPENING TO FULFILL THE WORDS OF THE PROPHETS.
WHEN THE DISCIPLES REALIZED THAT JESUS WAS GOING TO ALLOW THE SOLDIERS TO TAKE HIM AWAY, THEY FLED IN FEAR AND CONFUSION.

Peter Denies Christ
Matthew 26; Luke 22
THE SOLDIERS TOOK JESUS AWAY AND BROUGHT HIM TO THE COUNCIL OF ELDERS...
...WHILE PETER FOLLOWED QUIETLY BEHIND.
PETER SAT DOWN MISERABLY BY THE FIRE WITH SOME OF THE GUARDS, BUT A PASSING SERVANT GIRL RECOGNIZED HIM.
YOU ARE ONE OF THEM!
MY FRIEND, I AM NOT!
THIS MAN WAS WITH JESUS!
I DO NOT KNOW THAT MAN!
DIDN'T I SEE YOU IN THE GARDEN WITH HIM? YOU ARE ONE OF THEM.
I TOLD YOU, I DON KNOW HIM.

AFTER PETER DENIED JESUS THE THIRD TIME, A ROOSTER CROWED IN THE DISTANCE. PETER REMEMBERED WHAT JESUS HAD SAID AND BEGAN TO WEEP BITTERLY.

Jesus Before the High Priest

Mark 14–15; John 18

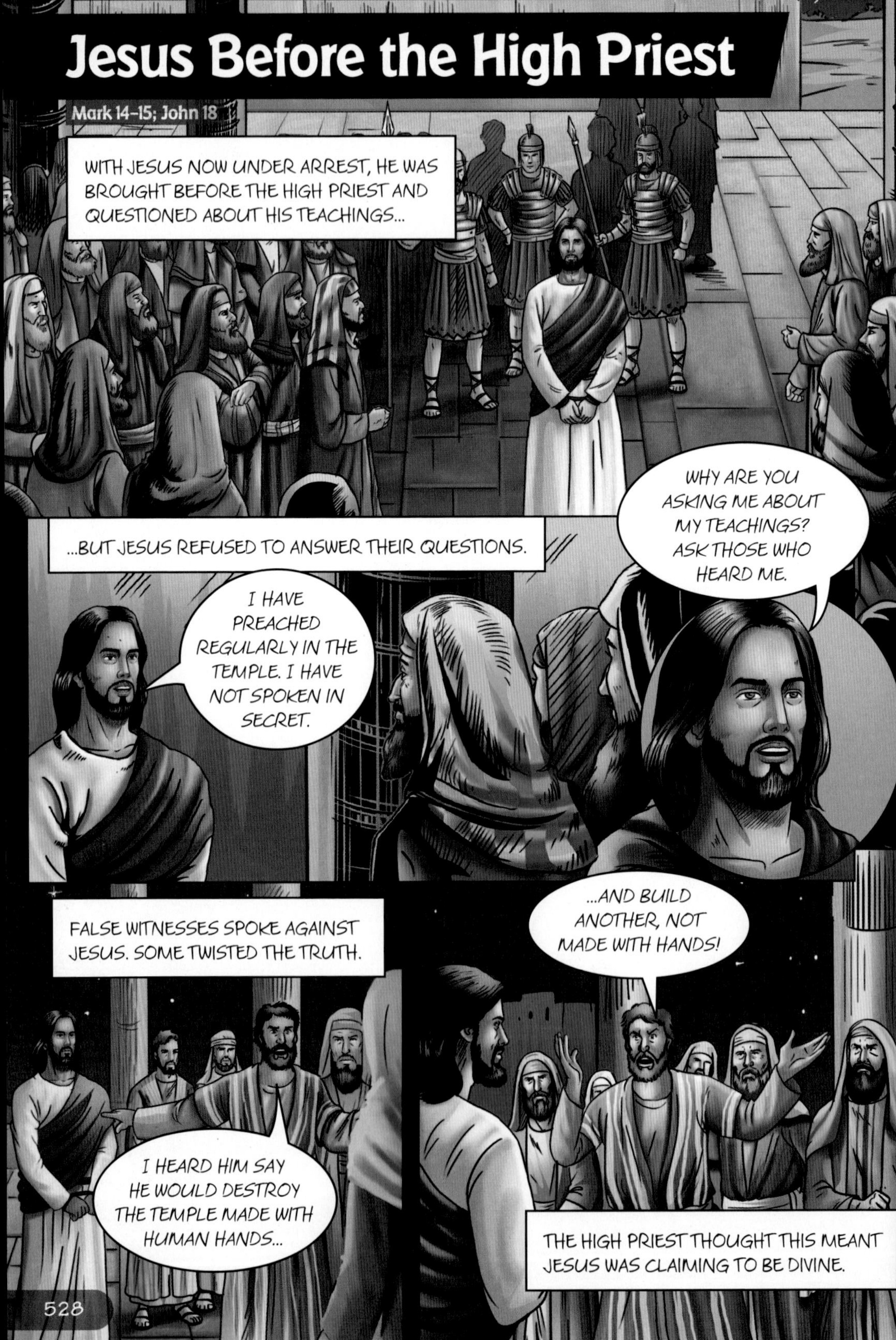

WHAT DO YOU HAVE TO SAY FOR YOURSELF?
JESUS AGAIN WAS SILENT.
ARE YOU THE MESSIAH, THE SON OF THE BLESSED ONE?
I AM.

MY BROTHERS, YOU HAVE HEARD HIS BLASPHEMY. WHAT IS YOUR VERDICT?
HE DESERVES TO DIE!
TAKE HIM TO PILATE! WE DON'T HAVE THE RIGHT TO EXECUTE HIM.
YES, HE IS PILATE'S RESPONSIBILITY NOW!

Pilate Washes His Hands
Matthew 27; Mark 15; Luke 23; John 18–19
PONTIUS PILATE WAS THE ROMAN GOVERNOR OF JUDEA. ONLY HE COULD SENTENCE JESUS TO DEATH.
ARE YOU THE **KING OF THE JEWS?**
THE LEADING PRIESTS ACCUSE YOU OF MANY THINGS. **WILL YOU ANSWER THEM?**
YOU HAVE SAID IT.
YOU SAY **NOTHING** IN YOUR DEFENSE?

THIS MAN IS NOT GUILTY OF ANY CRIME.
HE IS **CAUSING RIOTS** WITH HIS TEACHINGS!
THIS MAN IS FROM GALILEE. SEND HIM TO HEROD.
LET **HIM** JUDGE!

HEROD, THE RULER OF GALILEE, WAS GLAD TO SEE JESUS. HE HAD HEARD MUCH ABOUT HIM. HEROD QUESTIONED JESUS AT LENGTH, BUT HE, TOO, RECEIVED NO ANSWER.
SEND HIM BACK TO PILATE!
AND SO JESUS WAS BROUGHT BACK TO BE JUDGED BY PILATE.
I HAVE NOT FOUND THIS MAN GUILTY OF THE CHARGES YOU HAVE BROUGHT AGAINST HIM.
AND NEITHER HAS HEROD!
BUT THE RELIGIOUS LEADERS INSISTED JESUS MUST DIE.

AS IT HAPPENED, IT WAS A FEAST DAY. PILATE COULD RELEASE ANY PRISONER THE PEOPLE REQUESTED.
DO YOU WANT ME TO RELEASE BARABBAS OR THIS KING OF THE JEWS?
CRUCIFY JESUS!
RELEASE BARABBAS!
WHAT DO YOU WANT ME TO DO WITH THE MAN YOU CALL KING OF THE JEWS?
CRUCIFY HIM!!!
BARABBAS WAS A REBEL WHO HAD COMMITTED MURDER, BUT THE RELIGIOUS LEADERS AND THE MOB DEMANDED HIS RELEASE.

WHY? WHAT EVIL HAS HE DONE?
CRUCIFY HIM!
CRUCIFY HIM!
PILATE REALIZED THAT HE WAS GETTING NOWHERE. HE DIDN'T WANT TO BE RESPONSIBLE FOR JESUS' EXECUTION, SO HE TOOK SOME WATER...
...AND WASHED HIS HANDS IN IT IN FRONT OF THE CROWD.
I AM **INNOCENT** OF THIS MAN'S BLOOD! THE RESPONSIBILITY IS YOURS!
TO SATISFY THE CROWD, PILATE RELEASED BARABBAS. HE HAD JESUS FLOGGED AND HANDED HIM OVER TO BE CRUCIFIED.
AS FOR JUDAS, HE HAD FELT SO GUILTY WHEN HE REALIZED WHAT WAS HAPPENING THAT HE GAVE BACK THE MONEY THE PRIESTS HAD GIVEN HIM AND HANGED HIMSELF.

The Crucifixion

Matthew 27; Mark 15; Luke 23; John 18–19

THE SOLDIERS FORCED JESUS TO CARRY THE CROSS ON WHICH HE WOULD BE CRUCIFIED OUT OF THE CITY TO A HILL CALLED GOLGOTHA, THE PLACE OF THE SKULL.

BUT THE CROSS WAS HEAVY, AND JESUS WAS WEAK AND INJURED. THE SOLDIERS PULLED A MAN OUT OF THE CROWD, SIMON OF CYRENE...
...AND MADE HIM CARRY THE CROSS UP TO THE HILL.
DON'T WEEP FOR ME, BUT WEEP FOR YOURSELVES AND FOR YOUR CHILDREN.

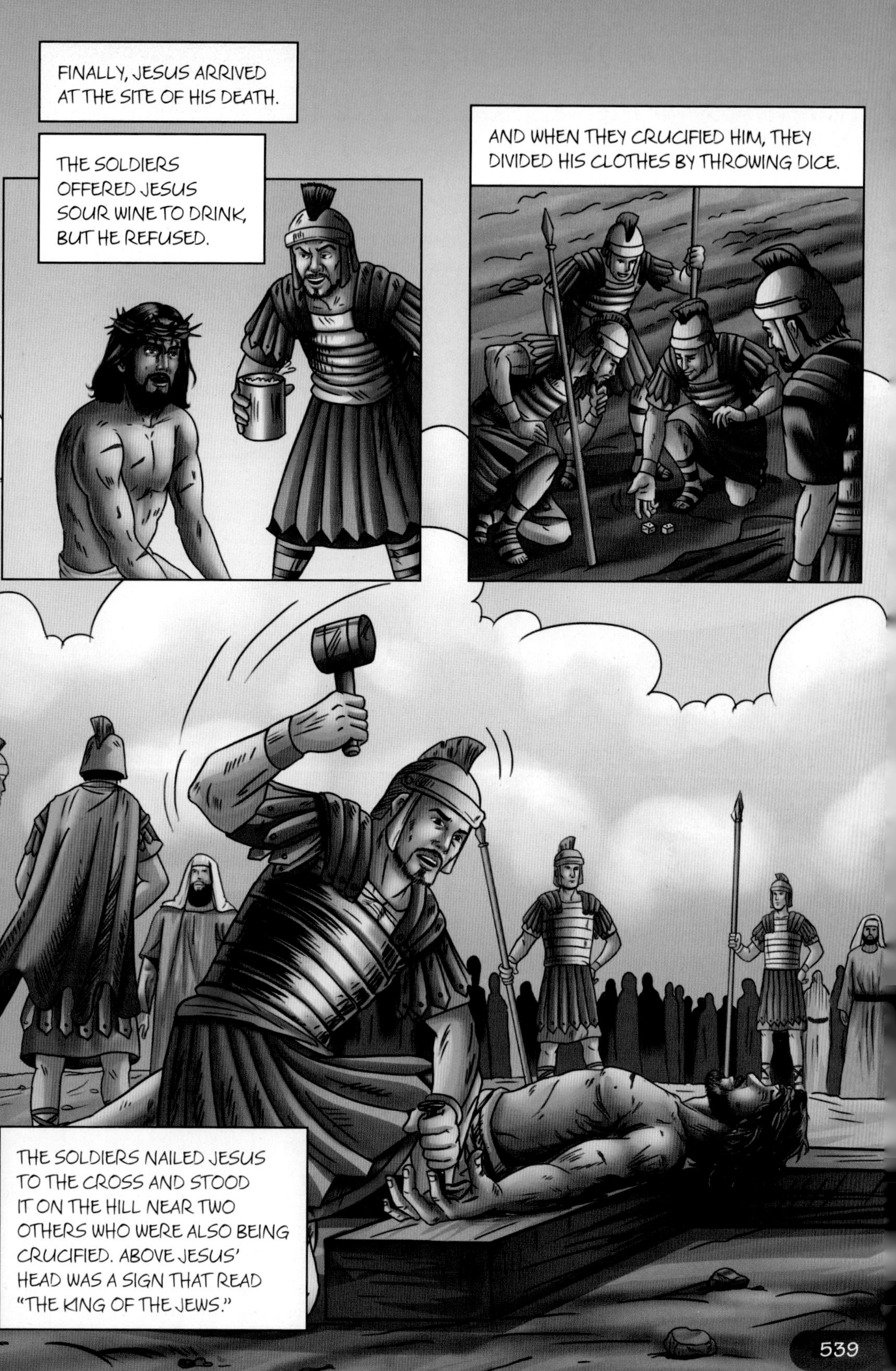
FINALLY, JESUS ARRIVED AT THE SITE OF HIS DEATH.
THE SOLDIERS OFFERED JESUS SOUR WINE TO DRINK, BUT HE REFUSED.
AND WHEN THEY CRUCIFIED HIM, THEY DIVIDED HIS CLOTHES BY THROWING DICE.
THE SOLDIERS NAILED JESUS TO THE CROSS AND STOOD IT ON THE HILL NEAR TWO OTHERS WHO WERE ALSO BEING CRUCIFIED. ABOVE JESUS' HEAD WAS A SIGN THAT READ "THE KING OF THE JEWS."

THE HOUR HAD COME.
ARE YOU NOT THE MESSIAH? SAVE YOURSELF AND US!
DON'T YOU FEAR GOD? WE DESERVE TO DIE FOR OUR CRIMES, BUT THIS MAN HASN'T DONE ANYTHING WRONG.
JESUS, REMEMBER ME WHEN YOU COME INTO YOUR KINGDOM.
TODAY YOU WILL BE WITH ME IN PARADISE.

AS HIS MOTHER WEPT AND OTHERS JEERED, A DARKNESS FELL ACROSS THE LAND.
SAVE YOURSELF IF YOU ARE KING OF THE JEWS!
MY GOD, MY GOD, WHY HAVE YOU ABANDONED ME?
I ENTRUST MY SPIRIT INTO YOUR HANDS!
AND THERE ON THE CRUEL CROSS JESUS TOOK HIS LAST BREATH.
JUST THEN, THE CURTAIN OF THE TEMPLE WAS TORN IN TWO FROM TOP TO BOTTOM.
THIS MAN TRULY WAS THE SON OF GOD!

The Resurrection

A MOVABLE FEAST

THE DATE OF EASTER SUNDAY VARIES FROM YEAR TO YEAR BECAUSE IT IS BASED ON THE LUNAR CALENDAR. IT IS CELEBRATED ON THE FIRST SUNDAY AFTER THE FULL MOON, ON OR AFTER MARCH 21.

THE ULTIMATE SACRIFICE

EASTER IS THE MOST IMPORTANT FESTIVAL IN THE CHRISTIAN CALENDAR AND THE STARTING POINT FOR CHRISTIAN FAITH. IT CELEBRATES GOD RAISING HIS SON, JESUS, FROM THE DEAD AND THE DESTRUCTION OF THE POWER OF SIN AND DEATH FOREVER. JESUS' SACRIFICE ENDED THE SEPARATION BETWEEN MAN AND GOD THAT SIN HAD CREATED.

Jesus Rises

Matthew 27–28; Mark 15–16; Luke 23–24; John 19–20

JOSEPH OF ARIMATHEA WAS A MEMBER OF THE COUNCIL BUT WAS SECRETLY A FOLLOWER OF JESUS. AFTER JESUS DIED, JOSEPH ASKED PILATE IF HE COULD PREPARE JESUS' BODY FOR BURIAL.

JOSEPH AND A MAN NAMED NICODEMUS WRAPPED JESUS' BODY IN LINEN.

THEY THEN BROUGHT JESUS TO A TOMB, PLACED THE BODY INSIDE, AND ROLLED A STONE OVER THE OPENING.

THE DAY AFTER JESUS DIED, THE PHARISEES WENT TO SEE PILATE.
MY LORD, WHILE THIS DECEIVER WAS ALIVE, HE SAID HE WOULD BE RAISED UP IN THREE DAYS.
WE THINK THE TOMB SHOULD BE GUARDED.
WE DON'T WANT HIS DISCIPLES TO COME AND STEAL THE BODY...
...AND THEN SAY HE HAS BEEN RAISED FROM THE DEAD.
PILATE AGREED, AND SOLDIERS WERE ASSIGNED TO GUARD THE TOMB.
ON SUNDAY, MARY MAGDALENE AND TWO OTHER WOMEN—SALOME AND MARY, THE MOTHER OF JAMES—WENT TO THE TOMB TO WASH JESUS WITH OILS, AS WAS THE CUSTOM.
WHO WILL ROLL AWAY THE STONE FOR US WHEN WE GET TO THE TOMB?

AS THEY APPROACHED THE TOMB, THE GROUND BEGAN TO SHAKE. THE WOMEN WERE SHOCKED TO SEE THAT THE STONE TO THE TOMB HAD BEEN ROLLED ASIDE.
WHY IS THE TOMB OPEN?
IT SEEMS STRANGE, DOESN'T IT?
THE WOMEN DID NOT KNOW THAT AN ANGEL OF THE LORD HAD COME DOWN FROM HEAVEN AND ROLLED BACK THE STONE. THE GUARDS WERE SO FEARFUL WHEN THEY SAW HIM THAT THEY BECAME LIKE DEAD MEN.

THE WOMEN CAUTIOUSLY APPROACHED THE TOMB. INSIDE THERE WAS NO SIGN OF JESUS, BUT INSTEAD THERE WERE TWO ANGELS SHINING BRIGHTLY. THE WOMEN WERE FILLED WITH FEAR.
DON'T BE AFRAID! WHY ARE YOU LOOKING AMONG THE DEAD FOR SOMEONE WHO IS ALIVE?
YOU ARE LOOKING FOR JESUS. HE IS RISEN FROM THE DEAD, JUST AS HE SAID WOULD HAPPEN. NOW GO AND TELL HIS DISCIPLES.

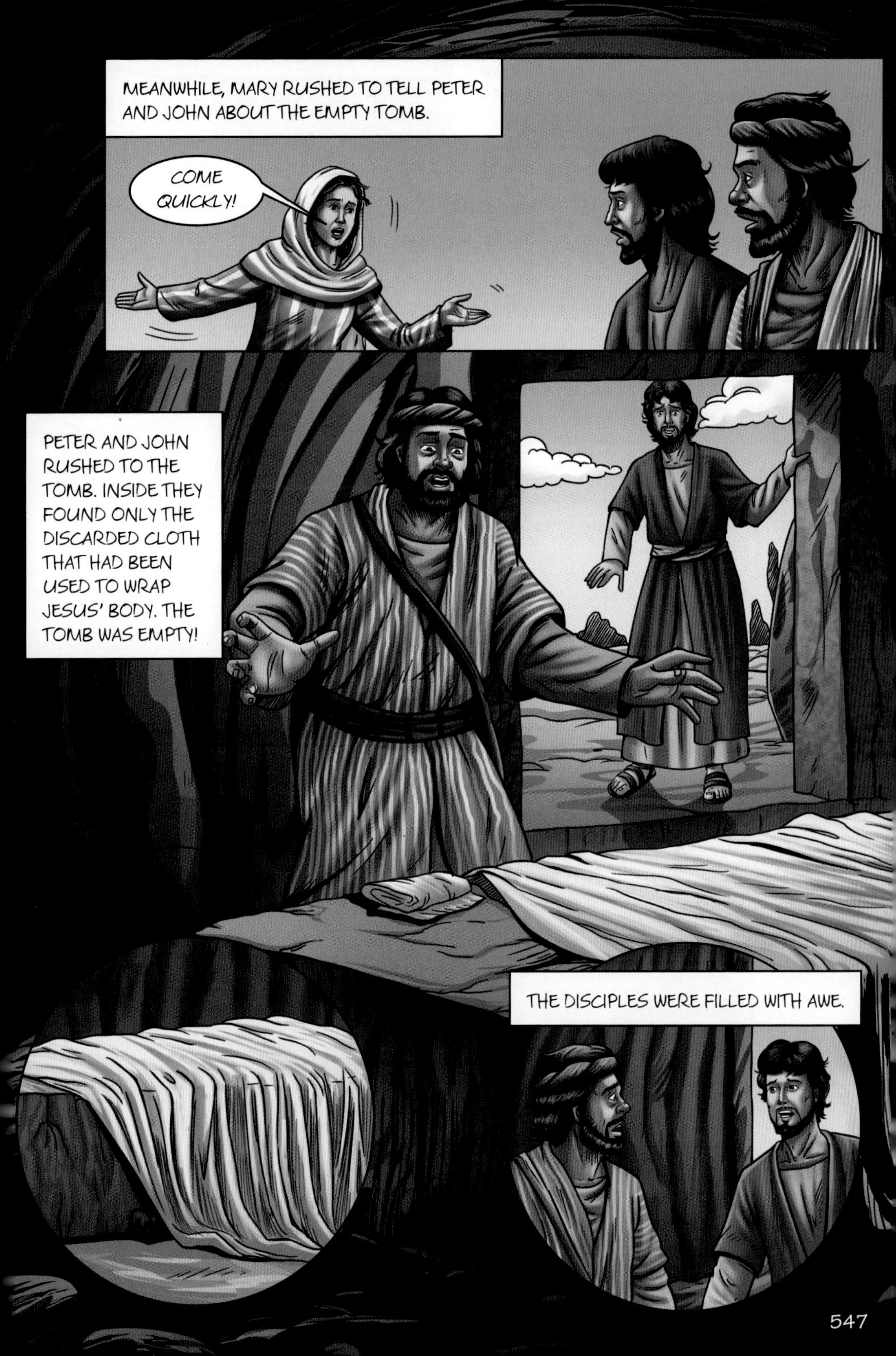
MEANWHILE, MARY RUSHED TO TELL PETER AND JOHN ABOUT THE EMPTY TOMB.
COME QUICKLY!
PETER AND JOHN RUSHED TO THE TOMB. INSIDE THEY FOUND ONLY THE DISCARDED CLOTH THAT HAD BEEN USED TO WRAP JESUS' BODY. THE TOMB WAS EMPTY!
THE DISCIPLES WERE FILLED WITH AWE.

MARY STOOD OUTSIDE THE TOMB ALONE, WEEPING QUIETLY. SHE DID NOT UNDERSTAND WHAT HAD HAPPENED, ONLY THAT HER TEACHER WAS GONE. SHE MISSED JESUS SO MUCH!
JUST THEN SHE HEARD STEPS BEHIND HER.
WHY ARE YOU CRYING? WHO ARE YOU LOOKING FOR?
SIR, IF YOU HAVE TAKEN HIM AWAY, TELL ME WHERE YOU HAVE PUT HIM.
IN REPLY, THE MAN ONLY SPOKE HER NAME, BUT INSTANTLY SHE KNEW WHO THIS WAS!
MARY!
TEACHER! CAN IT REALLY BE YOU?
DON'T CLING TO ME, FOR I HAVEN'T YET ASCENDED TO THE FATHER. BUT GO FIND MY BROTHERS AND TELL THEM.
FILLED WITH JOY AND AWE, MARY RAN TO TELL THE OTHERS THE AMAZING NEWS.

The Guards Are Told to Lie

Matthew 28

On the Road to Emmaus
Luke 24
THAT VERY DAY A MAN NAMED CLEOPAS AND HIS FRIEND WERE WALKING TO EMMAUS, A SMALL VILLAGE OUTSIDE JERUSALEM.
DID YOU HEAR? JESUS' BODY IS MISSING.
THAT'S VERY STRANGE. WHO WOULD TAKE IT?
AS CLEOPAS AND HIS FRIEND WALKED, A STRANGER JOINED THEM.
WHAT ARE YOU DISCUSSING AS YOU WALK ALONG?

YOU MUST BE THE ONLY PERSON IN JERUSALEM WHO HASN'T HEARD ABOUT THE THINGS THAT HAVE BEEN HAPPENING!
WHAT THINGS?
THE THINGS THAT HAPPENED TO JESUS, THE MAN FROM NAZARETH.
HE WAS A MIGHTY PROPHET AND TEACHER.

OUR RELIGIOUS RULERS HAD HIM ARRESTED.
THEY CONDEMNED HIM TO DEATH.
THEN THEY CRUCIFIED HIM.

SOME WOMEN FROM OUR GROUP WENT TO THE TOMB THIS MORNING.
THEY CAME BACK AND SAID HIS BODY WAS MISSING.
SOME OF OUR MEN RAN TO THE TOMB AND FOUND THINGS JUST AS THE WOMEN HAD SAID.

YOU FIND IT SO HARD TO BELIEVE ALL THAT THE PROPHETS WROTE. WASN'T IT CLEARLY PREDICTED THAT THE MESSIAH WOULD HAVE TO SUFFER ALL THESE THINGS BEFORE ENTERING INTO HIS GLORY?
THE STRANGER EXPLAINED WHAT MOSES AND ALL THE PROPHETS HAD WRITTEN ABOUT JESUS.
THE STRANGER WALKED WITH THE MEN. IT WAS GETTING LATE, SO THE MEN BEGGED THE STRANGER TO STAY FOR THE NIGHT.
IT'S GETTING LATE. WHY DON'T YOU STAY WITH US?
THE STRANGER AGREED AND WENT INSIDE...

...AND THE THREE MEN SAT DOWN TO EAT.
AS THE STRANGER BROKE BREAD, CLEOPAS AND HIS FRIEND REALIZED WHO THE STRANGER WAS.
MY LORD, IT IS YOU!
JESUS DISAPPEARED AS SOON AS CLEOPAS AND HIS FRIEND RECOGNIZED HIM.
CLEOPAS AND HIS FRIEND RACED TO JERUSALEM TO TELL THE OTHERS WHAT THEY HAD SEEN.
WHEN HE SPOKE TO US, IT WAS AS IF OUR HEARTS WERE BURNING!
THE LORD HAS REALLY RISEN!

Jesus Appears to the Disciples
Luke 24; John 20
AFTER JESUS' DEATH, THE DISCIPLES WERE AFRAID THE JEWISH AUTHORITIES WERE GOING TO ARREST THEM. THEY WERE CAREFUL NOT TO BE SEEN.
THIS WAY. BE QUIET. WE'RE MEETING THE OTHERS IN THE HOUSE DOWN THE ROAD. KEEP OUT OF SIGHT.
IT'S PETER. LET US IN.
KNOCK! KNOCK! KNOCK!
ALL OF US ARE HERE NOW, EXCEPT THOMAS.
JOHN, HAS ANYONE FOLLOWED US?
NO! I DON'T THINK SO, BUT I'LL KEEP AN EYE OUT.

AS THE DISCIPLES TALKED, A FIGURE SUDDENLY APPEARED IN THE ROOM.
PEACE BE WITH YOU.
IT'S A GHOST!
THE DISCIPLES WERE FRIGHTENED. SOME THOUGHT THEY WERE SEEING A GHOST.

WHY ARE YOU FRIGHTENED?
IT CAN'T BE! LORD, IS THAT YOU?
WHY ARE YOUR HEARTS FILLED WITH DOUBT?
TOUCH ME. GHOSTS DON'T HAVE BODIES, AS YOU SEE THAT I DO.
LOOK AT MY HANDS.

LOOK AT MY FEET.
IT IS YOU! IT IS REALLY YOU!

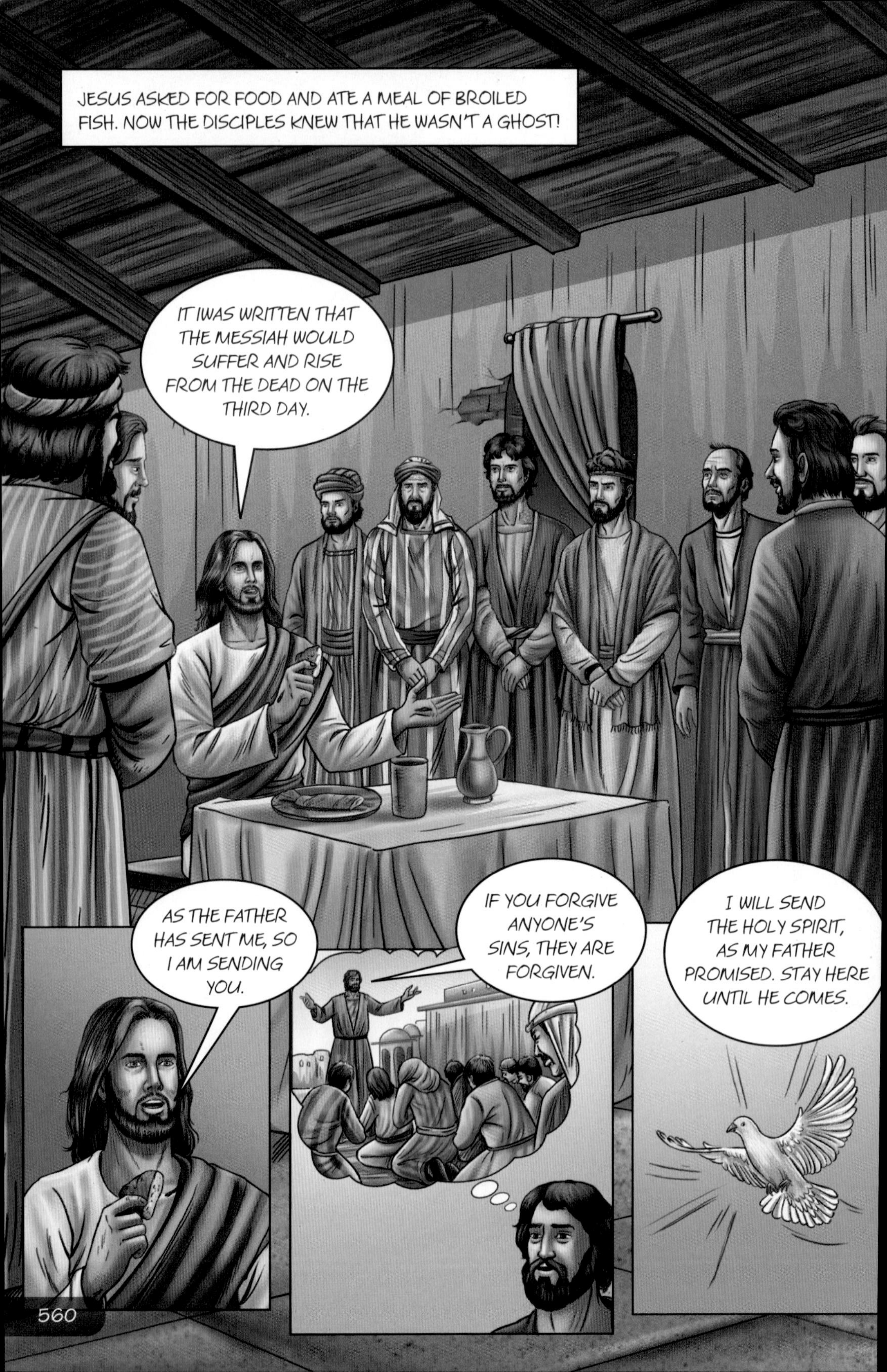
JESUS ASKED FOR FOOD AND ATE A MEAL OF BROILED FISH. NOW THE DISCIPLES KNEW THAT HE WASN'T A GHOST!
IT IWAS WRITTEN THAT THE MESSIAH WOULD SUFFER AND RISE FROM THE DEAD ON THE THIRD DAY.
AS THE FATHER HAS SENT ME, SO I AM SENDING YOU.
IF YOU FORGIVE ANYONE'S SINS, THEY ARE FORGIVEN.
I WILL SEND THE HOLY SPIRIT, AS MY FATHER PROMISED. STAY HERE UNTIL HE COMES.

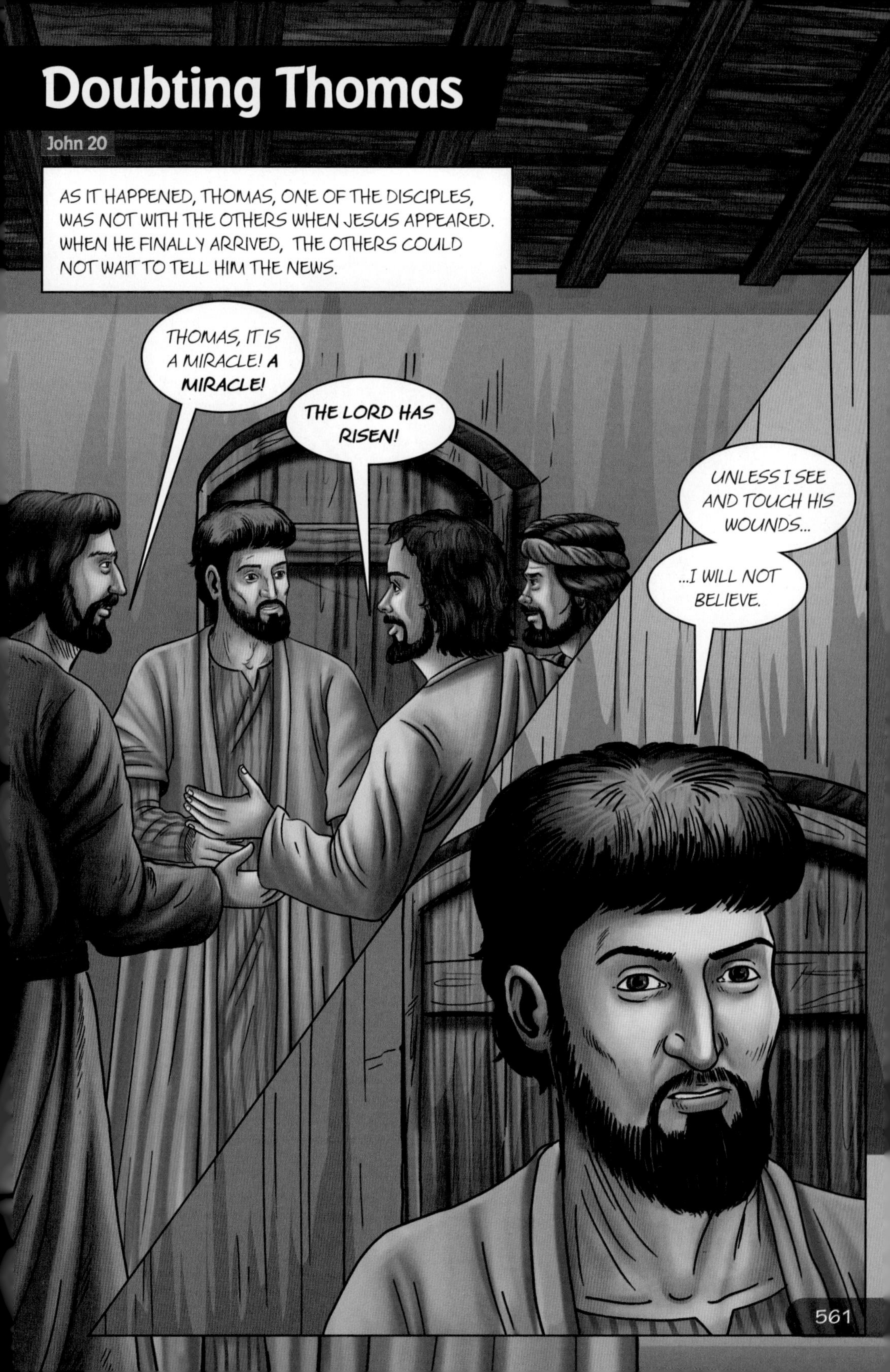
Doubting Thomas
John 20
AS IT HAPPENED, THOMAS, ONE OF THE DISCIPLES, WAS NOT WITH THE OTHERS WHEN JESUS APPEARED. WHEN HE FINALLY ARRIVED, THE OTHERS COULD NOT WAIT TO TELL HIM THE NEWS.
THOMAS, IT IS A MIRACLE! A MIRACLE!
THE LORD HAS RISEN!
UNLESS I SEE AND TOUCH HIS WOUNDS...
...I WILL NOT BELIEVE.

A WEEK LATER, JESUS APPEARED AGAIN AS THE DISCIPLES MET IN THE LOCKED ROOM.
PEACE BE WITH YOU!
LOOK AT MY HANDS.
JESUS TOLD THOMAS TO TOUCH HIS WOUNDS.
MY LORD AND MY GOD!
IT IS TRUE. YOU HAVE RISEN.
YOU BELIEVE BECAUSE YOU HAVE SEEN.
BLESSED ARE THOSE WHO BELIEVE WITHOUT SEEING ME.

"Simon, Do You Love Me?"

John 21

WHEN PETER REALIZED THAT JESUS WAS ON SHORE, HE JUMPED FROM THE BOAT AND WALKED TOWARD HIM. THE OTHERS FOLLOWED IN THE BOAT, THEIR NETS FULL OF FISH.
COME AND HAVE SOME BREAKFAST!
WHEN THE MEN FINISHED THEIR MEAL, JESUS SPOKE TO PETER.
SIMON SON OF JOHN, DO YOU LOVE ME?
YES, LORD. YOU KNOW I LOVE YOU.
FEED MY LAMBS.

SIMON SON OF JOHN, DO YOU LOVE ME?
YOU KNOW I LOVE YOU.
TAKE CARE OF MY SHEEP.
SIMON SON OF JOHN, DO YOU LOVE ME?
YOU KNOW EVERYTHING. YOU KNOW I LOVE YOU.
FEED MY SHEEP.
WHEN YOU WERE YOUNG, YOU WERE ABLE TO DO AS YOU LIKED. YOU DRESSED YOURSELF AND WENT WHEREVER YOU WANTED.
BUT WHEN YOU ARE OLD, OTHERS WILL DRESS YOU AND TAKE YOU WHERE YOU DON'T WANT TO GO.

FOLLOW ME!

Luke 24; Acts 1

ONE DAY, JESUS MET WITH HIS DISCIPLES IN BETHANY. THEY KNEW HE WAS THE TRUE MESSIAH AND ASKED HIM MANY QUESTIONS. THEY WANTED TO KNOW WHEN GOD WOULD FREE ISRAEL FROM THE ROMANS.

LORD, HAS THE TIME COME FOR YOU TO FREE ISRAEL?

AT THAT MOMENT, JESUS WAS TAKEN UP INTO HEAVEN IN A CLOUD.
TWO MEN IN WHITE ROBES STOOD BESIDE THE DISCIPLES.
MEN OF GALILEE, WHY ARE YOU STARING INTO HEAVEN?
JESUS HAS BEEN TAKEN FROM YOU INTO HEAVEN. HE WILL RETURN TO EARTH IN THE SAME WAY.

The Good News

AUTHOR OF BOOK OF ACTS: LUKE

WRITTEN: AROUND AD 60–65

OVERVIEW: GROWTH AND EXPANSION OF THE CHURCH AND IMPORTANT EVENTS IN THE LIVES OF SOME OF THE KEY APOSTLES, IN PARTICULAR PETER AND PAUL

FILLING THE GAP

AT THE BEGINNING OF THE BOOK OF ACTS WE ARE TOLD THAT THE DISCIPLES CHOSE ANOTHER MAN TO TAKE THE PLACE OF JUDAS ISCARIOT (WHO HAD HANGED HIMSELF FOLLOWING HIS BETRAYAL OF JESUS). THE MAN CHOSEN WAS MATTHIAS, WHO HAD BEEN A FOLLOWER OF JESUS SINCE HIS BAPTISM BY JOHN. WE DON'T KNOW MUCH ELSE ABOUT HIM.

MESSENGERS

THE TWELVE DISCIPLES OF JESUS (WITH THE EXCEPTION OF JUDAS ISCARIOT WHO WAS LATER REPLACED BY MATTHIAS) WERE KNOWN AS THE APOSTLES. THE WORD "APOSTLE" COMES FROM THE GREEK "APOSTOLOS," MEANING "MESSENGER," WHICH COMES FROM THE GREEK WORD "APOSTELLEIN," MEANING "TO SEND FORTH." THESE MEN WERE SENT BY JESUS TO PASS ON THE GOOD NEWS. OTHER APOSTLES ARE MENTIONED IN THE NEW TESTAMENT, MOST NOTABLY SAUL OF TARSUS, WHO WAS ALSO KNOWN AS PAUL.

The Coming of the Holy Spirit

Acts 2

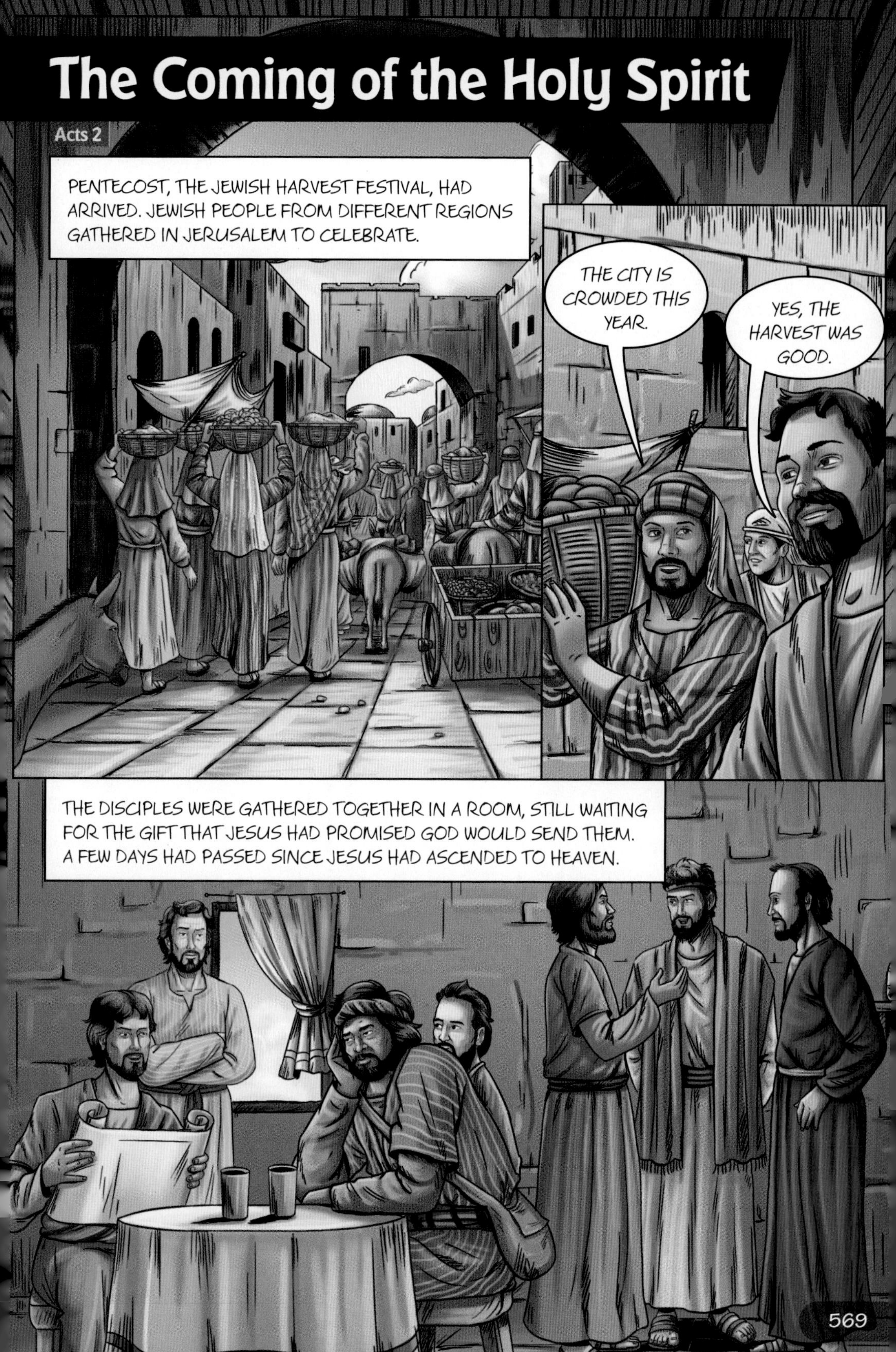

THEY HEARD A GREAT NOISE AS IF A HOWLING WIND WAS BLOWING THROUGH THE HOUSE. THEN BEFORE THEM THEY SAW WHAT SEEMED TO BE TONGUES, OR FLAMES, OF FIRE. THE FLAMES SETTLED ON EACH OF THEM.
THEY WERE FILLED WITH THE HOLY SPIRIT.
AND THEY BEGAN TO PRAISE GOD IN LANGUAGES THEY HAD NEVER SPOKEN BEFORE!

PEOPLE HEARD THE COMMOTION AND CAME TO SEE WHAT WAS GOING ON. WHEN THE APOSTLES CAME OUTSIDE, STILL SPEAKING IN DIFFERENT LANGUAGES, PEOPLE WERE CONFUSED. THEY KNEW THAT THESE MEN WERE FROM GALILEE, SO HOW WAS IT THAT THEY WERE ALL SPEAKING IN DIFFERENT LANGUAGES, PRAISING THE WONDERS OF GOD?

HOW DOES EACH OF US HEAR THEM IN HIS OWN NATIVE LANGUAGE?
WHAT DOES THIS ALL MEAN?
MAYBE THEY DRANK TOO MUCH WINE!

PETER STEPPED FORWARD AND ADDRESSED THE CROWD.
OF COURSE WE'RE NOT DRUNK! IT IS ONLY EARLY IN THE MORNING.
THE HOLY SPIRIT IS UPON US JUST AS THE PROPHET JOEL FORETOLD.
JESUS WAS A SPECIAL MAN. GOD SHOWED YOU THIS WITH ALL THE MIRACLES AND WONDERS AND SIGNS HE DID THROUGH JESUS. YET YOU KILLED HIM. YOU NAILED HIM TO A CROSS!
YET JESUS IS RAISED FROM DEATH! HE WAS LIFTED UP INTO HEAVEN AND SITS AT THE RIGHT HAND OF GOD. HE IS LORD AND MESSIAH!

THE PEOPLE FELT DREADFUL WHEN THEY HEARD PETER'S WORDS.
WHAT ARE WE TO DO?
TELL GOD YOU ARE SORRY FOR YOUR SINS! BE BAPTIZED IN THE NAME OF JESUS CHRIST!
GOD WILL FORGIVE YOU, AND THE HOLY SPIRIT WILL COME UPON YOU.
THAT DAY, THREE THOUSAND PEOPLE WERE BAPTIZED. THEY JOINED FOLLOWERS OF JESUS AND BECAME THE FIRST CHRISTIANS.

Peter Heals the Beggar
Acts 3–4
ONE DAY, JOHN AND PETER WERE GOING TO THE TEMPLE TO PRAY. BY THE STEPS WAS A MAN WHO HAD BEEN CRIPPLED ALL HIS LIFE.
SIR, WILL YOU HELP A POOR BEGGAR?
EVERY DAY, HIS FRIENDS CARRIED HIM TO THE TEMPLE SO THAT HE COULD BEG FOR MONEY.
FRIENDS, CAN YOU SPARE SOME MONEY FOR ONE CRIPPLED AT BIRTH?
I DON'T HAVE SILVER OR GOLD. BUT WHAT I DO HAVE I'LL GIVE YOU IN THE NAME OF JESUS CHRIST.

IN THE NAME OF JESUS CHRIST—GET UP AND WALK!
THEN PETER TOOK THE MAN'S HAND AND HELPED HIM UP.
LOOK AT ME! LOOK AT ME! I CAN JUMP!

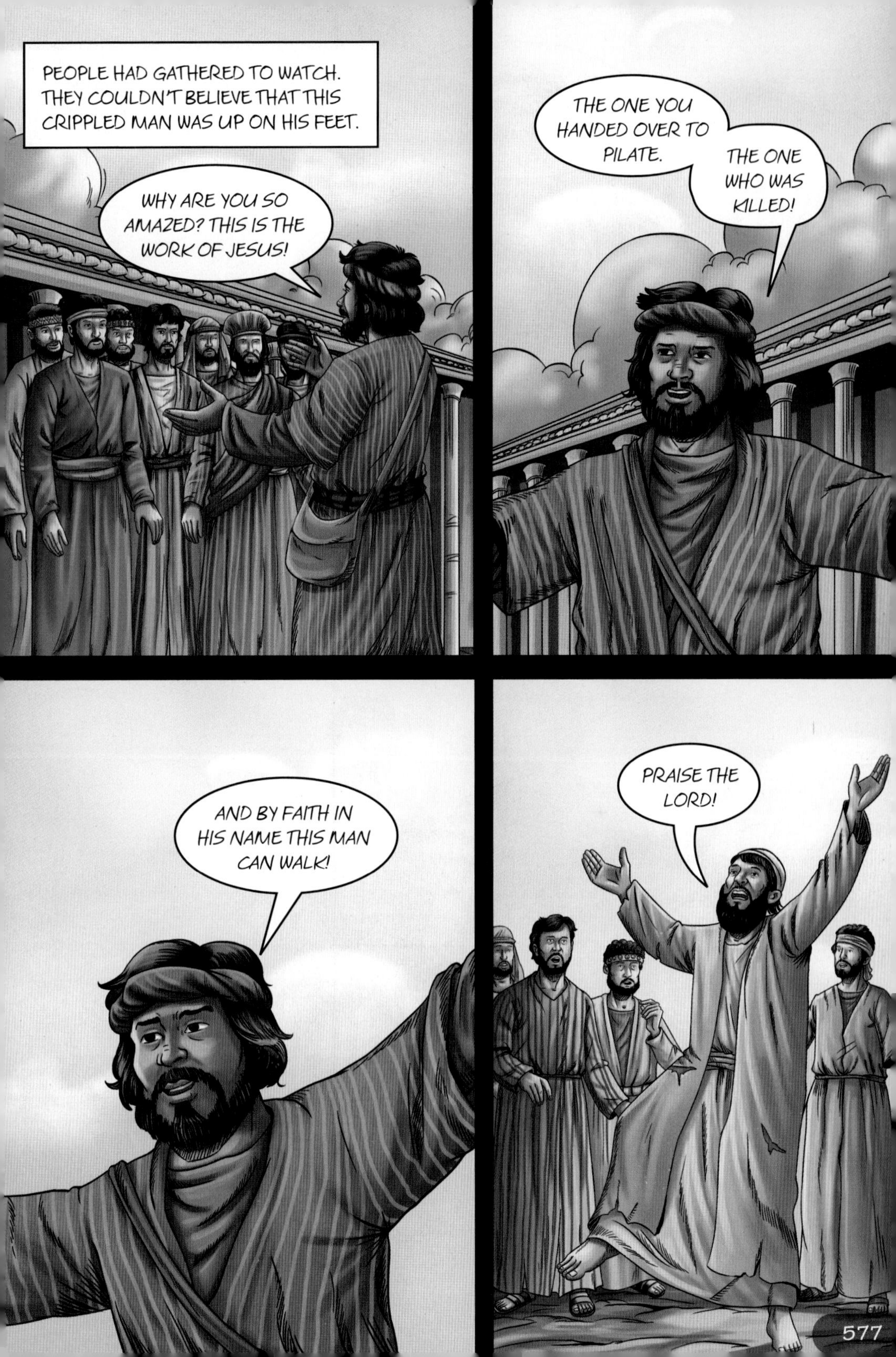

PEOPLE HAD GATHERED TO WATCH. THEY COULDN'T BELIEVE THAT THIS CRIPPLED MAN WAS UP ON HIS FEET.

AND NOW, BROTHERS, I KNOW THAT YOU ACTED OUT OF IGNORANCE...
...JUST AS YOUR LEADERS DID.
REPENT AND TURN TO GOD...
...SO THAT YOUR SINS MAY BE WIPED AWAY!
MANY WHO HEARD PETER SPEAK NOW BELIEVED, AND THE NUMBER OF CHRISTIANS GREW.

Arrested
Acts 4
THE PRIESTS AND JEWISH LEADERS WERE NOT SO HAPPY WITH WHAT WAS HAPPENING AND FELT THREATENED BY PETER AND JOHN.
SO THEY THREW THEM IN JAIL!
YOU WON'T STIR UP ANY TROUBLE IN THERE!
THE PRIESTS DEMANDED THAT THE APOSTLES TELL THEM WHO GAVE THEM THE POWER TO DO SUCH THINGS.
IT IS BY THE NAME OF JESUS CHRIST THAT THIS MAN HAS BEEN HEALED.
YOU NEED TO STOP ALL THIS TALK ABOUT JESUS!
SHOULD WE OBEY YOU OR GOD? WHAT WOULD GOD WANT? WE CANNOT KEEP QUIET ABOUT JESUS!
EVEN THE PRIESTS COULD NOT DENY THAT A MIRACLE HAD OCCURRED, AND IN THE END THE DISCIPLES WERE SET FREE. AND THEY CONTINUED TO TALK ABOUT JESUS EVERYWHERE THEY WENT!

Lying to God
Acts 5

THE NEW BELIEVERS WORKED CLOSELY TOGETHER. THEY SHARED THEIR BELONGINGS WITH ONE ANOTHER. SOME EVEN SOLD THEIR HOMES AND LAND SO THE MONEY COULD BE SHARED AND SO EVERYONE COULD HAVE WHAT THEY NEEDED.

ANANIAS AND SAPPHIRA WERE TWO OF THE BELIEVERS.

THEY SOLD SOME LAND AND PLANNED TO GIVE THE MONEY TO BE SHARED.
THIS IS A GOOD PLOT. IT'S FERTILE AND WILL SERVE YOU WELL.

BUT INSTEAD OF GIVING AWAY ALL THE MONEY FROM THE SALE, ANANIAS AND SAPPHIRA KEPT SOME FOR THEMSELVES.
NO ONE WILL NOTICE IF WE KEEP SOME BACK!

ANANIAS GAVE THE MONEY TO PETER, BUT PETER SAW THROUGH HIS DECEIT.
PETER, I SOLD MY LAND. HERE IS THE FULL AMOUNT.
ANANIAS, WHY ARE YOU LYING? SATAN HAS FILLED YOUR HEART. THE FIELD WAS YOURS AND THE MONEY WAS YOURS, BUT YOU CHOSE TO LIE ABOUT IT.
YOU'RE NOT LYING TO ME—YOU'RE LYING TO GOD!
ANANIAS HEARD WHAT PETER HAD SAID. HE IMMEDIATELY FELL TO THE FLOOR AND DIED.
SOME YOUNG MEN THEN CARRIED ANANIAS AWAY AND BURIED HIM.

THREE HOURS LATER, SAPPHIRA CAME TO SPEAK WITH PETER.
DID YOU SELL YOUR LAND FOR THIS AMOUNT?
OH, YES. THAT WAS THE PRICE.
YOU AND YOUR HUSBAND HAVE TESTED THE HOLY SPIRIT!
KNOCK!
KNOCK!
KNOCK!

THOSE WHO BURIED YOUR HUSBAND ARE HERE.
THEY WILL NOW BURY YOU!
SAPPHIRA FELL DEAD, JUST AS ANANIAS HAD.
THE MEN BURIED SAPPHIRA NEXT TO HER HUSBAND. WHEN OTHERS IN THE CHURCH HEARD WHAT HAPPENED, THEY WERE AFRAID.

Jail Break
Acts 5
THE APOSTLES CONTINUED TO TELL PEOPLE ABOUT JESUS AND TO HEAL IN HIS NAME. SO MANY CAME THAT THE PRIESTS BECAME INCREASINGLY WORRIED AND ANGRY, AND ONCE AGAIN THEY THREW THE APOSTLES IN PRISON.
IT'S A MIRACLE. PRAISE THE LORD!
BUT DURING THE NIGHT GOD SENT AN ANGEL TO FREE THE MEN.
THE ANGEL OPENED THE DOORS OF THE PRISON AND BROUGHT THE MEN OUT.
GO TO THE TEMPLE AND GIVE THE PEOPLE THIS MESSAGE OF LIFE!
WHEN THE PRIESTS FOUND OUT THE MEN HAD GONE, THEY WERE AMAZED. THEY SENT GUARDS TO FIND THEM AND BRING THEM BACK AND TRIED TO ORDER THEM TO STOP HEALING AND PREACHING, BUT IN THE END THEY HAD TO LET THEM GO.
WE HAVE TO OBEY GOD, NOT MEN!
AND OF COURSE, THE APOSTLES CARRIED ON JUST AS BEFORE!

Stephen, the Martyr

Acts 6–7

THE BELIEVERS WERE GROWING IN NUMBER DAILY. TO MAKE SURE EVERYTHING WAS SHARED FAIRLY, THEY CHOSE SEVEN GOOD MEN TO BE IN CHARGE OF DIVIDING THE FOOD SO THAT THE APOSTLES COULD CONCENTRATE ON TEACHING THE WORD OF GOD AND ON PRAYER.

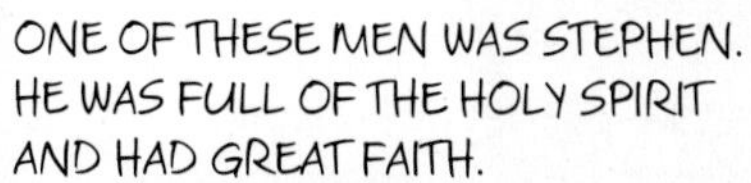

BUT STEPHEN'S ENEMIES MADE UP LIES ABOUT HIM, AND HE WAS BROUGHT BEFORE THE HIGH COUNCIL TO BE TRIED. HE FACED HIS ACCUSERS BRAVELY, HIS FACE SHINING LIKE THAT OF AN ANGEL.

YOU HAVE BETRAYED AND MURDERED GOD'S GREATEST MESSENGER. GOD GAVE YOU HIS LAW, BUT YOU DON'T OBEY IT.

LOOK! I SEE HEAVEN AND THE SON OF MAN STANDING AT GOD'S RIGHT HAND!

THIS WAS TOO MUCH FOR THE COUNCIL, WHO DRAGGED STEPHEN AWAY AND STONED HIM TO DEATH.

LORD, DO NOT CHARGE THEM WITH THIS SIN!

EVEN THEN, STEPHEN'S LAST THOUGHTS WERE NOT FOR HIMSELF.

Philip and the Ethiopian

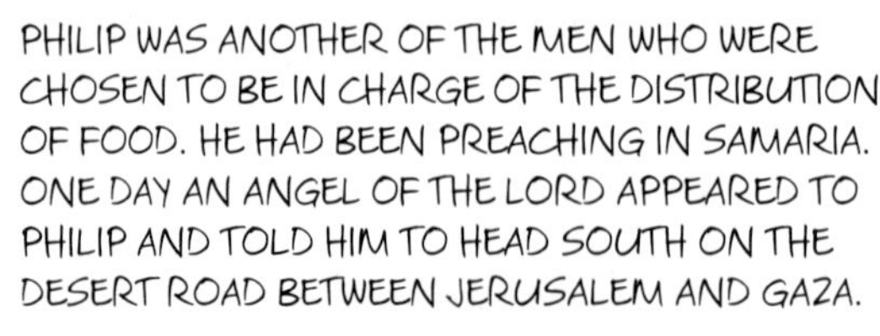

YOU ARE READING THE WORDS OF THE PROPHET ISAIAH.
HE IS TALKING ABOUT A MAN BEING LED TO HIS DEATH LIKE A LAMB TO THE SLAUGHTER.
HE IS SPEAKING OF THE MESSIAH, JESUS, WHO DIED TO SAVE US.
PHILIP TOLD THE ETHIOPIAN ABOUT ISAIAH'S WORDS, AND THEN HE WENT ON TO TELL HIM ALL ABOUT JESUS.

WHEN THEY APPROACHED SOME WATER, THE ETHIOPIAN ORDERED THE DRIVER TO STOP.
LOOK, THERE IS WATER. CAN I BE BAPTIZED?
PHILIP AND THE ETHIOPIAN WENT INTO THE WATER, WHERE PHILIP BAPTIZED HIM.
WHEN THEY RETURNED TO THE SHORE, THE SPIRIT OF THE LORD SNATCHED PHILIP AWAY. THE ETHIOPIAN NEVER SAW HIM AGAIN BUT CONTINUED ON HIS JOURNEY HOME, FILLED WITH JOY. AS FOR PHILIP, HE CONTINUED TRAVELING AND TEACHING.

A Special Woman

Acts 9

A Sheet of Animals
Acts 10
IN THE TOWN OF CAESAREA LIVED A ROMAN CAPTAIN NAMED CORNELIUS, A GOD-FEARING MAN WHO HELPED THE POOR.
MONEY FOR YOU, SIR.
MAY YOU LIVE A LONG LIFE, CAPTAIN!
ONE AFTERNOON, AN ANGEL OF THE LORD APPEARED TO CORNELIUS.
GOD WANTS YOU TO SEND SOME MEN TO JOPPA TO BRING BACK PETER.
HE IS STAYING WITH A TANNER NAMED SIMON.
GO TO JOPPA AND BRING BACK THE MAN NAMED PETER.

MEANWHILE IN JOPPA, PETER WENT UP TO THE ROOF BEFORE LUNCH TO PRAY. WHILE THERE, HE HAD A VISION. HE SAW A HUGE SHEET BEING LOWERED FROM THE SKY, AND IN IT WERE ALL KINDS OF ANIMALS. PETER REALIZED THAT THERE WERE ALSO ANIMALS JEWS WERE FORBIDDEN TO EAT, FOR THEY WERE CONSIDERED UNCLEAN.
THEN HE HEARD GOD'S VOICE TELLING HIM TO EAT.
I CAN'T DO THAT, LORD! I'VE NEVER EATEN ANYTHING UNCLEAN!
DO NOT CALL SOMETHING UNCLEAN IF GOD HAS MADE IT CLEAN.
THIS HAPPENED THREE TIMES. THEN PETER HEARD A KNOCK AT THE DOOR.

IT WAS CORNELIUS'S MEN. PETER INVITED THEM IN, AND THE NEXT DAY HE WENT WITH THEM TO CAESAREA, FOR NOW HE UNDERSTOOD HIS VISION.
PLEASE COME IN.
CORNELIUS WELCOMED PETER INTO HIS HOME.
ACCORDING TO OUR LAW, JEWS ARE NOT SUPPOSED TO ASSOCIATE WITH GENTILES.* BUT GOD HAS SHOWN ME THAT I SHOULDN'T CONSIDER ANYONE UNFIT OR UNCLEAN.
*A GENTILE IS A PERSON WHO IS NOT A JEW.
PETER SPOKE TO CORNELIUS'S FAMILY AND FRIENDS.
GOD DOESN'T SHOW FAVORITISM. HE DOESN'T CARE WHAT NATION YOU COME FROM. HIS MESSAGE IS FOR EVERYONE. HE WILL WELCOME ANYONE WHO BELIEVES IN HIM AND TRIES TO FOLLOW HIS LAWS.
THE HOLY SPIRIT HAS COME TO YOU. YOU CAN BE BAPTIZED TOO.
CORNELIUS AND THE OTHERS WERE BAPTIZED IN THE NAME OF JESUS CHRIST.

Freed by an Angel
Acts 12
HEROD AGRIPPA, WHO WAS KING OF JUDAH AT THAT TIME, HATED CHRISTIANS. HIS SOLDIERS ROUNDED THEM UP AND THREW MANY IN PRISON.
HEROD PUT TO DEATH JAMES, THE BROTHER OF JOHN...
...AND ARRESTED PETER. HEROD PUT HIM IN PRISON AND UNDER THE GUARD OF FOUR SQUADS OF SOLDIERS.
ON THE EVENING BEFORE HEROD WAS TO BRING PETER TO TRIAL, AN ANGEL APPEARED IN THE CELL AS THE GUARDS SLEPT.
QUICK! GET UP!

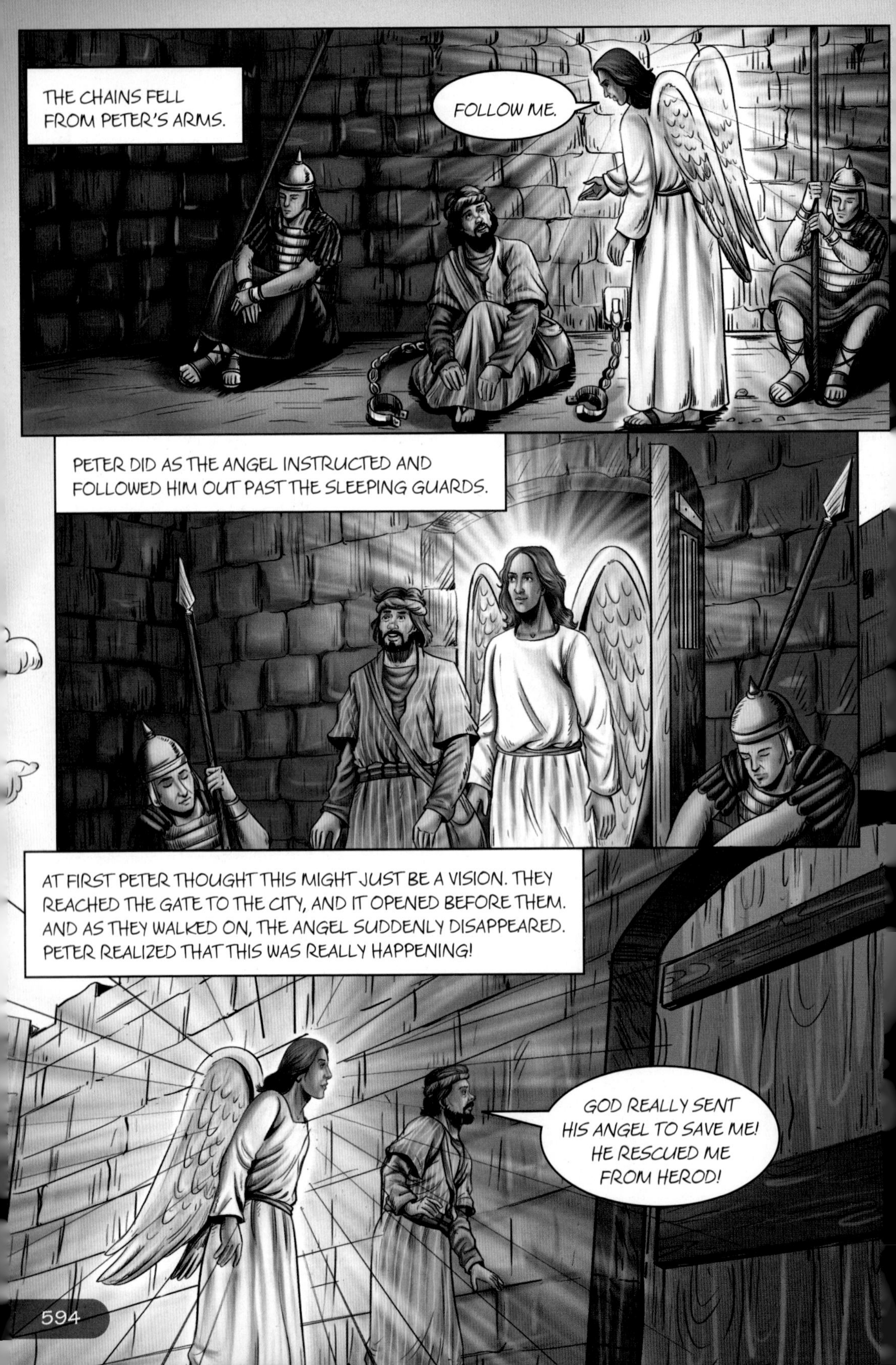
THE CHAINS FELL FROM PETER'S ARMS.
FOLLOW ME.
PETER DID AS THE ANGEL INSTRUCTED AND FOLLOWED HIM OUT PAST THE SLEEPING GUARDS.
AT FIRST PETER THOUGHT THIS MIGHT JUST BE A VISION. THEY REACHED THE GATE TO THE CITY, AND IT OPENED BEFORE THEM. AND AS THEY WALKED ON, THE ANGEL SUDDENLY DISAPPEARED. PETER REALIZED THAT THIS WAS REALLY HAPPENING!
GOD REALLY SENT HIS ANGEL TO SAVE ME! HE RESCUED ME FROM HEROD!

PETER MADE HIS WAY TO THE HOUSE OF ANOTHER FOLLOWER OF JESUS.
OPEN THE DOOR! IT'S ME!
THE SERVANT RECOGNIZED PETER'S VOICE AND RUSHED TO TELL THE OTHERS THAT HE WAS THERE, BUT IN HER EXCITEMENT SHE FORGOT TO OPEN THE DOOR!
PETER IS HERE!
YOU'RE OUT OF YOUR MIND, GIRL. YOU MUST BE IMAGINING THINGS!
BUT PETER KEPT KNOCKING, AND AT LAST THEY OPENED THE DOOR.
IT REALLY IS YOU!
LET ME TELL YOU HOW I ESCAPED.
HEROD WAS FURIOUS WHEN HE FOUND THAT PETER HAD ESCAPED, SO HE ORDERED THE GUARDS TO BE EXECUTED. BUT HE COULDN'T FIND PETER, FOR HE HAD ALREADY MOVED ON. DESPITE HEROD'S BEST EFFORTS, THE MESSAGE OF GOD WAS RAPIDLY SPREADING, REACHING MORE AND MORE PEOPLE.

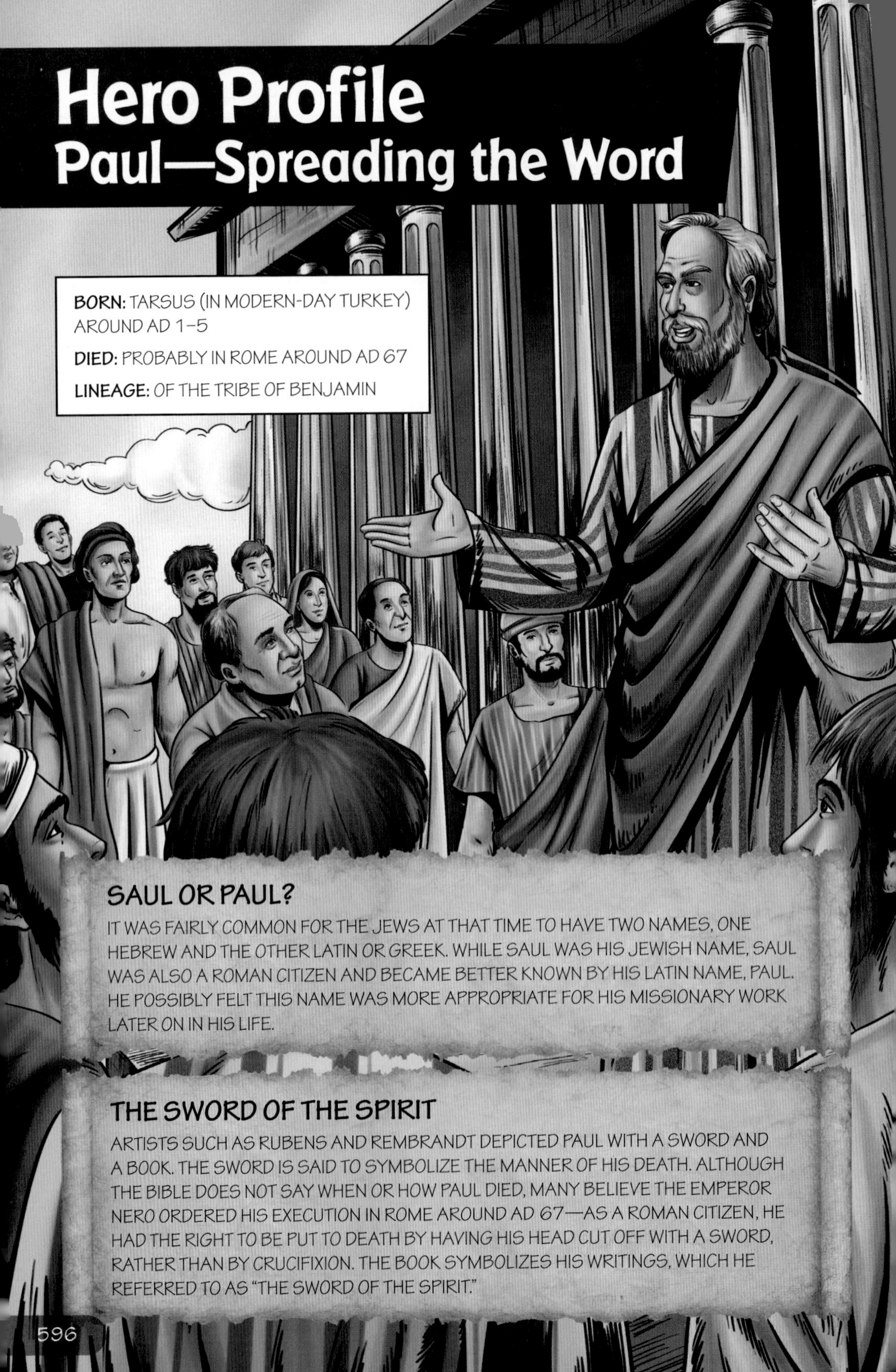

Hero Profile
Paul—Spreading the Word

BORN: TARSUS (IN MODERN-DAY TURKEY) AROUND AD 1–5

DIED: PROBABLY IN ROME AROUND AD 67

LINEAGE: OF THE TRIBE OF BENJAMIN

SAUL OR PAUL?

IT WAS FAIRLY COMMON FOR THE JEWS AT THAT TIME TO HAVE TWO NAMES, ONE HEBREW AND THE OTHER LATIN OR GREEK. WHILE SAUL WAS HIS JEWISH NAME, SAUL WAS ALSO A ROMAN CITIZEN AND BECAME BETTER KNOWN BY HIS LATIN NAME, PAUL. HE POSSIBLY FELT THIS NAME WAS MORE APPROPRIATE FOR HIS MISSIONARY WORK LATER ON IN HIS LIFE.

THE SWORD OF THE SPIRIT

ARTISTS SUCH AS RUBENS AND REMBRANDT DEPICTED PAUL WITH A SWORD AND A BOOK. THE SWORD IS SAID TO SYMBOLIZE THE MANNER OF HIS DEATH. ALTHOUGH THE BIBLE DOES NOT SAY WHEN OR HOW PAUL DIED, MANY BELIEVE THE EMPEROR NERO ORDERED HIS EXECUTION IN ROME AROUND AD 67—AS A ROMAN CITIZEN, HE HAD THE RIGHT TO BE PUT TO DEATH BY HAVING HIS HEAD CUT OFF WITH A SWORD, RATHER THAN BY CRUCIFIXION. THE BOOK SYMBOLIZES HIS WRITINGS, WHICH HE REFERRED TO AS "THE SWORD OF THE SPIRIT."

Saul Sees the Light

Acts 7–9

SAUL DISLIKED THE CHRISTIANS SO MUCH THAT HE ASKED THE HIGH PRIEST OF JERUSALEM TO SEND HIM TO DAMASCUS IN SYRIA SO HE COULD BRING BACK AND IMPRISON THE BELIEVERS.
IF I FIND ANYONE WHO BELIEVES IN THE WAY, I'LL BRING THEM BACK IN CHAINS.
THE HIGH PRIEST GAVE SAUL HIS BLESSING, AND HE BEGAN A JOURNEY TO DAMASCUS.

AS SAUL NEARED THE CITY, A BRIGHT LIGHT SHONE DOWN. HE FELL TO THE GROUND. AT THAT MOMENT, SAUL HEARD A VOICE.
SAUL! SAUL! WHY ARE YOU PERSECUTING ME?
I AM JESUS, THE ONE YOU ARE PERSECUTING! NOW GO INTO THE CITY, AND YOU WILL BE TOLD WHAT TO DO.
I...I...I CANNOT SEE! I AM BLIND!

THE MEN TRAVELING WITH SAUL TOOK HIM BY THE HAND AND LED HIM TO DAMASCUS.

ANANIAS DID AS GOD ASKED AND WENT TO SEE SAUL. SAUL HAD NOT HAD ANYTHING TO EAT OR DRINK FOR THREE DAYS.
SAUL, MY BROTHER, IT WAS JESUS WHO APPEARED TO YOU ON THE ROAD.
THE LORD SENT ME SO THAT YOU MAY REGAIN YOUR SIGHT AND BE FILLED WITH THE HOLY SPIRIT.
I CAN SEE! I CAN SEE!
SAUL WAS THEN BAPTIZED, AND WHEN HE HAD EATEN, HE SET OUT TO PREACH GOD'S WORD IN THE CITY.

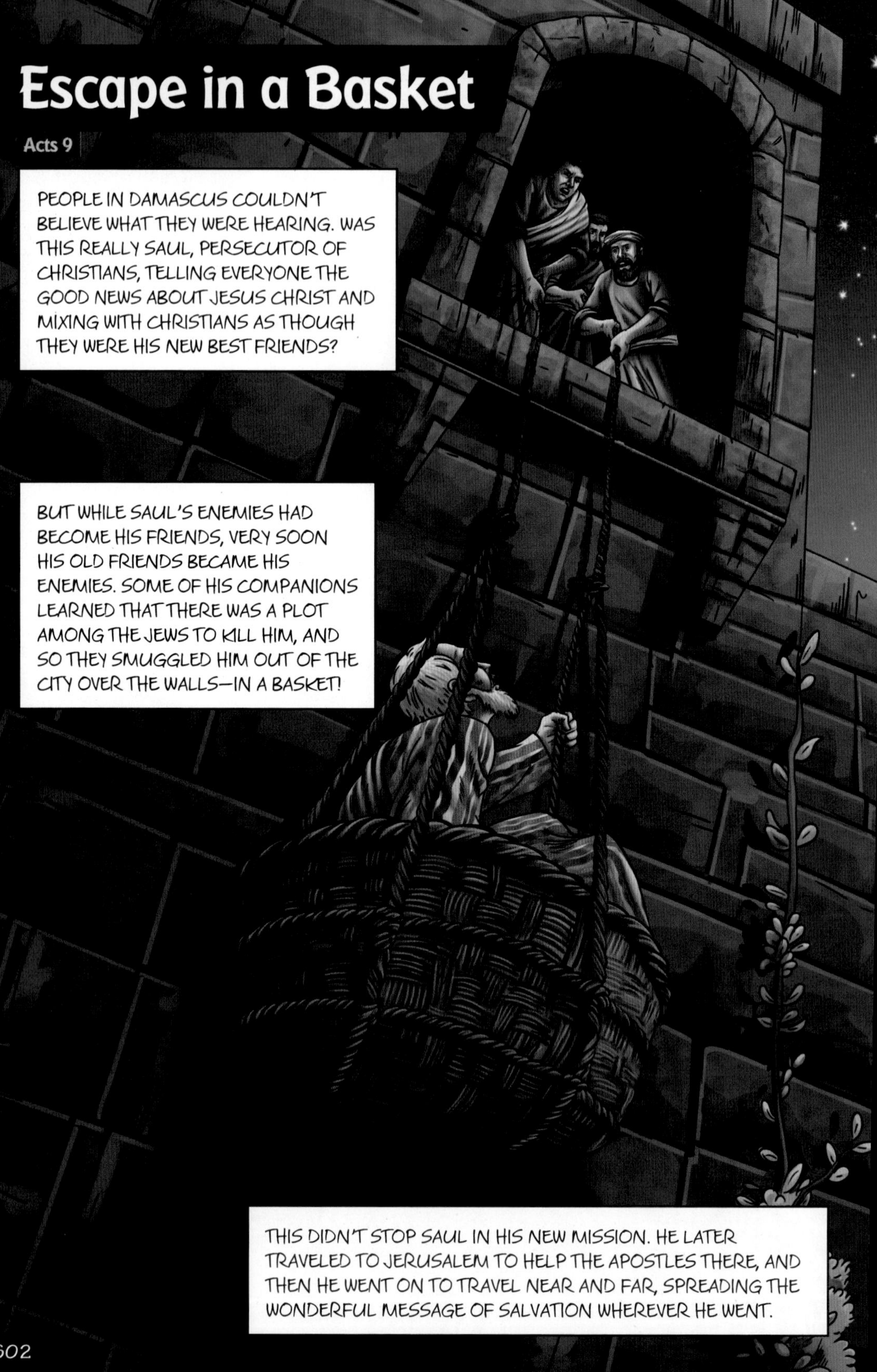
Escape in a Basket
Acts 9
PEOPLE IN DAMASCUS COULDN'T BELIEVE WHAT THEY WERE HEARING. WAS THIS REALLY SAUL, PERSECUTOR OF CHRISTIANS, TELLING EVERYONE THE GOOD NEWS ABOUT JESUS CHRIST AND MIXING WITH CHRISTIANS AS THOUGH THEY WERE HIS NEW BEST FRIENDS?
BUT WHILE SAUL'S ENEMIES HAD BECOME HIS FRIENDS, VERY SOON HIS OLD FRIENDS BECAME HIS ENEMIES. SOME OF HIS COMPANIONS LEARNED THAT THERE WAS A PLOT AMONG THE JEWS TO KILL HIM, AND SO THEY SMUGGLED HIM OUT OF THE CITY OVER THE WALLS—IN A BASKET!
THIS DIDN'T STOP SAUL IN HIS NEW MISSION. HE LATER TRAVELED TO JERUSALEM TO HELP THE APOSTLES THERE, AND THEN HE WENT ON TO TRAVEL NEAR AND FAR, SPREADING THE WONDERFUL MESSAGE OF SALVATION WHEREVER HE WENT.

Struck Blind
Acts 13
SAUL (CALLED PAUL) AND A MAN NAMED BARNABAS WERE CALLED BY GOD TO GO ON A JOURNEY TO SPREAD THE GOOD NEWS TO PEOPLE WHO HAD NOT YET HEARD ABOUT JESUS. THIS WAS THE FIRST OF PAUL'S MISSIONARY JOURNEYS.
PAUL'S MISSIONARY JOURNEYS
PAUL'S FIRST MISSIONARY JOURNEY
PAUL'S SECOND MISSIONARY JOURNEY
PAUL'S THIRD MISSIONARY JOURNEY
PAUL'S VOYAGE TO ROME
Rome
ITALY
Adriatic Sea
MACEDONIA
Black Sea
Philippi
Thessalonica
Berea
Troas
Aegean Sea
ASIA MINOR
SICILY
Syracuse
Athens
Corinth
GREECE
Ephesus
Antioch
Iconium
Derbe
PISIDIA
Lystra
MALTA
Myra
Antioch
CYPRUS
Salamis
CRETE
Salmone
Fair Havens
Paphos
Mediterranean Sea
Damascus
Tyre
Jerusalem
Alexandria
JUDAH
EGYPT
ARABIA
FIRST THEY WENT TO CYPRUS, WHERE THE ROMAN GOVERNOR SENT FOR THEM. ONE OF HIS ATTENDANTS WAS A SORCERER NAMED ELYMAS WHO TRIED TO STOP THE GOVERNOR FROM LISTENING TO PAUL.
THEY'RE TELLING YOU NOTHING BUT LIES!
YOU ARE THE SON OF THE DEVIL! YOU TRY TO TURN THE LORD'S TRUTHS INTO LIES! BUT YOU WILL BE STRUCK BLIND!
INSTANTLY, THE SORCERER'S EYES CLOUDED OVER, AND HE COULD SEE NOTHING.
I CAN'T SEE! I CAN'T SEE!
THE GOVERNOR WAS SO AMAZED THAT HE BECAME A CHRISTIAN.

On the Road

Acts 13

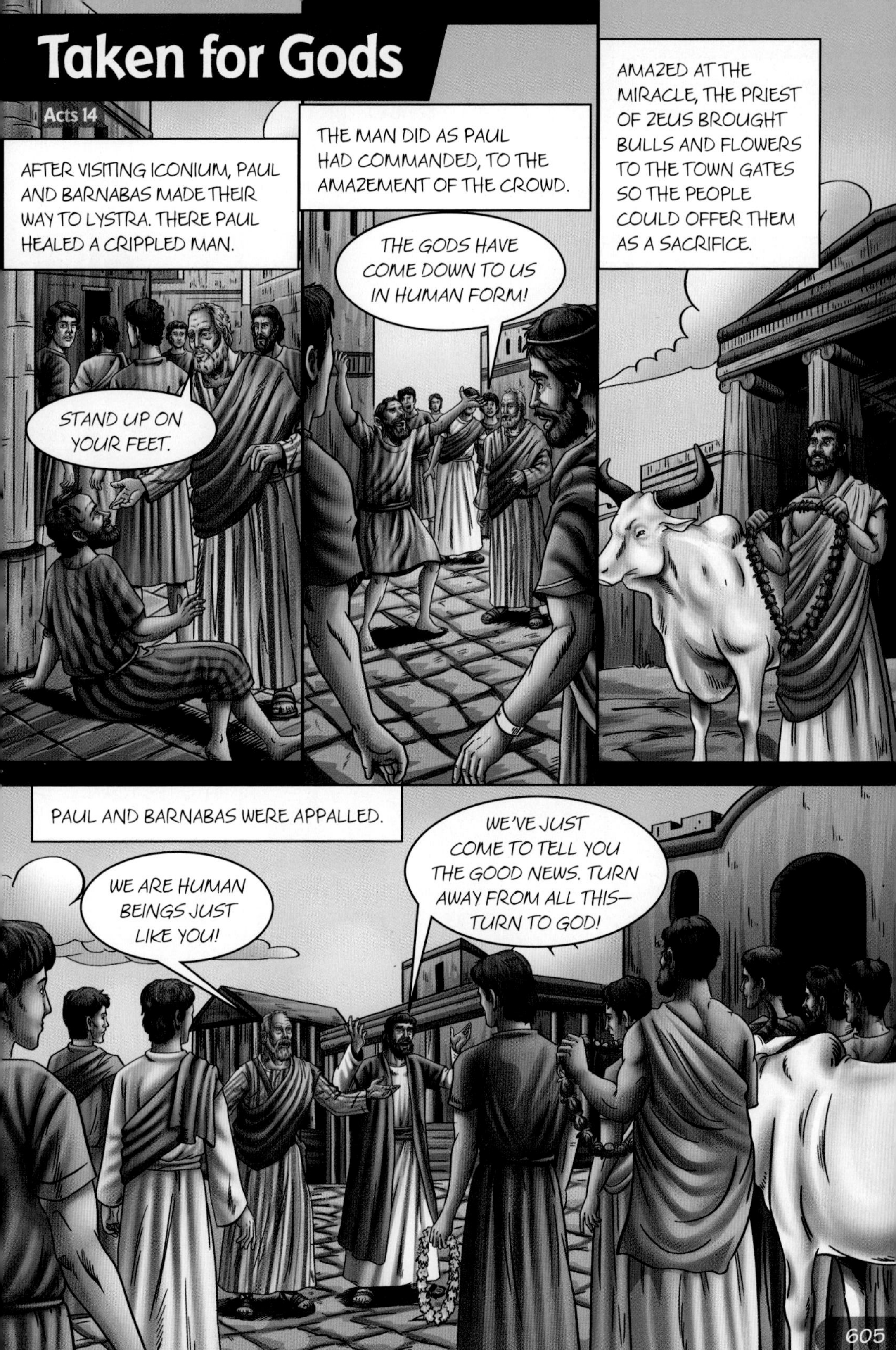
Taken for Gods
Acts 14
AFTER VISITING ICONIUM, PAUL AND BARNABAS MADE THEIR WAY TO LYSTRA. THERE PAUL HEALED A CRIPPLED MAN.
STAND UP ON YOUR FEET.
THE MAN DID AS PAUL HAD COMMANDED, TO THE AMAZEMENT OF THE CROWD.
THE GODS HAVE COME DOWN TO US IN HUMAN FORM!
AMAZED AT THE MIRACLE, THE PRIEST OF ZEUS BROUGHT BULLS AND FLOWERS TO THE TOWN GATES SO THE PEOPLE COULD OFFER THEM AS A SACRIFICE.
PAUL AND BARNABAS WERE APPALLED.
WE ARE HUMAN BEINGS JUST LIKE YOU!
WE'VE JUST COME TO TELL YOU THE GOOD NEWS. TURN AWAY FROM ALL THIS—TURN TO GOD!

THEN SOME JEWS CAME FROM ANTIOCH, AND THEY TURNED THE PEOPLE AGAINST THE APOSTLES. THE CROWD THREW STONES AT PAUL...
KILL THE TROUBLE-MAKER!
...AND THEN DRAGGED HIM OUT OF THE CITY AND LEFT HIM FOR DEAD.
BUT WHEN THEY HAD GONE, PAUL GOT UP AGAIN...
I THOUGHT HE WAS DEAD!
PRAISE THE LORD!
...AND WENT BACK INTO THE TOWN.
THE NEXT DAY, HE AND BARNABAS LEFT LYSTRA AND CONTINUED THEIR MISSION TO DERBE.

Off to Macedonia
Acts 15–16
SOME TIME LATER PAUL SET OFF ON ANOTHER MISSIONARY JOURNEY. THIS TIME HE TOOK A MAN NAMED SILAS WITH HIM. THEY WENT BACK TO SOME OF THE NEW CHURCHES THAT PAUL HAD SET UP TO HELP THE PEOPLE.
IT'S GOOD TO SEE YOU AGAIN!
TELL ME HOW YOU HAVE BEEN GETTING ON.
ONE NIGHT PAUL HAD A VISION. HE SAW A MAN FROM MACEDONIA ASKING FOR HELP.
COME TO MACEDONIA, PAUL! PLEASE HELP US!
PAUL AND SILAS TRAVELED TO MACEDONIA AT ONCE AND CAME TO THE CITY OF PHILIPPI. THERE THEY MET A WOMAN NAMED LYDIA, WHO OPENED HER HEART TO THE WORD OF GOD AND WELCOMED THE MEN INTO HER HOME.

IN THE CITY OF PHILIPPI, THERE WAS A SLAVE GIRL WHO WAS POSSESSED BY A DEMON. SHE MADE MONEY FOR HER OWNERS BY TELLING PEOPLE'S FORTUNES.
I CAN SEE VAST RICHES IN YOUR FUTURE.
THE SLAVE GIRL BEGAN TO FOLLOW PAUL AND SILAS AROUND.
THESE MEN ARE SERVANTS OF THE MOST HIGH GOD! THEY ARE HERE TO TELL YOU HOW TO BE SAVED.
I COMMAND YOU, DEMON, IN THE NAME OF JESUS CHRIST, TO **COME OUT OF HER!**

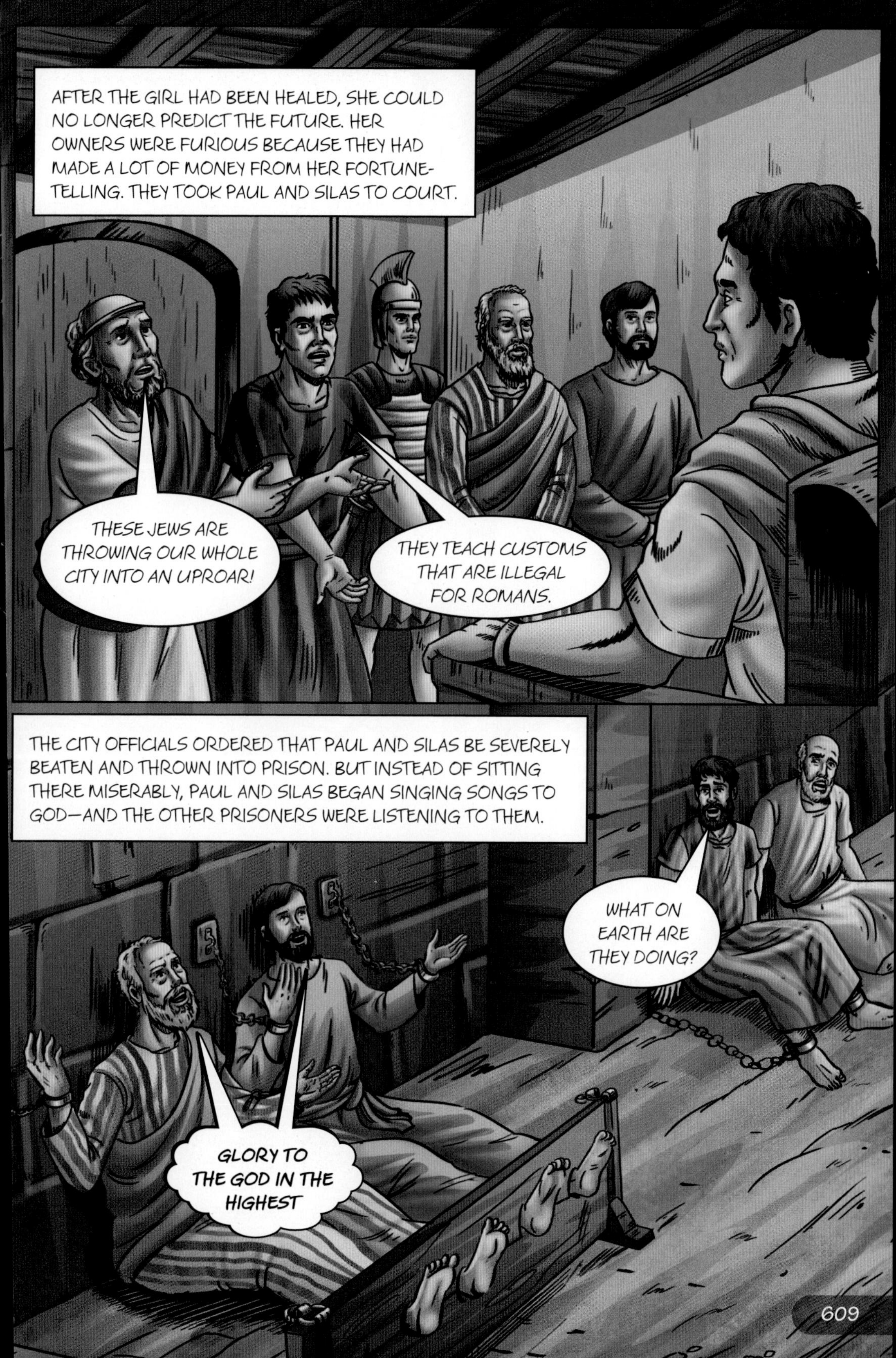
AFTER THE GIRL HAD BEEN HEALED, SHE COULD NO LONGER PREDICT THE FUTURE. HER OWNERS WERE FURIOUS BECAUSE THEY HAD MADE A LOT OF MONEY FROM HER FORTUNE-TELLING. THEY TOOK PAUL AND SILAS TO COURT.
THESE JEWS ARE THROWING OUR WHOLE CITY INTO AN UPROAR!
THEY TEACH CUSTOMS THAT ARE ILLEGAL FOR ROMANS.
THE CITY OFFICIALS ORDERED THAT PAUL AND SILAS BE SEVERELY BEATEN AND THROWN INTO PRISON. BUT INSTEAD OF SITTING THERE MISERABLY, PAUL AND SILAS BEGAN SINGING SONGS TO GOD—AND THE OTHER PRISONERS WERE LISTENING TO THEM.
GLORY TO THE GOD IN THE HIGHEST
WHAT ON EARTH ARE THEY DOING?

The Earthquake

Acts 16–17

...THAT PAUL AND SILAS WERE STILL INSIDE.
DO NO HARM TO YOURSELF! WE ARE STILL HERE.
SIRS, WHAT MUST I DO TO BE SAVED?
BELIEVE IN THE LORD JESUS.
THE NEXT DAY THE CITY OFFICIALS SENT WORD TO LET PAUL AND SILAS GO. BUT PAUL AND SILAS REFUSED. THEY TOLD THE JAILER THAT THEY WERE ROMAN CITIZENS WHO HAD BEEN BEATEN. THEY INSISTED THAT THE CITY OFFICIALS COME AND FREE THEM AS PUBLICLY AS THEY HAD IMPRISONED THEM. THE OFFICIALS WERE AFRAID WHEN THEY LEARNED THAT PAUL AND SILAS WERE ROMAN CITIZENS, AND THEY LET THEM GO. BUT THEY BEGGED PAUL AND SILAS TO LEAVE THE CITY. THEY LEFT AFTER SAYING GOODBYE TO LYDIA AND SOME OF THE OTHER BELIEVERS.

Riot at Ephesus
Acts 19
PAUL WAS IN EPHESUS ON THE THIRD OF HIS MISSIONARY JOURNEYS.
THINGS STARTED OFF FAIRLY WELL. HE BAPTIZED SOME OF THE NEW FOLLOWERS IN THE NAME OF JESUS AND SPENT TIME PREACHING IN THE SYNAGOGUE. WHEN PEOPLE REFUSED TO LISTEN, HE WENT INSTEAD TO A SPECIAL SCHOOL WHERE HE TALKED WITH PEOPLE EVERY DAY. HE WAS THERE FOR TWO YEARS, AND MANY HEARD HIS MESSAGE.

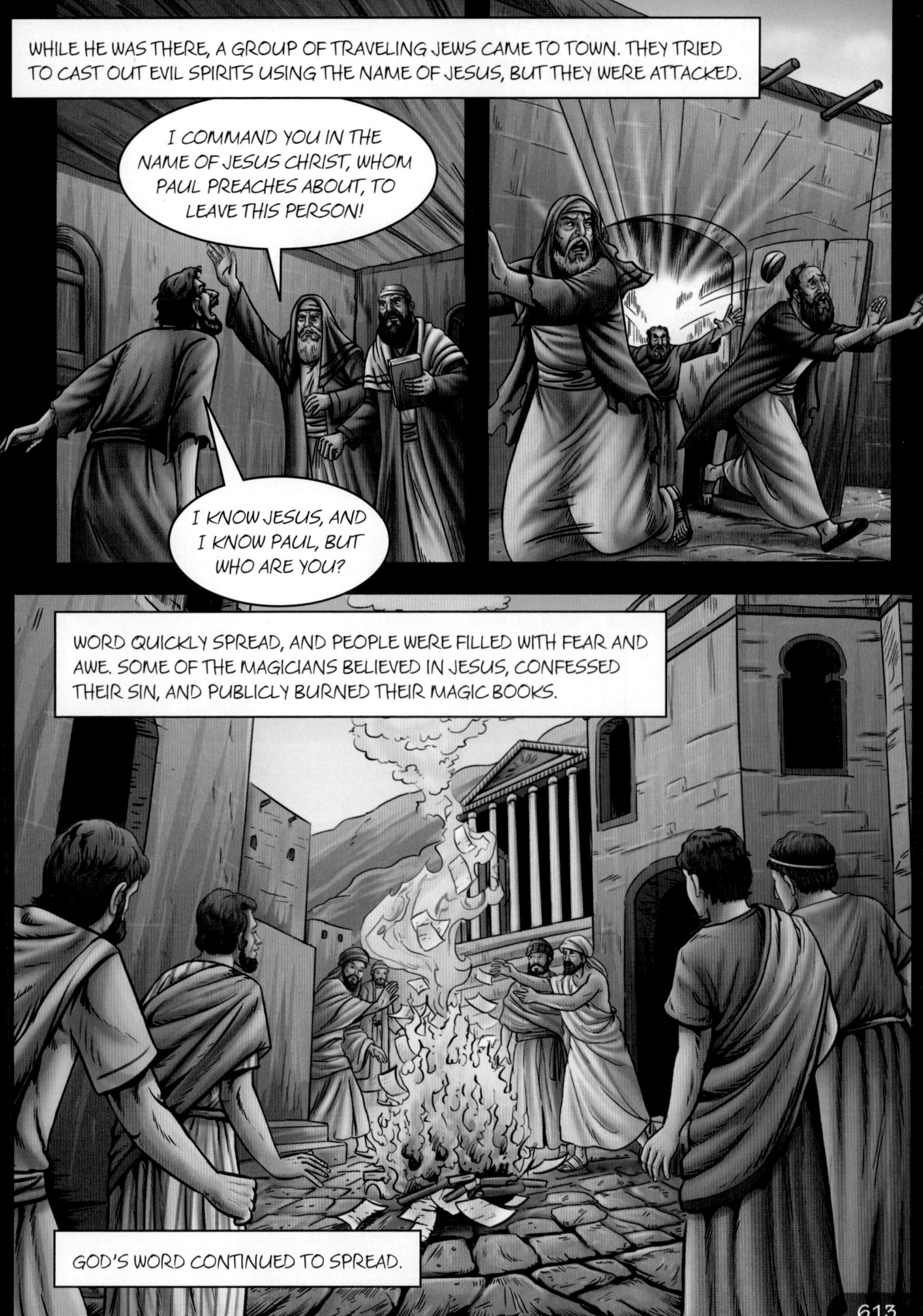
WHILE HE WAS THERE, A GROUP OF TRAVELING JEWS CAME TO TOWN. THEY TRIED TO CAST OUT EVIL SPIRITS USING THE NAME OF JESUS, BUT THEY WERE ATTACKED.
I COMMAND YOU IN THE NAME OF JESUS CHRIST, WHOM PAUL PREACHES ABOUT, TO LEAVE THIS PERSON!
I KNOW JESUS, AND I KNOW PAUL, BUT WHO ARE YOU?
WORD QUICKLY SPREAD, AND PEOPLE WERE FILLED WITH FEAR AND AWE. SOME OF THE MAGICIANS BELIEVED IN JESUS, CONFESSED THEIR SIN, AND PUBLICLY BURNED THEIR MAGIC BOOKS.
GOD'S WORD CONTINUED TO SPREAD.

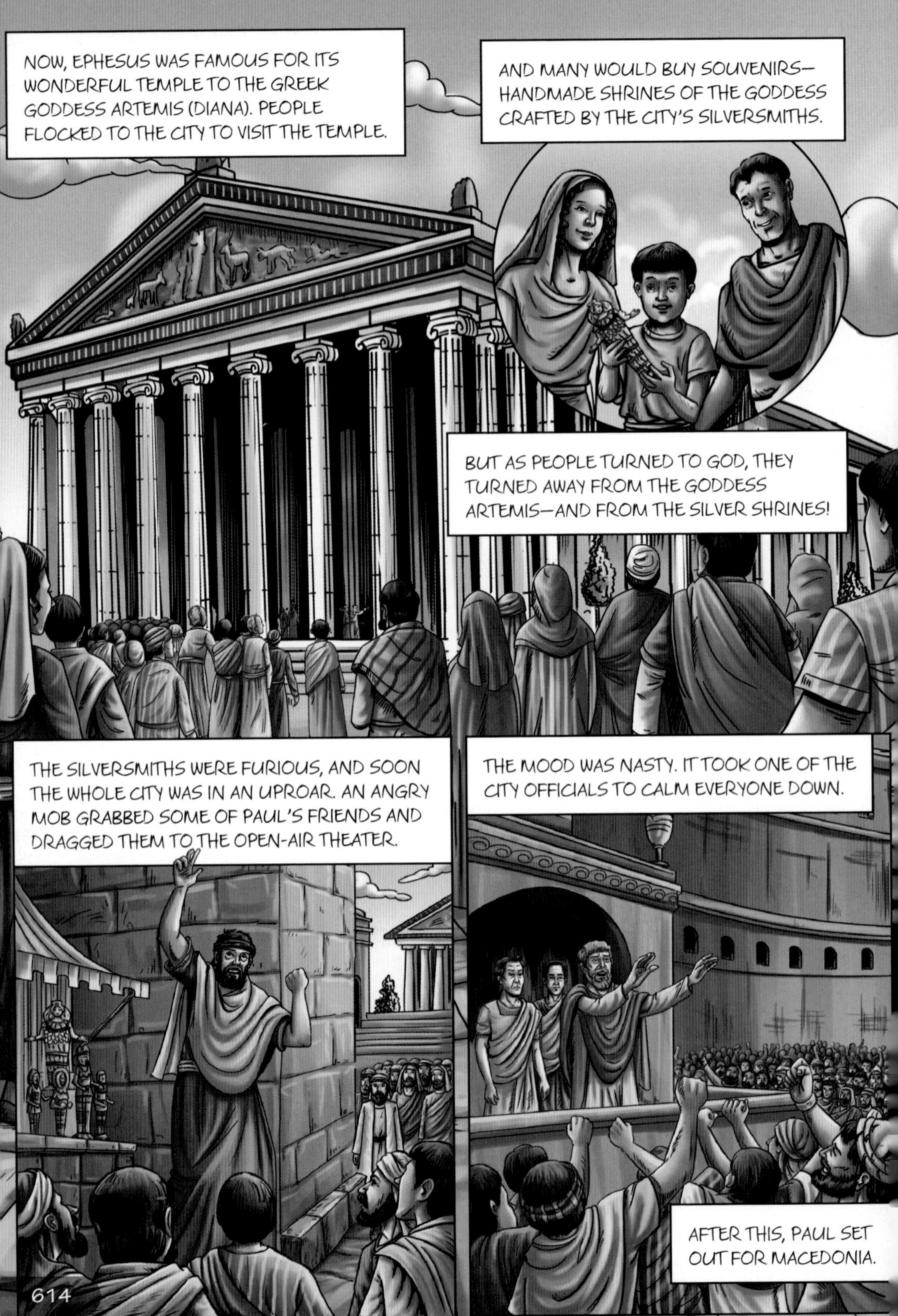
NOW, EPHESUS WAS FAMOUS FOR ITS WONDERFUL TEMPLE TO THE GREEK GODDESS ARTEMIS (DIANA). PEOPLE FLOCKED TO THE CITY TO VISIT THE TEMPLE.
AND MANY WOULD BUY SOUVENIRS—HANDMADE SHRINES OF THE GODDESS CRAFTED BY THE CITY'S SILVERSMITHS.
BUT AS PEOPLE TURNED TO GOD, THEY TURNED AWAY FROM THE GODDESS ARTEMIS—AND FROM THE SILVER SHRINES!
THE SILVERSMITHS WERE FURIOUS, AND SOON THE WHOLE CITY WAS IN AN UPROAR. AN ANGRY MOB GRABBED SOME OF PAUL'S FRIENDS AND DRAGGED THEM TO THE OPEN-AIR THEATER.
THE MOOD WAS NASTY. IT TOOK ONE OF THE CITY OFFICIALS TO CALM EVERYONE DOWN.
AFTER THIS, PAUL SET OUT FOR MACEDONIA.

Acts 20

IN THE ROOM WAS A YOUNG MAN, EUTYCHUS, WHO WAS SITTING ON A WINDOWSILL, TRYING DESPERATELY TO STAY AWAKE.

BUT EUTYCHUS DOZED OFF AND FELL OUT THE THIRD-STORY WINDOW.

IS HE ALL RIGHT?
NO! HE'S DEAD!
PAUL RUSHED DOWN TO SEE THE BOY.

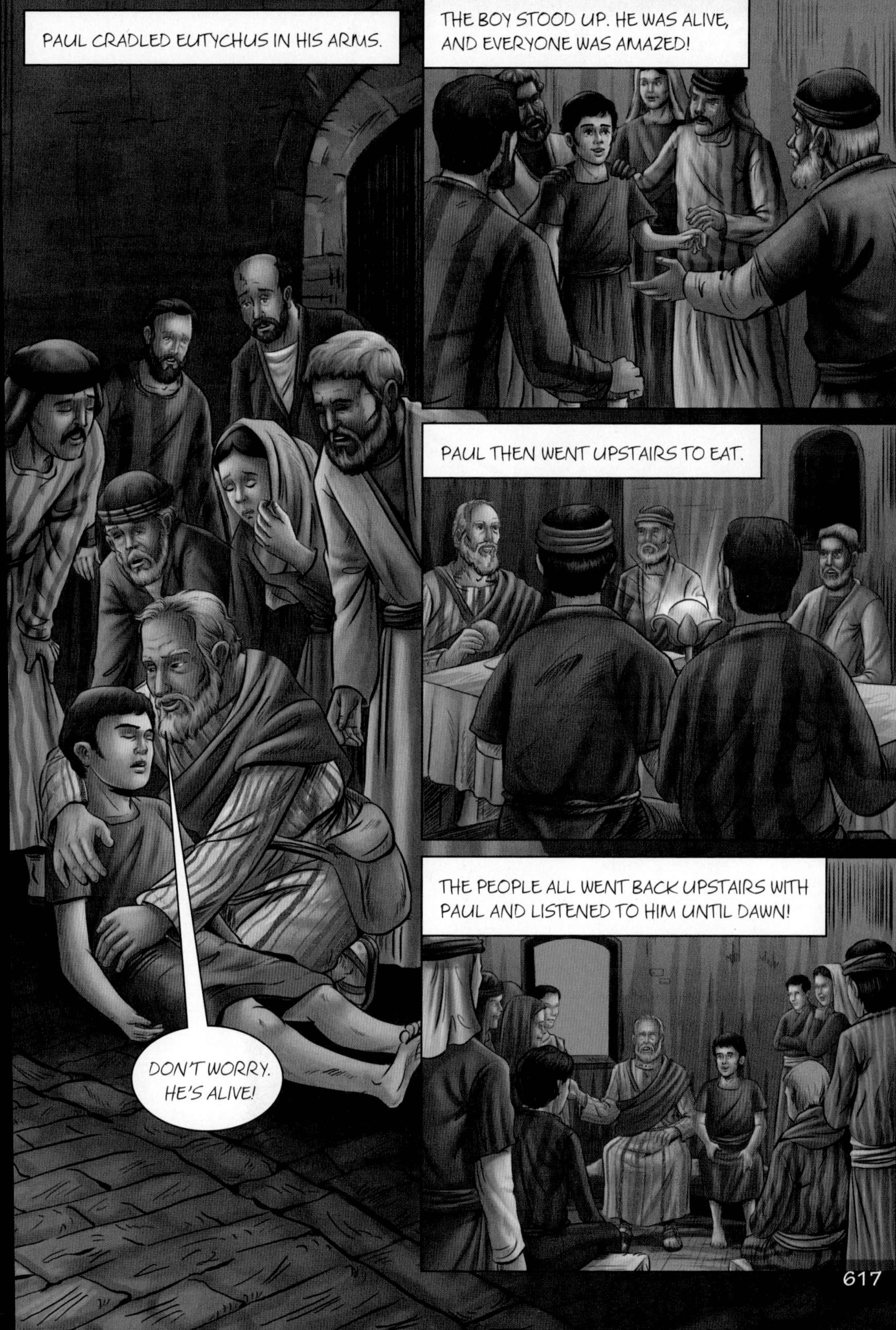
PAUL CRADLED EUTYCHUS IN HIS ARMS.
DON'T WORRY. HE'S ALIVE!
THE BOY STOOD UP. HE WAS ALIVE, AND EVERYONE WAS AMAZED!
PAUL THEN WENT UPSTAIRS TO EAT.
THE PEOPLE ALL WENT BACK UPSTAIRS WITH PAUL AND LISTENED TO HIM UNTIL DAWN!

Please Don't Go

Acts 20

PAUL'S FRIENDS DIDN'T WANT HIM TO GO TO JERUSALEM. THEY KNEW IT WOULD BE DANGEROUS FOR HIM THERE AND BEGGED HIM TO STAY.

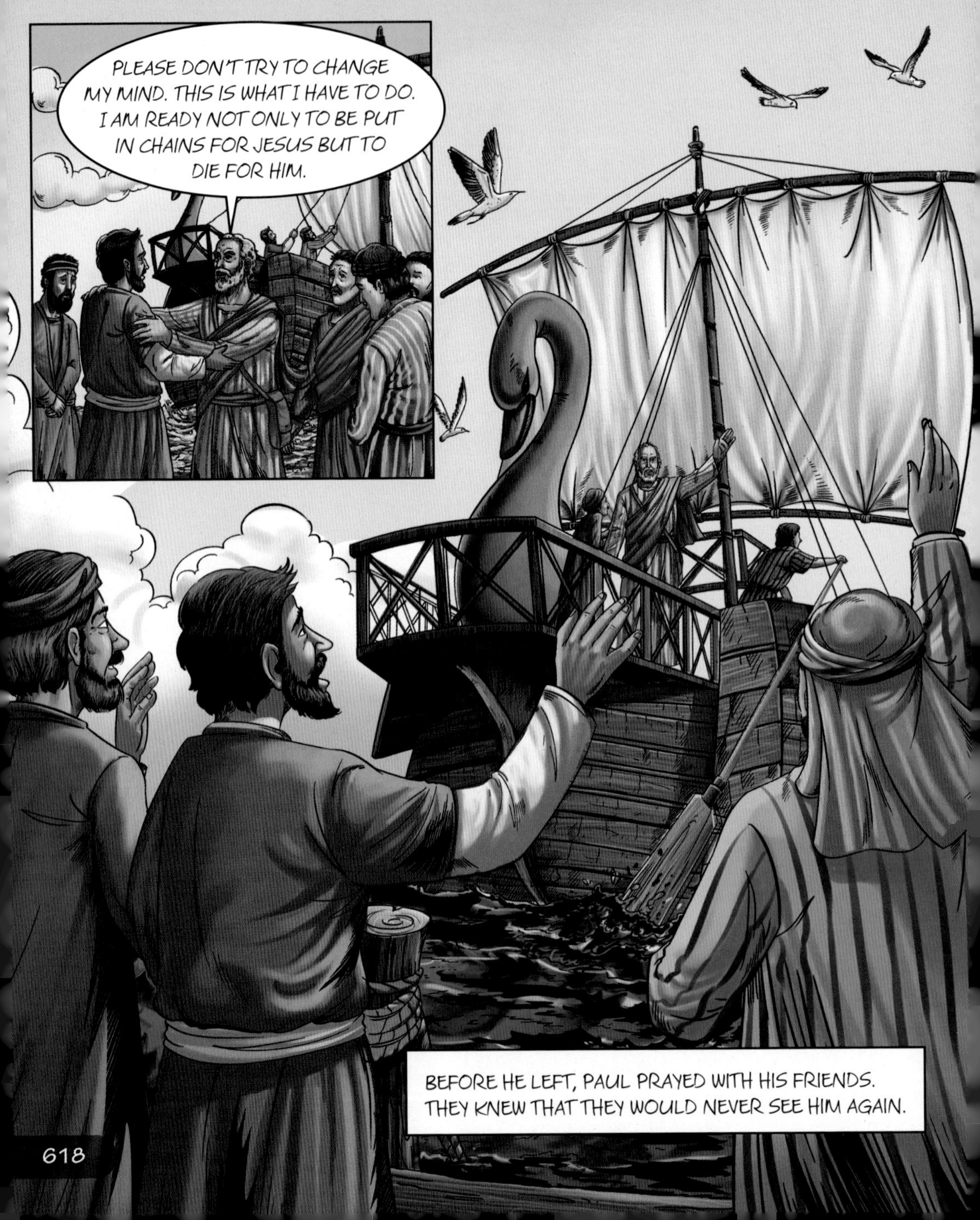

Trouble in Jerusalem

Acts 21–22

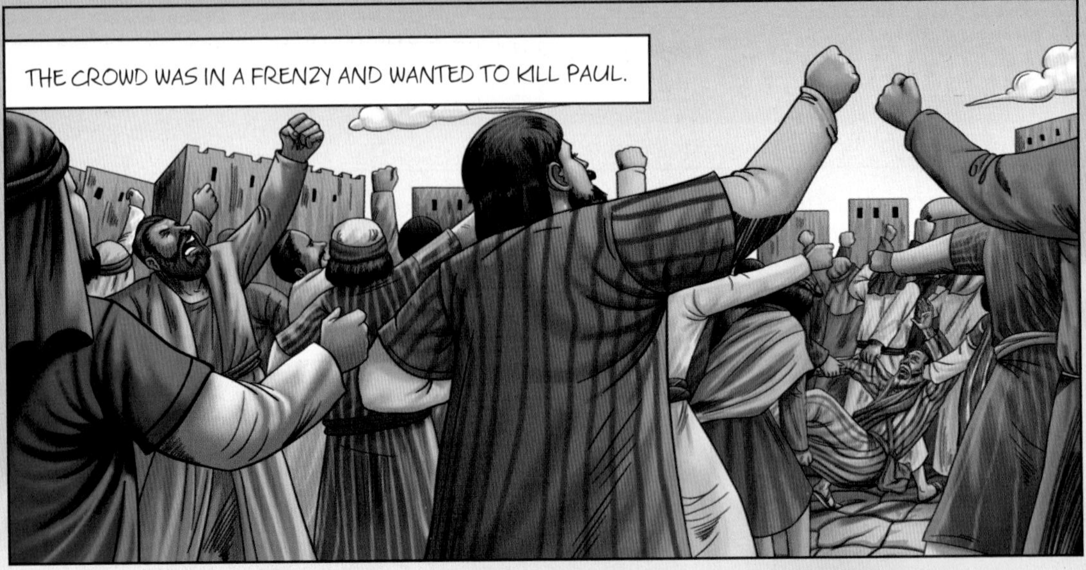

THE CROWD WAS IN A FRENZY AND WANTED TO KILL PAUL.

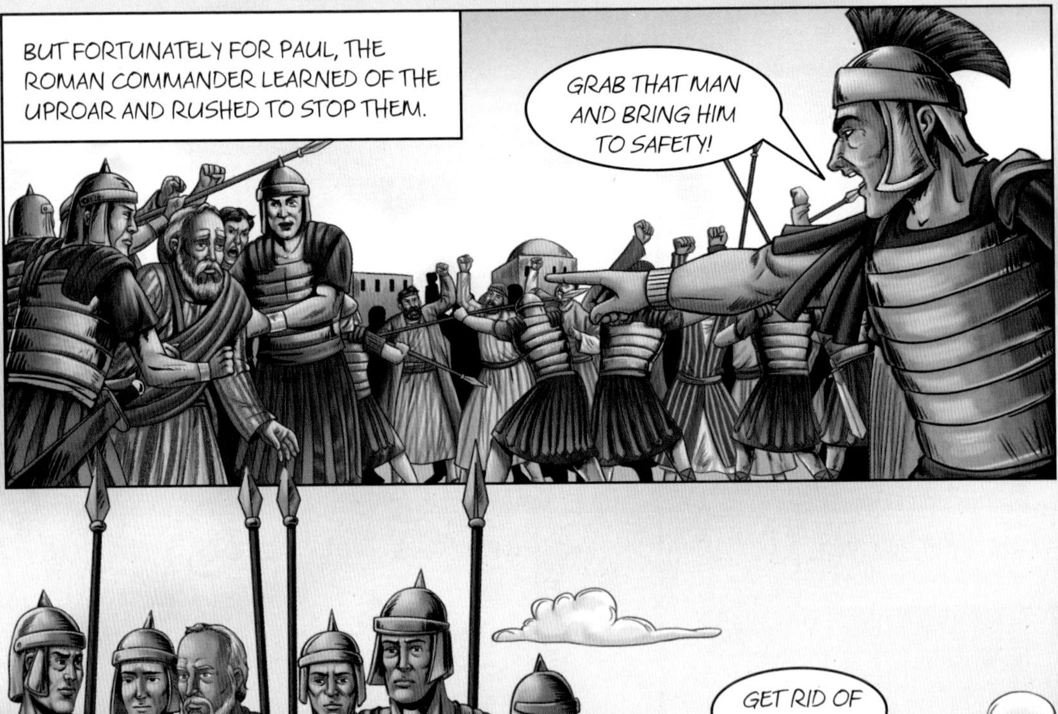

BUT FORTUNATELY FOR PAUL, THE ROMAN COMMANDER LEARNED OF THE UPROAR AND RUSHED TO STOP THEM.

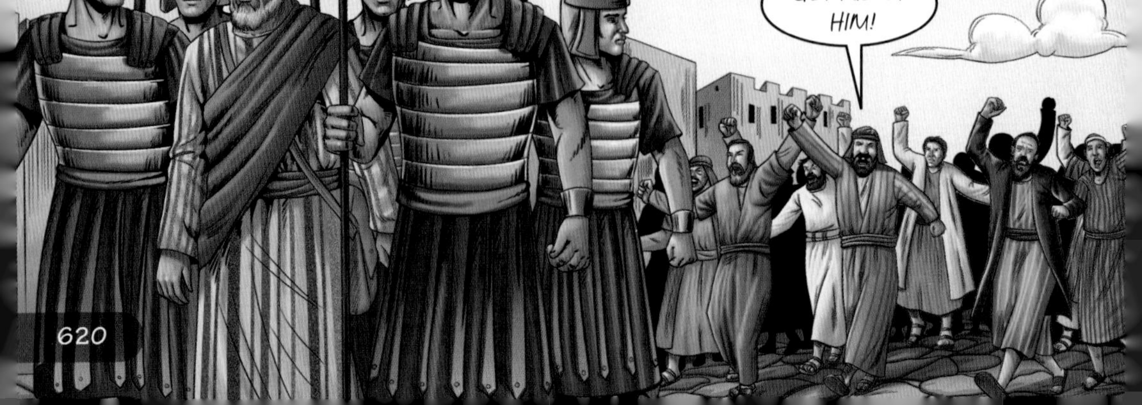

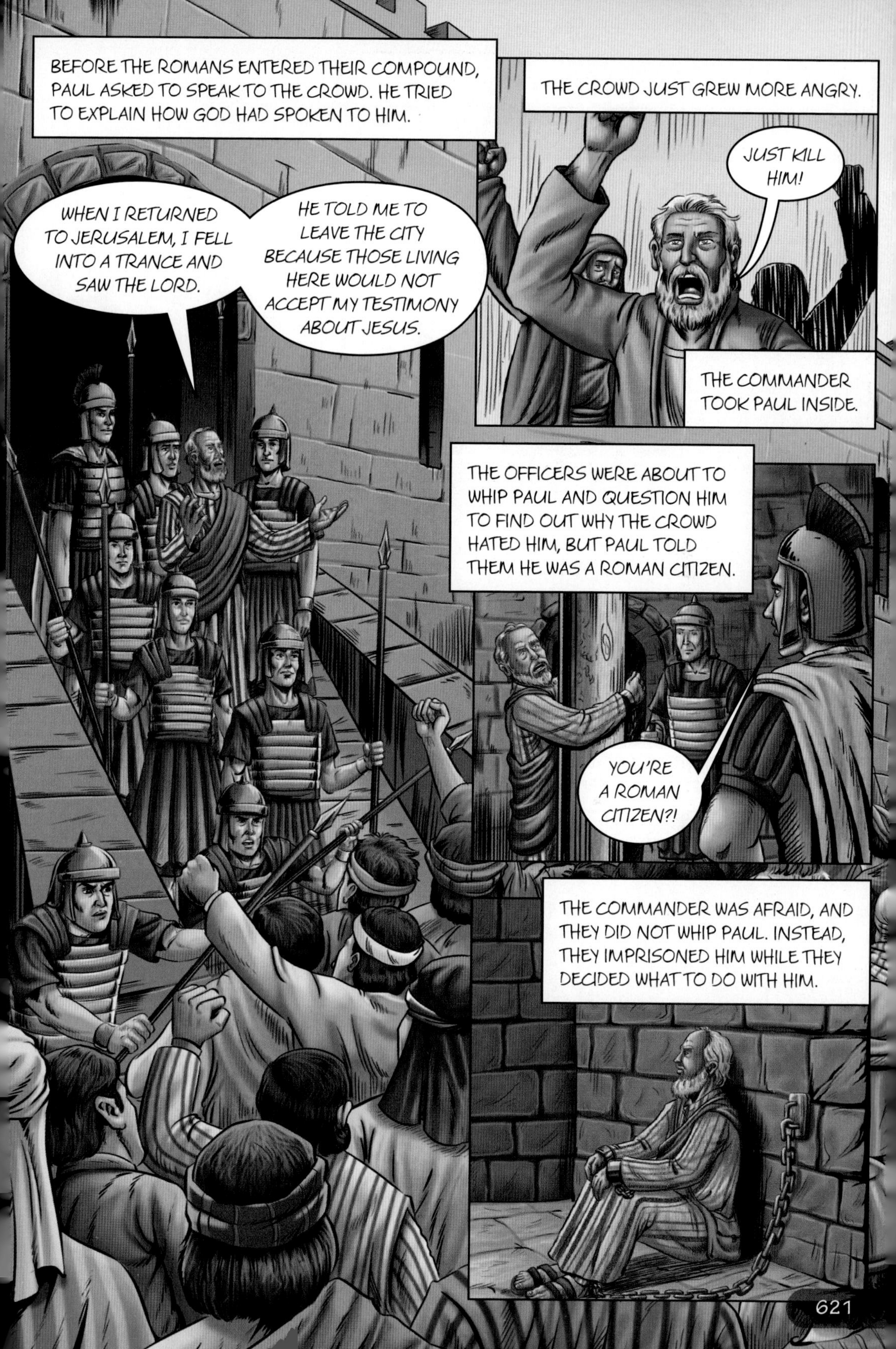
BEFORE THE ROMANS ENTERED THEIR COMPOUND, PAUL ASKED TO SPEAK TO THE CROWD. HE TRIED TO EXPLAIN HOW GOD HAD SPOKEN TO HIM.
WHEN I RETURNED TO JERUSALEM, I FELL INTO A TRANCE AND SAW THE LORD.
HE TOLD ME TO LEAVE THE CITY BECAUSE THOSE LIVING HERE WOULD NOT ACCEPT MY TESTIMONY ABOUT JESUS.
THE CROWD JUST GREW MORE ANGRY.
JUST KILL HIM!
THE COMMANDER TOOK PAUL INSIDE.
THE OFFICERS WERE ABOUT TO WHIP PAUL AND QUESTION HIM TO FIND OUT WHY THE CROWD HATED HIM, BUT PAUL TOLD THEM HE WAS A ROMAN CITIZEN.
YOU'RE A ROMAN CITIZEN?!
THE COMMANDER WAS AFRAID, AND THEY DID NOT WHIP PAUL. INSTEAD, THEY IMPRISONED HIM WHILE THEY DECIDED WHAT TO DO WITH HIM.

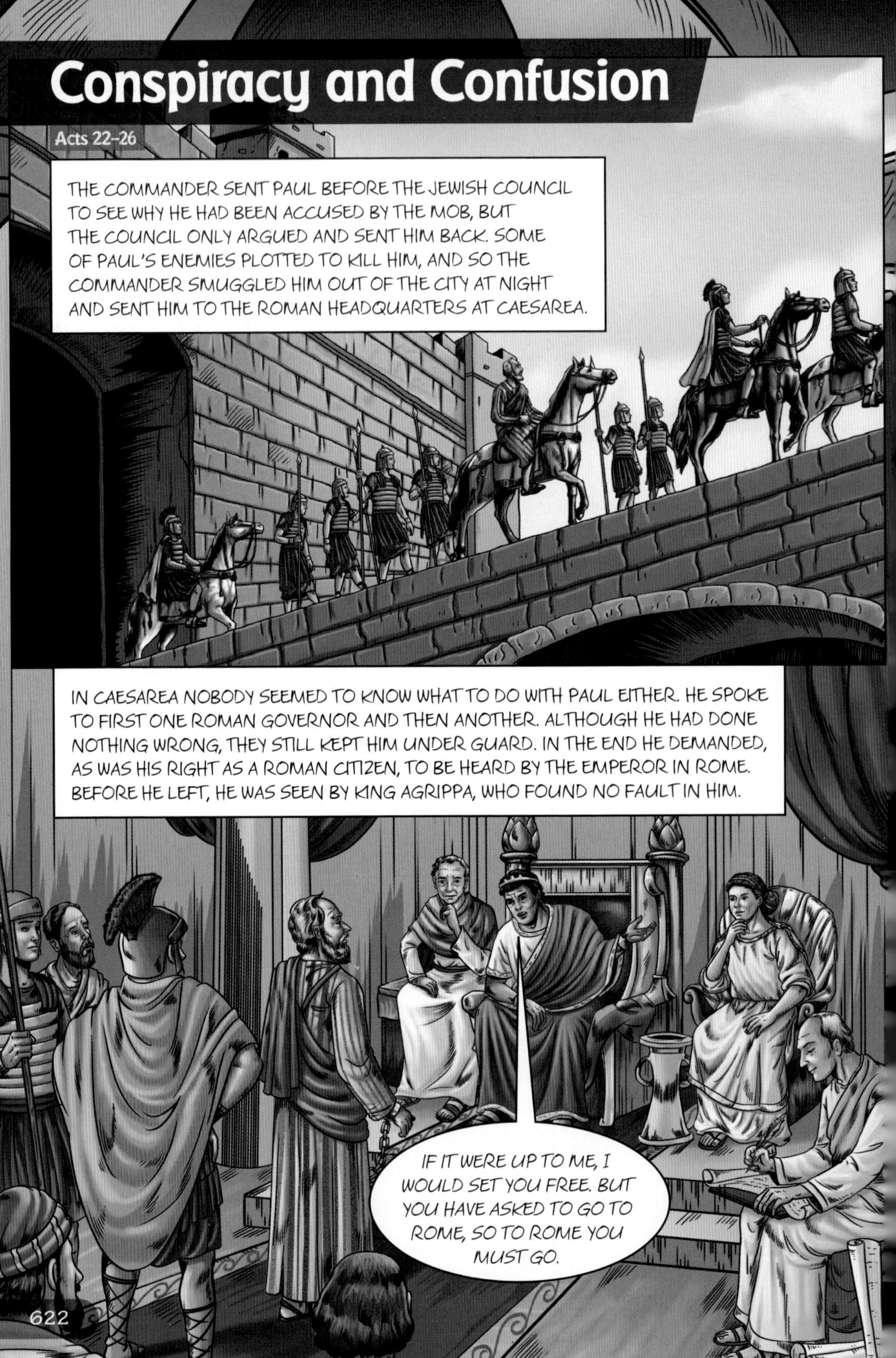
Conspiracy and Confusion
Acts 22–26
THE COMMANDER SENT PAUL BEFORE THE JEWISH COUNCIL TO SEE WHY HE HAD BEEN ACCUSED BY THE MOB, BUT THE COUNCIL ONLY ARGUED AND SENT HIM BACK. SOME OF PAUL'S ENEMIES PLOTTED TO KILL HIM, AND SO THE COMMANDER SMUGGLED HIM OUT OF THE CITY AT NIGHT AND SENT HIM TO THE ROMAN HEADQUARTERS AT CAESAREA.
IN CAESAREA NOBODY SEEMED TO KNOW WHAT TO DO WITH PAUL EITHER. HE SPOKE TO FIRST ONE ROMAN GOVERNOR AND THEN ANOTHER. ALTHOUGH HE HAD DONE NOTHING WRONG, THEY STILL KEPT HIM UNDER GUARD. IN THE END HE DEMANDED, AS WAS HIS RIGHT AS A ROMAN CITIZEN, TO BE HEARD BY THE EMPEROR IN ROME. BEFORE HE LEFT, HE WAS SEEN BY KING AGRIPPA, WHO FOUND NO FAULT IN HIM.
IF IT WERE UP TO ME, I WOULD SET YOU FREE. BUT YOU HAVE ASKED TO GO TO ROME, SO TO ROME YOU MUST GO.

The Storm and the Shipwreck

Acts 27–28

THE STORM GREW WORSE AS THE SHIP NEARED THE ISLAND OF CRETE.
YOU SHOULD HAVE LISTENED TO ME INSTEAD OF SAILING FOR CRETE.
BUT BE STRONG, NOT ONE OF YOU WILL LOSE YOUR LIFE!
PAUL SAID THAT AN ANGEL APPEARED TO HIM AND TOLD HIM NOT TO BE AFRAID, FOR ONLY THE SHIP WOULD BE LOST. PAUL TOLD THE MEN TO HAVE FAITH IN GOD.
THE STORM GREW WORSE, AND THE FEARFUL MEN THREW CARGO INTO THE SEA.
THEY THREW OVERBOARD THE SHIP'S GEAR AND ANYTHING ELSE THAT WOULD LIGHTEN THE SHIP.

DAYS PASSED, AND THE STORM CONTINUED TO RAGE. DESPERATE AND TERRIFIED, THE SAILORS TRIED TO LEAVE IN THE LIFEBOAT.
BUT PAUL WARNED JULIUS AND THE SOLDIERS THAT ALL MUST STAY WITH THE SHIP TO SURVIVE.
UNLESS THE MEN STAY WITH THE SHIP, THEY WILL DIE.
THE SOLDIERS LISTENED TO PAUL. THEY CUT THE ROPES OF THE LIFEBOAT AND SET IT ADRIFT.

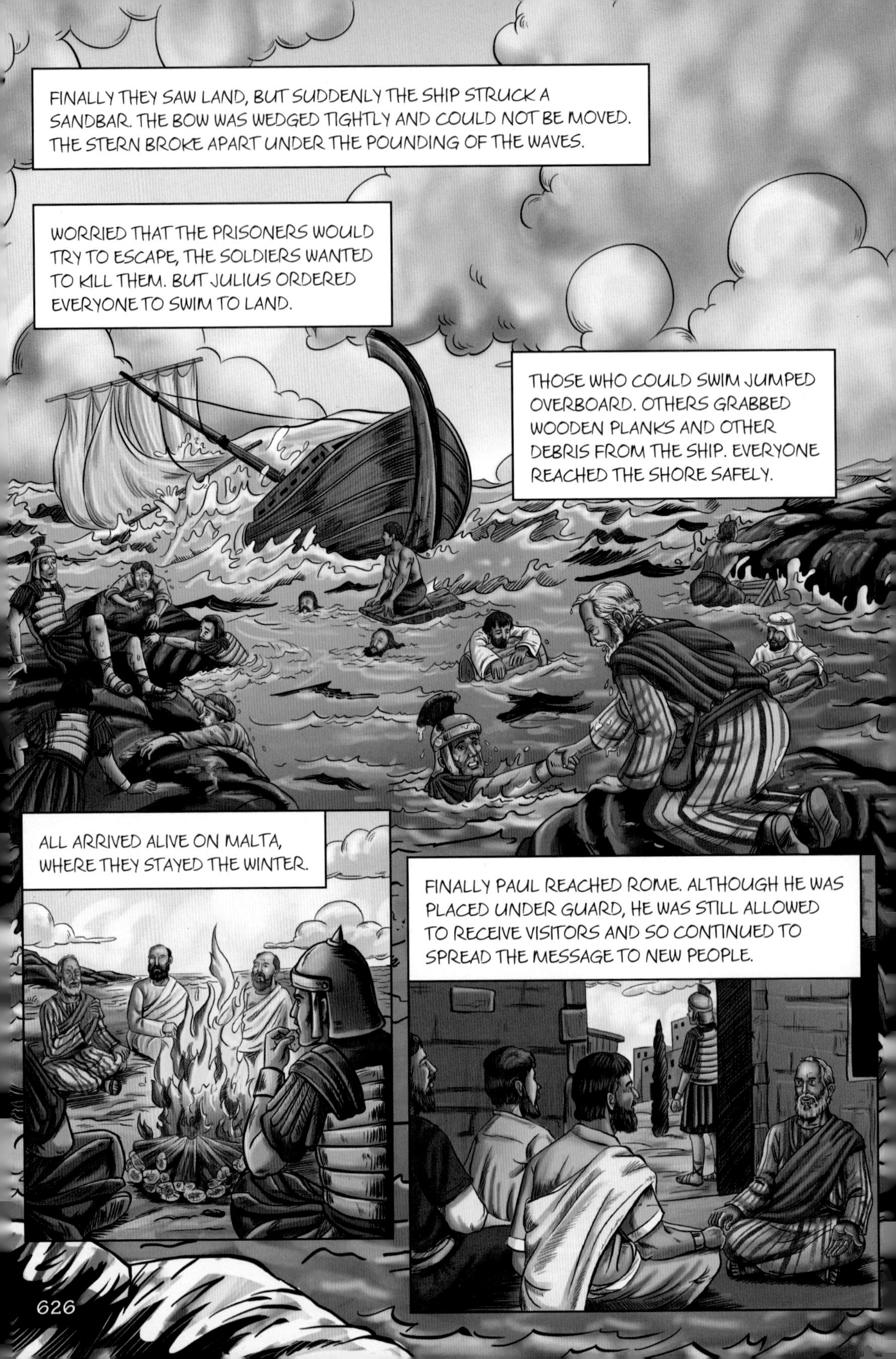
FINALLY THEY SAW LAND, BUT SUDDENLY THE SHIP STRUCK A SANDBAR. THE BOW WAS WEDGED TIGHTLY AND COULD NOT BE MOVED. THE STERN BROKE APART UNDER THE POUNDING OF THE WAVES.
WORRIED THAT THE PRISONERS WOULD TRY TO ESCAPE, THE SOLDIERS WANTED TO KILL THEM. BUT JULIUS ORDERED EVERYONE TO SWIM TO LAND.
THOSE WHO COULD SWIM JUMPED OVERBOARD. OTHERS GRABBED WOODEN PLANKS AND OTHER DEBRIS FROM THE SHIP. EVERYONE REACHED THE SHORE SAFELY.
ALL ARRIVED ALIVE ON MALTA, WHERE THEY STAYED THE WINTER.
FINALLY PAUL REACHED ROME. ALTHOUGH HE WAS PLACED UNDER GUARD, HE WAS STILL ALLOWED TO RECEIVE VISITORS AND SO CONTINUED TO SPREAD THE MESSAGE TO NEW PEOPLE.

The Epistles

KNOWN AUTHORS: PAUL, PETER, JOHN (APOSTLES)

JAMES, JUDE (FAMILY MEMBERS OF JESUS)

WRITTEN: AROUND AD 50–90

THE WORD "EPISTLE" COMES FROM THE GREEK WORD "EPISTOLE," MEANING "LETTER" OR "MESSAGE."

THE POWER OF THE PEN

OF THE 27 BOOKS THAT MAKE UP THE NEW TESTAMENT, 21 ARE EPISTLES—LETTERS WRITTEN TO CHURCHES OR INDIVIDUALS. PAUL IS BELIEVED TO HAVE WRITTEN AT LEAST 7 OF THEM, AND UP TO 13 HAVE TRADITIONALLY BEEN ATTRIBUTED TO HIM. THESE ARE REFERRED TO AS THE PAULINE EPISTLES.

THE OTHER BOOKS ARE KNOWN AS THE GENERAL EPISTLES AS THEY WERE NOT ADDRESSED TO SPECIFIC PERSONS OR CHURCHES BUT WERE MEANT FOR GENERAL CIRCULATION AMONG ALL THE CHURCHES. THESE INCLUDE JAMES, 1 AND 2 PETER, 1, 2, AND 3 JOHN, AND JUDE.

PRISON AND PASTORAL

OF THE PAULINE EPISTLES, SOME (EPHESIANS, PHILIPPIANS, COLOSSIANS, AND PHILEMON) ARE KNOWN AS THE PRISON EPISTLES BECAUSE THEY WERE WRITTEN WHEN PAUL WAS UNDER HOUSE ARREST IN ROME. OTHERS WERE WRITTEN TO INDIVIDUALS TO GIVE ADVICE ABOUT PROVIDING PASTORAL CARE AND ARE KNOWN AS THE PASTORAL EPISTLES.

The Greatest of These Is Love

Romans 5, 8; 1 Corinthians 12–13

PAUL WROTE MANY LETTERS. EVEN BEFORE HE WAS IMPRISONED IN ROME, HE WROTE LETTERS TO THOSE HE HAD MET ON HIS TRAVELS, OFFERING ADVICE, CRITICISM, ENCOURAGEMENT, AND LOVE. HIS HELP WAS IMPORTANT TO THOSE WHO WERE STARTING UP THE NEW CHURCHES, AND HIS ADVICE AND COMFORT ARE RELEVANT TODAY.

BEFORE HE TRAVELED TO ROME, PAUL WROTE TO THE BELIEVERS THERE:

Problems and trials help us develop endurance, strength of character, and hope. Yet what we suffer now is nothing compared to the glory God will reveal to us later.

If God is for us, who can ever be against us? Since he did not spare even his own Son but gave him up for us all, won't he also give us everything else? Nothing can ever separate us from God's love that is revealed in Christ Jesus our Lord—not troubles or persecution, or hunger, or poverty, or danger or death.

PAUL WROTE TO THE CHRISTIANS IN CORINTH:

A spiritual gift is given to each of us so we can help each other. All of you together are Christ's body, and each of you is a part of it. If I could speak all the languages of earth and of angels, but didn't love others, I would only be a noisy gong or a clanging cymbal. If I had the gift of prophecy, and if I had such faith that I could move mountains, but didn't love others, I would be nothing. Love is patient and kind. Love is not jealous or boastful or proud or rude. It does not demand its own way. It is not irritable, and it keeps no record of being wronged. It does not rejoice about injustice but rejoices whenever the truth wins out. Love never gives up. Three things will last forever—faith, hope, and love—and the greatest of these is love.

Faith in Christ

Galatians 2–5; Colossians 3; Ephesians 6

Fight the Good Fight

1 & 2 Timothy

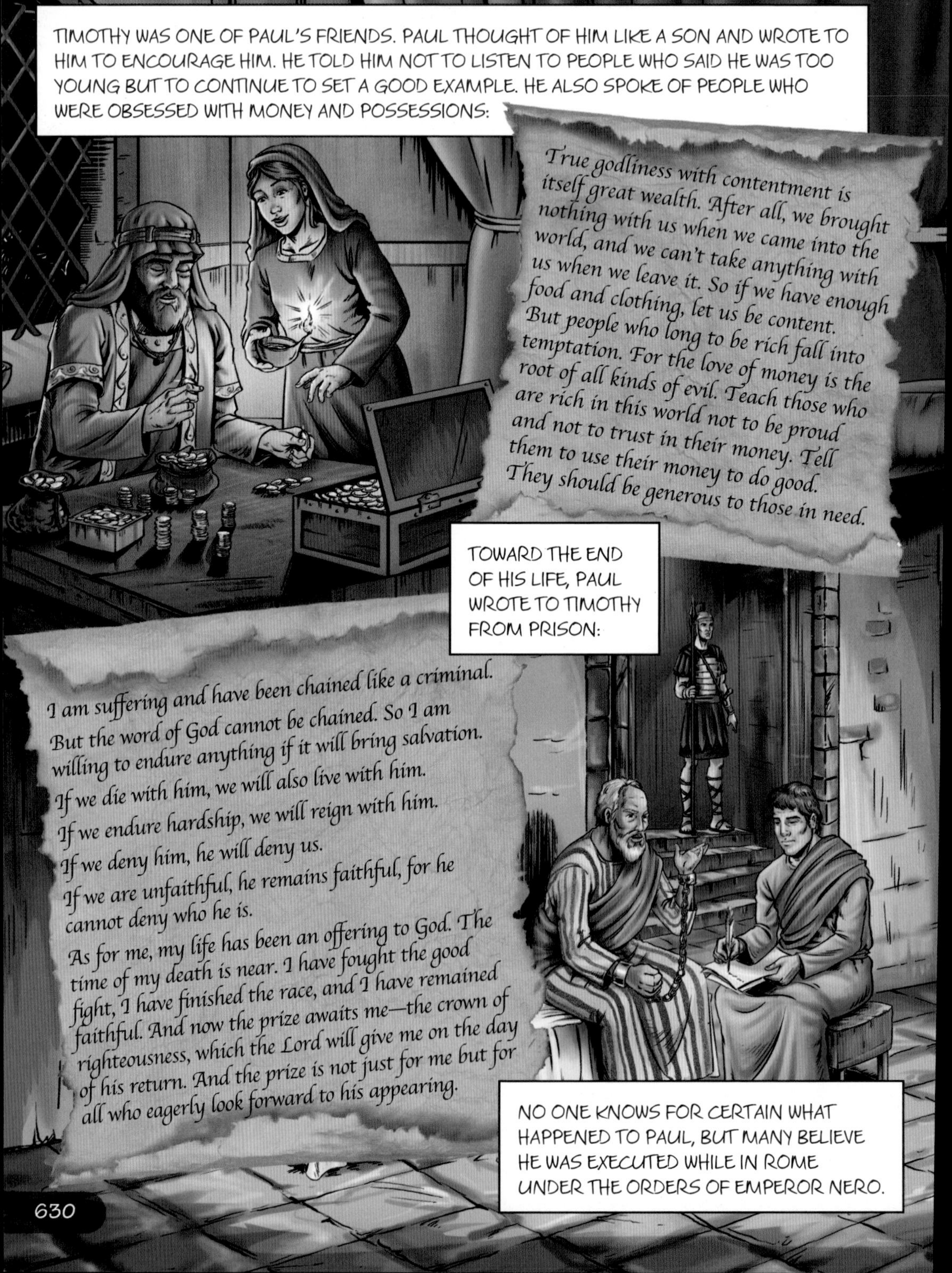

TIMOTHY WAS ONE OF PAUL'S FRIENDS. PAUL THOUGHT OF HIM LIKE A SON AND WROTE TO HIM TO ENCOURAGE HIM. HE TOLD HIM NOT TO LISTEN TO PEOPLE WHO SAID HE WAS TOO YOUNG BUT TO CONTINUE TO SET A GOOD EXAMPLE. HE ALSO SPOKE OF PEOPLE WHO WERE OBSESSED WITH MONEY AND POSSESSIONS:

True godliness with contentment is itself great wealth. After all, we brought nothing with us when we came into the world, and we can't take anything with us when we leave it. So if we have enough food and clothing, let us be content. But people who long to be rich fall into temptation. For the love of money is the root of all kinds of evil. Teach those who are rich in this world not to be proud and not to trust in their money. Tell them to use their money to do good. They should be generous to those in need.

TOWARD THE END OF HIS LIFE, PAUL WROTE TO TIMOTHY FROM PRISON:

I am suffering and have been chained like a criminal. But the word of God cannot be chained. So I am willing to endure anything if it will bring salvation.

If we die with him, we will also live with him.

If we endure hardship, we will reign with him.

If we deny him, he will deny us.

If we are unfaithful, he remains faithful, for he cannot deny who he is.

As for me, my life has been an offering to God. The time of my death is near. I have fought the good fight, I have finished the race, and I have remained faithful. And now the prize awaits me—the crown of righteousness, which the Lord will give me on the day of his return. And the prize is not just for me but for all who eagerly look forward to his appearing.

NO ONE KNOWS FOR CERTAIN WHAT HAPPENED TO PAUL, BUT MANY BELIEVE HE WAS EXECUTED WHILE IN ROME UNDER THE ORDERS OF EMPEROR NERO.

Run the Race

Hebrews; James; 1 & 2 Peter; 1 John

THE NEW TESTAMENT IS ALSO MADE UP OF LETTERS BY THE APOSTLES PETER AND JOHN AND BY JAMES AND JUDE, WHO WERE RELATED TO JESUS.

NO ONE CAN BE CERTAIN WHO WROTE THE LETTER TO THE HEBREWS, BUT IT ENCOURAGES THE READER TO BE FILLED WITH FAITH, LIKE NOAH, SARAH, AND MOSES:

Let us strip off every weight that slows us down and run with endurance the race God has set before us. We do this by keeping our eyes on Jesus, who gives us faith.

JAMES TOLD HIS READERS THAT IT WAS NOT ENOUGH TO SAY YOU HAVE FAITH:

What good is it if you say you have faith but don't show it by your actions? Can that kind of faith save anyone? Faith by itself isn't enough. Unless it produces good deeds, it is dead and useless.

PETER WROTE:

There is wonderful joy ahead, even though you must endure many trials for a little while. These trials will show that your faith is genuine. It is being tested as fire tests and purifies gold. The Lord isn't really being slow about his promise, as some people think. He wants everyone to repent. But the day of the Lord will come as unexpectedly as a thief.

THE APOSTLE JOHN WROTE:

God showed how much he loved us by sending his one and only Son into the world so that we might have eternal life through him. Since God loved us that much, we surely ought to love each other. God is love, and all who live in love live in God, and God lives in them. Such love has no fear, because perfect love expels all fear. We love each other because he loved us first.

John's Revelation

KNOWN AS: THE REVELATION OF SAINT JOHN THE DIVINE

THE BOOK OF REVELATION

THE APOCALYPSE (FROM THE GREEK WORD "APOKALYPSIS," MEANING "UNVEILING" OR "REVELATION")

WHICH JOHN?

TRADITIONALLY, THE BOOK OF REVELATION HAS BEEN ASSOCIATED WITH JOHN, THE APOSTLE, BUT MANY MODERN SCHOLARS DOUBT THAT. SOME IDENTIFY HIM AS "JOHN THE ELDER," BUT HE IS OFTEN SIMPLY REFERRED TO AS "JOHN OF PATMOS," IN RECOGNITION OF THE ISLAND ON WHICH IT IS GENERALLY BELIEVED THE BOOK WAS WRITTEN.

BOOK OF PROPHECY

IT IS THE ONLY PROPHETIC BOOK IN THE NEW TESTAMENT. JOHN'S VISION DESCRIBES FUTURE EVENTS AT THE END OF THE WORLD, INVOLVING THE FINAL REBELLION BY SATAN AT ARMAGEDDON, GOD'S FINAL DEFEAT OF SATAN, AND THE RESTORATION OF PEACE TO THE WORLD.

An Amazing Vision

Revelation 1–20

ON A GREEK ISLAND CALLED PATMOS, AN OLD MAN NAMED JOHN—IMPRISONED FOR PREACHING ABOUT JESUS—HAD AN AMAZING VISION. A VOICE SPOKE TO HIM AND TOLD HIM TO WRITE DOWN WHAT HE SAW AND TO SEND IT TO THE SEVEN CHURCHES.

JOHN TURNED AND SAW A FIGURE LIKE THE SON OF MAN, WITH PURE WHITE HAIR AND EYES LIKE BLAZING FIRE. HE WAS STANDING AMONG SEVEN GOLDEN LAMPSTANDS AND HELD SEVEN STARS IN HIS HAND.

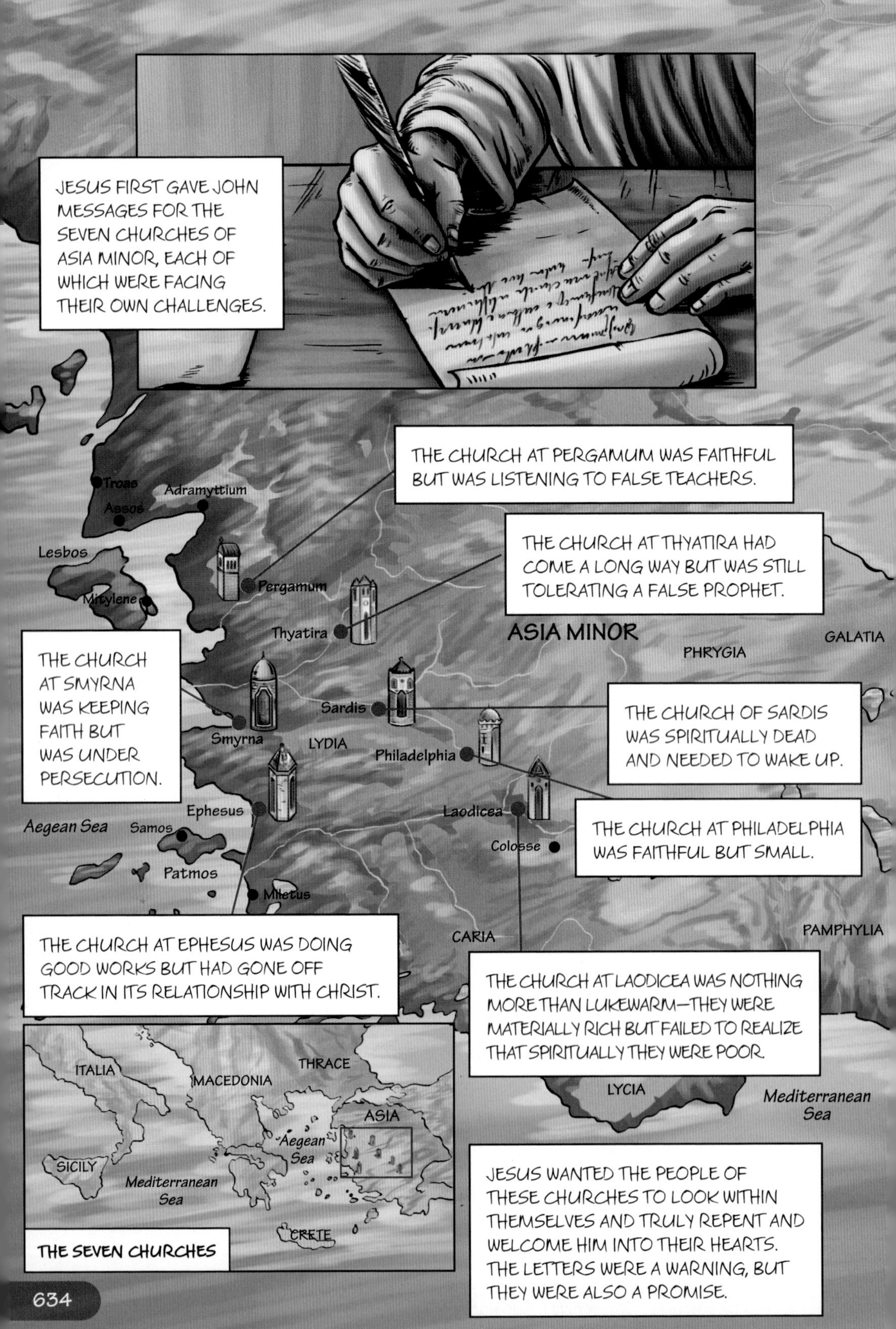
JESUS FIRST GAVE JOHN MESSAGES FOR THE SEVEN CHURCHES OF ASIA MINOR, EACH OF WHICH WERE FACING THEIR OWN CHALLENGES.
THE CHURCH AT PERGAMUM WAS FAITHFUL BUT WAS LISTENING TO FALSE TEACHERS.
THE CHURCH AT THYATIRA HAD COME A LONG WAY BUT WAS STILL TOLERATING A FALSE PROPHET.
THE CHURCH AT SMYRNA WAS KEEPING FAITH BUT WAS UNDER PERSECUTION.
THE CHURCH OF SARDIS WAS SPIRITUALLY DEAD AND NEEDED TO WAKE UP.
THE CHURCH AT PHILADELPHIA WAS FAITHFUL BUT SMALL.
THE CHURCH AT EPHESUS WAS DOING GOOD WORKS BUT HAD GONE OFF TRACK IN ITS RELATIONSHIP WITH CHRIST.
THE CHURCH AT LAODICEA WAS NOTHING MORE THAN LUKEWARM—THEY WERE MATERIALLY RICH BUT FAILED TO REALIZE THAT SPIRITUALLY THEY WERE POOR.
JESUS WANTED THE PEOPLE OF THESE CHURCHES TO LOOK WITHIN THEMSELVES AND TRULY REPENT AND WELCOME HIM INTO THEIR HEARTS. THE LETTERS WERE A WARNING, BUT THEY WERE ALSO A PROMISE.
Troas
Adramyttium
Assos
Lesbos
Pergamum
Mitylene
Thyatira
ASIA MINOR
GALATIA
PHRYGIA
Sardis
Smyrna
LYDIA
Philadelphia
Ephesus
Laodicea
Aegean Sea
Samos
Colosse
Patmos
Miletus
CARIA
PAMPHYLIA
LYCIA
Mediterranean Sea
ITALIA
MACEDONIA
THRACE
ASIA
Aegean Sea
SICILY
Mediterranean Sea
CRETE
THE SEVEN CHURCHES

IN HIS VISION, JOHN SAW A DOOR IN HEAVEN OPEN.
A VOICE INVITED JOHN TO COME LOOK CLOSER. THERE HE SAW A HUGE THRONE SURROUNDED BY TWENTY-FOUR OTHER THRONES, EACH WITH AN ELDER SITTING ON IT.
JOHN SAW FOUR LIVING CREATURES, EACH WITH SIX WINGS.

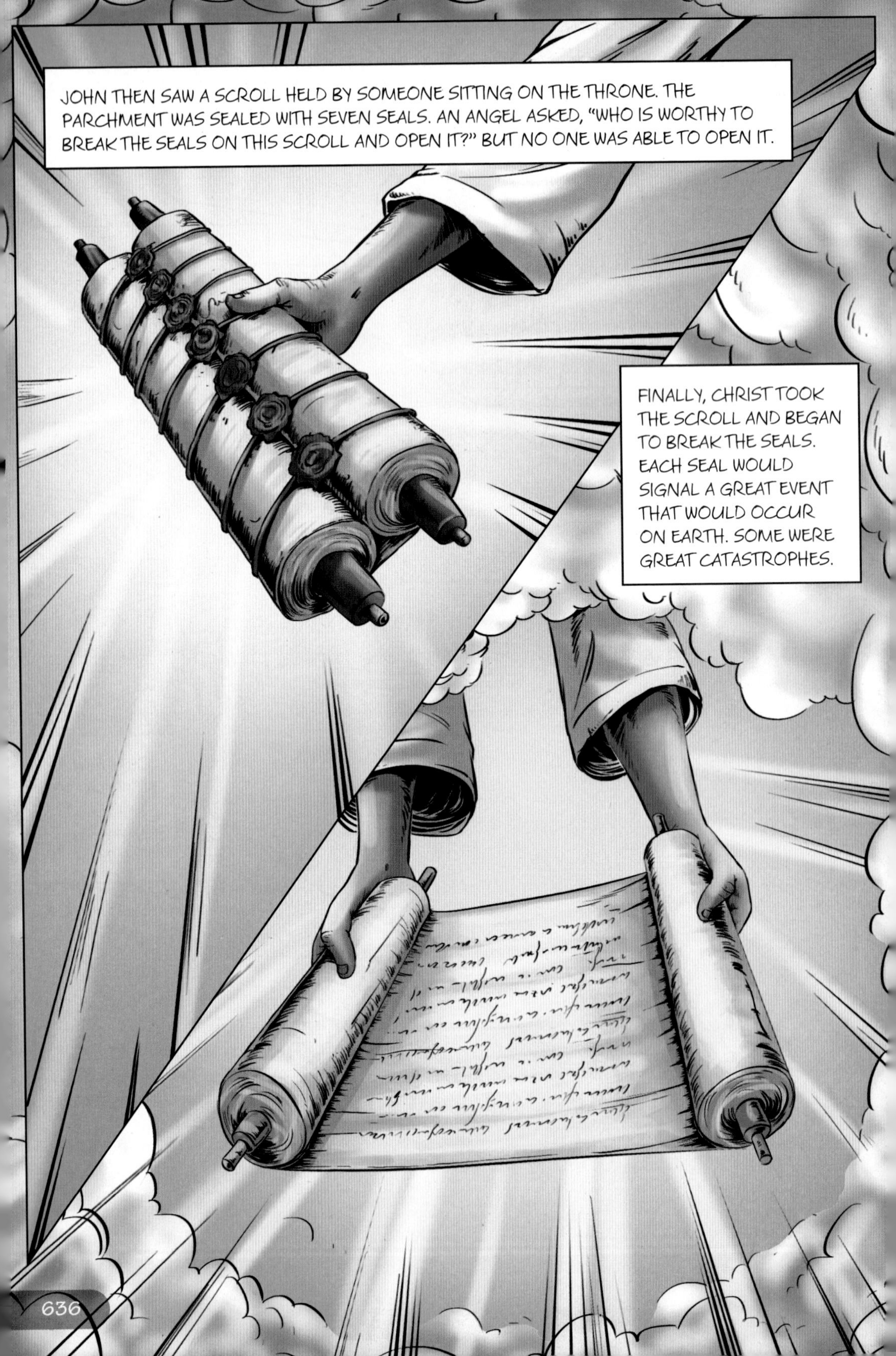
JOHN THEN SAW A SCROLL HELD BY SOMEONE SITTING ON THE THRONE. THE PARCHMENT WAS SEALED WITH SEVEN SEALS. AN ANGEL ASKED, "WHO IS WORTHY TO BREAK THE SEALS ON THIS SCROLL AND OPEN IT?" BUT NO ONE WAS ABLE TO OPEN IT.
FINALLY, CHRIST TOOK THE SCROLL AND BEGAN TO BREAK THE SEALS. EACH SEAL WOULD SIGNAL A GREAT EVENT THAT WOULD OCCUR ON EARTH. SOME WERE GREAT CATASTROPHES.

WHEN THE FIRST SEAL WAS BROKEN, A VOICE LIKE THUNDER CRIED OUT, "COME!" A RIDER ON A WHITE HORSE APPEARED. HE CARRIED A BOW AND WAS GIVEN A CROWN. HE WENT OUT TO CONQUER AND WON MANY VICTORIES.
WHEN THE SECOND SEAL WAS BROKEN, A RED HORSE APPEARED, AND ITS RIDER WAS GIVEN A GREAT SWORD. WAR WAS EVERYWHERE.

WHEN THE THIRD SEAL WAS BROKEN, A BLACK HORSE APPEARED. HIS RIDER CARRIED A PAIR OF SCALES IN HIS HAND. FOOD BECAME SCARCE AND EXPENSIVE.
WHEN THE FOURTH SEAL WAS BROKEN, A FOURTH RIDER ON A PALE-GREEN HORSE APPEARED. THE RIDER'S NAME WAS "DEATH," AND THE GRAVE FOLLOWED HIM.

WHEN THE FIFTH SEAL WAS BROKEN, THOSE WHO HAD BEEN MARTYRED RECEIVED WHITE ROBES. WHEN THE SIXTH SEAL WAS BROKEN, AN EARTHQUAKE ROCKED THE PLANET, THE SUN DARKENED, AND STARS FELL FROM THE SKY. WHEN THE SEVENTH SEAL WAS BROKEN, SEVEN ANGELS WITH TRUMPETS STOOD BEFORE GOD.
WHEN THE FIRST ANGEL BLEW HIS TRUMPET, HAIL, FIRE, AND BLOOD HURLED DOWN TO EARTH.
WHEN THE SECOND ANGEL BLEW HIS TRUMPET, A BURNING MOUNTAIN WAS THROWN INTO THE SEA.
AS EACH TRUMPET BLEW, A DIFFERENT CALAMITY STRUCK EARTH. THE ULTIMATE BATTLE BETWEEN GOOD AND EVIL HAD BEGUN.

JOHN'S VISION CONTINUED. AN ANGEL CAME DOWN FROM HEAVEN HOLDING IN HIS HAND THE KEY TO THE BOTTOMLESS PIT. HE SEIZED THE DRAGON, WHO IS THE DEVIL, AND CAST HIM INTO THE PIT. SATAN WOULD BE SHUT UP AND PEACE WOULD REIGN ON EARTH FOR A THOUSAND YEARS...
...BEFORE ONE FINAL, DREADFUL WAR BETWEEN SATAN AND THE PEOPLE OF GOD. BUT AT THE END SATAN WOULD BE CAST INTO A LAKE OF FIRE.

The Holy City
Revelation 20–22
JOHN SAW THE TIME OF THE FINAL JUDGMENT. HE SAW A GREAT WHITE THRONE AND THE ONE SITTING ON IT. HE SAW THE BOOK OF LIFE, WHICH WOULD BE OPENED, AND ALL WOULD BE JUDGED ACCORDING TO WHAT THEY HAD DONE. THEN THE WICKED WOULD ALSO BE CAST INTO THE LAKE OF FIRE, ALONG WITH DEATH AND THE GRAVE.
THEN JOHN GOT A GLIMPSE OF THE NEW HEAVEN AND EARTH. HE SAW THE HOLY CITY, COMING DOWN OUT OF HEAVEN LIKE A BEAUTIFUL BRIDE, AND HEARD A VOICE SPEAKING FROM THE THRONE.
GOD'S HOME IS NOW AMONG HIS PEOPLE! HE WILL LIVE WITH THEM, AND THERE WILL BE NO MORE DEATH OR SORROW OR CRYING OR PAIN.
I AM THE ALPHA AND THE OMEGA— THE BEGINNING AND THE END.

THE HOLY CITY SHONE WITH THE GLORY OF GOD. IT'S TEMPLE WAS THE LORD GOD ALMIGHTY AND THE LAMB. THE RIVER OF LIFE RAN THROUGH ITS CENTER. THE CITY HAD NO NEED FOR THE SUN OR THE MOON, BECAUSE THE GLORY OF GOD SHONE ON IT, AND THE LAMB WAS ITS LIGHT.
I AM COMING SOON!
AMEN! COME, LORD JESUS!